Jesus Tradition, Early Christian Memory, and Gospel Writing

JESUS TRADITION, EARLY CHRISTIAN MEMORY, AND GOSPEL WRITING

The Long Search for the Authentic Source

ALAN KIRK

WILLIAM B. EERDMANS PUBLISHING COMPANY

GRAND RAPIDS, MICHIGAN

Wm. B. Eerdmans Publishing Co.
4035 Park East Court SE, Grand Rapids, Michigan 49546
www.eerdmans.com

29 28 27 26 25 24 23   1 2 3 4 5 6 7

ISBN 978-0-8028-8295-0

Library of Congress Cataloging-in-Publication Data

A catalog record for this book is available from the Library of Congress.

Dedicated to

Kenton and Sheldina, Bill and Debbie,
Steve and Patri, Silas and Becky,

friends for a lifetime

Contents

Abbreviations

ABG	Arbeiten zur Bibel und ihrer Geschichte
AGJU	Arbeiten zur Geschichte des antiken Judentum und des Urchristentums
AYBRL	Anchor Yale Bible Reference Library
BBB	Bonner biblische Beiträge
BETL	Bibliotheca Ephemeridum Theologicarum Lovaniensium
BWANT	Beiträge zur Wissenschaft von Alten und Neuen Testament
BZNW	Beihefte zur Zeitschrift für die neutestamentliche Wissenschaft
ClQ	*Classical Quarterly*
ConBNT	Coniectanea Biblica: New Testament Series
CurBR	*Currents in Biblical Research*
DSD	*Dead Sea Discoveries*
EC	*Early Christianity*
ECHE	Early Christianity in Its Hellenistic Environment
ETL	*Ephemerides Theologicae Lovanienses*
FAT	Forschungen zum Alten Testament
FRLANT	Forschungen zur Religion und Literatur Neues Testaments
HibJ	*Hibbert Journal*
HTR	*Harvard Theological Review*
JBL	*Journal of Biblical Literature*
JR	*Journal of Religion*
JSHJ	*Journal for the Study of the Historical Jesus*
JSNT	*Journal for the Study of the New Testament*
JSNTSup	Journal for the Study of the New Testament Supplement Series
JSOTSup	Journal for the Study of the Old Testament Supplement Series
JTS	*Journal of Theological Studies*
LNTS	The Library of New Testament Studies
MThA	Münsteraner Theologische Abhandlungen
MTSR	*Method and Theory in the Study of Religion*

NovT	*Novum Testamentum*
NovTSup	Supplements to Novum Testamentum
NTS	*New Testament Studies*
NTTSD	New Testament Tools, Studies, and Documents
OLAW	Orality and Literacy in the Ancient World
OT	*Oral Tradition*
RJFTC	Reception of Jesus in the First Three Centuries
SCI	*Scripta Classica Israelica*
STDJ	Studies in the Texts of the Judean Desert
STRev	*Sewanee Theological Review*
TRE	*Theologische Realenzyclopädie.* Edited by Gerhard Krause and Gerhard Müller. Berlin: de Gruyter, 1977–
TSK	*Theologische Studien und Kritiken*
UNT	Untersuchungen zum Neuen Testament
WMANT	Wissenschaftliche Mongraphien zum Alten und Neuen Testament
WUNT	Wissenschaftliche Untersuchungen zum Neuen Testament
ZNT	*Zeitschrift für Neues Testament*
ZTK	*Zeitschrift für Theologie und Kirche*
ZWT	*Zeitschrift für wissenschaftliche Theologie*

Written Gospel or Oral?
Lessing, Herder, and the Road to Strauss

To a contemporary scholar viewing Synoptic variation and agreement in a synopsis it might hardly occur that the answers to the most basic questions in Christian origins are to be discerned in the restless movement of these ever-shifting patterns. But the synopsis is catching, as if in a photographic frame, a moment of a highly kinetic cultural-memory formation that leads us back ultimately into primitive Jesus commemoration and to the very germination of the tradition in the memory of Jesus. It is the Synoptic patterns of variation and agreement that allow us to navigate back toward these otherwise inaccessible points. In those patterns lies the answer to the perennial question of how the Jesus tradition mediates the past. In short, there is no more basic question in Christian-origins inquiry than the Synoptic problem.

For long periods this was recognized and indeed was the primary impetus in Synoptic scholarship. The question that engrossed nineteenth-century source criticism was the connection of the tradition to apostolic memory. Source criticism was the concerted effort to identify where that memory was to be found in its most unsullied form. Today the enterprise will strike many as dated. The Synoptic problem has come to be regarded as a subfield, a pursuit for scholars with a niche taste for textual minutiae, for a querulous source-critical debate that surely everyone knows to be an arcane exercise in futility. Is it not common knowledge that the Synoptic problem is stuck at a permanent impasse? The gospels offer promising fields for other, more cutting-edge methods of critical inquiry, for "interrogating" their texts! True, we must renounce the quest for knowing anything certain about the origins and history of the materials that these works contain, or even why they came into existence, but is that not just a chastened, sober estimate of the limits to our knowledge?

Historical Jesus research has likewise cut itself loose from what had long been understood to be its organic connection with the question of the history of the tradition, and thus with Synoptic-problem inquiry. This disconnect is due to the loss of confidence in the form-critical model for the history of the tradition, a model that arose in consequence of the failure of the nineteenth-century source critics in their quest for the pristine memory of Jesus. Form criticism reacted by severing the vitalizing connection between memory and the tradition, and with it the quest for the historical Jesus from the Synoptic problem altogether. Memory became identified with so-called authentic trace elements lying under or strewn among multiple strata of church-generated "tradition." Loss of confidence in form criticism was already far advanced when the present author was in graduate school early in the 1990s (albeit there were some for whom Bultmann was still a name to conjure with). The collapse of the form-critical model, however, has not been followed by any viable alternative. Historical Jesus scholarship has proceeded without any working theory of the history of the tradition, in other words—and paradoxically—without a theory of how the tradition actually mediates the past.

This conundrum is on display E. P. Sanders's explanation of his methodological program in his seminal 1985 volume *Jesus and Judaism*. Sanders in fact takes as his point of departure the failure of the form-critical method to identify an agreed, secure core of "authentic" materials. He follows Gerhardsson in rejecting the form-critical postulate that large quantities of the tradition were generated out of typical situations in the primitive churches, while confessing that "we do not have a persuasive alternative."[1] For him this means that the critic sidelines the problem of the tradition and relies instead upon a few indisputable "bedrock facts" about Jesus that can be connected to certain cultural and historical realities to further fill out the picture of Jesus. But then he immediately falls back into fretting about which of the traditions are authentic, and which are created by the church.[2] This is not a critique of Sanders's method or of his results and those of other contemporary Jesus scholars, but to point out the oddity, in the end the impossibility, of operating without some default theory of the tradition itself. Memory approaches have recently gained some traction in Jesus research, but applications typically have proceeded with only perfunctory reflection on the memory-tradition problematic, and certainly on the problem of variation and agreement in the Synoptic tradition not at all.

This is not a book on historical Jesus research. The point is that in continuing to follow the form critics in divorcing these questions from the Synoptic problem we have closed the door to our only point of entry for recovering

---

1. E. P. Sanders, *Jesus and Judaism* (Philadelphia: Fortress, 1985), 15.
2. Sanders, *Jesus and Judaism*, 13.

the history of the tradition and for cracking the problem of the relationship between memory and the tradition. The pressing question is: why the present impasse? Why did nineteenth-century source criticism run into its dead end in its source-history pursuit of the authentic memory of Jesus, exiting into form-critical skepticism and the all but complete exclusion of the memory factor from the formation of the tradition? There is nothing in the Synoptic profile that would indicate insuperable difficulties to solving the Synoptic problem. Its density in information is such as to strongly suggest otherwise. What is needed is a diagnosis of why the inquiry keeps failing.

The impasse in the Synoptic problem, and with it the abandonment of the project of recovering the history of the tradition, is due to the *defective media assumptions* that have fed into the formulation of source-history hypotheses in the nineteenth century and then reappearing on cue in the contemporary debate. Chief among these is the application of an *oral/written binary*, the effect of which is to foreordain that it will be impossible to reconcile the patterns of Synoptic agreements with the patterns of Synoptic variation. The persistence of these media assumptions is the reason why much of the contemporary debate turns out to more or less recapitulate the nineteenth-century debate. Widespread disciplinary amnesia about nineteenth-century source criticism hinders recognition of this. Good surveys of both the nineteenth-century and contemporary debates exist,[3] but the as yet untried angle is our proposed media/memory analysis—what role particular assumptions about *oral tradition* and *gospel writing*, and the intersection of both with *memory*, have played in the spinning out of proposed solutions to the Synoptic problem. And just as importantly: *what is at stake* when critics invoke media factors and memory in their histories of the Synoptic tradition and gospel writing. Putting Synoptic-problem inquiry on sound media premises holds the promise of breaking the impasse and recapturing for the Synoptic problem its long-lost centrality in research into Christian origins.

Though we begin with Lessing and Herder and continue down to the contemporary debate, this is *not* a history of Synoptic-problem research. Each of the source critics selected here for detailed analysis exemplifies diagnostically the media/memory problematic. We will drill down deeply into each to lay open to view the operative media assumptions.

—

3. The best is John S. Kloppenborg, *Excavating Q: The History and Setting of the Sayings Gospel* (Minneapolis: Fortress, 2000), chaps. 6 and 7.

The oral/written binary appears right at the commencement of critical reflection on the problem of Synoptic patterns of variation and agreement in
Gotthold Ephraim Lessing's (1784) and Johann Gottfried Herder's (1794) competing accounts of gospel origins. Lessing grounded his explanation in the
written medium, positing a written Urgospel; Herder in the oral medium, in
an oral Urgospel.

Gotthold Ephraim Lessing's Written Urgospel

Lessing argued for the early and spontaneous appearance of a written Aramaic Urgospel. Anonymous Jesus followers, "Nazarenes," collected and wrote
down orally circulating stories and sayings that they had heard from living
apostles and other eyewitnesses. The inscription enterprise was uncontrolled,
with numerous collectors and copyists involved. This gospel of the "Nazarenes"
therefore came to circulate in Palestine, alongside oral tradition, in expanded,
abbreviated, textually variant, and differently ordered exemplars. Though not
the author, the apostle Matthew was a contributor to this gospel. The break-
out of the movement to the Greek-speaking world precipitated the Synoptic Gospels. To meet this exigency, each evangelist extracted directly from
the Aramaic Urgospel, each in whatever form it was available to him (Mark's
version of the Urgospel, for example, being less complete), each making his
own selection and each his own translation into Greek—as Papias says, in his
own style.[4] Hence the patterns of agreement and variation in the Synoptic
Gospels: they arise in the *written* medium, the outcome of the contingencies
of collection, copying, extraction, translation, and stylistic shaping. Lessing
understands oral tradition as the oral testimony of living apostles and other
eyewitnesses to the "Nazarenes" of Palestine; its role is limited to providing the
Nazarenes raw material for their written Urgospel. Oral tradition as Lessing
conceives it is not an adequate medium for transmission of apostolic memory.
It is undifferentiated from direct apostolic recollection and thus not securely
transmissible beyond the confines of Palestine. Rather it is the Urgospel, in
its written tangibility, that bridges the thirty-year gap between Jesus and the
Synoptic Gospels.[5]

---

4. Gotthold Ephraim Lessing, "New Hypothesis concerning the Evangelists Regarded as
Merely Human Historians," in *Lessing's Theological Writings*, trans. Henry Chadwick (1784;
repr., Stanford: Stanford University Press, 1957), 65–81 (66–79).

5. Lessing, "New Hypothesis," 66–71.

JOHANN GOTTFRIED HERDER

Herder's Oral Urgospel

Reacting to Lessing several years later (1796–1797), Johann Gottfried Herder voiced skepticism that utilization of a *written* Urgospel source—and a single one at that—could possibly have generated the present range of Synoptic variation. Such a scenario, he says, actually worsens the difficulties raised by divergences and contradictions among the Synoptics. Herder's media assumption is that written source utilization will hew closely to the source. "By whose authority and on what grounds," he asks, "would they [the evangelists] have so modified their written *Urschrift*?"[6] He finds it incredible that any Urgospel could have come together through the inadvertent, ad hoc processes that Lessing proposes. Wide overlap in the materials of the Synoptics suggests intentionality and thus speaks against any such scenario. And in addition, he says, are we to imagine the evangelists, like toiling scribes, cobbling adventitious collections together to form coherent gospels? Why do so when with little effort they could get the materials direct from eyewitnesses, most of whom were still alive (*noch lebten*)? In any case, Herder alleges, any intra-utilization theory (*Benutzungshypothese*) has no prospects of success, and this dashes any hopes of recovering a hypothesized written Urgospel source.[7]

Herder therefore shifts to the other media pole. He points out that one errs by imputing the gospel bookrolls and lections of the second and third centuries to primitive Christianity.[8] It is more likely that an oral Urgospel (*mündliche Evangelium*) marks the beginning of the history of the gospel literature. The ontogenesis of the oral Urgospel lies in the preaching of Christ himself, but, more immediately, in the apostles' oral preaching in its kerygmatic outline.[9] The emergence of an Aramaic oral Urgospel in the primitive community (*älteste Christengemeinde*) is *a priori* likely, Herder thinks, not only in view of Jewish oral-tradition practices but also because of the "oriental" predilection for sim-

---

6. Johann Gottfried Herder, "Vom Erlöser der Menschen: nach unsern drei ersten Evangelien," in *Johann Gottfried Herder Theologische Schriften*; *Johann Gottfried Herder Werke*, ed. Christoph Bultmann and Thomas Zippert (1796–1797; repr., Frankfurt am Main: Deutsche Klassiker Verlag, 1994), 9.1:609–724 (679).

7. Herder, "Vom Erlöser," 676, 679.

8. Herder, "Vom Erlöser," 685–86; "Regel der Zusammenstimmung unsrer Evangelien, aus ihrer Entstehung und Ordnung," in *Sämmtliche Werke: Religion und Theologie*, ed. Johann Georg Müller (1797; repr., Carlsruhe: Büreau der deutschen Classiker, 1829), 1–68 (6).

9. Herder, "Vom Erlöser," 670–74.

ple oral narrative.[10] An oral gospel would have nucleated spontaneously out of evangelistic preaching and baptismal instruction, with its primary formation occurring in the instructional circles around the apostles themselves.[11]

Herder is keenly aware that the issue for an oral-gospel theory is identifying the grounds of the entity's coalescence and its durable cohesion. He argues that the Christian confession of faith, the apostolic kerygma attested in Acts 1:21–22, formed its spine, its ordering *Schema*, within and around which was configured a common fund of sayings, parables, and episodic materials. The Urgospel's schematic form and circumscribed stock of traditional materials assisted in its assimilation and wider dissemination by evangelists— that is, by "apostolic helpers," who were not personal eyewitnesses. Just like the Homeric cycles, this "apostolic saga" was narrated by the apostles and evangelists in quite uniform (*festgestellte*) ways, at times extending so far as verbatim agreement, due to its frequent repetition and to simple oriental practices of narration. On the other hand, this was not a matter of slavish, rote performance of a memorized text; the "gospel rhapsodes" exercised freedom in their oral enactments of the Urgospel. In its every line, says Herder, "there breathes the free spirit of the oral presentation, the *Spirit*, not the *Letter*."[12] This accounts for Synoptic variation: divergences in the *order* of the Urgospel because the sequencing of its constituent *Perikopen* was alterable, subject to the intentions and individual genius of a narrator; likewise the *wording* of its individual pericopes. The contingent transmission of the Urgospel along complex networks of oral tradents as well as its wide geographical dissemination further conduced to variation in wording and order.

In short: Herder conceives the oral Urgospel as a loose but nevertheless schematically cohering body of performed oral tradition, comprising a common fund of narratives, parables, and sayings that like the Urgospel itself had assumed stable traditional forms.[13] Given the powerful forces acting to generate variation, Herder admits that the challenge for the oral hypothesis is to explain the striking patterns of close agreements in order and wording. Parables and sayings, he notes, naturally maintain stability in their essential elements across variants. But the main factor producing Synoptic agreements is the kerygmatic schema of the primitive Christian saga. This ensures the

---

10. Herder, "Vom Erlöser," 685–86; "Regel," 18, 48.

11. Herder, "Vom Erlöser," 685–87; "Von Gottes Sohn, der Welt Heiland: nach Johannes Evangelium," in *Christliche Schriften von J. G. Herder. Dritte Sammlung* (Riga: Hartnoch, 1797), 1–273 (7–8).

12. Herder, "Vom Erlöser," 675–76, 686–87; "Regel," 7–10.

13. Herder, "Vom Erlöser," 697; "Regel," 7–13, 59–60.

oral Urgospel's long-term cohesion, and it suffices, Herder claims, to account for Synoptic agreements, especially in sequence.[14] But no doubt sensing that the kerygma schema is not quite up to the challenge he is constrained to adduce external factors: the Urgospel received its schematic arrangement and fund of traditions in the circumscribed instructional circles of the apostles in the primitive Jerusalem community. The apostolic helpers and evangelists received it in that set form and disseminated it in mission. These evangelists and teachers, not being personally acquainted with events and traveling far afield, required such for their own oral proclamation.[15]

Given the oral gospel's cohesion and utility, the fraught question (which will plague the oral-gospel hypothesis in all its iterations) is: why then the written Synoptics? Herder holds that the likely setting for the rise of written versions would have been baptismal instruction. What would have prevented a catechumen from writing down some iteration of the oral Urgospel conveyed in this setting? The Prologue to Luke's Gospel explicitly locates its origins in convert instruction. But Herder thinks that the "apostolic helpers" themselves—evangelists like Luke and Mark—would have found a written version of the oral gospel necessary to their work of instruction. Unlike the apostles they were not eyewitnesses, and their travels soon carried them beyond the radius of apostolic memory.[16]

There is a rather obvious clash here with his claim that the quasi-fixed oral gospel was apt for missionary purposes. Herder senses this and other problems that lurk in his hypothesis. Were written gospels at the initiative of catechumens or the evangelists themselves? If the evangelist, why, in view of the utility of the oral Urgospel, received directly from the apostles in a stable schematic form, for their mission? Did not the oral gospel itself emerge organically within the matrix of baptismal instruction? Herder suggests that Mark wrote down or dictated the oral gospel as an "off the cuff" memory aid.[17] But the schematic form of the oral gospel supposedly conduced to its assimilation to memory and transmission in that medium, especially for someone like Mark, on Herder's own telling a companion of the apostles. Elsewhere he says that Luke used the oral gospel for twenty years before he produced a written version.[18] The difficulties force Herder back on various ad hoc explanations,

---

14. Herder, "Vom Erlöser," 697; "Regel," 13–14, 31, 57–58.
15. Herder, "Vom Erlöser," 684–87; "Regel," 7–13, 60–61.
16. Herder, "Vom Erlöser," 679–80; "Regel," 7–8.
17. Herder, "Regel," 24.
18. Herder, "Regel," 48.

arguing that that the evangelists needed written versions to ensure the uniformity of the gospel, noting the susceptibility of an oral gospel to distortion by false teachers, and also suggesting that the rapid expansion of the movement had simply outstripped the capacities of an oral gospel.[19]

How does Herder imagine the relationship of the written Synoptics and the evangelists to the oral Urgospel? Mark and Luke belonged among the apostolic helpers and evangelists, by definition competent in the oral gospel, which—as the Lukan Prologue confirms—they had sought out direct from the mouths of the apostles and eyewitnesses. Matthew as an apostle was manifestly competent in the oral gospel. They wrote out their gospels drawing directly from the oral gospel in the version current for them, while adapting it to the exigencies of their divergent contexts.[20] We saw that Herder finds intra-utilization hypotheses (*Benutzungshypothesen*) and the corresponding scribal model of source utilization and editing ("laboriously cobbling materials together") absurd. How much easier for the Synoptic authors just to go speak to the many living eyewitnesses! Any intra-utilization scenario exacerbates the problem of variation: why would composers, so conceived, have produced such contradictions? Determining the logic of these direct utilization theories is impossible. "How is one to figure out which Evangelist copied, supplemented, abbreviated, tore apart, improved, degraded, and stole from the other?"[21] In Herder's polemic against *Benutzungs*-hypotheses one sees the acute problem that Synoptic variation posed in his cultural setting: it was grist for the scoffers and skeptics of his day. Written source-utilization hypotheses, he thinks, make matters worse. The oral gospel hypothesis, on the other hand, on the analogy of the saga neatly accounts for Synoptic variation: it arose naturally down an extended history of oral transmission by evangelist-performers ("rhapsodes") sensitive to their immediate settings, and inspired by their own genius and by the Spirit in the freedom of oral utterance.[22]

Herder, Markan Priority, and Apostolic Memory

Markan priority makes an early appearance here as a prominent feature of Herder's account. Dissenting acerbically from the Mark-as-epitomator theory,

---

19. Herder, "Vom Erlöser," 680; "Regel," 7–8, 65; "Von Gottes Sohn," 7–8.
20. Herder, "Regel," 26–29; "Von Gottes Sohn," 5–7.
21. Herder, "Vom Erlöser," 683.
22. Herder, "Regel," 57.

Herder argues that of the three Synoptics Mark is the earliest. Its shortness, unpolished expression, and Aramaic complexion indicate that it is very close to the form of the primitive (*urältesten*) Palestinian Urgospel, as the latter existed prior to its modifications and secondary expansions in its oral transmission and dissemination. This is confirmed by the intentionality of the references in Mark's materials to Peter, James, and John that signals their special status as principal eyewitnesses and the leading agents in the formation of the apostolic saga, and by the early patristic tradition that Mark received the oral gospel direct from Peter. In contrast to the pitiful, woodenly compiling Mark of the Griesbach theory (Herder asks, why would such a useless epitome, serving no evident purpose, even be passed down?), the Gospel of Mark is closest to the archetypal apostolic narrative; it renders it in its most unsullied form, "without admixture of subsequently motivated additions." This is to say that a not inconsiderable amount of the additional materials found in Matthew and Luke is not original to the Urgospel, such as the Nativities and elements like those found in Matthew 18 that reflect later church formation and concerns. In fact, on the assumption that Mark is its best representative the divergences of the other evangelists from the primitive gospel are easily explicable.[23] Mark's complexion reflects its direct derivation from vivid oral storytelling; this also accounts for its thinness in didactic materials, which Herder takes to be less suitable to oral narrative utterance.[24] The primitive oral Urgospel, best conserved in Mark, is the basis, the "unadorned center column," for agreements in order and wording in the common tradition of the three Synoptics.

It follows that the Gospel of Mark is "witness to the first entrance of the historical gospel into the world."[25] Of the Synoptics it is the purer derivative of the oral Urgospel, which is the efflux of apostolic memory, of the eyewitness proclamation of Peter, James, and John in particular. Indeed, the simple pericopal form of the oral gospel's constituent traditions is the mode in which "people like the apostles" would have recollected and expressed memorable events and sayings.[26] Herder's source-critical enterprise anchors a strategy for securing the historical grounds of the gospel in apostolic memory and for distinguishing primary from secondary elements of the Synoptic tradition.

---

23. Herder, "Regel," 14–15, 18–24, 33–34, 61–63 (quotation 19); "Vom Erlöser," 677–78; "Von Gottes Sohn," 3–5.

24. Herder, "Vom Erlöser," 688.

25. Herder, "Regel," 61–66 (quotation 61).

26. Herder, "Regel," 59–60.

Herder's Proto-Matthean Gospel and the Double Tradition

But though the most pristine representative of the oral Urgospel, Mark's Gospel was not the first *written* gospel. In Herder's view that distinction goes to the Aramaic Gospel of the Hebrews (or Nazarenes), fragmentarily attested in patristic citations but more fully albeit only approximately represented, in Greek translation, in our Gospel of Matthew, a translation undertaken subsequent to the appearance of the Gospel of Mark. This Gospel of the Hebrews was composed in the primitive Jerusalem community, perhaps by the scribally trained Matthew himself—thus Herder interprets Papias's reference to Matthew's λόγια—with input from other eyewitnesses. Like the Gospel of Mark, it took the oral Urgospel as its baseline: hence the pattern of agreements between Matthew and Mark. This it subjected to some alterations and supplemented with messianic proofs.[27]

Luke, though aware of his colleague Mark's written gospel, likewise drew directly upon the oral Urgospel in the version that had descended to him, rendering it in polished Greek. The oral gospel thus is the medial term between Mark's Gospel and Luke's Gospel.[28] But Herder thinks it possible that Luke also used the primitive Gospel of the Hebrews, whose translation into Greek as our Gospel of Matthew had not yet occurred when Luke wrote. This would account for the materials that the Gospel of Luke shares with the Gospel of Matthew. But on balance Herder thinks it more likely that Luke did not use the Gospel of the Hebrews, for this is difficult to square with his very different arrangements of the double tradition. Instead, he directly accessed the primitive body of sayings and narratives that the Gospel of the Hebrews had drawn upon. In comparison to Matthew the double tradition's dispersed (*zerstreut*) arrangement in Luke more closely approximates to its primitive mode of circulation.[29]

Tradition, Memory, and Media in Herder's Source History

In the course of arguing his oral gospel hypothesis, Herder becomes acutely aware of the complexity of the media problematic that will beset Synoptic-problem scholarship. It is no surprise, therefore, that all the lines of subsequent source-critical development are to be found incipiently in his three essays. One finds, on the one hand, a sharp repudiation of the Griesbach hypothesis and,

27. Herder, "Regel," 26–29, 63–66; "Vom Erlöser," 677–78, 683–84, 694.
28. Herder, "Regel," 51–55, 64.
29. Herder, "Regel," 41, 49–50, 64; "Vom Erlöser," 692–93.

on the other, incipient forms of both the two source hypothesis and what to-day would be called the Farrer hypothesis. Herder affirms Markan priority in principle, the only difference being that the triple tradition is mediated to Matthew's and Luke's gospels via the oral Urgospel (Matthew's via the Gospel of the Hebrews). The oral Urgospel, that is to say, is a kind of proto-Mark. The double tradition is distinct from the mostly narrative tradition transmitted in the oral Urgospel. Matthew's double tradition comes to him via the Gospel of the Hebrews. Luke gets his either from the Gospel of the Hebrews (a Matthean prototype) or directly from the double-tradition sources of the Gospel of the Hebrews. Herder judges the latter—in effect a rudimentary Q hypothesis—to be the more likely.[30] As regards the medium of the double tradition itself Herder is less clear, though odds are he imagines it as circulating orally and unaggregated.

This nuanced media scenario notwithstanding, it is true that Herder places heavy emphasis on the oral factor. His analogy from oral saga gives him powerful leverage on the phenomenon of Synoptic variation. His awareness of the orality factor and its outsized cultural effects in the ancient world anticipates twentieth-century developments in research on ancient media realities. It is what leads him to warn against the error of projecting second-century practices with respect to written gospel books back into the first-century period of their emergence—a caution very needful today. He works with a robust conception of oral tradition, noting that it circulates in a range of genres, or forms, that persist into their initial textualization in the Gospel of Mark, and also that its self-contained pericopal forms help account for certain Synoptic phenomena, such as the contingent order of the Synoptic Gospels.[31] He recognizes that the sensitivity of oral tradition to social and historical contingences is a principal factor in the rise of Synoptic variation.[32] Synoptic writing, he notes, interacts with the ambient field of oral tradition.[33] Herder also works out a theory of the memory-tradition nexus. The primitive oral traditions are the tangible forms of apostolic memories (*Denkwürdigkeiten*), the linguistic forms of apostolic utterance. First-person eyewitness perspectives are absent in the tradition because its originators were bearing witness not to themselves but to Christ. Nevertheless, in the prominence it gives to Peter, James, and John, the proto-Markan Urgospel discloses its eyewitness originators.[34]

30. Herder, "Regel," 50.
31. Herder, "Regel," 59.
32. Herder, "Regel," 33–34.
33. Herder, "Regel," 24.
34. Herder, "Regel," 16.

Notwithstanding his grasp of the media complexity of the Synoptic problem, ultimately Herder does not escape a binary media perspective. He objects to Lessing's written Urgospel because he thinks that written source utilization cannot cope with the range of Synoptic variation. He rejects intra-Synoptic utilization hypotheses because he cannot conceive the evangelists subjecting their written Synoptic sources to such alterations. His binary puts him in the awkward position of having to claim that Luke probably "knew" but did not "use" his written predecessors (Gospel of Mark; Gospel of the Hebrews), allowing nonetheless that Luke, where his own style permitted, was influenced by "his friend [Mark's]" Semitic Greek style and wording.[35] In other words, Herder acknowledges tacitly that his scenario of the evangelists directly utilizing their versions of the Aramaic Urgospel cannot cope with the actual patterns of agreements in Greek.

He posits instead an oral Urgospel that by virtue of its oral properties accounts for the Synoptic variation yet, like an oral saga, is stable enough in its transmission to account for agreements. But in order to encompass variation and agreement Herder must claim simultaneously that the oral Urgospel was open to free variation and that it was fixed (*festgestellt*).[36] Herder masterfully identifies the powerful centripetal forces in oral tradition that generate variation. Every element of the tradition, "from the most inconsequential circumstantial details to the most important formulas," is grist for free variation; each recitation, each audience, and the "genius" of each individual narrator is occasion for such.[37] But as countervailing factors he is able to muster only the apostolic origins of the Urgospel, its point of origins in a primitive community around a single kerygma, the observable tendency of oral tradition to vary less in key motifs than in circumstantial details, and the simple, repetitive manner of "oriental" narration.[38] Whether these factors suffice to account for the close and extensive agreements in sequence and in wording may be doubted, especially given Herder's romantic celebration of the "free spirit" of the oral tradition. Similarly, we saw that on the oral gospel hypothesis Herder struggles to answer the natural question: Why then the written Synoptics? He is not able to come up with a compelling account of gospel writing.

Like Lessing's written Urgospel, Herder's oral-gospel hypothesis is a counter to the cultural skepticism of his time, an effort to identify solid his-

35. Herder, "Regel," 55, 64; also "Erlöser," 682–83.
36. Herder, "Erlöser," 686.
37. Herder, "Erlöser," 686–87, 697; "Regel," 57–59.
38. Herder, "Vom Erlöser," 697.

torical foundations for the religion of Christ. It traces the written Synoptics and their constitutive tradition back to a singular point of origins in apostolic memory. The traditions themselves are the tangible forms of apostolic memory. It is oral-traditional forces in the oral gospel's transmission that explain the problematic divergences among the Synoptic Gospels. We see here, right at its outset, the high cultural stakes in the critical inquiry into the Synoptic problem, and particularly in the roles that critics will assign to oral tradition, writing, and memory in their source histories. For both Herder and Lessing, Synoptic-problem analysis is a quest to identify historically trustworthy Ur-sources that transmit apostolic memory.

But it is the religion of Jesus that they seek to recover in these sources, not the Christ of church dogma. For Herder, Jesus's religion stood against Pharisaic legalism and empty cultic ritualism, against pointless theological speculation, and against the nationalistic particularism of official Judaism. Jesus taught simple childlike trust in God's provident care, manifestly evident in blessings received, and imitation of God's magnanimous love.[39] It is a religiosity native to Galilee, a region romanticized by Herder as "far from Judea and haughty Jerusalem," populated by a lively, common-sense people, from which humble classes, receptive to his simple preaching and message, Jesus took his disciples, not from the educated disciples of the rabbis with their pedantic, hypocritical piety.[40] From this opposition between Judea and Galilee arose the conflict that claimed Jesus as its victim.

Lessing and Herder simply reconnoitered the Synoptic media terrain. It would fall to Eichhorn to work out Lessing's written Urgospel proposal to its fullest extent, to Gieseler to do the same for Herder's oral Urgospel proposal. But Herder also worked out an incipient form of Markan priority, and at the same time suggested distinct origins for the double tradition. This brings us to Herbert Marsh (1801).[41]

39. Herder, "Vom Erlöser," 712.
40. Herder, "Vom Erlöser," 641–42.
41. Gottlob Christian Storr, in *Ueber den Zweck der evangelischen Geschichte und der Briefe Johannis* (Tübingen: Herbrandt, 1786), is another early advocate for Markan priority. He reasons from agreements in order that Luke used Mark, while his non-Markan materials are "oral reports" that he received from eyewitnesses in Jerusalem. Storr thinks that Luke was aware of an Aramaic Matthew, written by the apostle, but did not use it, owing to this proto-Matthew's arrangement of the material. Aramaic Matthew likewise used Mark, supplementing it with additional sayings (*Reden*) and episodes from the Palestinian tradition. Subsequently a translator made it available to Greek-speaking believers. Instead of "oral tradition" Storr speaks of "oral reports": testimony direct from eyewitnesses. This explains why he thinks Mark appeared as soon as the movement spread beyond the aural radius

CHAPTER 1

HERBERT MARSH

Writing in 1801, Herbert Marsh reacts to Herder as well as to Griesbach.[42] But he also engages Eichhorn (see below), whose essay "Ueber die drey ersten Evangelien: einige Beyträge zu ihrer künftigen kritischen Behandlung" appeared in 1794. While Marsh sharply criticized elements of Eichhorn's source history, his own account likewise features written sources intermediating between the apostolic proclamation and the Synoptics. Both therefore stand in a lineage descending from Lessing.[43]

Marsh's Multi-Document Source History

Marsh rules out intra-utilization hypotheses in principle because he thinks it impossible that "successive Evangelists copy[ing] from the preceding" could have produced the observable patterns of Synoptic variation. That they sometimes contradict each other; that they frequently describe events "in different, but synonymous terms"; that they randomly contain more, or less, than their putative sources; that their circumstantial descriptions diverge so markedly: all this is unintelligible on any direct-utilization scenario.[44] Similarly for an Aramaic Urgospel of Matthew as the source of three Greek Synoptics: such cannot explain why Mark and Luke passed over so much significant material (36). On similar grounds he also rejects the Griesbach hypothesis: it has difficulty supplying intelligible reasons why Mark would have proceeded as he did (17). Of Herder's oral-gospel hypothesis he notes that it skirts the problem of Synoptic agreements in wording, and that years of oral transmission would have made nonsense of any notion of a "common Gospel" (37–38). Because he shares Eichhorn's model of multiple intermediating written sources, his criticism of Eichhorn's source theory is muted, limited to pointing out that

---

of the apostolic eyewitnesses in Jerusalem. Luke's and Matthew's non-Markan materials likewise come to them direct from eyewitnesses. This media framework explains why Storr does not inquire further into the sources of the double tradition.

42. Herbert Marsh, *A Dissertation on the Origin and Composition of Our Three First Canonical Gospels* (Cambridge: Burges, 1801).

43. Marsh's *Dissertation* appeared in German as "Abhandlungen über die Entstehung und Abfassung unserer ersten drey kanonischen Evangelien," in *Herbert Marsh's Anmerkungen und Zusätze zu Joh. David Michaelis Einleitung in die göttlichen Schriften des Neuen Bundes*, trans. Ernst Friedrich Karl Rosenmüller (Göttingen, 1803), 135–331. I have found mentions of Marsh's work in German source critics down to about 1850 or so.

44. Marsh, *Dissertation*, 39, also 154 (hereafter page citations will be in the text).

14

Eichhorn's expedient of translation variants falls far short of accounting for the patterns of variation in Synoptic parallels (34, 166–69).

What does Marsh propose in the place of these theories? He starts from the striking patterns of agreement in the triple tradition. Matthew and Luke never agree in order except where both are in agreement with Mark; similarly, Mark never agrees verbally with Luke except where Matthew also agrees with Luke, and Matthew and Luke invariably diverge verbally except where both agree with Mark. As the ground of these agreements Marsh posits (with a nod to Eichhorn) a written Aramaic Ursource, א: from "communications of the apostles" a "short narrative was drawn up" comprising the principal episodes in the life of Jesus, beginning with Jesus's baptism and ending with his passion (196). Subsequently the Ursource א began to be variously augmented by "new communications from Apostles and other eyewitnesses," added to copies of א first as marginalia and then subsequently to the text itself. Because it had already diverged into different lines of transmission its various exemplars came to display different admixtures and combinations of additions, which are manifest in various double agreement configurations of the Synoptic Gospels.

Marsh further differentiates these various supplements to א into shorter, close-agreement circumstantial additions, labeled α, β, γ, and longer episodic sectional additions, labeled A, B, and Γ, which do not necessarily display close verbal agreement (Matthew's and Mark's parallel versions of the Death of John the Baptist, for example). Matthew/Mark agreements of the former kind he labels α augmentations, of the latter kind A augmentations; likewise, Mark/Luke agreements he labels β and B, Matthew/Luke agreements γ and Γ. Accordingly, in what Marsh describes as the "genealogy of these transcripts," the Gospel of Matthew is א+αγAΓ; the Gospel of Mark is א+αβAB; the Gospel of Luke is א+βγBΓ. The α/A augmentations (Matt/Mark agreements) were made to one copy of the Ursource, the β/B (Mark/Luke agreements) to a different copy. Along a branching stemma of transmission these two versions came to be combined and merged in a third copy—to form the proto-Mark Aramaic exemplar. Along separate, diverging branches of transmission to the forerunner א+αA and א+βB exemplars the γ/Γ materials (Matt/Luke agreements) were added independently—to form the proto-Matthew and proto-Luke Aramaic exemplars (176–77, 200).

These exemplars descend, along these separate lines, to the evangelists. None worked with knowledge of the others. The evangelist Matthew (the apostle) in working with his exemplar wrote in Aramaic, whereas Mark and Luke independently translated their Aramaic exemplars into Greek. This helps account for the verbal variation in their respective parallels. As Marsh recognizes, however, translation cannot account for verbal agreements in Greek—he criticizes Eichhorn on precisely this point. Accordingly, he argues that Mark and Luke used as an aid a Greek translation of א made before it had suffered any αβγABΓ additions: thus Mark and Luke's close triple-tradition agreements in Greek. After their gospels were in circulation, an unknown person translated the apostle Matthew's Aramaic gospel into Greek. In executing the project he used Mark's Greek gospel as an aid to render passages that Matthew and Mark shared in common (hence triple-tradition verbal agreements), and he turned to Luke's Greek gospel for assistance *only* for cases in which Mark and Matthew had no material in common (double-tradition verbal agreements). This expedient allows Marsh to explain why Matthew and Luke rarely agree verbally against Mark in triple-tradition passages: "The translator of St. Matthew's Hebrew Gospel made no use of St. Luke's Gospel, where he could derive assistance from St. Mark" (215–16).

Distinguishing features of the γ/Γ (double tradition) materials attract Marsh's attention. He notes that a subset, specifically the Sermon and the Healing of the Centurion's Servant, falls in coherent narrative order in both Matthew and Luke. These he designates Γ^1, reasoning that they were transmitted to Matthew and Luke as additions to א. But "by far the most numerous" of the γ/Γ materials appear in very different places in Matthew and Luke, respectively; these Marsh designates Γ^2. The best way to explain these distinctive Γ^2 materials and their "non-correspondent" patterns of distribution, Marsh thinks, is to suppose that they come from a distinct Aramaic document, ב, "a collection of precepts, parables, and discourses," a "Γνωμολογια" as primordial as the narrative source א, and like the latter "formed by continual accretions of new matter" (234–35). Matthew's and Luke's respective versions of this source had diverged in transmission; that is, it came to them in what amounts to ב[Matt] and ב[Luke] (177–78). Since it had no narrative order, and since Matthew and Luke had no knowledge of each other, they distributed ב materials into their narrative א source on different principles. Drawing on his eyewitness expertise, Matthew attached them to the appropriate narrative settings, though also opting to expand the א Sermon with materials drawn from various locations in the ב source. Lacking this eyewitness intelligence, Luke retained them mostly in the original order of the ב source, inserting the bulk between 9:51 and 18:14, supplementing them, as well as א sequences, with materials picked up from his own enquiries (thus L^S materials) (203–6, 235–36). Matthew and Luke display verbal agreements in these γ/Γ passages because Matthew's translator consulted Luke's translation in rendering them (203–9, 235–36).

Marsh and the Problem of Synoptic Variation

Marsh's account encounters complications in the variation patterns in the triple tradition and double tradition, especially passages where "the same thing is related in different words," that is, where *ex hypothesi* the evangelists (and the Matthean translator) consulted shared Greek translations. Marsh's initial response to this anomaly is to betake himself to what will ever be the source critic's most impregnable refuge: the subjective intentionality of the evangelist, or in this case of the Matthean translator. The translator was not pleased by the Gospel of Mark's periphrastic style. Nor did he think it necessary "at all times to consult St. Mark's Gospel" (212–13).

Notably, however, Marsh goes beyond this appeal to authorial subjectivity to invoke manuscript realities: because of unbroken, unformatted script it would have been a "greatly complicated" matter for the Matthean translator to distinguish passages in Mark's gospel—"to discover in one Gospel the passages, which correspond to those of another" (212). And in any case, he points out, one errs in imputing source-critical sensibilities, source-collating activities, or even the interests of a fourth-century Eusebius with his canons, to these Synoptic writers. Because of these media realities the Matthean translator would not have been making continuous close use of Mark's Greek text (156, 212–18). *A fortiori* the differently ordered passages in Matthew 8–9 would be high variation (e.g., their abbreviated profile), it being even more troublesome for the Matthean translator to locate these visually in Mark's Greek text.

How does Marsh bring verbal variation and agreement patterns in γ/Γ (double tradition, from source ב) parallels under his hypothesis? The Matthean translator, he says, upon encountering in Aramaic Matthew a γ/Γ addition—that is, a passage where "St. Mark's Gospel deserted him"—simply "look[ed] into" the Gospel of Luke for translation assistance (221). The difficulty is that numerous of the high-agreement γ/Γ parallels are found in Luke in a very different order. This is contrary to what Marsh's explanation of high-agreement triple-tradition passages leads one to expect. Marsh is therefore forced ad hoc to claim that the different order of the γ/Γ materials placed upon the Matthean translator the necessity of going "to greater pains" to locate the respective Lukan parallels, their concentration in the travel section easing this task somewhat. But then, suddenly, he switches to the out-of-order expedient to explain the high-variation Parable of the Pounds/Talents (Matt 25:14–30// Luke 19:11–27) (227–28). The Matthean translator goes to pains to locate the Lukan parallels—until he doesn't!

We see that Marsh's strictly written-source account cannot cope with Synoptic variation. It lands him in an impossible tangle of ad hoc qualifiers. Marsh's media outlook is refracted through a media binary that attributes variation to the oral medium, textual fixation in the mode of source copying to the written medium. Faced by Synoptic variation and agreement, and having judged against Herder that the patterns of agreements are the more determinative, Marsh works out a Synoptic history that is written source from A to Z. Synoptic variation arises through complex processes of written transmission.

Media and Memory in Marsh's Source History

Marsh's model is scribal manuscript transmission. Written sources א (narrative source) and ב (gnomologium) form the starting points for the history of the tradition. Oral tradition, understood as "apostolic communications," is a nominal factor, serving only as an initial placeholder and to furnish the necessary materials for writing operations. These are enterprises that originate in the primitive community. Along divergent and intersecting stemmata of transmission, "transcripts" of these initial drafts get augmented through additional "communications from Apostles and eyewitnesses" on the model of scribal marginalia, subsequently integrated into the text. Patterns of verbal variation arise in translation (Aramaic to Greek, periphrastic and literal), in various combinations of Aramaic and Greek *Vorlagen*, and in inexact recollection of remote passages in the source. Intentional modification of the written text is countenanced in one instance—for the apostle Matthew, who rearranged and redacted an exemplar of א on the basis of his eyewitness knowledge. Its ingenuity notwithstanding, this writing-based account simply gets overwhelmed by Synoptic variation. It is handicapped at the outset by Marsh's crude working conception of oral tradition: "communications of the apostles," a placeholder and negligible factor in Synoptic developments, an entity fugitive to memory and thus likely to be quickly fixed in writing (196–204).

Notwithstanding these complications, Marsh's sharp observation of the patterns of sequential and verbal agreement, his recognition that such require the written medium for their transmission, his recognition of the distinctive patterns of triple-tradition and double-tradition agreement, and the economical resolution of these patterns into Ursources א (narrative source) and ב (gnomologium) make him a pioneer of the two document hypothesis (2DH). Reconstituted on the basis of triple-agreement episodes, the Ursource א amounts to a kind of proto-Mark: a short narrative comprising the principal episodes in the life of Jesus, beginning with Jesus's baptism and ending with his passion, that is augmented along divergent stemmata of transmission and in thus differentiated exemplars forms the basis of Matthew, Mark, and Luke, with Mark the medial term of the other two.

JOHANN GOTTFRIED EICHHORN

Johann Gottfried Eichhorn first published his source history in 1794 and continued to present it, with revisions, in the various editions of his *Einleitung*. We will take his 1794 "Ueber die drey ersten Evangelien" and the 1820 edition of his *Einleitung* as our points of reference.

Eichhorn's Multi-Document Source History

In his 1794 essay Eichhorn points out that a common oral tradition is incapable of mediating Synoptic patterns of agreement in wording and episodic order. These patterns indicate documentary mediation. The options then are either direct-utilization relationships among the Synoptics, or their independent use of common written sources.[45] The former is improbable, he argues, because of divergences among the Synoptics in wording, scene depictions, and sequence. If Matthew were copying from Mark, why would he shorten and mangle Mark's scenes, for example in the Sea-Crossing episode (Mark 4:31–35//Matt 8:18–27) carelessly omitting Mark's notation, essential to the logic of the narrative, that Jesus was asleep at the stern? Why would he put down that there were two demoniacs rather than one? Why would he write "carpenter's son" rather than "carpenter"? Conversely, why would Luke and Mark diverge so sharply on the paralytic's passage through the roof? Why does Luke know nothing of Mark's Call of the Disciples (Mark 1:16–20)? If an evangelist had the works of the others before his eyes, would such frequent divergences in expression and sequence occurred? Hardly! The only explanation for these patterns of agreement and divergence is that they are both drawing from a primitive Aramaic writing (*Urschrift*).[46]

But how to reconstitute this primitive writing? Where the order of all three Synoptics in their common episodes agrees, one is securely in touch with the *Urschrift*. Where two out of three agree in order against the third, and a

45. Johann Gottfried Eichhorn, "Ueber die drey ersten Evangelien: Einige Beyträge zu ihrer künftigen kritischen Behandlung," in *Allgemeine Bibliothek der biblischen Literatur*, vol. 5 (Leipzig: Weidmann, 1794), 760–996 (765–66, 926–27).
46. Eichhorn, "Evangelien," 766–68, 773–75, 841–42, 929.

reason can be given for the latter's divergence, one has recovered yet more of it. Eichhorn supposes that as a kind of rough first draft (*ein roher Entwurf*), this *Urschrift* would have had a rather raw, primitive form, a bare-essentials content, and an unevenness of episodic arrangement. At times one Synoptic, at times another, has what appears to be the most primitive form of their common tradition. None of the three therefore preserves the *Urschrift* in its purity. Doubly attested (Mark/Matt and Mark/Luke) pericopes found in the common triple sequence are additions to the *Urschrift* in the course of its documentary transmission in branching and intersecting stemmata of development. It has descended to the evangelists in a stemma of three separate exemplars: an exemplar "A" used by Matthew that contained a number of additions, an exemplar "B" used by Luke, with a set of different additions, and an exemplar "C" used by Mark that had combined the additions found in the A and B exemplars, respectively.[47]

We see that Eichhorn will try to explain the rise of Synoptic variation on the model of variants arising cumulatively in the course of scribal transmission of a manuscript. Synoptic variation is parsed out among proliferating exemplars plotted on a three-branched stemma connecting our Synoptics back to the *Urschrift*. The *Urschrift*'s primitive, first-draft profile and its deficiencies in content invite supplementation and other interventions by copyists in the course of its dissemination.[48] In Eichhorn's view the shortest form of a given pericope is also the most primitive. The *Urschrift*'s pericopes therefore prompted expansion. The exemplar used by Matthew best preserves its short-pericope character.[49] Stubs of instructional elements in the *Urschrift* prompted supplementations with like materials: its short Mission Instruction, for example, was enlarged to the proportions observable in Matthew 10. A copyist of an early exemplar supplied the *Urschrift*'s truncated Temptation pericope with the three temptations. The stemmatic branch of that exemplar descended to Matthew and Luke, to the latter, though, in a variant exemplar that had transposed the temptations.

Copyist-tradents frequently supplemented their exemplars with materials from their own knowledge of the life of Jesus, either as eyewitnesses or from eyewitness informants, particularly when such would rectify narrative deficiencies of the *Urschrift*. A case in point is the insertion of Jesus's move from

47. Eichhorn, "Evangelien," 797–800, 826, 961–62.
48. Eichhorn, "Evangelien," 790; *Einleitung in das Neue Testament*, 2nd ed. (Leipzig: Weidmann, 1820), 1:29–30.
49. Eichhorn, "Evangelien," 836–37.

Nazareth to Capernaum upon his return to Galilee in an exemplar in the line descending to Matthew and Luke. Sometimes it was a matter of a tradent exchanging an element in the text with a variant originating in Jesus's own teaching or a variant current in the tradent's immediate context. At times tradents substituted a favorite expression for the one in their exemplar or expanded it with analogous material. Occasionally modifications of the *Vorlage* were a matter of copyists reacting with their contemporary historical contexts—for example, the modification of "Zachariah son of Jehoida" to "Zachariah son of Berechiah," the latter murdered by Zealots before the destruction of the Temple (Matt 23:35b//Luke 11:51a).[50]

In other words, Eichhorn positions *Urschrift* tradents in an ambient memory field of tradition that constantly impinged on their tradent activity.[51] A special case of this is Eichhorn's claim that the apostle Matthew was the redactor of an exemplar of the primitive Aramaic source positioned early in its line of transmission to the Gospel of Matthew. Matthew occasionally corrected his exemplar on the basis of his eyewitness knowledge. This is how Eichhorn explains the Markan transpositions in Matthew 8–12: the Markan order has been adjusted to the correct chronology. Several small-scale Matthean variants receive the same explanation, an instance being the mother of the sons of Zebedee, not James and John themselves, asking for their preferment (Matt 20:20).[52] Inserting additions into an exemplar, whether by an apostolic redactor like Matthew or by anonymous tradent-copyists drawing from the ambient memory field, often required editing of adjacent materials. This generated further variants.

But how does Eichhorn explain variation in wording? In his 1794 essay he invokes translation variants—consistently with his practice of finding the origins of every Synoptic variant in some documentary operation. Variation in wording among the Synoptics is so extensive, he thinks, that the evangelists cannot have been working from Greek originals, for why would they have so extensively departed from the text of the Greek *Vorlage*? Each has independently translated the Aramaic *Urschrift*, in the particular form it has come down to him, into Greek.[53] The diverse wording of the arrival of the women at the tomb—Ὀψὲ δὲ σαββάτων, τῇ ἐπιφωσκούσῃ εἰς μίαν σαββάτων κ.τ.λ.

---

50. Eichhorn, "Evangelien," 974.
51. Eichhorn, "Evangelien," 790–96, 821–23, 877–82, 890.
52. Eichhorn, "Evangelien," 780–81, 855–60, 942; *Einleitung*, 437–38.
53. Eichhorn, "Evangelien," 782–84.

(Matt 28:1); Καὶ διαγενομένου τοῦ σαββάτου κ.τ.λ. (Mark 16:1); τῇ δὲ μιᾷ τῶν σαββάτων ὄρθρου βαθέως κ.τ.λ. (Luke 24:1)—are independent renderings of the baseline Aramaic text.[54] Eichhorn extends the translation variant explanation to the entire range of lexical variation in the Synoptics. Matthew's tauter, more concise Greek comes from his more literal translation of the Aramaic text, whereas Mark's verbose, periphrastic style reflects his freer approach to translation.[55] The translation variant device, in concert with the variations that have developed among the A, B, and C exemplars through a multi-branched stemmatic transmission, allows Eichhorn to reconcile the Synoptics' widely variant wording with their broad agreement in order, a perennial conundrum for Synoptic source criticism.

The translation-variant theory showed serious strains already in 1794 when Eichhorn first adumbrated it. As otherwise sympathetic critics like Herbert Marsh pointed out, it had difficulty coping with contradictory variants, a case in point being Mark's "dug through the roof" and Luke's "through the tiles" in the Healing of the Paralytic (Mark 2:4b//Luke 5:19b), which Eichhorn is forced to attribute ad hoc to "an underlying obscurity of the Aramaic text."[56] The main objection, however, was that independent translation could not explain the extensive verbatim or even close verbal agreements in Greek. Added to this was that the Synoptics sometimes agreed in Greek citations of the Old Testament that diverged from the LXX, and also in rare Greek words and unusual expressions—for example, πτερύγιον τοῦ ἱεροῦ (Matt 4:5//Luke 4:9) and ζημιόω (Matt 16:26//Mark 8:36//Luke 9:25).[57]

Accepting the justice of these critical objections Eichhorn in subsequent expositions of his hypothesis introduced an amendment to it, one that Marsh had tried out in 1801. Shortly after the appearance of the Aramaic *Urschrift* a bilingual early Christian teacher and companion of the apostles made a Greek translation to facilitate outreach in bilingual regions of Syria. This Greek translation was disseminated and came down to the evangelists. They kept it at hand as an aid (*Hülfschrift*) as they translated their respective Aramaic

---

54. Eichhorn, "Evangelien," 835–37, 919.

55. Eichhorn, "Evangelien," 930, 937–49.

56. Eichhorn, "Evangelien," 846; see Marsh, *Dissertation*, 34, 166–69.

57. According to Gieseler it was Hug that pointed out that Eichhorn's independent translation-variant hypothesis could not account for Synoptic agreements in trivial or rare Greek words and in OT citations neither from the Hebrew nor from the LXX. See Johann Carl Ludwig Gieseler, *Historisch-kritischer Versuch über die Entstehung und die frühesten Schicksale der schriftlichen Evangelien* (Leipzig: Engelmann, 1818), 43–44, citing Hug, *Einleitung in die Bücher des N. T., Erstes Heft* (Basel, 1797), 60–68.

exemplars. Their practice was to follow this common Greek *Hülfschrift* where its text matched closely the text of their respective Aramaic exemplars, but to translate direct from their Aramaic exemplars where the latter diverged from the Greek text. This produces the Synoptic patterns of alternating agreement and variation.[58] This contrivance, rather than getting rid of its difficulties exacerbates the core problem of Eichhorn's utilization hypothesis: its dizzying proliferation of intermediating written sources to cope with the range and profile of Synoptic variation. Now Eichhorn adds yet another stemma for the Greek version of the *Urschrift* running parallel with the stemma of the Aramaic *Urschrift* and intersecting with its branches at numerous points.

As if this documentary array were not complex enough, Eichhorn also now posits a D exemplar—a version of the *Urschrift* used by Matthew and Luke that contained their *double-tradition* expansions (we will return to Eichhorn's explanation of the double-tradition problem below). He tries to simplify this by proposing the existence of an Aramaic Matthew E, a combination of A and D, subsequently translated into Greek.[59] But his account collapses under the weight of the sources and ad hoc hypotheses he must posit to prop it up. It succumbs to the fate of any utilization hypothesis that operates strictly within the confines of the written medium and documentary practices: the proliferation of sources to encompass Synoptic variation, for the origin of each variant can only lie in some documentary action.

Eichhorn on Tradition and Memory

The converse of Eichhorn's strictly documentary-media approach is his impoverished notion of oral tradition. Oral tradition for Eichhorn is simply a subsidiary term for direct apostolic eyewitness testimony, hence an entity proprietary to the individual apostles. He connects it to no artifactual form other than "oral instruction" (*mündlicher Unterricht*). It follows that its effective range is those within earshot of the apostles or other eyewitnesses, though it can also be mediated via direct informants. This is why Eichhorn has the primitive Aramaic source appearing immediately upon the movement's being carried by apostolic helpers and teachers beyond the boundaries of Palestine after Stephen's martyrdom, "three to four years after Jesus' death."[60] This primitive work is a "memoire" (*Denkschrift*), its materials are memory elements

58. Eichhorn, *Einleitung*, 196–200.
59. Eichhorn, *Einleitung*, 366–70.
60. Eichhorn, *Einleitung*, 4, 548–49.

(*Denkwürdigkeiten*).[61] Its antecedents lie in the practice of Jewish rabbis and their students to write down memoranda—for memory-aid purposes—of their oral tradition.[62] As such the *Urschrift* is subliterary and artless, the artifact of uneducated men unpracticed in composition, a rough draft of the life of Jesus following the outline of the narrative kerygma, with a basic selection of episodes rendered in a truncated form.[63] In other words, the *Urschrift* is the virtually unfiltered expression of unmediated apostolic memory.

To be sure, the unknown composer of the *Urschrift* was no apostle himself, for an eyewitness would hardly have recorded such a profusion of miraculous and legendary elements, which show that popular interpretation has already mingled with the historical material. Eichhorn nevertheless pays his respects to the Papias testimony: the apostle Matthew was an early redactor of the *Urschrift*.[64] This further secures the eyewitness credentials of the *Urschrift*, which in its Matthean line of transmission subsequently experienced considerable developments.[65] The evangelists Mark and Luke also have apostolic bona fides. Eichhorn rejects as legendary the patristic report that Mark's Gospel was direct from Petrine preaching traditions, noting the sparseness of its references to Peter. The patristic testimony is dispensable here because it conflicts with Eichhorn's utilization scenario, which has Mark dependent on a much-modified, much-transmitted version of the *Urschrift*. Nevertheless, the evangelist is the historical John Mark known from Acts, thus in a position to assess the trustworthiness of his source materials. The historical trustworthiness of Luke's Gospel ultimately derives from the *Urschrift*, but as Paul's companion on his last journey Luke would also have come into contact with eyewitnesses of Jesus's words and deeds.[66]

We now see more clearly what is at stake in Eichhorn's three-way configuration of eyewitness memory, the primitive Aramaic source, and documentary transmission in complex branching stemmata. The *Urschrift* is the taproot of apostolic memory, of the primitive Aramaic-speaking community. Put differently, analysis of Synoptic variation and agreement that has made it possible to trace and reconstitute the *Urschrift* at the same time has brought us into touch with the life of Jesus in its purest (*gereinigtes*) form.[67] By the same token,

61. Eichhorn, *Einleitung*, 259–60.
62. Eichhorn, *Einleitung*, 3–5.
63. Eichhorn, *Einleitung*, 5, 177–78; "Evangelien," 778.
64. Eichhorn, *Einleitung*, 9–10, 176, 611, 691.
65. Eichhorn, *Einleitung*, 474, 495–97, 548.
66. Eichhorn, *Einleitung*, 598–603, 611–12, 644; "Evangelien," 798.
67. Eichhorn, *Einleitung*, 154–59.

it has put us in touch with the faith of the primitive community, which does not need a virgin birth to connect Jesus to God and manages fine with few of the miraculous, legendary elements that would soon so profusely overrun the tradition. Eichhorn's source history distinguishes the "apostolic" from the "nonapostolic," the essentials of faith from the nonessentials. As such it serves as a bulwark for the gospel sources against the calumnies of the skeptics.[68]

Eichhorn's Media Assumptions

We have seen that the Eichhorn model of variation arising from cumulative, incremental editorial modifications of an *Urschrift*, on the analogy of scribal manuscript transmission, must proliferate intermediating sources to handle the copiousness of Synoptic variation. The reason is that Eichhorn's media assumptions allow him to conceive of written transmission only as close copying. The result is open-ended multiplication of intervening sources. The anomaly is that Eichhorn, in some tension with his media model, often recognizes that significant transformations of the written tradition can plausibly be attributed to the evangelists and—on his model—to earlier tradents of the *Urschrift*. The evangelist Mark is responsible for the "periphrastische" expansion and free rendering of *Urschrift* pericopes; Luke similarly. Both substitute favorite expressions, and both have transposed the Decalogue order (Mark 10:16 and Luke 18:20).[69] In the Wicked Husbandmen Matthew has "paraphrased his *Urtext* in . . . verse 41, appended an unambiguous application to the Jews to verse 43, and . . . transposed the statements at the end of the pericope."[70] Eichhorn pays his debts to his media model by professing agnosticism over whether such modifications are to be attributed to an evangelist or "to an earlier copyist [*Abschreiber*]." Yet he also says that "the most significant, most extensive modifications may stem from the evangelists themselves."[71] But once he allows room for redactional autonomy, he has undermined his warrants for rejecting direct-utilization relationships among the Synoptics.

Eichhorn's difficulties can be traced to a media binary that takes variation to be the index property of oral tradition, close agreement the index property of the written medium, and these modes of transmission as mutually exclusive of each other. Eichhorn, we saw, lacks any robust conception of oral

---

68. Eichhorn, *Einleitung*, 445–50, 498–500.
69. Eichhorn, "Evangelien," 809, 897–98.
70. Eichhorn, "Evangelien," 904.
71. Eichhorn, "Evangelien," 939.

tradition. He regards variant second-century patristic citations of Synoptic materials, for example, as drawn *either* directly from oral tradition independent of the Synoptic Gospels *or* directly from some written gospel. Because these quotations vary from their Synoptic parallels, the patristic writer cannot be quoting directly from one of our Synoptics. He can only be citing from other gospel books, which must be relics of the *Urschrift*, the transmission of which continues into the second century and surfaces in various apocryphal gospels.[72] Eichhorn is trying to deflect the objection: why have the vast branching stemmata of *Urschrift* exemplars that he posits disappeared without a trace? Characteristically, he generates yet more exemplars: distinct written sources behind patristic variants.

Eichhorn's Rudimentary Two Document Hypothesis

Eichhorn applies the sound criterion that the common order of the triple tradition is the order of the primitive Aramaic source: where all three agree, and where two agree against the third and reasons can be given for the divergence of the third. By the same token, comparing Mark/Matt parallels, and Mark/Luke parallels, he recognizes that Mark is medial. His Markan evangelist of course uses a version of the *Urschrift* (C) that had combined the versions used, respectively, by Matthew (A) and Luke (B). Eichhorn notes though that of the three, Mark adheres to the *Urschrift* "the most faithfully."[73] Preventing him from a closer approach to Markan priority is alternating primitivity, a standard problem for any Markan priority theory. But playing an outsized role in Eichhorn's determinations of primitivity is his axiom that the "shortest, most incomplete, most deficient" parallel will always stand closest to the *Urschrift*.[74] Hence he thinks that the abbreviated pericopes in the Gospel of Matthew best preserve *Urschrift* forms, subjected by Mark in every case to periphrastic expansion. Against Eichhorn's media horizon the evangelists do not exercise the level of redactional autonomy that would make Matthew's and Luke's direct utilization of Mark even a theoretical possibility.

This brings us to Eichhorn's attempt to solve the source-critical problem presented by the double tradition. Given his media framework, reckoning with its puzzling combinations of close verbal agreements and wildly different order gives him no end of trouble. He never quite successfully copes with it, and his

72. Eichhorn, *Einleitung*, 102–3, 128–31, 153.
73. Eichhorn, "Evangelien," 828.
74. Eichhorn, "Evangelien," 789.

explanations shift across the various iterations of his source history. We will look at his first (1794) and final (1820) accounts.

In 1794 Eichhorn treats the double tradition in different but sometimes overlapping subsets:

(1) Matthew and Luke's close agreements against Mark in the Preaching of John the Baptist indicate their common dependence upon "some written source or other" (*aus einerley schriftlicher Quelle zugeflossen*). Eichhorn takes three-way agreements in Mark 1:7–8//Matt 3:11//Luke 3:16 (The Stronger One) to indicate that the primitive *Urschrift* must have been the original baseline (*Grundlage*) for these double-tradition additions. Luke's divergences from Matthew, not least his expanded form of John's preaching, make his derivation of them from Matthew or the Matthean exemplar unlikely.[75] In the case of another overlap passage, the Beelzebul Accusation (Matt 12:22–29// Mark 3:22–30//Luke 11:14–23), Eichhorn surmises from the agreements with Mark that Matthew's version must come from his *Urschrift* exemplar. Out of concern for chronological accuracy, however, an early eyewitness redactor has relocated the episode to Matthew 12. Luke on the other hand takes his version from "another memoir" (*eine andre Denkschrift*) and to avoid redundancy has dropped the Mark 3 doublet. His placement of the Accusation (Luke 11:14–23) in a very different narrative sequence from Mark's version, and (presumably) its lack of agreements with Mark indicate that Luke takes his Beelzebul episode from this source and passes over the version attested by Mark (so in Luke's "B" version of the *Urschrift*) to avoid creating a doublet. That a parallel to Jesus's True Family (Mark 3:31–35) is found in Luke 8:19–21 confirms Luke's awareness of the Beelzebul episode's narrative contextualization (attested by Mark) in the *Urschrift*. Eichhorn of course notices that on this account of things the close Matt/Luke agreements against Mark are anomalous. To explain them he hypothesizes some early cross-fertilization from the pre-Matthean exemplar stemma into the separate Lukan *Denkschrift* line.[76]

(2) Eichhorn demarcates another set of double-tradition materials, among them the Temptation (Luke 4:1–13//Matt 4:1–11); Healing of the Centurion's Servant (Luke 7:1–10//Matt 8:5–13); Jesus's Discourse on John the Baptist (Luke 7:18–35//Matt 11:2–19); the pre-mission call stories (Luke 9:57–62// Matt 8:18–22); Woes (Luke 11:37–52//Matt 23); and Parable of the Entrusted Money (Luke 19:11–27//Matt 24:14–30). Matthew's and Luke's disagreements in these passages, and their highly divergent arrangements, rule out direct

75. Eichhorn, "Evangelien," 809–11.
76. Eichhorn, "Evangelien," 860–65; see also *Einleitung*, 259–60.

dependence of one on the other. These materials come *either* from commonly expanded *Urschrift* exemplars descending to Matthew and Luke, respectively, *or* from other sources, distinct from the *Urschrift* but rough narrative *bioi* just like it. Eichhorn judges the latter scenario the more likely on the grounds that the narrative logic of Luke's contextualization of these materials is superior to Matthew's.[77] He does not speculate on where these parallel materials come from or how they came to different *Urschriften*.

(3) Eichhorn proposes that Luke's travel section 9:51–18:14 is a distinct Lukan source which the evangelist has inserted as a block, a memoir written down by a companion of Jesus on his final journey to Jerusalem. This source contained double-tradition elements such as the Mission Instruction; the Our Father; Ask, Seek, Knock; the Beelzebul Accusation (here Eichhorn gets around to identifying Luke's distinct source for that episode); Return of the Evil Spirit; Demand for a Sign; Lamp of the Body; the Woes (which earlier he has assigned to a parallel *Urschrift* composition); Do Not Be Anxious; Divisions; and Settling with an Opponent. But if Luke has a unique source for these, how does Eichhorn explain the Matthean parallels, many of them in the Sermon on the Mount? He notes that the close verbal agreements in these parallels, and the close internal motif-cohesion displayed by a number of them, require a written source connection of some sort, which means that Matthew and Luke must be using a common source (*gemeinschaftlich einerlei Denkschrift gebraucht*).[78] This is the same solution that Eichhorn offered for the Preaching of John the Baptist. So is this common *Denkschrift* Luke's travel source? But the latter is a unique Lukan source, and limited to the final journey. Eichhorn's account is getting incoherent. The double tradition is eluding his grasp.

The 1820 edition of his *Einleitung* registers Eichhorn's final effort to solve the problem. He now consolidates quite a bit of the double tradition into a separate version of the *Urschrift*, the "D" exemplar. In one list he includes the Temptation; Sermon elements; the Healing of the Centurion's Servant; the Luke 9:57–62 call stories; Jesus's discourse on John the Baptist; elements of the Beelzebul Accusation, including the Return of the Unclean Spirit and Demand for a Sign; from the Mission Instruction, the Woes against the Galilean Cities; the Woes, including the Announcement of Judgment and Lament over Jerusalem; Faithful and Unfaithful Servants; Bold Proclamation (Luke 12:2–8); and the Entrusted Money. The common denominator of these parallels is high agreement, though with enough disagreement to rule out direct utilization

---

77. Eichhorn, "Evangelien," 965–67.
78. Eichhorn, "Evangelien," 992–93, also 977–78.

of one by the other. Therefore Matthew and Luke must be using a common written source (*von einer gemeinschaftlichen schriftlichen Quelle abhängen*). Eichhorn rules out that it might be a self-contained double-tradition source, a sayings source. Why does he reject this possibility out of hand? He professes not to see how these various double-tradition materials might cohere to constitute a source, but his more fundamental reason is his belief that the archetypal early Christian genre can only have been a *narrative*, a *Leben Jesu*. Much more likely therefore is a "D" version of the *Urschrift* with double-tradition expansions that has descended separately to the Matthean and Lukan evangelists, to the former in a combined A + D exemplar "E."[79]

Eichhorn now attempts to square this with Matthew's and Luke's divergent arrangements, the principal cause of which, he argues, is early interventions by the apostolic *Urschrift* redactor Matthew and final interventions by the "final arranger" (*letzte Ordner*) of the Gospel (presumably the Matthean evangelist). Eichhorn seems to imagine the double tradition coming into the *Urschrift* in two waves. Some elements came in so early that they were in the *Urschrift* exemplar redacted by the apostle Matthew. The latter shifted a number of these to more chronologically accurate narrative contexts; still others got shifted around in the wake of his Markan transpositions. Another quantity was added (along with a number of M materials) by the final arranger, who was also principally responsible for giving the Gospel the schematic topical arrangement that is its emblematic feature (Eichhorn therefore regards the Lukan arrangement of the double tradition as the more original). A subsidiary factor was the Lukan evangelist's preference on occasion for a doublet (e.g., the Luke 11 Woes and the Luke 12 Faithful and Unfaithful Servants).[80] This is effectively a Q hypothesis, the difference being that the Matthean final arranger reorders the double tradition of a Matthew-redacted Urgospel relative to the latter's triple-tradition narrative spine.

This revised account of the double tradition, however, lands Eichhorn back in his original difficulties. Eichhorn wants to make Matthew's "final arranger" responsible for the addition of a large quantity of the M materials, because of their high quotient of elements with legendary coloration.[81] But he also thinks, given the close integration of some M materials with Matthean double tradition (e.g., in the Sermon on the Mount), that the final arranger brought in a fresh quantity of double-tradition materials along with the M materials.

79. Eichhorn, *Einleitung*, 365–67.
80. Eichhorn, *Einleitung*, 368, 491–97, 544–45.
81. Eichhorn, *Einleitung*, 474.

Suddenly the differently contextualized Lukan parallels—one need only think of the Sermon on the Mount—become a problem again! Eichhorn again identifies the travel section, dense in Sermon on the Mount parallels, as a unique Lukan source. But he observes that the numerous close-agreement parallels to the Sermon's elements demand some kind of written-source connection. The Matthean arranger therefore must have had some written aid (*etwas Schriftliches*), some source or other (*einerley Denkschrift*) in common with Luke, before his eyes when incorporating these additions.[82] He leaves the difficulty of the double tradition there, no further toward resolution than in 1794.

In sum: we have here, in 1794, and again in 1820, a rudimentary version of the two document hypothesis, with several of its main pieces in place, including that Luke's Gospel best preserves the order of the double-tradition materials in the common source, and that Matthean redactors have carried out a rearrangement under the guidance of specific editorial principles. Eichhorn is impeded from identifying it as a sayings source because his *Urschrift* hypothesis requires narrative to be the archetypal primitive Christian genre.

JOHANN CARL LUDWIG GIESELER

The abrupt compensating shift to the other media pole occurs in Johann Carl Ludwig Gieseler's *Historisch-kritischer Versuch über die Entstehung und die frühesten Schicksale der schriftlichen Evangelien* (1818). Gieseler follows Herder and argues that the Synoptic Gospels are adventitious byproducts of oral practices, independent realizations of an oral Urgospel.[83]

Gieseler's Oral Gospel Hypothesis

Gieseler shares Eichhorn's premise that written utilization is a matter of close copying of the source. Therefore, he is in accord with Eichhorn in peremptorily rejecting direct utilization among the Synoptics. Synoptic patterns of variation are inexplicable on such theories. They would entail a writer sometimes obscuring and even contradicting his source, substituting defective for clearer depictions, carrying out bewildering transpositions of words, phrases, and indeed

---

82. Eichhorn, *Einleitung*, 544–45, 648–50.

83. Gieseler identifies J. Chr. R. Eckermann, *Erklärung aller dunkeln Stellen des Neuen Testaments*, Theil I (Kiel, 1806), xi–xii (also *Theologische Beiträge*, vol. 5 [Altona, 1796], 155–209) as a forerunner; also Gottlieb Christian Philip Kaiser, *Die biblische Theologie*, Theil 1 (1813), 224 (*Versuch*, 83–85).

entire passages, "turning the pages of his predecessor now here, now there," here holding exactly to source wording and sequence, there randomly varying, here omitting, there adding materials.[84] But on Eichhorn's theory of mediating Greek translations one would expect much closer agreement (41).

In Gieseler's view the only alternative is the oral medium. Gieseler builds his case mainly on extraneous considerations, chief among which is the pervasiveness of ancient orality. We must guard, he says, against projecting our contemporary literate realities back into the ancient world. Jewish practice in ancient Palestine favored oral tradition almost exclusively. The rabbis transmitted their tradition orally, feeling no need "to fix it in writing" until AD 200. If orality so dominated the practices of the elite literate rabbis, how much more the earliest believers, who were of the humble classes! Capability, let alone interest, in writing can hardly be imputed to simple Galilean fishermen, unschooled in difficult Aramaic letters, unpracticed in the cumbrous writing materials and accoutrements, and strangers to the laborious work of the scribe. But more to the point, the artificiality and deadness of writing is the antithesis of free, life-filled orality. The enthusiastic (*begeisterte*) Aramaic-speaking community of simple "Orientals" would hardly have "chained" their "living memory" of Jesus, uttered in inspired charismatic fervor, to "dead letters" (*todte Buchstaben*) (60–66). (Here we have another early debut of the romanticized primitive Palestinian community, the *Urgemeinde*, destined for a long career in Synoptic source criticism.) The apostle Paul knows of nothing but the oral proclamation of the gospel (75). Variant patristic quotations indicate that these second-century writers were still using a widely received body of oral tradition rather than written gospels (147–49, 153–73).

As it was for Herder, Gieseler's challenge is to explain the rise of a cohering oral Urgospel solely out of early Christian oral practices. The oral tradition itself, Gieseler begins, emerged directly from the eyewitness testimony of the apostles, expressed in their Spirit-inspired preaching and community instruction. In these activities their memories of the details of Jesus's life and his sayings merged with messianic interpretation of the Old Testament to form the primitive tradition, which orbited around the christologically interpreted Scriptures just like the rabbinic oral tradition orbited around the Torah (70–80). To counter the powerful centrifugal forces of orality that would generate uncontrolled variation, this oral tradition received tight narrative forms (*feste Erzählungsformen*) (102).

It is one thing to describe the origins of the tradition (there is much to like in Gieseler's account above), quite another the origins of a stably co-

---

84. Gieseler, *Versuch*, 35–36 (hereafter page citations will be in the text).

hering oral Urgospel persisting as an identifiable entity for decades, in wide dissemination, despite these same oral forces of variation, such that it can account for the patterns of close agreements among the Synoptic Gospels. This is where Gieseler starts to lose his footing. "The identical order of the Synoptic episodes," he says with some bravado, "makes the least difficulty." Why? Because it was of "highest importance" to the apostles, who shaped the oral gospel in their preaching, that the events of Jesus's life unfold in correct order (88). Eyewitnesses could come to one another's aid in establishing the most faithful order (100). Through rehearsal this order became fixed. The set oral forms assumed by the tradition, Gieseler says, limited the range of verbal variation. Somewhat counterintuitively (variants typically arise across multiple enactments) Gieseler claims that the apostles "always repeated things in the same words" (95). His analogies are to singers like Homer, whose reenacted sagas maintained consistent form, and also to Old Testament messengers who faithfully repeated their messages. Also conducing to lexical uniformity was the Aramaic language's (alleged) poverty in synonymous expression: a given content could only take form within a limited lexical range of expression. The "simplicity" (*Einfachheit*) of the apostles and the primitive community, as well as their singularity of focus on the events to which they bore witness, also tended toward a certain uniformity (*Gleichheit*) in the lexical profile of the oral Urgospel. The "high importance" of the matters to which the episodes bore witness was likewise a formidable factor strengthening lexical cohesion (88–94).

Gieseler is not so naïve as to imagine that these factors could produce the extensive lexical agreements, in words and word order, displayed by many Synoptic parallels. Rather, the quasi-fixed form (*feste Form*) taken by the oral gospel was in consequence of its repeated rehearsal in the primitive community. That this occurred orally neatly explains the differential levels of Synoptic agreement. High agreement narrative parallels were those regarded as more important than the low-agreement parallels, hence more frequently rehearsed and thus more exactly imprinted in memory (*je wichtiger . . . desto übereinstimmender*), whereas more the content than the form was preserved of less important narratives. The same goes for the high agreements in sayings elements vis-à-vis narrative elements, an additional factor being the tight linguistic forms of sayings and their innate memorability. And like the disciples of the rabbis, those sitting under the apostles would have repeated their instruction with exactitude (90, 98–99).

But perhaps sensing problems with the analogy, given the at best intermittent exactitude in Synoptic parallels, and given his categorical contrast of elite literate circles with the living orality of the unlettered primitive community, Gieseler throws the accent back upon the latter. Uttered in their midst by eyewitnesses in a state of charismatic exultation (*begeisterte Augenzeugen*), the traditions resounded in the inner being of the gathered believers, aroused their affects to high pitch, and deeply imprinted their memories (*aufs festeste einprägen*). Early Christian memory for Gieseler is an affect, a state of exultation, the cognitive counterpart of community enthusiasm (*Begeisterung*). Oral memory—and the cohesive form of the primitive oral gospel—is the manifestation of community life borne upon the afflatus of the Spirit, not the artifice of the dead letter, the artifact of formal apostolic agreements and laborious memorization (92–99).[85] This body of oral tradition coalesced in the oral gospel, its episodic and lexical bonds forged and reinforced in its careful repetition in discipleship circles gathered around the apostles and informed by the ethos of unbroken master/disciple succession (Gieseler abruptly shifts back to the rabbinic analogy). Thus rendered resistant to orality's propensity to variation, its form sanctioned by usage, and cultivated in cultural contexts accustomed to passing down tradition by memory, it was capable of durable, long-term transmission. It was apt for quick memory assimilation by nonapostolic evangelists and teachers whose travels disseminated it beyond Palestine (68–69, 88–97, 105–7). Its tight coherence in order and wording accounts for the striking patterns of agreements of the Synoptic Gospels.

Solving one difficulty—how an oral gospel can assume a *feste Form*—gives rise to another: ironically, accounting for the considerable variation in Synoptic parallels. How does Gieseler explain this, given his insistence on the oral gospel's baked-in resistance to variation? The claim that the oral Urgospel's constituent episodes fell on a scale of greater or less "importance," the less important being rehearsed less often and thus more variable, was his preemptive response to this problem. The oral gospel that emerged from Jerusalem, therefore, in its individual pericopes was actually just "more or less" uniform (*gleichförmig*) (103). Also, its dissemination beyond the geographical and cultural confines of Palestine and the rise of the Gentile mission introduced diverging vectors of development (110). Gieseler also reaches for Eichhorn's expedient: translation variants from Greek translations of the Palestinian Urgospel. A fluent Greek translation realized in Antioch under the auspices of "Hellenists" such as Barnabas, and omitting Jewish-exclusive passages, passed into the Pauline mission and hence to Luke. A Semiticizing Palestinian trans-

---

85. Gieseler is emphatic that an apostolic *collegium* is not required to account for the *feste Form* of the oral Urgospel; the Urgospel self-organizes.

CHAPTER 1

lation, under the auspices of the apostles Matthew and Peter, was the basis for the Gospels of Matthew and Mark (i.e., Peter), accounting for why they agree more closely with each other in wording than with Luke (113–16, 123–27).

Gieseler and the Appearance of the Written Synoptics

Given the sufficiency of the oral Urgospel, its long-term transmissibility in *feste Form*, and its versatile utility in mission and teaching, the appearance of the written Synoptics after just a few decades seems like an anomaly. There was no obvious need that such answered to; indeed, Gieseler thinks that the oral gospel was still the gospel of the churches in the second century. He gives the only explanation he can of this phenomenon: it was wholly adventitious. With the oral gospel's wide dissemination in the literate Greek world, inevitably there would be some to whom it occurred to write it down, among whom were the writers of the Synoptics. Luke refers to this in his Prologue. There was no programmatic intent (*höhere Bestimmung*) in these writing projects; they were merely for private use (*Privatschriften*), handy aids (*Hülfsmitteln*) for assimilation of the oral Urgospel to memory or as prompts to assist a teacher or evangelist in its oral delivery (116–17).

The Synoptics were formed by these evangelists drawing independently upon the oral Urgospel. Given the lengths to which he goes to secure a *feste Form* for the Urgospel, how does Gieseler explain the differences in content among the Synoptics (MarkS, MattS, LukeS) as well as in the Mark/Matt, Mark/Luke, Matt/Luke parallels? The oral Urgospel, he says, copiously contained all the Synoptic content; the evangelists drew upon it selectively, guided by the needs of their respective audiences. Why, in view of the apostolic sanction that it bore, did they take the liberty to draw from it selectively? Because, Gieseler says, its content was not the consequence of a conciliar decision but of usage, a convention. Their divergences in order are due to the natural freedom of variation that "an oral narrative schema" permits (87–89).

Gieseler's oral gospel hypothesis entails that the Synoptics in their origins have the status of accidental writings, *Privatschriften*, that upon their appearance did not encroach one bit into the oral gospel's domain, which lasted into the second century. Though the Synoptics were doubtless locally known, they lacked comparable authority: variant parallels and absence of citation formulae to written gospels confirm that the patristic writers were using an oral source, the Urgospel. "Hence it is clear that the earliest Christian era held the written Synoptics to be of no value [*keinen Werth*]; the evangelists' oral tradition was more important" (171). How then to explain the sudden canonical apotheosis of the Synoptics beginning in the mid-second century? Gieseler has little choice but to put this down solely to contingency: it was an expedient to combat the heretics and their written gospels (147–48, 197–201).

The Oral Gospel and Gieseler's Media Framework

Gieseler is uncannily contemporary in his grasp of the pervasiveness of orality in the ancient world. His description of the tradition emerging from the nexus (*Zusammentreffen*) of the memory of Jesus with scriptural messianic interpretation, its formation around christological and moral nucleation points in primitive Christ groups, achieves a high level of insight into tradition-formation. Gieseler likewise recognizes that oral tradition takes shape in forms that bring stability and variation into equilibrium and ensure the secure memory-based transmission of essential cultural information.

Nevertheless, his attempt to explain Synoptic phenomena exclusively with reference to the oral medium fails as completely as Eichhorn's exclusive appeal to the written medium. Eichhorn's model could not account plausibly for Synoptic variation. Gieseler's oral hypothesis cannot explain the patterns of close agreement. Attempts to derive close agreements in wording from the apostles' uniformity of perspective, from their oriental "simplicity," from Aramaic's alleged poverty in synonymous expression are obviously specious—and they make variation anomalous. But also on the face of it dubious is Gieseler's baseline explanation: the more important a tradition, the higher its agreement levels. In any case, once variation is allowed into any elements of the oral Urgospel, once its units are differentiated and individuated on the basis of importance and the frequency of rehearsal, its *feste Form*, so crucial to the success of the hypothesis, is compromised. The oral tradition breaks back up into individual units.

Gieseler's difficulties arise from defective media assumptions that take orality and writing to be mutually exclusive modes of transmission. He dismisses out of hand direct utilization relationships because—like Eichhorn—he cannot conceive that such variance can arise out of one evangelist utilizing another. In Gieseler's case the media dichotomy is hardened even more by his romanticization of the primitive Palestinian community, placing its enthusiastic orality in structural antithesis to the lifeless artificiality of writing and elite literacy. But he is forced by brute Synoptic realities, the patterns of variation and agreement, to impute properties of the written medium to the oral gospel (its quasi-fixed form) and properties of the oral medium to the evangelists (their freedom in in selection and ordering of materials). But the more he emphasizes the *feste Form* of the oral gospel, the more difficult it becomes—ironically—to accommodate the patterns of variation. The hypothesis fails at explaining what should give it the least difficulty. Gieseler does not really grasp that variation is a core property of the oral medium, essential to the situational responsiveness of oral tradition and hence to its long-term viability. The fixation uniquely enabled by the written medium becomes a norm transferred to the oral gospel. Variation receives ad hoc explanations. The appearance of the written Synoptics and their canonization remain unaccountable anomalies.

Gieseler rejects written utilization scenarios out of hand. His imputation of properties of the written medium to the oral Urgospel means, however, that he does work out a utilization scheme of sorts. In his scenario the Greek oral gospel that the evangelist Mark uses shares with the Greek oral gospel version used by Matthew the distinction of hewing closest to the original Aramaic Urgospel. Luke's gospel is derived from an early, Gentile-friendly oral translation of the Urgospel, leavened by influence from the more Semiticizing Greek oral Urgospel from which Matthew's and Mark's versions derive. The faintest hint of a Q hypothesis lies in Gieseler's insistence that the primitive community focused on the narratives of Jesus life (*die Begebenheiten seines Lebens*) and his sayings (*seine Reden*) as being of equal importance (100).[86]

Ernst Sartorius

Though not particularly influential, the contribution (1820) of Ernst Sartorius merits brief treatment because of his attention to the factors of oral tradition, written tradition, and memory in an attempt to reckon with Synoptic realities. He opens with a trenchant commentary on the intractability of the Synoptic variation-and-agreement profile to one-track media solutions. The difficulty, he says,

> lies in the dense intermingling of two contradictory phenomena—the most diverse variation with the most exact agreement, and in every possible combination and gradation, such that the one cancels out any explanation one attempts to give of the other. . . . The [Synoptic] problem presents us not so

---

86. In 1812 Alois Gratz published his *Neuer Versuch, die Entstehung der drey ersten Evangelien zu erklären* (Tübingen: L. F. Fues, 1812). Like Eichhorn's Gratz's theory is beholden to the written medium, but it bears marks of Marsh's influence in particular. He posits two sources for the Lukan double tradition, one being a gnomologium and reflected in the travel section. These materials are found dispersed in Matthew. Gratz therefore conjectures that Matthew made use of a gnomologium related to Luke's.

much with a single knot as a snarl of knots, where unravelling one without fail has the effect of creating more. Here and there a few wholly identical verses, but shortly little variations resurface—in particles, transitional and connective formulas, synonyms, verb tenses and the like—that are all the more conspicuous the more difficult it is to identify any grounds for an author, supposedly slavishly following another, to diverge in such trifles— most of which can hardly be construed as improvements.[87]

This induces Sartorius to rule out any direct-utilization relationship. But he also rejects Marsh's and Eichhorn's "complex labyrinth" of sources.[88] Nevertheless Marsh demonstrated incontrovertibly, Sartorius believes, that the Synoptics are dependent on the same Greek source or sources. The notion of a primitive Aramaic gospel rests upon confused patristic testimony (21–22, 35–39). But Sartorius emphatically rejects the idea of a Greek Urgospel: the triple-tradition order of episodes only rarely agrees in all three Synoptics in contextualization of component episodes. For Sartorius these realities mean that one cannot get back to an Urgospel without reverting to the untenable solution of intermediating sources (14–20, 41–42).

How does Sartorius account for these Synoptic patterns? He reduces the history of the tradition to the terms of the written medium. Oral tradition as he conceives it is inherently prone to distortion and disintegration. Its dysfunctional properties prompted the rapid gathering of Jesus sayings and narratives into provisional written collections (*Aufzeichnungen*), an enterprise centered on the apostolic collegium in Jerusalem. Oral tradition was a feasible medium for the gospel only in the mode of the direct eyewitness testimony of the apostles. The precipitating occasion for the written tradition therefore was the rapid expansion of the movement beyond the borders of Palestine and thus out of the aural range of the preaching of the Jerusalem apostles. These first written collections therefore were not in Aramaic but Greek (41–52, 66–69).[89] By this means Sartorius reconciles the primitive Palestinian origins of the tradition with the indefeasible evidence that the Synoptics are dependent on Greek sources. With the same stroke he dispenses with the Aramaic Urgospel hypothesis.

87. Ernst Sartorius, "Ueber die Entstehung der drey ersten Evangelien," in *Drey Abhandlungen über wichtige Gegenstände der exegetischen und systematischen Theologie* (Göttingen: Dieterische Buchhandlung, 1820), 9–126 (11–12).

88. Sartorius, "Entstehung," 25–26 (hereafter page citations will be in the text).

89. Sartorius extends Luke's motive of ἀσφάλεια (in the Prologue) to these primitive writing projects that he hypothesizes.

The contingent origins of these provisional collections in convert instruction accounts for other striking features of the Synoptic profile. Little consideration was given to matters of historical chronology or coherent connections among constituent elements. This source history is registered in the "abrupt, fragmentary" profile of the Synoptics. The transitional elements that serve to connect units form a chronological-geographical framework of only the most sketchy kind. The attempt to find a coherent historical line of development in the Synoptics is futile. The paucity of the Synoptic material relative to what must have been the abundance of historical occurrences is likewise explicable with reference to the primitive written collections: episodes and sayings were selected that brought home most sharply and strikingly the points of ethical, practical, and christological significance (56–63).

How will Sartorius explain Synoptic variation? Acknowledging a debt to Herder, he moves in an innovative, cross-media direction. The evangelists were "companions of the apostles," particularly charged with memorizing the various written collections of apostolic traditions and reciting them as time, place, and occasion required. They deeply internalized these collections, and their repeated oral enactments of them increasingly came to bear their individual imprint. It was also inevitable that in repeated oral enactment, these memory-internalized materials—originally distinct, provisional collections (*Aufzeich-nungen*)—would gradually merge into a single narrative unity. A common baseline order emerged. Each evangelist adapted and supplemented his version with additional materials acquired through their individual connections with various apostles (70–73). By these means Sartorius accounts economically not only for the origins but also the profile of the Synoptic Gospels—they are aggregations of smaller Greek collections, displaying patterns of agreement and variation in diction, sequence, and content.

Mark's medial position is due to the evangelist, a companion of both Paul and Peter, drawing on variant collections associated with Paul and Peter, respectively. This explains his alternating agreements with Luke's Gospel (Paul's companion) and Matthew, whose gospel Sartorius associates with Petrine materials (he does not explain why). This account has a Griesbachian flavor— Mark alternately drawing on Matthean and Lukan materials—but because dependence exists at the level of the primitive collections accessed by all three, Mark is no epitomizer, as Sartorius makes a point of saying. Because their three-way relationship is mediated through Mark, the companion of both Paul and Peter, there is a sense in which Sartorius construes Mark as prior. In fact, he identifies Mark as "the oldest gospel," on the grounds that it lacks an infancy narrative and allusions to the fall of Jerusalem (126). What about the double tradition? Sartorius identifies the block of material Luke 9:51–18:15 as one of these pre-Synoptic collections, "a distinct collection [*Sammlung*] of the sayings of Jesus" (64). This collection was constituted out of numerous smaller collections, which explains why the parallels in the Gospel of Matthew are found dispersed (97–98).

Sartorius's source history, centered on pre-Synoptic written collections, is the product of a media model in which oral tradition is little more than the aural dimension of apostolic testimony. Once out of effective aural range of the Jerusalem apostles any oral traces immediately become subject to whimsy and random distortion. It is this negative property of oral tradition, so conceived, that triggers Synoptic writing—the provisional collections that eventually issue in the Synoptic Gospels. The memory-internalized provisional collections in repeated oral enactment develop divergent profiles. In effect, picking up suggestions of Herder, Sartorius advances a primitive theory of how orality can affect written transmission.

Friedrich Schleiermacher, 1817

The first to propose a multiple-collections solution to the Synoptic problem, however, was Friedrich Schleiermacher, in 1817, three years before Sartorius's monograph.[90] Sartorius does not reference Schleiermacher, but a derivative relationship of Sartorius to Schleiermacher seems probable.

Schleiermacher's Multiple-Collections Hypothesis

Schleiermacher rejects direct-use hypotheses because in his view they entail capricious utilization practices that are simply unintelligible on any supposition of direct copying. Eichhorn's solution posits multiple gospel sources that mysteriously have disappeared without a trace.[91] Schleiermacher says that Eichhorn also will have us imagine "our good Evangelists, surrounded by four, five, six rolls and books, in different languages, all opened, now looking into one, now looking into another, collating passages. Methinks I find myself transported rather into an eighteenth- or nineteenth-century book workshop in Germany than back into the primitive era of Christianity" (14–15). More

---

90. Friedrich D. E. Schleiermacher, "Ueber die Schriften des Lukas: Ein kritischer Versuch," in *Friedrich Daniel Ernst Schleiermacher: Exegetische Schriften*, ed. Hermann Patsch and Dirk Schmid (1817; repr., Berlin: de Gruyter, 2001), 1–179.

91. Schleiermacher, "Schriften," 11–13 (hereafter page citations will be in the text).

basically, Eichhorn's primitive Aramaic source reconstituted from triple-agreements is an anomaly, "a wholly fantastical and disproportionate thing, elaborately detailed in some parts, incomprehensibly meager in others" (14). In any case, disruptions in sequence among the three (the different order of the materials Matthew 8–9 in particular; the absence of long sequences from Luke altogether) and the very different contextualizations of pericopes belie the notion of common triple-tradition order. Schleiermacher rejects Gieseler out of hand, arguing that his applying of the term εὐαγγέλιον, construed as a genre—"an ordered collection of episodes from Jesus' life"—to the most primitive era of Christianity is an anachronism (9–10).[92]

The unpredictable patterns of agreement and divergence, so refractory to Urgospel and direct-utilization solutions, are easily explicable, Schleiermacher argues, on the hypothesis that the evangelists (Matthew and Luke in particular) fit together multiple written collections of Jesus materials, some available to two or all three evangelists, some to just one (15–17). The origins of these collections lie in the desire of converts to have the narratives about Jesus and his sayings available in writing, as well as in the exigency of spreading the gospel beyond the aural radius of eyewitness testimony. The primary agents in this enterprise were not eyewitnesses themselves but persons in immediate contact with eyewitness informants. The resulting collections were diverse: many were organized on topical grounds; other collections simply registered miscellaneous materials as they came spontaneously from informants. The earliest were more like snippets, which invited combination into longer collections (17–20). Drawing from this field of primitive written collections, the evangelists fit them together such that they formed coherent gospel artifacts. Synoptic relations are mediated by these collections. This explains the curious patterns of variation and agreement that they display.

Taking the Gospel of Luke as his basis for comparison with Matthew and Mark, Schleiermacher argues that *Schlußformeln* (formulaic closing elements) and *Ausgangsformeln* (formulaic opening elements) allow the critic to demarcate the primitive collections that Luke has gathered together into his gospel. Luke 4:15–16 ("and Jesus returned in the power of the Spirit into Galilee,

92. It is curious that Schleiermacher in 1817 makes reference to Gieseler's work, published in 1818. The reference appears in Schleiermacher's *Vorrede* (dated Easter 1817). Schleiermacher's footnote allows us to identify his source as: J. C. L. Gieseler, "Ueber die Entstehung und frühesten Schicksale der schriftlichen Evangelien," in *Analekten für das Studien der exegetischen und schematischen Theologie*, ed. Carl August Gottlieb Keil and Heinrich Gottlieb Tzschirner (Leipzig: Johann Ambrosius Barth, 1816), 3.1:31–87. This fifty-six-page essay looks like a précis of Gieseler's 1818 volume.

and a report about him spread through all the country round about, and he was teaching in their synagogues, being praised by all"), for example, is the formulaic conclusion of a collection, also used by Matthew and Mark, that extended from the Baptism to the Temptation and centered on Jesus's call and authorization (40–41). Schleiermacher analyzes Luke 4:31–7:10 into two composite collections of shorter episodic sequences conspicuous by residual *Schlußformeln* that make redundant references to the spread of Jesus's fame or opening elements that lack connections to what precedes. The first, a collection of Capernaum healings, extended from 4:31 to 5:16; the second, a collection of Capernaum stories with sayings, extended from 5:27 to 7:10, with the Healing of the Paralytic, which combines pronouncements with a healing, perhaps serving to bind the two collections together at a pre-Lukan stage (47–50). The order of episodes in Matthew 4–9 differs from the order of the parallels in this two-collection Lukan section because Matthew used different collections of these materials, stemming from different eyewitness informants (64–65). The Lukan travel section is a composite of two collections (101, 120, 146–50).

How does Schleiermacher deal with the more fine-grained, localized patterns of alternating variation and agreement? He appeals mostly to what we can call "differential recollection": behind the various parallel and overlapping collections stand different eyewitnesses. Matthew 20:29 and Mark 10:46 have the Healing of Bartimaeus at Jesus's departure from Jericho, Luke 18:35 at his approach: the eyewitness informant behind Luke's source recollected things more accurately (140–45). The Matthean and Lukan versions of the Sermon stem from the different informants behind the two collections; the informant for the collection used by Luke was perhaps less advantageously placed to hear the Sermon, or perhaps more time had elapsed between the event and his recollection of it (62). Schleiermacher attributes the wide divergence between the Two Ways/Narrow Door parallels to Jesus's giving the teaching on two occasions in different words (121). The even more incongruent variants "whitewashed tombs" of Matthew 23:27 and "concealed tombs" of Luke 11:44 stem from faulty recollection on the part of the Matthean informant (115).

Differential recollection is Schleiermacher's one-size-fits-all explanation for variant parallels, but eventually he runs up against cases that strain credulity. Here he falls back on ancillary explanations. In one or two difficult cases he is forced to invoke redactional intervention by an evangelist—Luke's Sermon is short in part because the evangelist struck Jewish-Christian elements from the longer version in his collection (62). The curious bursts of verbatim verbal agreements in otherwise variant parallels, from different collections—that is, stemming from different informants—are due to the particular memorability of those elements. Frequently these coincide with Jesus's own speech and sayings. He has little to say, though, about cases of close verbal agreement in descriptive elements. To explain variants in otherwise close-agreement sequences of Jesus's own words he appeals partly to different understandings of the original Aramaic, partly to editorial intervention (142).

Posited to account for divergences in order, Schleiermacher's distinct-collections account runs into difficulties explaining agreements in order. How do independent collectors, consulting different eyewitness informants, produce collections that frequently agree in the order of independent episodes, whose connections with each other seem wholly contingent? It is also not easily squared with his view that the collections were formed on topical principles—collections of healings, of sayings, of stories with sayings, and the like (47–48). Schleiermacher's explanations are ad hoc, even conflicting. Likewise, his identification of certain passages as the *Ausgangsformeln* and *Schlußformeln* that demarcate collections is frequently arbitrary and strained.[93] The ease with which contingently originating collections can be snapped together to form coherent narrative lines, their convenient overlap in content, and the coincidence in the order in which the evangelists independently line up the collections strains credulity. Schleiermacher tries to make the different phases of Jesus's life a factor in the formation of the collections: a kind of virtual gospel is serving as the framework for their origins. Some collectors were interested in Call and Authorization episodes; others sought informants in and around Capernaum, creating Capernaum Ministry collections; some eyewitnesses wrote memoranda of journeys, which formed the travel section collections; other collectors were interested in Jesus's last days, hence Passion narrative collections. It seems that an Urgospel is not so easily dispensed with after all![94]

Schleiermacher's Multiple Collections and the Triple Tradition

The alert reader will have noticed that Schleiermacher talks little about Mark; his analysis proceeds mostly at the level of a Luke/Matthew comparison.

93. E.g., καὶ ἰδοὺ (Luke 23:50) as the *Ausgangsformel* for the Joseph of Arimathea episode, attached here by Luke to a Crucifixion account ("Schriften," 178).

94. As an evangelist Luke is little more than a collector and arranger (*von Anfang bis zu Ende nur Sammler und Ordner*), figuring out ways to fit prefabricated written collections together chronologically and topically in intelligible ways ("Schriften," 180). Thus Luke's own account of his work in his Prologue: καθεξῆς γράψαι ("Schriften," 100). But we have seen that Schleiermacher is forced to attribute some redactional activity to Luke and to the other evangelists, a concession that seems fatal to his hypothesis.

There is a reason for this. Schleiermacher wants to undermine the premise of Urgospel hypotheses: the existence of a common triple-tradition order. By comparing Matthew and Lukan order primarily, with particular attention to the stark divergences in order in Matthew 5–12 and then to the long block of missing material in Luke (the Great Omission), and leaving Mark out of the picture, he is able to depict a far more discontinuous triple-tradition sequence and thereby defang the principal argument for an Urgospel. He manages this by adopting a quasi-Griesbach approach to Mark's relation to Matthew and Luke. Sometimes he asserts that Mark is alternately using Matthew and Luke (100). In other cases he has Mark's agreements with Matthew and Luke mediated through their collections; for example, Mark agrees in order with Luke against the Matthew 5–12 sequence because he has at his disposal the same two collections that Luke uses in this section. This is still a Griesbach Mark; the direct utilization is simply at the level of Luke's and Matthew's collections. Mark, Schleiermacher says, is "too dependent and subordinate to come into consideration" (101). This conveniently clears the way for him to appraise triple-tradition order on the basis of a two-way comparison of Lukan order and Matthean order.

Schleiermacher's Multiple Collections and the Double Tradition

How does the Schleiermacher of 1817 handle the double tradition? It is incorporated into his system of collections. No gnomologium lies behind Luke's travel section. Rather, this section of Luke, which he argues extends through to the Judean journey (to Luke 19:48), comprises two collections, joined together (the seam is 13:21–22) at a pre-Lukan stage. In his opinion it lacks the genre profile of a sayings collection: it contains narrative materials, especially in 18:15–19:48, and any gnomologium *Schlußformel* is absent (101–2, 136). One cannot fail to notice that the narrative episodes in question are actually triple-tradition materials. Likewise, no gnomologium stands behind the Matthew 5–7 and Luke 6 Sermons. The extended, detailed speeches with their vivid openings are—in Schleiermacher's view—incongruous for a sayings collection. The Matt/Luke agreement in the order Sermon + Healing of the Centurion's Servant is the historical sequence of events (71).

Schleiermacher's Media Assumptions

What media assumptions inform Schleiermacher's analysis? The oral tradition equates to eyewitness testimonies mediated directly into the primitive written collections via individuals consulting with eyewitness informants. In a few instances eyewitness and collector are the same person. The eyewitness informants are not identical with the already over-extended apostles but are "friends and observers of the outer circle [*der zweiten Ordnung*]." Likely this is how Schleiermacher explains what he takes to be the eyewitness vividness of the Synoptic narratives but at the same time why they lack first-person perspective. For Schleiermacher *oral* tradition is quite literally the eyewitness voice (*Stimme*): if not recorded in writing it dies away (*verhallt*) with the soundwaves of its utterance. This is what precipitates the enterprise of written collections (70–71). Oral tradition is a kind of transitory placeholder, because of its contingent and precarious nature swiftly yielding to writing. Written transmission runs along a completely separate track; its definitive mode of transmission is close source copying. Verbal variation cannot be squared with source copying, so it arises from differential eyewitness recollection.

WILHELM MARTIN LEBERECHT DE WETTE

Synoptic source criticism in the 1820s was in flux. That the Griesbach hypothesis was a major force at the time is evident from Heinrich Saunier's 1825 *Ueber die Quellen des Evangelium des Markus*.[95] It also survived the 1830s upsurge in Markan priority theories to be taken up into early Tübingen *Tendenzkritik*. In our analysis, however, we give the Griesbach hypothesis only occasional mention. We are viewing nineteenth-century source criticism from the vantage point of the contemporary debate, in which the Griesbach hypothesis is no longer a force to be reckoned with.

95. Heinrich Saunier, *Ueber die Quellen des Evangelium des Markus: Ein Beitrag zu den Untersuchungen über die Entstehung unsrer kanonischen Evangelien* (Berlin: Ferdinand Dümmler, 1825), observes that Eichhorn's *Urschrift* is a deformed anomaly, whereas Gieseler asks us to accept the anomaly of a fixed oral gospel. Written mediation in Greek, Saunier observes, is required to produce this pattern of protracted agreements in order and wording: Mark combining and abbreviating Matthew and Luke. To get around the difficulties in this utilization scheme Saunier takes frequent refuge in ad hoc explanations and appeals to the inscrutability of Mark's intentions, as well as to Mark's redactional freedom. He admits that it is nevertheless difficult to understand some of Mark's passages as reworkings of the Synoptic parallels; in these cases Mark is drawing directly from a number of primitive sources, oral and written. In short, Saunier is unable to impute consistent editorial procedures to Mark. He is not even able to maintain that Mark is secondary. Saunier says that the question of Matthew's and Luke's relationship constitutes a separate problem. The Griesbach hypothesis is in fact principally an account of the origins of the Gospel of Mark. In theory it is compatible with any hypothesis that denies Markan priority.

In his 1826 *Lehrbuch* Wilhelm Martin Leberecht de Wette developed a hybrid source theory that combined the Griesbach hypothesis with the oral hypothesis,[96] an influential synthesis that D. F. Strauss adopted as the source-critical basis for *Das Leben Jesu*. De Wette's study merits our attention because it confronts head-on the media questions that are the concern of our study, and it also struggles mightily with the source-critical problems presented by the double tradition.

De Wette's Combination of the Griesbach and Oral Gospel Hypotheses

Writing in 1826, de Wette witnesses to the collapse of the multiple-source source histories associated with Eichhorn and Marsh. He begins where Eichhorn and indeed most Synoptic source criticism begins, with a description of Markan mediality, embracing Griesbach's explanation of the phenomenon.[97] But de Wette is in fact less interested in Mark than he is in the early history of the tradition and in Matthew and Luke's relationship. For this also he takes Griesbach's account as his point of departure (137). He is aware that the Griesbach hypothesis does not account for Synoptic origins or for the phenomenon of variation and agreement in Synoptic parallels, which the Eichhorn/Marsh approach at least purported to do. For a solution he turns to the oral hypothesis.

The intuition of the oral hypothesis, de Wette says, was correct—a widely diffused oral proclamation is the grounds of our three Synoptics. Saga-like elements in the Synoptics (e.g., Matt 27:8, 53) corroborate this. But an integrated gospel could not possibly have coalesced in the oral medium. The range of variation among Synoptic parallels is simply too great. It is better to understand this oral entity as a loosely cohering body of common oral tradition, in Greek (owing to its diffusion beyond Palestine). De Wette pointedly refers to it as an "oral presentation, performance" (*mündliche Vortrag*) rather than as a "gospel" (*Evangelium*) (98–99, 143–45). As such it simply cannot account for variation and agreement patterns in the Synoptics.

The written medium therefore must be brought into the picture. In due course there were efforts to bring the oral *Vortrag* into writing, as we learn from the Lukan Prologue. The effect of these provisional writing projects (*Aufzeichnungen*) was not only to fix the materials but to bring them into a more

---

96. Wilhelm Martin Leberecht de Wette, *Lehrbuch der historisch kritischen Einleitung in die Bibel Alten und Neuen Testaments* (Berlin: G. Reimer, 1826).

97. De Wette, *Lehrbuch* (1826), 132 (hereafter page citations will be in the text).

coherent, i.e., gospel-like, order. Importantly, these written artifacts in turn had a feedback effect upon the oral *Vortrag* in its ongoing oral transmission, affecting its organization and tightening up its cohesion, *and* upon subsequent gospel-writing projects. The latter occurred not only directly but also indirectly, via the feedback effects of these primitive writing projects on the oral *Vortrag* (145–46).

This accounts for the origins of Matthew and Luke, and for their relationship. De Wette says we learn from the Prologue that Luke drew upon these proto-gospel artifacts, and also from the stabilized oral *Vortrag* itself—which because of its now writing-influenced form we can start calling the oral gospel (de Wette starts referring to the *Evangelien-Vortrag*). The Matthean evangelist likewise drew upon the oral gospel. This elucidates Matthew and Luke's relationship and the variation profile of their parallels: their relationship is mediated by the now-stabilized oral gospel. They share a basic narrative sequence, with striking but localized divergences. But it is the pattern of variation in their common pericopes—low variation in sayings and essential episodic details, high variation in ancillary elements—in particular that indicates that a body of oral tradition, mediated by memory, must be their middle term. De Wette finds it hard to imagine direct written-source utilization producing these patterns (146).

Matthew and Luke's common sequence of narrative episodes is the sequence of the oral gospel. This sequence commences in their John the Baptist materials, and it continues, with localized disruptions, through to the Passion and Resurrection accounts. The disruptions in the order of their common episodes in the Galilean ministry (i.e., the Markan transpositions) amount to oral variants in order, owing to the weak bonding capacity of the oral medium.

The situation is rather different in their common sayings materials. A large number of these are found concentrated in Luke's travel section, provided with perfunctory historical settings, but their Matthean parallels appear in extended topical arrangements in different contexts. All these materials derive from the oral gospel, but Luke's disposition of them is mediated by his *Gewährsmann*: the person responsible for drawing up the written instantiation of the oral gospel which Luke uses had configured them into a different arrangement. The divergent dispositions of the Sermon and Mission materials likewise are due to the alternative arrangement of Luke's source. Viewed panoramically, Matthew has their common sayings materials in large blocks in chapters 5–7, 10, 13, 18, 23–25; Luke's are dispersed. Matthew's arrangements likely owe something to the Matthean evangelist himself (148–55). The ultimate source for the Matt/Luke common sayings tradition, however, is the oral *Vortrag*, not a *Spruch-sammlung*, as Marsh held, nor a separate travel narrative (*Reisebericht*), as Schleiermacher (1817) argued (156).

This is a serious attempt to deal with the media conundrum posed by Synoptic patterns of agreement and variation. It makes Matthew and Luke the products of complex cross-influences of oral and written sources. De Wette recognizes that an oral gospel *simpliciter* cannot be the grounds of their agreement patterns. Whoever the first writing evangelist might have been, this person brought these units into coherent narrative order, one that concentrated the bulk of its episodes artificially into a Galilean ministry. This order had a feedback effect on the oral *Vortrag* in its subsequent transmission, and so was also the order followed by subsequent writing evangelists. This Urevangelist could not have been Luke: he says as much in his Prologue, and his travel section interrupts the primitive narrative sequence. That it was the Matthean evangelist—and that Luke then utilized the Gospel of Matthew directly—cannot be satisfactorily demonstrated. The most that can be said is that the order of the Gospel of Matthew—or the order of a precursor gospel taken up by the Gospel of Matthew—influenced the oral *Evangelium-Vortrag*, and via this oral route fed into the Gospel of Luke, who was also influenced, however, by another written version of the oral *Vortrag* that had their common sayings material in different arrangements. These routes of influence explain the Matt/Luke patterns of agreement and variation in sequence and wording of parallels.

In the end de Wette's is a theory of Matthean priority and complexly mediated Matthean influence on Luke. For his part, Mark draws upon and combines Matthew and Luke, hence his alternating agreement with them in the order of their common narrative episodes. But so arbitrary is Mark's pattern of alternation and so variant is his wording from theirs that he cannot have their gospels before his eyes. Rather, he is using them by memory, a procedure that generates the same profile as oral utilization. This also explains why Mark lacks their didactic traditions, for these are harder to retain in memory. The often quite significant extent of Mark's variation from Matthew and Luke, and his frequent surplus in local details, as well as his small store of unique pericopes, indicates that he also drew directly—likewise by memory—from the oral tradition (159–60, 169).

Triple Tradition and Double Tradition in de Wette's Source History

How successful is de Wette's source history? De Wette combines a diminished oral hypothesis with Matthean priority and makes Luke dependent on Matthew via the middle term of the oral *Vortrag* that has been shaped by a Matthew-like written gospel artifact. To this source-critical array de Wette appends the Griesbach hypothesis to account for the Gospel of Mark, but this is an arbitrary conjunction: his Griesbach account of Mark has no organic connection with his account of Matthew and Luke. More significantly, de Wette's oral gospel—the middle term between Matthew and Luke—turns out to look more like an *Urmarkus*, a phantom Mark expanded by double tradition narrative episodes such as the Preaching of John the Baptist. Other than a few localized transpositions, its narrative sequence tracks the triple-tradition order.

The corollary is that de Wette fails to accommodate the double tradition successfully to his theory of a proto-Matthean oral gospel. He is forced to the expedient that Luke is using an alternative written instantiation of the oral gospel, one with a different configuration of the double-tradition materials, though remarkably this source sticks with the triple-tradition order, and though its existence clashes with de Wette's claim that the Gospel of Matthew was the principal organizing influence on the oral *Vortrag*. But then, oddly, de Wette also identifies Luke 9:51–18:14 as a Lukan insertion, though saying elsewhere that the Sermon on the Mount parallels in the travel section are due to Luke's special gospel source. That is, de Wette is not quite clear about the origins of Luke's disposition of the double tradition. His explanation for Mark's omission of the double tradition—that didactic materials could not be so easily grasped in memory—runs counter to his postulate that the oral gospel mediates (via memory) Matthean influence to Luke. If the double tradition presents special problems to oral mediation, then the oral *Vortrag* must have looked more like a proto-Mark than a proto-Matthew. De Wette in fact concedes that his Griesbach Mark must have had direct recourse to the oral tradition as well as to Matthew and Luke. In de Wette's system this can only have been the oral gospel. But if Mark had access to the oral gospel, why did he bother with Matthew and Luke at all?

In short, the double tradition is the Achilles heel of de Wette's hypothesis. He is not able to accommodate it to his proto-Matthew oral gospel. His oral gospel looks more like a phantom Mark, and behind the account he gives of the double tradition one sees something more like a phantom Q.

Nevertheless this is a serious attempt to reckon with the media complexities of the Synoptic problem. De Wette recognizes that the Synoptic profile must have been generated in some sort of interaction of orality and writing. He recognizes that the tendency of agreements in parallel pericopes to converge on essential details is an indicator of oral, memory-based transmission. Positing an oral gospel, stabilized by the feedback effects of a Matthew-like written artifact, as the middle term between Matthew and Luke is a serious attempt to cope with the unmistakable marks of orality in their parallel materials. This solution remains bound, however, to a media binary conception: variation patterns can only be due to the effects of an intermediating oral entity. Orality and writing remain segregated media modalities.

In subsequent editions of the *Lehrbuch* de Wette continued to affirm his source theory in its essentials while vacillating over how to construe Matthew's influence on Luke. In the 1830 edition he repeats that Luke in his triple and double tradition appears to be giving secondary renderings of more primitive Matthean versions. De Wette thinks that this indicates memory influence from Matthew, but different from 1826 he now allows that Luke occasionally has what appears to be the more primitive tradition—for example, the Lord's Prayer (Luke 11:1–4), the Sign of Jonah (Luke 11:29), and the Woes (Luke 11:37–42). Luke therefore obtained these directly from a pre-Matthean source stage.[98] It is not clear that de Wette continues to think of an oral gospel as the middle term between Matthew and Luke. Instead, he seems to conceive of Luke operating under direct memory influence from Matthew. In the 1842 edition of the *Lehrbuch* de Wette describes Luke's Sermon as a "deforming excerption" of the Sermon on the Mount. Luke has arbitrarily (*willkürlich*) redistributed the elements of Matthean sayings discourses and given them historical settings. He took his cue from Matthew's Nativity to develop his own Nativity, and similarly for his version of the Rejection at Nazareth (Luke 4:16–30) and Call of the Disciples (Luke 5:1–11).

But some of Luke's double tradition comes from a sayings collection (citation to Marsh) that had at some point been supplemented with scattered (*zerstreute*) excerpts from Matthew.[99] In the fifth German edition (1848, ET 1858) de Wette reverts to suggesting that the Matt/Luke agreement in narrative (triple tradition) sequence is mediated by an oral source, and he seems more receptive to Gieseler's notion of a stable narrative sequence that becomes established in an oral source though repeated oral delivery.[100] On the whole, though, the Gospel of Matthew appears to be more primitive than the Gospel of Luke, and in general Luke looks like "an elaboration of the first [gospel]." However, he reiterates his view that Luke has also used a written source, "which we may, with Marsh and others, regard as a collection of discourses [that] seems to have been enriched by scattered and unarranged excerpts from Matthew before it fell into Luke's hands; and despite his acquaintance with Matthew, he preferred to follow it, and to give some of the discourses in a

98. Wilhelm Martin Leberecht de Wette, *Lehrbuch der historisch kritischen Einleitung in die Bibel Alten und Neuen Testaments*, 2nd ed. (Berlin: G. Reimer, 1830), 162.

99. De Wette, *Lehrbuch der historisch kritischen Einleitung in die Bibel Alten und Neuen Testaments*, 4th ed. (Berlin: G. Reimer, 1842), 181–84.

100. De Wette, *An Historico-critical Introduction to the Canonical Books of the New Testament*, trans. Frederick Frothingham (Boston: Crosby & Nichols, 1858), 150.

less fitting connection."[101] The double tradition, its different arrangements in Matthew and Luke, continues to give de Wette headaches, and he finds himself pushed toward a Q-like solution.

De Wette's *Lehrbuch* in its various editions is an early effort to argue for Lukan dependence on Matthew. The main challenge of such an undertaking—giving an economical account of Matthew's and Luke's very different dispositions of the double tradition—is evident in de Wette's various complicated and ad hoc workarounds. He never successfully squares the divergent double-tradition arrangements and the corresponding question of double-tradition origins with the primitive oral-*Vortrag*/oral-gospel element of his source theory. The oral *Vortrag* in the end really serves only to account for the triple tradition, and thus amounts to a kind of proto-Mark. The Griesbach explanation of Markan origins is simply an unintegrated addendum to de Wette's analysis of Matthean and Lukan origins.

FRIEDRICH SCHLEIERMACHER, 1832

Schleiermacher's 1817 proto-Synoptic collections theory is the backdrop to his more famous 1832 essay on the Matthean λόγια mentioned in the Papias fragment on the origins of the Synoptic Gospels.[102]

Schleiermacher's Logia Source and Proto-Markan Source

According to Papias, Ματθαῖος μὲν οὖν Ἑβραΐδι διαλέκτῳ τὰ λόγια συνετάξατο, ἡρμήνευσεν δ᾽ αὐτὰ ὡς ἦν δυνατὸς ἕκαστος (Eusebius, *Hist. eccl.* 3.39.14–17). Schleiermacher identifies the root meaning of the Greek term τὰ λόγια as "oracles of God" (*Gottessprüche*). Papias, he says, is referring not to the Gospel of Matthew but to a collection (*Sammlung*), comprising individual sayings (*Sprüche*) and longer instructional sequences (*Reden*), compiled and written down by the apostle Matthew.[103] Subsequently an unknown redactor made this Logia source a major structural element of a gospel (the Gospel of Matthew) by attaching minimalist narrative frames to its discourses, using materials drawn adventitiously from "oral traditions of evangelists" (not apos-

---

101. De Wette, *Introduction*, 162–63.

102. Friedrich D. E. Schleiermacher, "Über die Zeugnisse des Papias von unsern beiden ersten Evangelien," in *Friedrich Daniel Ernst Schleiermacher: Exegetische Schriften*, ed. Hermann Patsch and Dirk Schmid (1832; repr., Berlin: de Gruyter, 2001), 229–54.

103. Schleiermacher, "Zeugnisse," 232–37 (hereafter page citations will be in the text).

tles but vocational messengers of the apostolic proclamation). The secondary narrative frames Matthew 4:23–25 and 7:28–8:1, for example, made a sermon on a mountain out of what had been the first section of the primitive gnomologium (as Schleiermacher is now prepared to call it). The gnomologium format made it an uncomplicated matter for the redactor to break into the sequence of logia at various places to make narrative insertions. The large Matthean discourses roughly preserve the collection's original sequence and structure. As a gnomologium it lacked narrative materials; hence it did not contain the Preaching of John the Baptist or the Temptation in Matthew 3–4, or the Beelzebul Accusation sequence in Matthew 12. The Matthean redactor seems to have pulled his narrative materials (healing stories, feeding stories, triumphal entry, and so forth) from a source or sources in which they already stood in narrative relations to each other (238–42).

On the other hand, the dispersed arrangement and different contextualizations of the double-tradition parallels in Luke show that Luke could not have used the Logia source; it is exclusive to the Gospel of Matthew. In Luke the parallel materials appear in their actual (*wirklich*) narrative connections, in sharp contrast to the topical organization of the Matthean Logia and the artificial narrative frames that attach logia discourses to the narrative ductus of the Gospel (247).

This brings Schleiermacher to Papias's comments on Mark. Papias's informant, he argues, could not have been referring to the Gospel of Mark, nor to John Mark of Jerusalem, an eyewitness himself of sorts. The Mark referred to by Papias's informant is an otherwise unknown companion and translator of Peter who transcribed the elements of Peter's ad hoc, to-the-occasion teachings in whatever order they came to his recollection. The described activity, Schleiermacher points out, would hardly have produced the present Gospel of Mark with its basic *bios* narrative sequence; indeed, Papias says explicitly, "but not in order." Rather, the work of this Mark would have amounted to a provisional collection, in Greek, of narratives mingled with sayings, though predominantly narratives, which are more suited for preaching (249–50). In other words, Schleiermacher interprets Papias's testimony about Matthew's λόγια and Mark as Peter's transcriber as a corroboration of his "provisional collections" source theory. The effect is that, in no small shift from his 1817 essay, he posits a Logia collection and a proto-Markan narrative collection, though without ruling out—in a nod to his 1817 essay—the existence of other mixed, ad hoc collections of the Markan type, attested in some of the Lukan sequences. Relations among the Synoptic Gospels, that is to say, continue to be mediated by these proto-Synoptic collections (250–54).

But this is accompanied by qualifications that likewise signal shifts from 1817. Abandoning his Griesbach-lite construal of Mark, Schleiermacher entertains the notion that the author of the Gospel of Mark uses the proto-Markan collection as his principal source. The Matthean redactor thus could be drawing triple-tradition materials directly from the Gospel of Mark, but just as easily from the same proto-Markan collection, for we have no certainty that Mark's Gospel appeared before Matthew's Gospel. The same applies to the Lukan evangelist: the Gospel of Mark could be among the writings he mentions in the Prologue, but he could be drawing upon the proto-Markan collection. Under any scenario the latter is the Gospel of Mark's principal source, but on the equal odds the gospel was written after Matthew and Luke the Markan evangelist could have drawn in addition from these predecessors. Either scenario would account for the triple-tradition pattern of alternating agreement. Schleiermacher astutely notes that Matthew and Luke's own dependence on the proto-Markan collection would hardly have been evident to the Markan evangelist's eye—the evangelists are not proto-modern source critics (252–53)!

The upshot is that Schleiermacher adopts Markan priority, *mediated through the proto-Markan collection*, while leaving open the possibility, in his view undecidable, of direct utilization. He also makes a fundamental triple-tradition/double-tradition distinction between a *narrative source* and *sayings source*, with narrative double-tradition elements excluded from the sayings collection on genre purity grounds. The Logia is now the chief source of Matthew's double tradition, whereas Luke's—as in the 1817 essay—continues to be various proto-Synoptic collections that, like the proto-Markan collection, mingle sayings materials with narrative pericopes (251). This explains the salient features of the double tradition's dispersed arrangement in Luke, which in Schleiermacher's view also preserves its more original historical settings. The multiple collections of 1817 therefore maintain a residual presence in Schleiermacher's 1832 source history, serving mostly to account for Luke's double and special tradition. But he does not inquire into how Luke's use of the proto-Markan collection (or Mark directly) might correlate with his use of these other collections, or for that matter with the patterns of agreement in the double tradition. To all intents and purposes his multiple-collections theory is moribund, and the question of Luke's source for the double tradition remains open.

Schleiermacher's revised source history continues to trace a direct line from the Synoptic Gospels back to apostolic memory via the proto-Synoptic collections, but now two principal ones. These diverge by genre and roughly correspond to the triple and double tradition, respectively: a collection of predominantly narrative episodes from the apostolic helper Mark and the Logia, from the apostle Matthew himself. Schleiermacher continues to associate the Synoptic tradition without qualification with apostolic eyewitness testimony: the proto-Synoptic sources are "collected apostolic remembrances" (*gesammelte einzelne apostolische Erinnerungen*). In a noteworthy turn of phrase, he characterizes the multiple collections in aggregate as the "collective memory of the apostolic church" (*Gesammtgedächtnis der apostolischen Kirche*) (254).

The Myth of Schleiermacher and the Logia

Not infrequently critics of the two document hypothesis claim that the Q postulate originates in Schleiermacher's mistaken construal of the Matthean λόγια mentioned by Papias as a gnomologium. Since λόγια actually means "oracles," not "sayings" (λόγοι), so it goes, Schleiermacher committed an error: Papias could be referring to a gospel. Schleiermacher's error was benightedly taken over by subsequent scholarship and became a crucial factor in the emergence of the two document hypothesis. Two document hypothesis scholarship, that is to say, is predicated on an interpretative error by Schleiermacher.

But it is this account of matters that rests on errors. Rudiments of the two document hypothesis, and in particular the tendency to distinguish the triple and double tradition by genre and source, are evident as early as Herder. The gnomologium hypothesis itself goes back at least to Marsh, and it surfaces in German scholarship repeatedly well before Schleiermacher. There is actually not much in Schleiermacher's source history without some antecedent.

His consequential innovation is this: he grounded the sayings-collection theory in the testimony of Papias. Papias's testimony on gospel origins was widely taken in nineteenth-century source criticism to be stipulative, before Schleiermacher and after. Many source critics took it as their point of departure; others interpreted it in light of their results. Schleiermacher's reading of Papias therefore would certainly have given a boost to emergent two-document scholarship, but it can hardly be taken as its starting point. In point of fact Schleiermacher notes that the root meaning of λόγια is "oracles" (not "sayings," as though confusing λόγια with λόγοι). Interpreting it as *Gottessprüche*, he then draws the inference to a sayings collection (232). He was already putting forward the sayings-collection theory in 1817. The version of it that he promulgates in 1832 owes more to his multiple-collections hypothesis than to any interpretation of Papias.

But even more importantly: by identifying Papias's Matthean λόγια as a Matthean sayings collection, and basing the identification in observable features of the double tradition, Schleiermacher provided an alternative to Matthean Urgospel theories (which in any case kept turning out to look more like proto-Marks). By interpreting Papias to be referring to a Matthean Logia source rather than to a Matthean Urgospel, Schleiermacher cleared the way for the clean emergence of Markan priority, and with it the source-critical problematization of the double tradition. His interpretation also explained the conundrum of why the narratives in the Gospel of Matthew, if they descend from a Matthean Urgospel, lack even residual traces of direct eyewitness recollection. A Matthean sayings collection does not run up against that difficulty.[104]

KARL CREDNER

We devote space to Karl Credner's 1836 source history because it is an illuminating case study of the effects of media and memory variables in Synoptic-problem theorizing. Credner emphatically rejects the hypothesis of a written Aramaic Urgospel supposedly authored by the apostle Matthew: the theory rests on nothing more than misinterpretations of Papias's testimony.[105] The prevailing conviction now, he says, is that oral tradition is the principal source for the Synoptic Gospels (referencing Herder and "above all" Gieseler).[106] Credner's account of the oral gospel's formation nevertheless diverges from Gieseler's. It emerged in the Aramaic-speaking apostolic community out of the dynamic cultivation of memories of Jesus's deeds and teachings (187). Ow-

104. We note briefly Friedrich Ludwig Sieffert's study, *Ueber den Ursprung des ersten kanonischen Evangeliums: Eine kritische Abhandlung* (Königsberg: J. H. Bon, 1832). Because his book was published in 1832, Sieffert is not familiar with Schleiermacher's essay. His source theory combines elements of the Griesbach hypothesis and Gieseler's oral hypothesis in a way that attempts to accommodate Papias's testimony about Synoptic Gospel origins—e.g., in composing his gospel the apostle Matthew draws upon the oral body of tradition. Particularly notable, though, for an era that tended simply to identify oral tradition with apostolic eyewitness testimony is Sieffert's clear-eyed acknowledgment that the units of the tradition do not fit the profile of eyewitness testimony. His attempt to account for this is insightful, even prescient. He observes that the Synoptic materials lack the episodic detail that is invariably part of eye- and ear-witness recollections. Instead, "only what is important and valuable gets communicated and propagated" (77–78) along with circumstantial information of only the most general sort. This metamorphosis occurs as a matter of course in the functional shift from immediate eyewitness recollection to the deployment of the materials in instructional settings. The effect is to give the units of the tradition an autonomy that makes it possible to bring them freely into different combinations.

105. Karl August Credner, *Einleitung in das Neue Testament* (Halle: Buchhandlung des Waisenhauses, 1836), 70, 92.

106. Credner, *Einleitung*, 178 (hereafter page citations will be in the text).

ing to its reception by the "Hellenists," the oral gospel almost immediately morphed into a Greek version. Though its emergence was spontaneous, the Greek oral gospel took on a "stereotyped" form. Nevertheless, it was only "partially uniform." Because it was an oral gospel, it gave scope for variation and for its tradents to exercise freedom in its enactments. The order of its episodes was contingent and variable according to occasion. It was no formally cohering gospel (189–93). It was longer, more copious, and more detailed than our present Synoptics. Standing in such intimate connection to living apostolic witness, its constituent pericopes expressed the immediacy and full episodic detail of eyewitness testimony. Its uniformity began to increase markedly, however, in proportion to its increasing distance from the eyewitnesses as the geographical radius of its dissemination expanded, and as the apostles themselves began to pass from the scene. As the connections to living eyewitness memory began to dissolve, the need for a more invariant oral gospel became an influential factor in its transmission. In due course it achieved the level of fixity mirrored in the patterns of agreement among the Synoptic Gospels (197–98).

What, then, prompted the shift to written gospels? Here is where the unresolved orality/writing issue generates an unintegrated source account. The principal factor, Credner says, was the fraying connections to eyewitness memory, which had sustained the oral-gospel tradition in its fullness and historical authenticity (*Vollständigkeit und Lauterkeit*). To its breakdown corresponded a degeneration in the historical quality of the oral-gospel tradition. This included widespread loss of eyewitness details, such as specific names, times, and places. Conversely, miraculous, legendary, or just historically inauthentic elements, along with contemporizing and dogmatic tendencies, filtered into the tradition. The eyewitness oral gospel was rapidly degrading into oral saga. Only the sayings tradition—Jesus's authentic teachings—was not susceptible to this tendency. These factors combine to account for the shift of the oral gospel to the written medium and the appearance of the Synoptics (193–201).

On Papias's authority Credner posits the priority of two written sources (*Schriften*), one direct from the apostle Matthew, and another from Peter via Mark. Matthew composed τὰ λόγια, an Aramaic sayings collection. Subsequently it was taken up into the narrative gospel, composed by a Palestinian Christian, that became known as the Gospel of Matthew. This unknown evangelist also utilized a Markan *Schrift*—not the Gospel of Mark, but a provisional written collection (*unzusammenhängende Aufzeichnung*) a certain Mark had made of Peter's testimonies. The Matthean evangelist's third source was "the oral tradition" (123, 201–5). The Markan evangelist took the Petrine *Schrift* and put it in a more coherent order, adding some oral materials. The provisional collection drawn up by Papias's Mark therefore effectively amounts to an Urmarkus. Credner, however, offers no accounting for the agreements in order of Mark with Luke and Matthew. Perhaps we may assume that he sees them as mediated through the proto-Markan collection. On the other hand, he refers to the evangelist Mark "abbreviating" and "omitting" materials from and "adding" others to the arrangement (*Anlage*) that he shares with Matthew (108) and also to him "excluding . . . the myths and sagas" of Luke 1–2 (155). This has a Griesbach ring to it, but on the other hand Credner thinks that the evangelist Luke is familiar with Matthew and Mark. Getting a completely clear picture of Credner's source history is hampered by the brevity of his discussion of the Synoptic problem in his *Einleitung*.

Luke's sources are likewise somewhat of an unsorted medley. It is "quite possible," indeed "hard to deny," Credner says, that the evangelist is acquainted with the Gospels of Matthew and Mark. But "with greater certainty" it can be assumed that the apostle Matthew's λόγια and the Petrine collection of Papias's Mark were known to him (156–57, 206). He had "long mastered" the elements of these written sources that suited his schema for his gospel, taking them up into his work "alongside the oral tradition" (206). On the other hand the form and shape of Luke's gospel had gestated for a long time "in his head and in his heart" (157). This is how Credner accounts for the different arrangement of the double tradition in Luke.

Credner's utilization model is beset with obscurities, but when all is said and done, it amounts to a two document hypothesis. Two written sources (*nur zwei Schriften*) underlie the Synoptic Gospels: a Logia source and a Markan source, conceived as an unordered collection principally narrative in profile (201–6). The Markan source functions as a kind of Urmarkus, put in coherent order and supplemented by all three evangelists. The evangelist Matthew utilizes both the Logia collection and the proto-Markan collection. In the main Luke draws upon them as well, though Credner countenances the possibility that Luke is also using Matthew and Mark. Though certainly influenced by Schleiermacher's interpretation of the Papias testimony, Credner predicates his Logia source and proto-Markan source on the respective genre distinctions of the double tradition and the triple tradition.

We see confirmed that the effect of Schleiermacher's identification of Papias's λόγια with a sayings collection was to rid source criticism of the Matthean Urgospel chimera and thereby clear the way for recognition of Markan priority. A corollary effect, already evident in Credner's account, is that the role of pristine apostolic Ursource now begins to pass to the λόγια source. The sayings traditions are the voice of Jesus himself and—as Credner notes—innately less susceptible to variation and to legendary and dogmatic tendencies. To be sure, Credner's proto-Markan collection is Petrine, but it is mediated by his noneyewitness companion.

After working up an elaborate account of an oral Urgospel and its primacy, Credner never really finds a place for it in his source-utilization scenario. In the end he has the triple tradition mediated principally through the proto-Markan written collection; the double tradition through the Matthean λόγια collection. The function of the oral Urgospel seems to be to connect the Synoptic materials to an origin in apostolic memory. Credner identifies the early oral tradition with oral eyewitness testimony *simpliciter*: "the voice of the apostles" (*die Stimme der Apostel*); it circulates as individual items (*Einzelheiten*) that coalesce into the oral gospel (187). Originally these had the very form of precisely detailed eyewitness testimony. The meagerness in details, lack of specific names, the geographical and chronological indeterminacy that characterize the observable tradition, and the presence within it of legendary and dogmatic elements attest to the tradition in a degenerative state, the consequence of its transmission beyond the effective range of the eyewitness voice and the dying away of that voice itself. Credner tries to account for the conspicuous differences between eyewitness testimonies and the actual forms of the Synoptic traditions. He ends up imputing a tendency toward the legendary, the miraculous, and the otherwise historically inauthentic to the tradition itself, affecting all its elements. Only the sayings materials are immune.

KARL LACHMANN

We briefly note Karl Lachmann's 1835 analysis because it shows the productive effects that follow from dispensing with a Matthean Urgospel. Lachmann welcomes the demise of Matthean Urgospel hypotheses.[107] He embraces Schleiermacher's interpretation of Papias's λόγια but declares that the hypothesis of a Logia source stands on its own.[108] The crux at which Lachmann proposes to show the power of the hypothesis is the odd interruption in triple-tradition agreement in order in the sequences that fall between Matthew 4:24 and 13:58 (Mark 1:21–6:13). Lachmann's analysis takes the Logia source as a premise; it

---

107. Karl Lachmann, "De ordine narrationum in evangeliis Synopticis," trans. N. H. Palmer, in "Lachmann's Argument," *NTS* 13 (1967): 368–78 (372). Originally published in *TSK* 8 (1835): 570–90. Citations will be to "Lachmann," with the pagination from Palmer's *NTS* article.

108. Lachmann, 373.

therefore amounts to an early test of its explanatory power. He argues that the Matthean evangelist adjusted the *narrative* sequences of his (proto) Markan source to the *logia* sequence of the apostolic Logia source as Schleiermacher conceived it (its arrangement in Matthew).

As with all critical reasoning, Lachmann's analysis is hypothesis laden: he considers an intractable difficulty in the light of the theory of a Logia source. He finds that the theory, when configured with the postulate of Markan priority, can generate an economical explanation of this the most perplexing crux in triple-tradition order. The increased viability of Markan priority theories is the effect of Schleiermacher's Logia theory, eliminating notions of a Matthean Urgospel, thereby freeing scholarship from the tyranny of Papias's testimony in their source-history hypothesizing. Though not the logical corollary, the Logia source theory is a natural corollary of Markan priority. Source theories that embrace Markan priority but reject Logia hypotheses must compensate with unparsimonious accounts of the double tradition. Lachmann offers a clinic in how source criticism ought to proceed: showing that a particular hypothesis offers a more elegant, more economical solution to a difficult problem than other hypotheses.

D. F. Strauss

D. F. Strauss's *The Life of Jesus Critically Examined* (1835/1836) is dramatic confirmation of how source criticism, theories of tradition origins, and historical criticism converge and alter each other's trajectories. Strauss grounded his revolutionary theory of the tradition in certain source-critical hypotheses, and the tremors he sent through Synoptic scholarship were felt with particular force in Synoptic-problem criticism. His account of the origins of the tradition remains influential, even regulative.

The Strauss Revolution I: The "Mythical Standpoint" and the Oral Hypothesis

Strauss views the tradition from the "mythical standpoint": myth is the principal factor in its formation. He denies that his approach is entirely novel, and he has a point: with few exceptions pre-Strauss criticism imputes to the tradition innate tendencies toward the legendary and the dogmatic. Herder drew the fundamental analogy between the Synoptic tradition and oral saga as it was conceived in German Romanticism. The saga analogy with its concomitant—the prerational folk community—also serves as the baseline premise of

Strauss's account. It is not going too far to say that Strauss's history of the tradition depends on the viability of that analogy. On the other hand, pre-Strauss source critics were sure to identify an unpolluted Ursource of the tradition, oral or written, and as its font a primitive Palestinian community (*Urgemeinde*) that had formed around the apostles and other eyewitnesses. The tendency was to take the tradition, in its emergent form, as indistinguishable from eyewitness testimony. Strauss will break with previous criticism by remorselessly destroying this connection between memory and the tradition.

The source hypotheses with the widest currency at this time were still the Griesbach hypothesis and the oral hypothesis. Like de Wette (and Sieffert), Strauss configures both into his account. The Griesbach hypothesis renders the important service of giving him his pretext to discount Papias's testimony of a memory link between the Gospel of Mark and the apostle Peter. He rejects Schleiermacher's Matthean λόγια source on the grounds that Papias in his comments about Mark uses the term to encompass Jesus's teachings *and* deeds (τὰ ὑπὸ τοῦ Χριστοῦ ἢ λεχθέντα ἢ πραχθέντα).[109] Destruction of the tradition's memory links is essential to reconstituting it as myth.

The Griesbach hypothesis plays no further role for Strauss. The oral hypothesis, on the other hand, is essential to his account. Strauss agrees with Gieseler that patristic citations are residues of an oral Urgospel, and that noncanonical gospels such as the Gospel of the Hebrews are relics of initial efforts at its textualization, an undirected enterprise that produced "many revisions and rearrangements" before finally issuing in the present Synoptics.[110] The Synoptic materials with their condensed, economical forms, vague time-and-place designations, and ad hoc associative connections point, Strauss notes, to a long history of oral transmission (350, 387). If for Strauss the Griesbach hypothesis serves to sever the Gospel of Mark from eyewitness testimony, the oral hypothesis serves to separate all three Synoptics from eyewitness origins by a prolonged period of oral transmission in turn followed by a long, haphazard process of textualization. Combined with the saga model and the presence of legendary, supernatural elements in the Synoptic tradition, the oral hypothesis supplies Strauss with his baseline premise: oral transmission is innately a process of mythologization.[111]

---

109. David Friedrich Strauss, *The Life of Jesus Critically Examined*, 4th ed., trans. George Eliot (1846; repr., Philadelphia: Fortress, 1972), 71. Originally published as *Das Leben Jesu: Kritisch bearbeitet*, 2 vols. (Tübingen: C. F. Osiander, 1846), 1835-36.

110. Strauss, *Life of Jesus*, 73 (hereafter page citations will be in the text).

111. On this point see Erich Fascher, *Die formgeschichtliche Methode: eine Darstellung und Kritik, zugleich ein Beitrag zur Geschichte des synoptischen Problems* (Gießen: Töpelmann,

Oral saga had shaped conceptions of the oral tradition in prior Synoptic criticism, but critics hedged its saga-like tendencies by connecting the tradition in its origins directly to eyewitness testimony and by pushing written-collection enterprises (*Aufzeichnungen*) back into the eyewitness era. Strauss severs the memory connection all but completely and makes myth formative of the oral tradition. As we noted, denying the former is essential to affirming the latter; hence Strauss's concerted attack on arguments for eyewitness origins of the tradition. Vivid realism does not mean that the narrator is an eyewitness; there is no evidence of primitive written collections; there is no reason to think that eyewitnesses were ubiquitously connected with the formation of the tradition, or that they were omniscient of the historical details, or even to think that they were immune to mythologizing tendencies (69–74, 388).

In fact, Strauss argues, for people in the prerational stage of human culture, like those of the primitive community in which the tradition formed, myth is the mode of cognition. The community was governed not by the principle of historical rationality but by the mythical imagination, by intense religious feeling and enthusiasm, upwelling in "creative vigour" (74–75). Its precursor was Jesus's Galilean following, the "simple and energetic minds of Galilee, less fettered by priestcraft and Pharisaism" (270). The oral medium itself, the paradigm for which is oral saga, is the corollary of the mythical mindset. Myth therefore is no accretion to the tradition but its substance; myth goes all the way down. The graphic narratives of the tradition are just appearance, a "semblance" (*Vorstellung*), narrative garments woven from a spiritual "idea," a concept (*Begriff*), for myth is the mode in which prerational people absorb concepts. Historicizing a narrative element of the tradition, trying to recover a historical core, is to violate its basic property as myth and to destroy its capacity as a vehicle of a deeper truth (546).

The leading idea generating the mythical representations of the tradition was the "messianic concept." As soon as belief that Jesus was the Messiah took hold, his followers simply transferred messianic motifs from the Old Testament to him, with some accommodation to impressions left by Jesus's character and teachings. To be sure, the crucifixion threatened to quench this messianic enthusiasm, but it resurged as resurrection belief under the influence of Scriptural intimations of messianic exaltation, helped along by female susceptibilities and by visions that stimulated the disciples to febrile mental states. Messianic belief therefore generated the resurrection narratives (84–86, 742–43).

1924), 28–29, noting, however, that Strauss's identification of oral tradition per se with myth was a sharp departure from Gieseler.

There are no historical nuclei at all in the Synoptic healing narratives. With the possible exception of some exorcisms the entire cycle was generated whole cloth by transferring to Jesus legendary motifs of Old Testament prophets healing blind, lame, paralyzed, and leprous persons (440). The "general idea" that the Pharisees were offended at Jesus's friendly relations with sinners received narrative representation in the Feast at Matthew's House. Call stories were woven out of Old Testament narratives such as Elijah's call of Elisha. The Fishers of Men story may have as its historical germ that some apostles were formerly Galilean fishermen, which became a metaphor for their apostolic calling. Its further mythical elaboration in the Lukan parallel (5:1–11) is confirmation of the tradition's myth-forming tendency. The Call of Matthew gives graphic narrative representation to the idea of discipleship as abandoning an old life and entering upon a new; it may have as a historical germ a memory that publicans numbered among Jesus's followers (311–22). Similarly, Peter's walking on the water is "allegorical and mythical representation" of Jesus's statement to Peter: "I have prayed for thee, that thy faith fail not" (502). The saying, "He that doeth the will of God is my brother and my sister and mother," generated two legendary settings (Mark 3:31–35; Luke 11:28–29). The Woes in Luke have generated the narrative setting of dinner with a Pharisee (Luke 11:37–39). The historical grounds of the Last Supper, however, are firmer: it is plausible that intensifying conflict with the hierarchy gave Jesus a presentiment of his imminent death, and that with the sayings of institution he gave a commemorative meaning to this last meal (363, 396, 634).

Strauss, however, privileges the sayings materials as the most stable, authentic, indeed the most primitive elements of the tradition. Unlike the narrative tradition with its thin (at best) historical residue, they are not generated by mythical elaboration. To the contrary: as immediate expressions of ideas and concepts they are seeds that generate the mythical (i.e., narrative) elements of the tradition, so much so that Strauss even comes close to distinguishing the sayings from the "oral tradition," myth by definition. The presence of any historical residue in the narrative materials can be ruled out completely for episodes dominated by the messianic idea or centered on miraculous occurrences (i.e., the healings tradition). The existence of a factual "kernel" can sometimes be supposed but rarely demonstrated with confidence (91). A singular exception is the Sermon, dominated of course by Jesus's sayings, which likely ("we have no reason to doubt") rests on an episode of Jesus preaching (336).

As noted, Strauss has little interest in source-critical questions. He employs the Griesbach hypothesis to neutralize Papias's testimony about the Gospel of Mark. He predicates his account of the tradition on Gieseler's oral-gospel hypothesis—using it to justify clearing written sources of any significance out of the first century. It has no interest for him as a solution to the Synoptic problem. Rather, it plays a crucial enabling role in his theory. One sees why critics like C. H. Weisse and others will regard source criticism as an effective angle of counterattack. Strauss's principal effect on Synoptic-problem scholarship therefore was to give renewed, energized stimulus to the source-critical enterprise. It explains its sharp post-Strauss shift away from the oral to the written medium. Conversely, his trenchant analysis of the narrative tradition pushed critics further toward the sayings tradition as the securely authentic element in the tradition and—eventually—toward the Logia source theory, though to be sure, Synoptic critics had habitually privileged the sayings tradition long before Strauss.[112]

The Strauss Revolution II: Myth and Memory in the Synoptic Tradition

The effects of Strauss's account of the tradition continue into the present. Strauss recognizes that the formal features of the Synoptic materials—their indefinite framing, the ad hoc inter-connectors, the formulaic summaries, their parsimony, their brevity, the topical arrangements given them by the evangelists—indicate that the Synoptics are close derivatives of oral tradition. But where he really makes a Copernican advance is his recognition not just of the large-scale infusion of the symbolic world of the Old Testament into the tradition but that this symbolic world is a principal factor in the *formation* of the tradition. Intimately connected to this is his recognition that the narrative episodes are not naïve historical description but ideal scenes that give condensed symbolic depiction to a set of emergent norms. In other words, he recognizes the symbolic properties of the tradition, that it serves in the first instance not historical description but the formation of a particular cultural and moral identity grounded in a particular Christology. The predominance of the sayings in the tradition, his observation that even the narrative traditions to no small extent serve as vehicles for Jesus's pronouncements, corresponds to this alignment of the tradition to norm-inculcation. In sum, Strauss recognizes

---

112. Strauss does briefly break stride to observe that the Sermon on the Mount appears to be an expansion of the more original version in Luke 6, using analogous materials found in dispersed locations in Luke, and to note in connection with the dinner at the Pharisee's house in Luke 11:37–38, which introduces the Woes, that "we again find Luke in his favorite employment of furnishing a frame to *the discourses of Jesus* which tradition had delivered to him" (Strauss, *Life of Jesus*, 336, 341 [quotation 363, emphasis added]).

the autonomy of the tradition, that it functions at the *cultural* level and as such is dynamic, open to autonomous development.

That said, there are problems with this account of the tradition, its *reductio* of the tradition to myth formation, its defining the tradition *per se* as "a process of transmuting the abstract into the concrete" (322). Myth in this scenario is the fundamental formative dynamic; the tradition itself is construed as a *process* that spins ideas into mythical garments. That a narrative might contain residues of a historical occurrence for Strauss is of import only to the extent that such might correlate to the germ idea—for example, Jesus's "accidental" riding of a donkey into Jerusalem as possibly a trigger cuing the messianic idea and a narrative woven of the corresponding prophetic motifs. But he holds that such is by no means essential; the messianic idea itself, in concert with the dogmatic belief in Jesus's omniscience, is sufficient to have generated this narrative out of Old Testament motifs (559).

Strauss, however, frequently fails to show in any convincing way that a given Synoptic narrative can be reduced to Old Testament motifs. The healing traditions are a case in point. The prophetic motif of the Messiah as healer and the corresponding list of afflictions from passages such as Isaiah 29:18; 35:5; 61:1, or from stories like Elisha curing diseases from a distance, simply cannot account for the texturing of the individual Synoptic healing narratives. Strauss is driven to this expedient on the one hand because of his philosophical naturalism, and on the other because he finds rationalistic explanations like Paulus's risible. In view of the strained nature of his own account, one must impute historical grounds to these narratives. His model for the formation of the tradition therefore does not resolve the longstanding problem of miraculous elements in the tradition. Strauss attempts to derive the feeding stories from the wilderness feedings in the Pentateuch and the story of Elijah multiplying the widow's meal and oil, but he concedes that the motifs do not all line up, and he overlooks the conspicuous eucharistic motifs, the presence of which indicates a formative vector coming into the tradition from another direction (517–18). As noted, he accords a nominal cuing effect to historical occurrences, but elsewhere he goes further, acknowledging that Old Testament messianic motifs were "modified" to accord with "the personal character, actions, and fate of Jesus," indeed, identifying Jesus's person, ministry, and fate as one of "two sources" that generated "*the pure mythus* of the Gospel" (86). That Jesus's enemies demanded a sign from him is explicable if "he had given himself out and was believed to be the Messiah, or even merely a prophet" (414). The Cleansing of the Temple episode is too independent of the passage in Malachi to be derivable from it, hence "it seems necessary to suppose an actual opposition on the part of Jesus to this abuse in order to account for the fulfillment of the above prophecies by him being represented under the form of an expulsion of buyers and sellers" (402). To account for divergences among five narratives of Jesus's encounters with women (the anointings of Mark 14:3–9, Luke 7:36–50, and John 12:1–8; the adulteress in John 8:1–11; Mary and Martha in Luke 10:38–42), Strauss posits two historical events at their origins (412). But if historical events are a formative factor in these narratives, why not in others? Strauss's mythical approach is predicated on the severing of the tradition from memory. But in his analysis of the Passion narrative he notes that Mark's identification of Simon the Cyrenian as "the father of Alexander and Rufus" (15:21) indicates that the latter "were noted persons in the primitive church," tacitly acknowledging an eyewitness connection (677). Since the Passion narrative is replete with Scriptural motifs, this eyewitness presence complicates Strauss's simple derivation of the tradition from myth.

Likely Strauss would not see any difficulty, for these historical, perhaps eyewitness elements are just inert residues, facts that perhaps as occasional topics of conversation became points of departure for myth formation. The exception, as noted, is the sayings materials, which because they encapsulate pure concepts serve as germination points for the narrative tradition. The dynamic force generating the oral tradition is myth, the primitive mode of cognition of the creative community. Myth is an autonomous creative force. The tradition is myth *simpliciter*. This means that the mythical elements and the historical elements, tradition and memory, remain discontinuous and unintegrated within the body of the tradition. Oral tradition and memories are entities alien to each other; they have separate origins. The narrative episodes of the tradition and their arrangements do not display the qualities of eyewitness testimony; they do not represent "the course of real life" (321). In fact, their generic, vaguely framed forms positively mark them as legend, as do any vivid details of the episodes themselves, which far from indicating eyewitness testimony amount to "arbitrary fictions [substituted] for the historical reality which is lost"; they are graphic representations of an idea, e.g., "a man's exit from an old sphere of life, and his entrance into a new one" (Call of Matthew) (388–89). The Synoptic tradition is, accordingly, a bifurcated entity: a few authentic historical residues, traces of eyewitness memories, overlaid by the "oral tradition," understood as a dynamic process of mythicizing and legend-building, the two elements alien to each other and standing in an at best incidental relationship. The corresponding hermeneutic is "the mythical mode of interpretation," penetrating to the deeper truths mythically depicted by the tradition, "relinquishing the historical reality of the sacred narratives in order to preserve to them an absolute inherent truth." Strauss raises this hermeneutic as a bulwark against the naturalistic *reductios* of the Rationalists and "the jesting expositions of the Deists," both of which drain the gospel of "all divine meaning" (65).

The habit of previous critics was simply to assimilate the oral tradition, in its early stage, to eyewitness testimony. With Strauss we have a Synoptic critic who is unsparingly forthright about the wide phenomenological distance between eyewitness testimony and the forms of the tradition. Observing the diffusion of Old Testament symbolism in the tradition as well as its density in miraculous and dogmatic elements, he naturally draws the conclusion that the tradition and memory are alien entities and that the latter is incidental to the former. Strauss's solution to the problem of the memory-tradition nexus is that there is no nexus. He does not regard oral tradition, taken as a cultural artifact, as a vehicle for memory, which he simply identifies with eyewitness testimony. From this it follows that he cannot see how memory can have traversed the great distance between eyewitnesses and the evangelists (on the oral hypothesis a particularly extended interval). The force of myth, cognitively embodied in the creative community (*Urgemeinde*), is the sole generator of the tradition. Strauss's theory of the memory-tradition nexus is itself a consequence of identifying oral tradition *per se* with the genre of oral saga, the artifact of communities at a prerational stage of culture and therefore subject to the cognitive impetus of the mythical imagination.

Strauss's theory gives us a dichotomous gospel tradition, one unable to integrate its elements. It is unlikely that this would trouble him: historical criticism can look for traces of authentic history in the gospel tradition just like it looks for them in the *Iliad*, the *Edda*, or the *Song of Roland*. But we have seen that elements of his own analysis contradict it, most strikingly in his granting that Old Testament motifs have been "accommodated" to the historical reality of Jesus and in fact were so already in the public response to him (84). By common consent the Passion narrative has been shaped by Old Testament motifs like no other part of the tradition, yet it is in the Passion narrative that Strauss seems the readiest to acknowledge underlying historical realities and indeed at least one reference to an eyewitness. The casting of lots for Jesus's garments and his taunting by observers "very probably really happened"; the corresponding elements from the Psalms have been "applied . . . to the sufferings of Jesus" (686). Historical events, that is, are exerting a strong gravitational pull on the Old Testament symbolism, which for its part reacts interpretively with the events. Strauss thinks it likely that the Last Supper, including the words of institution, is historical. But the Last Supper is shot through with

Scriptural symbolism. The cultural and social environment, the *Lebenswelt*, of Jesus's own activities was already saturated in Scriptural symbolism, narrative patterns, and language. History and the semantics of cultural symbolism in the tradition cannot be so easily parsed. The formative vectors come from various directions: from cultural symbolism, from historical events, and—as we see in the eucharistic symbols in the feeding stories—from commemorative practices in the primitive community, and intersect in the formation of the tradition. Strauss's account does not do justice to the realities of the tradition. It cannot cope with the cultural and commemorative forces at work in its formation.

Nevertheless, Strauss's account marks the turn of an era—indeed, eighty years later Bultmann will simply refurbish it—and there could be no retrograde return to the prior more or less naïve understandings of the tradition. Previous criticism explicitly or by implication distinguished historically more authentic Ursources, embodiments of apostolic memory, from their increasingly dogmatic and supernaturalistic reworkings. Strauss severs the tradition itself from memory. Memory is overlaid by "tradition." The primitive, enthusiastic community (the ever-indispensable Palestinian *Urgemeinde*), for prior scholarship the font of unsullied apostolic memory, modulates into the creative community, the generator of myth. Its forerunner is the "simple and energetic minds of Galilee." With adjustments Strauss's account of the tradition was mediated to contemporary scholarship by form criticism. We still live in the era of Strauss.

CHRISTIAN HERMANN WEISSE, 1838

Christian Hermann Weisse is usually singled out as the first to formulate the two document hypothesis in its classic form. At times it is alleged that he formulated it in response to Strauss's radical skepticism. There is an element of truth in both claims, if tempered with recognition that as early as Herder, rudiments of the 2DH were already circulating, and that with the Schleiermacher-precipitated decline of Matthean Urgospel hypotheses an environment more favorable to Markan priority existed—with the consequence that the double tradition now became a more acute source-critical problem. Writing in 1838, Weisse confirms this assessment of things. He points out that he was ruminating on his 2DH schema before the appearance of Strauss's work, which prodded him to work out his ideas out in detail.[113]

---

113. Christian Hermann Weisse, *Die evangelische Geschichte kritisch und philosophisch bearbeitet*, 2 vols. (Leipzig: Breitkopf and Härtel, 1838), 1:iii.

Weisse: *The Two Source Hypothesis versus the Oral Hypothesis*

Because it was appropriated by Strauss as the principal support of his theory, the oral hypothesis comes in for fierce attack. Strauss, Weisse says, gave hostages to fortune by taking over the oral hypothesis uncritically.[114] Weisse first claims that the hypothesis arose because of the failure of written Urgospel hypotheses to explain Synoptic variation and as such functioned *a priori*, that is, it was not well grounded in analysis of Synoptic parallels. But, he continues, a more lethal problem is that it analogized the Synoptic tradition to oral saga. Saga was taken to be the paradigm for oral tradition. For Herder and for Gieseler it was therefore the most natural thing for an oral gospel to emerge in the primitive community as a cohering entity, like an oral saga cultivated by rhapsodes. Since sagas are highly mythical, the "mythical perspective" on the tradition followed ineluctably. Weisse makes the obvious point that the Synoptic tradition is not epic poetry. It lacks the formal features such as meter that give epic its cohesion and transmissibility. Construing the oral gospel as a body of teaching that received fixed, memorized form is just a feeble attempt to compensate for this breakdown in the analogy (*Geschichte*, 1:12–14).[115]

Weisse argues that Markan priority is congruent with Papias's testimony about the origin of the Gospel as an οὐ τάξει transcription of the Petrine oral tradition. Mark's appearance is intelligible as a programmatic response to the crisis triggered by the passing of the apostolic era and the dissolution of living memory. Its somewhat ad hoc arrangements of self-contained episodes (*Bruchstücke*) corroborate its immediate derivation from oral preaching. Mark's narrative sequencing and the resulting narrative *Gestalt* are clearly of his own devising, though perforce following the historical course of Jesus's ministry from his public appearance to crucifixion.[116]

Weisse is aware that Schleiermacher's interpretation of Papias's statement about the Matthean λόγια is controvertible: the term does not unambiguously designate a sayings or instructional (*Reden*) collection. Nevertheless, he says, the term more commonly applied to a *bios*-type work was *apomnemoneumata*, and in fact *logia* is inappropriate for such a work. With all due caution, Schleiermacher's theory should be followed out to see where it leads, an experimental enterprise already initiated, Weisse notes, by Lachmann with good results (1:35–38).

---

114. Weisse, *Geschichte*, 1:6–9 (hereafter page citations will be in the text).

115. Weisse, *Die Evangelienfrage in ihrem gegenwärtigen Stadium* (Leipzig: Breitkopf und Härtel, 1856), 65–69.

116. Weisse, *Geschichte*, 1:35–38.

Weisse's approach is to show that the two document hypothesis makes sense at the general level of the Synoptic patterns rather than, like Lachmann, applying it to specific Synoptic cruxes. Against Strauss's skepticism he wants to sketch out a source-critical basis for the reconstruction of the historical ministry of Jesus. The combination of a Logia source and a Markan *bios* gospel in more comprehensive gospels is a foreseeable line of development, realized in Matthew and Luke (1:47–48). The Gospel of Mark bears other indications of priority. Its focus is the public ministry of Jesus; the Nativities and other legendary materials in Matthew and Luke are the saga-building of the next generation. The first string of episodes in Mark, beginning with the call of the disciples and continuing into the Sabbath events and healings, have a Capernaum focus and specificity of detail that, different from the Markan Baptism and the Temptation, suggest derivation from eyewitness testimony. It is no coincidence that the sequence begins with the call of named disciples Peter, Andrew, James, and John, and that they are present at subsequent events (1:56–67, 126).

In contrast to their agreement with Mark in triple-tradition order, Matthew and Luke diverge completely in their arrangements of their double-tradition materials, which nevertheless manifest strong topical and verbal agreements. This is intelligible on the theory that Matthew and Luke are using a Logia source; because a Logia source coheres not narratively but topically, its elements are far more open to rearrangement. The travel section (Luke 9:51–18:15) is a Lukan contrivance. Its travel notices are superficial and accord with Luke's practice of providing secondary historical settings for his materials. Luke has taken the journey notice in Mark 10:1 as a prompt to insert a mass of materials taken from the Logia collection and from his special materials (1:87–89). Matthew better conserves the source's sequence and wording; Luke has rearranged the materials and given them discrete historical settings. Weisse bases this judgment in his affirmation of the source's connections to the apostle Matthew (he frequently refers to it as the *ächte Matthäus*: "authentic Matthew") (1:90; 2:4, 28). On these grounds he also assigns Matthew's special traditions to the source.

As a source-critical argument Weisse's account is more in the nature of a prospectus: he sketches in the lines of a clean 2DH and attempts to see provisionally how it might in broad strokes provide an economical account of the observable Synoptic phenomena. In this connection he shows that the 2DH makes good sense of the instructional profile of the double tradition and the narrative profile of the triple tradition. Genre can account, that is, for the triple-tradition agreements in order and the lack of such in the double tradition, and for why the double tradition nevertheless features large-scale verbal agreements. The postulated Logia source itself contains such brief narrative notices as are needed to give pretext for a particular sequence of sayings (2:9).

Of particular interest is Weisse's observation that the narrative tradition would have nucleated in the eucharistic setting; that is to say, the Passion narrative is the primordial gospel narrative tradition (1:16–22). This makes sense: eucharistic celebration was the ritual actualization of the social and cultural identity of the emergent community, an identity that—just as with the Passover narrative—is symbolically refracted through a corresponding narrative. The Passion narrative is therefore the quintessential early Christian narrative pattern, and as such the orientation point for the subsequent narrative alignment of the Synoptic tradition. We will return to this point in chapter 6.

Weisse: Tradition, Memory, and Myth

Weisse's concerns lie in countering Strauss's historical skepticism arising from his assimilation of the tradition to myth. He holds that the 2DH does just that. Though questioning the saga analogy, he nevertheless regards oral tradition as a dangerous entity and thus to be banished from what is an entirely literary source history. By binding the Markan and Logia materials tightly to apostolic memories and to writing, he insulates them from what he continues to regard as the legend-forming tendencies of oral tradition. The Gospel of Mark and the Logia source are, respectively, the dual witnesses to Jesus's life and teaching.[117] The Logia source, compiled by Matthew, is a direct transcription of apostolic memory. It captures the very Aramaic utterances of Jesus. The Gospel of Mark's connection is at one remove, mediated by a noneyewitness companion of Peter. Its episodic connectors and metanarrative framing are of the evangelist's own construction. In the gospel's episodic liveliness undoubtedly there reverberates something of the eyewitness origins of its traditions, but this likely owes quite a bit to the depictive powers of the evangelist. Though derivative of eyewitness memory, the Markan episodes do not present themselves in the form of eyewitness testimony. They are subsequent formulations, and among them the evangelist has occasionally sown differently sourced (*fremdartige*) traditions. The Gospel of Mark therefore needs critical sifting to separate out historical from less historical elements. Nevertheless, it is still largely free of the touch of the mythical or the legendary (1:46–47, 69–70, 94, 109; 2:3). Weisse readily grants that Old Testament motifs were infused into the materials in the apostolic preaching, but different from the Lukan and Matthean Nativities these materials have not been *generated* by myth. Jesus's cultural *Lebenswelt* and his own actions were oriented to Old Testament narrative coordinates: his

---

117. On Weisse's programmatic marginalization of oral tradition see Fascher, *Methode*, 30–33.

calling the first disciples (Mark 1:16–20) was perhaps consciously patterned on the Elijah/Elisha call story (2:476). The Gospels of Luke and Matthew, on the other hand, fall outside the generational space illuminated by living apostolic memory. Thus they suffer from the effects of the tradition's innate tendency toward the legendary and a susceptibility to infiltration of inauthentic elements (2:168). Their special materials with their denser legendary coloration come from oral tradition, not from written sources with eyewitness credentials like Mark and the Logia. In consequence they lack the purity and integrity (*Reinheit und Integrität*) of the written source materials (2:134–35).

As Weisse therefore imagines it, the Synoptic materials originated as unfiltered eyewitness testimony. The sayings of the Lord immediately imprinted themselves upon the disciples' memory. Likewise, their minds served as a wholly neutral medium for their recollections of Jesus's activities (1:110).[118] These circulated in the form of memorable units fitted for repeated utilization. Mark did not transcribe Peter's teachings as a personal memory aid, for they were securely lodged in his memory. Rather, he wanted to publish them (1:42, 110). But Weisse notes that though they retain distinct markers of their eyewitness origins, the traditions do not display the *form* of direct eyewitness testimony, of Petrine recitations. It is Mark who gave these materials their *Gestalt*, to give them durability (*Bestehen*) and cohesion (*Haltung*) (1:58, 66–67). This is Weisse's theory of the nexus between memory and the episodic materials in their observable Markan forms.

Yet, as we have seen, he also posits an entity, "oral tradition," that circulates apart from eyewitness control and is prone to myth-forming tendencies. This he contrasts with the eyewitness-derived materials, which though influenced by Old Testament epic have not been fundamentally formed by it, at least not on the scale one observes in the Nativities (1:516–17). Weisse grants Strauss's claim about the effects of myth and dogma on the tradition (not a novel claim), but in the main localizes its generative influence to traditions circulating autonomously of eyewitness lines of transmission that descend to the evangelists via the Logia source and the Gospel of Mark. But the form in which the evangelist Mark casts these testimonies is not different in profile from the inauthentic traditions. Weisse therefore does not succeed in coming up with a coherent account of the tradition.

118. Also *Evangelienfrage*, 170.

CHRISTIAN HERMANN WEISSE, 1856

Weisse revisited these questions eighteen years later, in *Die Evangelienfrage in ihrem gegenwärtigen Stadium.*

Weisse, 1856: On Memory and the Tradition

In this volume Weisse reaffirms the privileged connection of the Logia source and the Gospel of Mark to apostolic eyewitness memory.[119] As in the 1838 account the Logia source is privileged over Mark by virtue of its immediate apostolic derivation, but now Weisse makes the differential ranking even more pronounced. The authenticity of the Logia source is self-manifest; its sayings express the deepest meanings of the corollary historical events. Indeed, it serves as the plumb line for evaluating the authenticity of the narrative traditions, and that includes those of the Gospel of Mark (79). The Markan evangelist, on the other hand, is neither an eyewitness nor a historian but a naïve transcriber caught in the grip of faith and religious enthusiasm. The sparseness of chronological and geographical detail in the narrative traditions shows that the leading factor in their formation was christological fervor rather than historical or biographical interest. Many of the miracle narratives have originated out of deep emotional response (*tiefe Gefühl*) to a particular saying or parable of Jesus. No amount of critical sifting will ever recover a biography of Jesus from the Markan gospel (92–93, 107). But this is not the problem it might seem to be, for the essence of Jesus's ministry lies in Jesus's *words*, his sayings. These are transmitted authentically in the Logia source.

In another shift from 1838 Weisse now takes a more expansive view of the oral tradition. His previous critique of the oral hypothesis, he says, ought not be taken as denying that a quantum of the tradition prior to its inscription long circulated in the oral medium. But he reiterates his category distinction between memory and tradition. Oral traditions constitute "a part" of the materials in our present Synoptics. Oral tradition is an inherently deforming (*umgestaltende*) medium, due to its being borne along in the fervid religious subjectivities of the early believers, coupled with its circulation in only sporadic connection to living apostolic memory. The Logia source, however, is not oral tradition but unfiltered apostolic recollection (*Erinnerung*) untouched (*unberührt*) by external influences. Mark on the other hand is hybrid: its core

---

119. Weisse, *Evangelienfrage*, 90–91 (hereafter page citations will be in the text).

elements are direct utterances of Peter, but among his fragmentary transcribed memories of these utterances the evangelist has layered in "oral traditions." All the Markan materials without exception have been filtered through the evangelist's religious subjectivity and without the external control of the lately departed Peter's living memory (132–34).

The consequence is again the sharpest bifurcation between memory elements and "tradition" elements in the Synoptic materials, despite there being no observable phenomenological distinction between the materials in these two categories. Weisse describes authentic elements as "encased" (*in der Hülle*) in unhistorical tradition; elsewhere as "intermingled" (*vermischt*) with these "alien" (*fremdartige*) elements (391). Hence the indispensability of the Logia source. This state of affairs, Weisse acknowledges, makes historical reconstruction a fraught enterprise. Even eyewitness testimony is no certain basis for historical veracity (92). Weisse shares with Strauss this sharp bifurcation between memory elements and "tradition" elements in the Synoptic materials. This marks a departure from the tendency in pre-Strauss scholarship simply to assimilate tradition to memory.[120]

Weisse, 1856: Urmarkus

In 1856 Weisse shifts to an Urmarkus position that influenced Holtzmann in his 1863 work. Weisse now regards it as a defect of his 1838 work that it assigned all the double tradition to the apostolic *Spruchsammlung*—"sayings collection" (as he now refers to it) (88). His main grounds for recanting this position is the notion of genre purity: as a sayings collection the *Spruchsammlung* cannot tolerate narrative elements, not even narrative traces. The effect is to exclude on *a priori* grounds the Preaching of John the Baptist, the Temptation, the Healing of the Centurion's Servant, Jesus's discourse on John the Baptist sequence (which commences with John's embassy in Luke 7:18–20), and the Beelzebul Accusation (156–57). Their source is instead an Urmarkus. Genre purity is essential to Weisse's heightened emphasis upon the Logia as immediate apostolic recollection, innocent of the deforming touch of "tradition"—by which he means the narrative tradition (90). Weisse's Urmarkus theory is effectively an artifact of his antithesis between "recollection" (*Erinnerung*) and "tradition" (*Überlieferung*).

Weisse pushes the genre essentialism further. As a sayings collection, constituent sayings of the Logia source can only have been loosely and unsystematically

120. Repeated with exactitude by Nineham one hundred years later: "two very different types of source" (D. E. Nineham, "Eyewitness Testimony and the Gospel Tradition," *JTS* 9.1 [1958]: 13–25 [17]).

ordered: by catchword in perfunctory topical arrangements. Correspondingly, the principal feature of Matthew's and Luke's utilization of Mark is their adherence to Mark's narrative sequence, whereas the principal feature of their Logia utilization is their divergence in order. It follows, Weisse thinks, that where Matthew and Luke agree in narrative placement of double-tradition materials, those materials are not from the Logia. This displaces the Preaching of John the Baptist and the Temptation into Urmarkus. But the Sermon also is found attached to a similar narrative setting in Luke and Matthew, and in both it is followed by the Healing of the Centurion's Servant. In its short form the Sermon too must be from Urmarkus. The intelligible ordering of the Sermon's common baseline sequence is also anomalous for a sayings collection. Matthew, however, has incorporated many Logia sayings into the Urmarkus Sermon (90–91, 157–60).

One senses here palpable strain on the Urmarkus hypothesis. Does the Matthean evangelist largely reproduce the Logia arrangement? Or does he incorporate loosely organized (*hie und da zerstreut*) Logia materials into a rump (*Grundstamm*) speech found at a certain point in the Urmarkus narrative? Likewise for the Mark 4//Matt 13 parable discourse, the Mark 6//Matt 10 Mission Instruction, and the Matthew 24 Apocalypse, formed by incorporating Logia sayings into the *Grundstamm* of the Mark 13 speech, sayings that Luke separately arranged into his own eschatological speech in Luke 17 (160, 167).

The more an Urmarkus is expanded with double tradition the more it begins to resemble an Urgospel, and we are back to Urmatthew hypotheses. Weisse's hypothesis also entails that our present Mark is not an orderly revision but a mangled version of Urmarkus. Weisse offers no explanation of why or how this mangling occurred. The theory really serves no other purpose than to purge the Logia source of narrative elements, consistent with Weisse's categorical distinction between memory and tradition. In 1856 Weisse's reservations about the historical qualities of the Gospel of Mark seem to have increased. He responds with a further apotheosis of the Logia.

Christian Gottlob Wilke

We rewind to 1838, when Christian Gottlob Wilke likewise published a detailed defense of Markan priority, though, it appears, not in reaction to Strauss, whom he never mentions.[121] Wilke had actually come out categorically in

---

121. Christian Gottlob Wilke, *Der Urevangelist, oder exegetisch kritische Untersuchung über das Verwandtschaftsverhältniß der drei ersten Evangelien* (Dresden & Leipzig: Gerhard Fleischer, 1838).

favor of Markan priority in 1829 in an essay on the Workers in the Vineyard (Matt 20:1–16).[122] From his accompanying short demonstration it is clear that Wilke had worked out the basics of his theory, though he would not give it its full exposition until 1838.

Wilke's Attack on the Oral Hypothesis

The oral hypothesis still occupied large space on the horizons of Synoptic scholarship, though awkwardly sharing that space with the Griesbach hypothesis. Wilke dismisses the notion of an oral Urgospel. No uniform oral gospel could have emerged from the free-form and contingent apostolic proclamation.[123] But more to the point, an allegedly orally *fixierte* Urgospel cannot encompass the range of variation on display in Synoptic parallels. In oral transmission narrative elements of the tradition are subject to a wide range of variation. That close agreements, reaching even to insignificant expressions, should exist in narrative elements of Synoptic parallels indicates the effects of the written medium. Similarly for the striking agreement in order of episodes that constitutes, moreover, a coherent narrative arc (28–30, 107–10, 124). These phenomena require the unique properties of the written medium (*ihr allein eigenthümliche Kennzeichen*)—its capacity to bind heterogeneous materials together in coherent relations (*Zusammenhänge*) in the materiality of the medium—and detached, reflective authorial (*schriftstellerische*) agency for their realization. Likewise, the systematic organization of *sayings* materials durably in tight, elaborative relations requires written mediation (121–23, 128–29).

Wilke's sweeping dismissal of the oral hypothesis is predicated on his sharply polarized media binary. Oral traditions as he conceives them are unformed, the immediate effusions of feeling (*Gefühl*). The divide between oral tradition and writing is as absolute as the divide between *Natur* and *Kunst* (artifice). Oral tradition is something given by the first Christian preachers in the form of immediate recollections. Like any recollection it momentarily receives an intelligible expression but no stable, marked form such as could persist in oral transmission and into the written medium (122–24, 130, 160, 304). The sayings, to be sure, would stick securely in the memory of those who heard Jesus utter them. The sayings therefore are the memory elements (*gedächtnismässig*) of the tradition.

122. Christian Gottlob Wilke, "Ueber die Parabel von den Arbeitern im Weinberge Matth. 20, 1–16," *ZWT* 1 (1829): 71–109.
123. Wilke, *Urevangelist*, 152 (hereafter page citations will be in the text).

The narrative materials, on the other hand, do not reflect the naïve immediacy, the realism, the idiosyncratic detail of individual recollection. The call of Levi and the dispute with the Pharisees that follows, for instance, is manifestly a highly artificial (*künstlich*) representation, not a realistic account from direct recollection. From Wilke's media premises it follows that Synoptic narrative units are products of *authorial artifice*, of the sort needed to give the recollected factual events (*Tatsachen, Nachrichten*) their narrative form and style. They are products of authorial reflection (*reflexionsmässig*), of writing, of *Kunst*. The form as much as the coherent overall ordering of Synoptic episodes originates in authorial (*schriftstellerische*) activity; both stem from the same authorial initiative. Moreover, the memory-medium materials—the sayings—are very frequently the dominant element of these short narratives, numerous of which clearly serve principally to give these elements their narrative occasions (3, 28–30, 129–33).

It is the oral-gospel hypothesis that Wilke has in his sights. But his categorical distinction between memory-mediated and writing-artificed elements in the Synoptics also plays into his explanation of the patterns of variation and agreement in the Synoptic parallels. On his model Synoptic narratives are by definition the artifacts of reflective writing. More precisely, they are the work of the Urevangelist. Whence therefore does variation arise? When the subsequent evangelists, utilizing the Urevangelist's gospel, exercise their own reflective artificing prerogatives in rendering their source. Patterns of agreement in wording and order come to exist because they are operating upon a common source (472–75).

In short, Wilke makes redaction, calculated operations of the evangelists upon a Greek source, virtually the exclusive factor in the rise of Synoptic variation. This permits him to offer an exclusively written-medium account of Synoptic phenomena without, as he notes, falling into the morass of intermediating sources that drowned Eichhorn's hypothesis (258, 529). He grounds this claim in close study of the parallels, arguing that intelligible redactional intent can be seen to be generating variants, among other things in "the effort to give the material a more precise expression, or to strengthen or improve the connections, or in the case of additional material being inserted, to further elaborate upon an element in the common text, or to substitute an alternative" (299). These are accompanied by editorial modifications required to connect inserted materials coherently into the context as well as stylistic modifications attributable to the evangelists. He breaks decisively with the view that close copying is the normative mode of written-source utilization. What would be the point, he asks, of the evangelists woodenly copying out (*bloß abschreiben*) their source? To what purpose and to what end? On the other hand, if the evangelists are working from a common source, one would expect patterns of agreement in order and wording to predominate, to constitute the continuous substratum of the three Synoptics. This, he says, is in fact what we observe. Redactional modifications are reliably explicable as arising out of the common material (290, 529). A set of coherent redactional principles is readily imputable to an evangelist from observation of the evangelist's modifications.

Wilke admits that a quantum of variants exists that appears unmotivated (*unabsichtlich*): no redactional rationale can be found for them (292, 658–59). He dimly senses that there are additional factors at work generating the patterns of variation and hypothesizes: "The common Synoptic *Grundelement* receives different forms in the same way that words and phrases of a speech heard and then recited from memory undergo all sorts of combinations and transpositions, giving the speech a new form of expression" (406). The evangelists, he says, were concerned more about the general meaning and content of the material; its form and wording were modifiable (107). Wilke comes close here to recognizing oral factors at work in the utilization of written tradition. His media binary—*either* oral *or* written utilization—as well as his badly deficient concept of oral tradition obstruct him from going further down that promising path.

Wilke and the Triple Tradition: Markan Priority

The prominence that Wilke's media model gives to writing plays directly into his source-utilization theorizing. Matthew and Luke, he observes, generally agree in the order and disposition of their triple-tradition materials, even when these fall in no natural narrative order, but they frequently diverge in the way that these materials are connected up to each other. Similarly, in individual pericopes, Matthew's and Luke's observable redactional traits never show up in close-agreement blocks of words, only in the respective variations. The inference: a common source, an *Urtext*, "a coherent whole constituted of intelligibly ordered materials," which Matthew and Luke occasionally transpose and into which they insert additional materials, and the distinctive text of which remains visible through the variations and always resurfaces as the common textual stratum (560, also 316–17). The contours of the *Urtext* emerge in the patterns of three-way agreements and two-way agreements in wording and order. Even units with three-way disagreements in expression share recognizably the same content (344).

Mark, he observes, is the middle term in these patterns of agreement, reliably in agreement with both Matthew and Luke or with one against the other. The materials constituting these three-way and two-way agreements, moreover, are integral: they do not bear obvious marks of being expansions or abbreviations. The Gospel of Mark is closest to this text type, for in contrast to Matthew and Luke its materials are rarely susceptible of being understood as expansions, abbreviations, or insertions (293–97, 413). Matthew and Luke display alternating primitivity in their triple tradition, with Mark consistently co-attesting the primitive reading. When both Matthew and Luke simultaneously offer clarifying variants in these materials, neither shows awareness of the redaction of the other.

Once one recognizes that the evangelists are bold redactors, Wilke says, a different profile of the *Urtext* emerges, one very close to the text of Mark (384–93, 413). In fact no meaningful distinction exists between the *Urtext* and the Gospel of Mark. Mark coincides with the original "Quantum" to which all three texts are reducible, the substratum running through additions and abbreviations. Nothing distinguishes Mark's style, configuration, and overall aim from the *Urtext*. Accordingly, the Gospel of Mark is the *Urtext*; Mark is the *Urevangelist*. The sparse Mark-only materials are not such as to require positing an Urgospel to account for them. Markan priority makes sense of Synoptic phenomena with economy and elegance, whereas its rival hypotheses are riven by explanatory problems and conundrums (417, 429, 457–68, 551, 655, 680).[124]

Wilke and the Double Tradition

Wilke observes that the double tradition has an instructional complexion, in particular noting that it exists in Matthew mostly without any narrative supports. Accordingly, it is distinctive vis-à-vis the mostly narrative materials of the Markan tradition (11, 19–20). The most striking of several curious aspects of the two-gospel manifestation of these materials is their quite different arrangements in Matthew and Luke. In Matthew they are "braided around" and "attached" to the narrative stem of the triple-agreement materials; in Luke they appear mostly as block insertions interrupting the narrative sequence and falling into a very different order than in Matthew. Luke has omitted quite a few Markan narrative elements and abbreviated others, evidently for the purpose of including the more copious instructional material he has at his disposal, and also to avoid doublets. Matthew for his part seems in chapters 4–12 to have reordered Markan sequences for the purpose of accommodating double-tradition materials (12, 170–71, 595–606).

---

124. Wilke gives a cutting critique of the competing Mark-as-medial hypothesis, the Griesbach, that is well worth the read (432–42).

Wilke further observes that the sayings of the double tradition exist in tight didactic sequences. As such the sequences are products of authorial reflection and exist by virtue of the fixing properties of the written medium. They must come from a written source (128–29). But though he thinks it likely that the λόγια Papias references correspond in some way to the double tradition, he rejects Schleiermacher's reading of Papias and rules out a Logia source. In his view the only viable options can be Luke borrowing from Matthew or Matthew from Luke. Whether these λόγια circulated prior to the Synoptics in the form of provisional collections (*Aufzeichnungen*) may be left undecided—Wilke is noncommittal on this. What is decisive for him is that, in his judgment, when separated out from their Matthean and Lukan contexts, it is difficult to see that the double-tradition materials fall together into a cohering, connected source. This is Wilke's principal objection to a Logia source (175). What Wilke seems to mean is that the respective double-tradition instructional sequences lack redactional connectives—that is, the evidence of reflective authorial activity— between them analogous to those that serve to bring triple-tradition pericopes into a coherent sequence. As corroboration Wilke points to the disposition of the double-tradition materials in Matthew: their connectivity is contingent on the Markan sequence that "bears them and holds them"; lacking it, he argues, they would simply disintegrate into separate elements (685). A double- tradition source therefore can only have been a gospel-like entity containing narrative materials to hold together the sayings (691).

It follows that either Luke or Matthew is borrowing these materials from the other—Wilke decides that Matthew takes them from Luke. He gives little space to demonstrating this—eight pages out of over seven hundred. In the scholarly environment of the 1830s it clearly was a far more pressing matter to make a case for Markan priority against the oral and Griesbach hypotheses. In his foreword, however, he confesses the need for deeper inquiry into the source of Luke's double tradition and announces his plans for a work dedicated to this question, which unfortunately never came to fruition (vi).

Wilke on the Memory Nexus

Here we are brought back to Wilke's critique of the oral gospel hypothesis, and to his polarized media model. The "gospel reports" (*die evangelischen Nachrichten*), i.e., the Synoptic narrative pericopes, certainly bear traces of apostolic memory (*Spuren apostolischer Erinnerung*), and they reflect the nar- rative perspective of the disciples (39). But they do not fit the profile of eye- witness recollection. No tradition issuing direct from apostolic eyewitnesses would display so much conflicting variation, such imprecision and vagueness in time and place, such meagerness of detail, so many historical gaps. What eyewitness report would begin, "It happened one day . . ."? In their observable form the narrative episodes issue not from memory but from the artifice of the evangelist. The direct memory elements of the tradition are the sayings: easily imprinted on the memories of the disciples, directly uttered by Jesus. The narrative elements of the tradition are in fact mostly subordinated to the sayings, serving to frame them. This state of affairs means that the Gospel Mark is itself an authorial artifact (*künstliche Komposition*), not a documentation of apostolic eyewitness testimony and preaching (28–30, 40–48).

Wilke's reasoning on these matters is conditioned by his polemic against the oral gospel hypothesis. He shares the premise of Gieseler's oral hypothesis that the forms of a tradition derived from memory correspond to the eyewitness expression of that memory. He turns this back with great effect against the hypothesis, pointing out the lack of correspondence between narrative pericopes and eyewitness testimony. But continuing to reason from that premise, he infers that the narrative elements are not memory elements (*gedächtnismässig*) but authorial contrivances (*reflexionssmässig*). Only the sayings are unambiguously memory elements of the tradition.

This is to say that Wilke has no real model for oral tradition, no concept of oral genres. He has no model for the nexus of memory with the formation of an oral tradition. There is little to indicate that Wilke thinks historical skepticism follows from his analysis, but his lack of a robust model for oral tradition leaves him unable to stipulate how information contained in the Synoptic narratives came down to the artificing evangelist.[125] The evangelists receive their information (*Kunde*) of events from "rumors" or "reports" (*Gerüchte, Nachrichten*) that have reached them or through eyewitness recollections, whether mediated or heard direct Wilke does not say (34). For Wilke the *Urtext* (= Mark) is not a privileged source of apostolic memory. The closest thing to that is the sayings tradition, which Luke gets from an indeterminate source or sources.

Wilke recognizes the unique media properties of writing: its capacity to consolidate and stabilize an extended, complex text in a material substratum, that such a work, requiring meditated reflection detached from the immediacy

---

125. Wilke never bangs the drum of historical skepticism, and nowhere does he push his inferences in a skeptical direction (he ended his life as a convert to the Catholic Church). He is simply drawing out the logical inferences from his particular account of the origins of the tradition; his target, such as it is, is Gieseler's oral Urgospel.

of oral enactment, can only be realized in the written medium.[126] This insight powers his critique of the oral hypothesis and leads him to his important documentary inferences. Over against this, however, stands an understanding of oral tradition that we recognize to be badly defective. His not distinguishing it from immediate eyewitness recollection is a first indicator of a more comprehensively flawed conception. As it was for Gieseler, for Wilke oral tradition is the "natural" that stands in sharp structural antithesis to artifice (110, 128–30). Accordingly, early Christian oral traditions in recollection and preaching were all but formless; the shaped Synoptic narrative pericopes, on the other hand, are artifacts of authorial reflection. Early Christian oral traditions had no stable transmissible forms (no *stehende Form*); the narrative pericopes are not residues of oral traditions (160, 304).

So great is the media polarization that Wilke is not able to bridge the gap that it opens up between apostolic memory and Synoptic writing. Only the sayings cross the gulf; other information comes in nondescript "rumors" and "reports." He cannot solve the problem of early Christian memory and the Synoptics, notwithstanding that he regards the *Urtext* (Mark) as a memory project.[127] His model generates incommensurable representations of the writing activity of the evangelists: on the one hand they are authors—especially the Urevangelist—creating narratives from "rumors" and "reports"; on the other hand they are transmitters and cultivators of a written tradition—Matthew and Luke as redactors of the Markan materials. Notwithstanding his fondness for the authorial characterization, Wilke recognizes that Matthew and Luke behave more like tradents in their treatment of Mark than like autonomous authors. That is, they treat their written materials as *tradition*, something trustworthy (*glaubwürdig*) that they have received and are constrained by, something that even in the transformations they visit on it they strive to mediate faithfully and comprehensively (18–19, 467–71).

Wilke's defective model for oral tradition takes some of the edge off his critique of the oral hypothesis. Conversely, it forces him to reduce all Synoptic variation to redaction. With his sharp media binary he must account for Synoptic phenomena solely in terms of editorial operations, which he attempts to manage through the model of Matthew and Luke as active redactors, while

---

126. Wilke, *Urevangelist*, 121–23, his programmatic statement on this.

127. "We understand the *Urschrift* as an effort towards an ordered presentation of the leading events [*Hauptthatsachen*] of the messianic life and ministry of Jesus, accordingly as a work that . . . brings together and aligns under a single perspective *that which is about to vanish from memory*" (656, emphasis added).

nevertheless conceding the existence of a surplus of variation that cannot be accounted for on any redactional rationale. On occasion, however, he comes close to dismantling the media binary and recognizing oral forces at work in the utilization of written tradition. Reflecting on the *Metamorphosen* of Mark in Matthew and Luke he writes: "The way in which the base text has been rendered in other forms is not unlike the case of someone who re-narrates [*wiedererzählt*] by ear and memory: in the mouth of the narrator the words undergo all sorts of recombinations and coalesce into a unique form" (406). But his media binary blocks any further inquiries in this direction.

After Strauss, Weisse's and Wilke's analyses appeared to put source criticism on the cusp of a new era. Their independent convergence on Markan priority seemed the culmination of lines of development that took their start from Lessing and Herder—from Herder in particular. But this is hindsight. In fact, source-critical matters were still in flux. Weisse's analysis was not probative, and Wilke's inability to connect Synoptic writing to the tradition opened his account of Markan priority to exploitation by a skepticism more radical than Strauss's.

Tendenzkritik: Drifting Back to Mark

B Y 1838 MARKAN PRIORITY seemed on the verge of breakthrough. Yet it would be exiled to the wilderness for more than a decade, rejected by the early Tübingen school, which tied its *Tendenzkritik* method to the Griesbach hypothesis. In 1856 Weisse is still identifying himself as the only critic who had followed through with Lachmann and Schleiermacher to work out a consistent 2DH position.[1] Why this sudden stall in the movement toward hypotheses featuring Markan priority? Weisse faulted his failure to ground his 1838 analysis in detailed analysis of Synoptic parallels.[2] But Wilke's argument for Markan priority was exhaustively text-based. Why did his results fail to gain traction?

One reason is that the Griesbach hypothesis was not dead. In fact, it received an extended lease on life from its suitability to *Tendenzkritik* accounts of Synoptic origins. The other reason was the publication in 1841 of *Kritik der evangelischen Geschichte der Synoptiker* (1841) by archskeptic Bruno Bauer.[3] Bauer predicated his radical historical skepticism on Markan priority, appealing to Wilke in particular. Markan priority was discredited by association— and with Markan priority out of favor, prospects were dim for the 2DH. In 1843 Albert Schwegler of the Tübingen school wrote a combined critical review of Wilke's *Der Urevangelist* and Bruno Bauer's *Kritik der evangelischen Geschichte*.[4] This review helps us understand why Markan priority ran into a wall of resistance.

1. Weisse, *Evangelienfrage*, 82.
2. Weisse, *Evangelienfrage*, 146.
3. Bruno Bauer, *Kritik der evangelischen Geschichte der Synoptiker*, 3 vols. (Leipzig: Otto Wiegand, 1841).
4. A. Schwegler, "Die Hypothese vom schöpferischen Urevangelisten in ihrem Verhältniss zur Traditionshypothese," *Theologische Jahrbücher* 2 (1843): 203–78.

Schwegler says that Wilke failed to demonstrate that Mark is the Urevangelist, the common source of Matthew and Luke. The postulate explains their agreements, but not their patterns of variation. How does one explain the "innumerable variants in phrasing and word order that are in no way derivable from any intelligible authorial intention?"[5] Patristic testimony connects any *Urevangelium* to the name of Matthew, not Mark.[6] Schwegler grants the justice of Wilke's observation that the stylistic, linguistic, and theological distinctives of Matthew and Luke do not appear in Mark, but argues that as an epitomator Mark would naturally want to produce a neutral (*farblos*) text by culling the distinguishing features of his sources.[7] In any case, Schwegler continues, a solution to the Synoptic problem will never emerge from analysis of the complexities of agreement and variation among the existing Synoptics. The only way out of the impasse is *Tendenzkritik*: correlating their distinctives to dogmatic developments in early Christianity. *Tendenzkritik* confirms the truth of the Griesbach hypothesis: Mark charts a neutral path, eliminating the Jewish Christian elements of Matthew and the Pauline, Gentile-Christian elements of Luke.[8]

But in Schwegler's view, particularly discreditable to the theory is the foundational role that Bruno Bauer gave it in his *Kritik der evangelischen Geschichte*. Schwegler sees Bauer's radical skepticism as the consequence of Wilke's analysis.[9] Scholars after Schwegler likewise identified association of Markan priority with Bruno Bauer's skepticism as the principal factor in its long marginalization.[10] Bauer singled out Wilke for special approval as the one whose "extraordinarily thorough" textual analysis "established for all time that Mark is the

---

5. Schwegler, "Hypothese," 210.

6. Schwegler, "Hypothese," 231–33.

7. Schwegler, "Hypothese," 229.

8. Schwegler, "Hypothese," 235–39.

9. Schwegler, "Hypothese," 241, 252.

10. Weisse said that the strong negative reaction to Bruno Bauer badly damaged the prospects of Markan priority (*Evangelienfrage*, 82). For similar judgments see Adolf Hilgenfeld, *Die Evangelien nach ihrer Entstehung und geschichtlichen Bedeutung* (Leipzig: Hirzel, 1854), 18–19; Albrecht Ritschl, "Über den gegenwärtigen Stand der Kritik der synoptischen Evangelien," *Theologische Jahrbücher* 10 (1851): 480–538 (Bauer's appeal to Wilke brought Markan priority into "Misskredit" [508]); Bernhard Weiss, "Zur Entstehungsgeschichte der drei synoptischen Evangelien," *TSK* 34 (1861): 29–100, 646–713 (688); Karl Veit, *Die synoptischen Parallelen und ein älterer Versuch ihrer Enträtselung* (Gütersloh: Bertelsmann, 1897), Weisse and Wilke had the "bad luck" of association with Bruno Bauer (15); Julius Wellhausen, *Einleitung in die drei ersten Evangelien*, 2nd ed. (Berlin: Georg Reimer, 1911), 154–55, who notes that Bauer's exploitation of Wilke was the consequence of Wilke's failure to reconcile Mark's tradition-groundedness with the authorial factor.

source of Matthew and Luke."[11] Weisse, he complains, still tried to connect the tradition directly to Jesus through the two sources of Mark (the apostle Peter) and the Logia source (the apostle Matthew). Because he showed (to Bauer's satisfaction) that the double tradition in Matthew derived from Luke, Wilke dispensed forever with the notion of a second source and thereby identified the Gospel of Mark as the point of departure for the tradition.[12] We recall that Wilke attributed the observable forms of the narrative tradition to the authorial activity of Mark. In consequence he could not clarify the connection between the written Markan materials and the pre-Markan tradition; indeed, he could not conceptualize oral tradition as anything other than momentary utterance. Bauer seizes on this: the materials of the Gospel of Mark are authorial creations; thus they are the afflatus of the genius of the writer. The existence of a pre-Markan oral tradition is fanciful. The transmission of any alleged pre-Markan tradition is in any case beyond the cognitive capacities of human memory—just try to recite the Parable of the Sower from memory![13] The Gospel of Mark does not deliver any "positive," i.e., real, information about the historical Jesus at all.[14] The Gospel is the free creation (*freie Schöpfung*) of the community's "self-consciousness," channeled by the genius of the author who renders this "self-consciousness" in narrative symbols.[15]

For Schwegler it is absurd to the face of it to trace the origins of a world-historical religion to the factitious narrative of an unknown "Mark," rather than to "an overpowering personality who from the outpouring of his inner life brought into existence a living community."[16] The same can be said of Bauer's fatuous denial of the possibility of a memory-mediated oral tradition: how then is he to explain the great oral sagas, the oral epics and poems found in Homer and Hesiod, the *altdeutsche* poems and sagas, of unknown origins and passed down unwritten through generations? Why should primitive Christians not have similarly passed down a living oral tradition in their gatherings? How can authorial creation be squared with the fragmentary, disjointed qualities of the Markan materials? Why should only "ideas" and "principles" form the contents of primitive Christian consciousness, and not also memories and historical traditions? Why should early Christian memory have left traces only in a couple hundred sayings?[17]

11. Bauer, *Kritik*, 1:xii.
12. Bauer, *Kritik*, 1:xi–xii.
13. Schwegler, "Hypothese," 257, with citations to Bauer, *Kritik*, 1:357; 2:336.
14. Bauer, *Kritik*, 1:xiii–xv.
15. Bauer, *Kritik*, 1:xv–xvi.
16. Schwegler, "Hypothese," 249.
17. Schwegler, "Hypothese," 257–65, 274.

To be associated with such a far-fetched piece of scholarship would indeed have been a mighty disability for the Markan hypothesis.

F. C. Baur

Baur positions *Tendenzkritik* as the only effective response to Strauss's negative historical-critical results. Strauss's theories, he says, could flourish only in the prevailing environment of uncertainty about Synoptic origins and source relations. Bypassing this problem was, however, his great methodological error. But a solution is not to be found in the old method of analysis of patterns of variation and agreement, which brought criticism nowhere but to the impasse exploited by Strauss. Comparative analysis of the *content* of the Synoptics must be brought into the picture if the source-critical impasse is to be broken.[18]

Baur's Tendenz-Driven Source History

Baur agrees with Wilke that the answer lies in direct-utilization relationships among the Synoptic Gospels, but he rejects Markan priority. It is much more likely that Mark is the epitomator of the other two gospels.[19] But only *Tendenzkritik* can settle the debate. The party conflicts prevailing in early Christianity when a particular evangelist writes will be vectored into a particular theological *Tendenz* that determines that evangelist's reception of his source. The approach is to align the Synoptic Gospels to a dogma-history schema that begins with particularistic Jewish Christianity, which generates its sharp antithesis in law-free Pauline Christianity, a conflict that then resolves in the mediating catholic Christianity of the second century (73–74, 530).

From its strong Jewish-Christian complexion it follows that the Gospel of Matthew, that is, Matthean priority, will anchor this system. Baur commences, however, with its antithesis, law-free Pauline Gentile Christianity. As the manifestation of this *Tendenz* he posits a primitive proto-Luke that later was received by the radical Paulinist Marcion, who found its pronounced anti-Judaism amenable. Canonical Luke then is a mediating, "irenic" redaction of this primitive proto-Lukan gospel, the product of a catholicizing *Tendenz* evident also in the Acts of the Apostles. Marcion's gospel cannot (as Irenaeus and Tertullian mistakenly thought) have been a heretical truncation of canonical

---

18. Ferdinand Christian Baur, *Kritische Untersuchungen über die kanonischen Evangelien: Ihr Verhältnis zu einander, ihren Charakter und Ursprung* (Tübingen: Ludwig Friedrich Fues, 1847), 51, 56, 71–72.

19. Baur, *Untersuchungen*, 69–70, 561–62 (hereafter page citations will be in the text).

Luke. Marcion's "omissions" are more intelligible as disruptive Lukan inter-
polations into a simpler, more coherent gospel. A number of the culling edits
that are alleged lack a rationale in Marcion's doctrinal system. Bracketing them
as Lukan additions reveals a primitive gospel with a radical Pauline dogmatic
Tendenz. This *Tendenz* powers proto-Luke's excision and effacement of Jewish-
Christian motifs in the Gospel of Matthew, its principal source (217–18, 404,
411, 423–24, 507, 520–24).[20] More pertinently for our purposes, it accounts
for his drastic divergences from Matthew's finely wrought arrangements. This
evangelist eliminated outright from the Sermon not only all its affirmative
statements about the law but also, owing to its strong Judaistic complexion,
the polemic against the Pharisees. He demoted the Sermon from its prominent
Matthean position, assigning it a later position in his gospel (Luke 6), replaced
it with an exorcism (signifying the gospel's reaching into the demonized realm
of the Gentiles), reduced it markedly in size by redistributing many of its elements, and symbolically downgraded it to a sermon on a plain (456–61).[21] He
shifted the Healing of the Centurion's Servant (Matt 8:5–13//Luke 7:1–10) into
proximity to Jesus's sayings about John the Baptist (Matt 11:2–19//Luke 7:18–35)
because both denounce obdurate Israel (59–63). Dividing the Matthean Commissioning (Matt 10) into a mission of the Twelve (Luke 9) and a mission of
the Seventy (Luke 10) depicts the displacement of the mission to the Jews,
led by Jesus's Jewish disciples, mediocrities all, by the Pauline mission to the
Gentiles. With the travel section, his boldest departure from the Matthean *Vorlage*, proto-Luke shifts the entire narrative center of gravity away from Jewish
territory (Galilee) to Gentile territory (Samaria), at the same time symbolically
transplanting to this journey through Gentile territory the bulk of the didactic
elements taken from Jewish-Christian Matthew (431–32, 445, 469–72). And so
forth. Theological *Tendenz* is the principal factor driving source utilization.

Canonical Luke on the other hand mediates between the opposing *Tendenzen* of the Pauline gospel and the Jewish-Christian Matthew. The redactor manages this by interpolating materials of Judaizing coloration into proto-Luke,
such as the Nativity and the Triumphal Entry. It is still a Pauline gospel, but the
effect is to take the edge off proto-Luke's uncompromising antithesis to Jewish
Christianity. True, there are some passages not found in the proto-Luke gospel

20. In 1851, responding to Hilgenfeld's critique, Baur concedes that Marcion probably did
redact out some passages from this source for dogmatic reasons, but insists that canonical
Luke is redacting the primitive gospel, not Marcion's redaction. See F. C. Baur, *Das Markus-
evangelium nach seinem Ursprung und Charakter, nebst einem Anhang über das Evangelium
Marcions* (Tübingen: Ludwig Fues, 1851), 208, 225–26.

21. Also *Markusevangelium*, 8–9.

that seem to contradict this scheme of things, such as the Rejection at Nazareth (Luke 4:16–30). But this episode, Baur says, reflects the Jewish rejection of the gospel, a motif also dominant in Acts, not the early dogmatic antithesis between Jewish Christianity and Pauline Christianity (217–18). Canonical Luke draws some of his mediating materials from special sources, but for significant chunks he turns back to the Gospel of Matthew for materials omitted by the proto-Luke evangelist. This includes quite a bit of double tradition, though Baur admits it is not clear why the redactor continued—like the proto-Luke evangelist—to relocate these from their Matthean arrangements. He surmises that the canonical evangelist had no other choice, given the departures of his source (the radical Pauline gospel) from the Matthean narrative order (i.e., the canonical redactor was willy-nilly dragged into proto-Luke's double-tradition redistribution scheme). This redaction did not happen until the middle of the second century: the Pauline-*Tendenz* proto-Luke gospel had to be current enough for Marcion to receive it, and it was in the second century that the catholicizing reconciliation of the primitive *Tendenzen* occurred (513–23).

For his part the Markan evangelist excerpts selectively from the Gospel of Matthew and the Pauline gospel, his utilization policy being to create a neutral, hence colorless, "indifferent" (i.e., without a pronounced *Tendenz*) gospel by eliminating the sharp *Tendenz* characteristics of his two sources. Thus he omits Luke's travel section, with its tendentious focus on Gentile Samaria, as well as Matthew's law-friendly Sermon on the Mount, and individual pericopes such as the Zacchaeus episode (too reminiscent of Paul's conversion) (563–67).[22] In 1851, under the pressure of Hilgenfeld's criticism that this *Tendenz*-neutrality policy fails to account for the full range of Mark's editorial operations, Baur adds that Mark also wanted to create a continuous historical narrative. Among other things this explains his omission of the Nativities (to avoid the leap from childhood to adult ministry), his passing over long sequences of didactic materials like the Sermons, as well as his sudden shifts from the order of one gospel to the other.[23]

This brings Baur at last to the Gospel of Matthew, for him the place to find the *fons et origo*, "the most primitive documentary source," of the gospel tradition. Appealing to patristic testimony Baur posits, as the Gospel's baseline tradition, an Aramaic Urmatthew, perhaps authored by the apostle, known to antiquity as the Gospel of the Hebrews, which eventually comes to circulate in various Greek translations. Just as the dogma-history schema would predict,

---

22. Also *Markusevangelium*, 2, 88, 143–46.
23. Baur, *Markusevangelium*, 137–46.

this primitive Aramaic source had a particularistic Jewish *Tendenz*; as such it expressed Christianity in its earliest form (577–58). Notably, though rejecting Schleiermacher's interpretation of Papias's Matthean λόγια as strictly a sayings-collection, Baur nevertheless holds that this Matthean Ursource was predominantly sayings. He takes Papias's λόγια terminology as confirmation of this and agrees with Schleiermacher that its original discourse format is reflected in the Gospel of Matthew. One does not need to posit a sayings collection (*Spruchsammlung*) source for Matthew and Luke: proto-Luke's appropriation of Matthean materials is satisfactorily explained by his *Tendenz* (581–87).[24]

This Urmatthew, predominantly sayings, is the source for our knowledge of Jesus's authentic teaching. It has a very high grade of authenticity (*Glaubwürdigkeit*). This is due not so much to its proximate eyewitness origins but because any distorting *Tendenz* barely registers in it. Further, sayings are less susceptible to the mythicizing, saga-forming impulse that Baur, agreeing with Strauss, thinks has generated much of the Synoptic narrative tradition (602–5, 620–21). To be sure, the source does have a Judaistic, law-positive tendency, but this is a "spiritualized" (*vergeistigt*) Judaism, the law finding its *telos* in pure morality (*reine Sittlichkeit*) purged of all Jewish dogmatism and legalism (585). In its very particularism, therefore, the source has an immanent universalizing impulse, a dynamic that it communicates to the Gospel of Matthew and, escaping the claustrophobic confines of Jewish orthodoxy, comes to full expression in Christianity. The incorporation of this source gives the Gospel of Matthew a heightened authenticity relative to the other Synoptics. Nevertheless, the gospel is the product of authorial (*schriftstellerische*) interests and saga-forming impulses. Old Testament messianic ideas have shaped its narrative (578–92, 609–14).

Oral Tradition and Synoptic Writing in Baur

Though Baur acknowledges the existence of an oral tradition with ongoing prestige, his *Tendenzkritik* is a written-medium, authorial-agency account of all aspects of the Synoptic profile. In part he is reacting against the use Strauss made of the oral hypothesis, but *Tendenzkritik* by definition identifies the reflective evangelist, the instrument of a particular dogmatic *Tendenz*, as virtually the sole factor generating small- and large-scale variation. Oral tradition, which he conceives to be an innately mythicizing, saga-like entity, is singled

---

24. Also *Markusevangelium*, 164. Francis Watson's L/M (Luke/Matthew) hypothesis will revive this view of the Gospel of Matthew's source.

out by Baur as the source from which the Matthean evangelist pulled a significant portion of his narrative tradition. For Luke it is a source for some of his special material (33, 458, 517).[25] The oral medium plays no further role in Baur's source history. Variation patterns among the Synoptics are the consequence of evangelist *Tendenzen*; they are "the living, concrete expression of the opposing dogmatic interests contending at the time that a particular gospel came into existence" (523). These historically conditioned interests find embodiment in the evangelist, in the creative authorial impulse (*schöpferische Geist*) that has configured the gospel as a work and its elements under a leading conception (*den Stoff beseelendes und gestaltendes Princip*), which therefore come to bear the impress of that conception.[26]

Baur's Tendenzkritik *and Luke's Utilization of Matthew*

Baur's is perhaps the earliest thorough-going attempt to give an account of Luke's Matthew utilization. Baur recognizes that theologically and historically conditioned authorial intentionality is a factor in Synoptic agreements and variation. But his attempt to explain the two Lukan evangelists' far-reaching rearrangements of Matthew as the workings of *Tendenzen* simply fails. Almost any utilization operation whatsoever on whatever source hypothesis can with some ingenuity be explained in terms of an authorial *Tendenz*, or as Baur often puts it, in terms of Luke's subjective intentionality (*Absicht*). Did the radically Pauline proto-Luke shift the Sermon on the Mount to Luke 6 and redistribute many of its elements? He wanted to deprive Matthew's law-centric Sermon of its frontispiece position, excise its law-friendly elements, and reduce its stature by even further reducing it in size and moving it down from a mountain to a plain. But why are numerous of Sermon elements relocated specifically to the travel section? Because he wanted to shift didactic materials to the Gentile setting of Samaria. Why did he nevertheless leave a substantial rump of the Sermon in Jewish Galilee? He must have felt he needed (*die Absicht . . . zu haben scheint*) to make a gesture to the significance accorded the Sermon in his source (461). The sheer complexity of Lukan operations upon Matthew eventually outruns Baur's inventiveness. His explanations tumble into the ad hoc and tautological. Why did the evangelist break up Matthew's didactic discourses and disperse their elements? Because his compositional "interests" were opposed to Matthew's (473). Why has he *augmented* the Sermon with

---

25. Also *Markusevangelium*, 157–58, 173.
26. Baur, *Markusevangelium*, 174–75.

6:39, 40, 44, 45 from Matthew 15:14, 10:24–25, and 12:33–35? Why has he shifted Matthew 7:25 to 6:31? Baur does not say. He is unable to bring the evangelist's diverse operations upon Matthew under any coherent editorial policy. Proto-Luke divides the Matthew 10 Commissioning into a Jewish Mission (Luke 9) and a Gentile Mission (Luke 10) to show the latter displacing the former. But why does he move some of the Matthew 10 materials in other locations, such as Luke 21? Because he proceeded "eclectically"; it simply "lay in the plan of his composition to temporarily pass over certain materials that might fit in a subsequent location, and at that point to reach back for it" (469). Characterizing Luke's editorial procedures as "eclectic" is Baur's euphemism for being unable to stipulate an intelligible editorial rationale for Luke's operations on Matthew.

Baur's Authentic Urmatthew Source

Baur's difficulties are a harbinger of the challenges that hypotheses positing Luke's dependence on Matthew will run into. His chief concern, however, is to find his way back through a *Tendenz*-driven source history to a historically reliable stratum, a point of departure for the tradition beyond the reach of Strauss's skepticism. His *Tendenzkritik* leads him back to Urmatthew, "the original, authentic historical source" (571). As noted, Urmatthew was a collection (*Sammlung*) of the teaching of Jesus, and though Papias had in mind the Gospel of Matthew, his term λόγια is an apt descriptor for what was in fact the Gospel's baseline source (581). The sayings making up this source are the pristinely authentic (*ächteste*) elements of the tradition; they issue right from the mouth of Jesus. It is in Jesus's teachings that the essentials of the gospel are to be found. And *qua* sayings they were less susceptible to the mythicizing tendency operating so powerfully in the narrative tradition. To be sure, Urmatthew does have a Judaistic, law-positive tendency, but as noted it is a "spiritualized" Judaism, expressing a "pure morality" from which all Judaistic dogmatism and legalism has been refined out (585–86). The source therefore has a universalizing impulse. The Gospel of Matthew despite hewing close to its authentic baseline source has a more pronounced *Tendenz* complexion. It incorporates a significant amount of narrative tradition, that is, materials (healing and miracle stories especially) shaped by the mythicizing forces of oral saga (602–5, 619–20). Dogmatic *Tendenzen* are the principal forces generating inauthentic materials in written transmission. Baur's source history amounts to a history of the tradition's degeneration from its historically authentic point of departure (Urmatthew) into rapidly increasing dogmatic distortion and adulteration by inauthentic elements. But conversely, *Tendenzkritik* is the means to work back to that authentic bedrock.

Baur's *de facto* Two Source Hypothesis

Ostensibly predicated on the Griesbach hypothesis, Baur's source history presents a more complicated state of affairs. His Urmatthew more or less corresponds to Schleiermacher's Logia source: a sayings-based, predominantly didactic source. In our terms it would have contained the bulk of the double tradition and quite a number of M materials, finely arranged in the five-discourse structure that is visible in the Gospel of Matthew. It began at Matthew 4:12, and thus with the Sermon, the programmatic set piece of Jesus's teaching on the interiority and universality of the kingdom (584).

Baur however rejects the Gospel of Luke's dependence this primitive source as an unwarranted complication. The theological *Tendenzen* of the proto-Luke evangelist and the canonical Lukan redactor account parsimoniously for their far-reaching rearrangements of Matthew (and, we might add, Luke's dependence on the Urmatthean source would make a poor fit with Baur's dogmatic history).[27] Baur in fact ends up spreading Lukan utilization of Matthew over two phases and two *Tendenzen,* proto-Luke's and the canonical redactor's—both for some unknown reason coinciding in the policy of redistributing Matthew's instructional materials (513). By these means these and other utilization problems are technically dispensed with, but at the cost of attributing a complex array of editorial motives and actions to two different redactors and destroying any claim for the parsimony of the hypothesis. That Baur posits a collection of Jesus's teachings as Matthew's source portends how hard it will be for source scenarios that posit Luke's utilization of Matthew to manage to do without a Q-like entity of some sort or other to account for the double-tradition phenomenon.

On Baur's *Tendenzkritik* source history, with its Griesbach assumptions, the Gospel of Matthew is also the source of the Lukan evangelist's narrative tradition (i.e., triple tradition). Here too "authorial interests" account for his utilization actions.[28] Baur notes that the Gospel of Mark, understood as an excerption and abbreviation of Matthew and Luke, is a pedestrian piece of work, without independent value. Only as motivated by a *Tendenz* can a reason be given for the project in the first place.[29] In the place of Markan priority Baur posits a *narrative oral tradition* as the source of Matthew's triple tradition, *qua* oral tradition shaped by the mythicizing forces innate to saga described by

---

27. Baur, *Markusevangelium*, 164–65.
28. Baur, *Markusevangelium*, 174.
29. Baur, *Untersuchungen*, 561–62.

Strauss and as such of a much inferior grade of authenticity compared to the instructional materials of the Urmatthew source.[30]

Baur ends up with a *de facto* two-source hypothesis: a written Urmatthew, overlapping by and large with the double tradition, and a narrative oral tradition corresponding more or less to the triple tradition. The Gospel of Mark lagging in the rear of this source history seems mainly to be the artifact of Baur's Griesbach scenario, required by his *Tendenzkritik* to secure Matthean priority. Baur acknowledges the difficulty of identifying a rationale for the existence of the work, and he struggles to give a coherent *Tendenzkritik* account of its utilization of Matthew and Luke. It will not be surprising to find subsequent Tübingen critics drifting back toward Markan priority.

ADOLF HILGENFELD

Adolf Hilgenfeld published *Das Markusevangelium* in 1850 and *Die Evangelien nach ihrer Entstehung und geschichtlichen Bedeutung* in 1854, significantly modifying his 1850 source history. We will begin with his 1850 analysis, and then assess his amended version in *Die Evangelien*. As it was for Baur, for Hilgenfeld *Tendenzkritik* is the effective response to Strauss's *Das Leben Jesu*, the fatal vulnerability of which was its inattention to the source-history question. Dogma-history conflicts in early Christianity, channeled through the individual evangelists, are the leading factors in their source utilization.[31]

Hilgenfeld's Source History, 1850

In a departure from Baur, Hilgenfeld rejects the "tortured" Griesbach account of the Gospel of Mark.[32] But he rejects Markan priority just as emphatically, though (as he admits) with less effort at justification.[33] He contents himself with claiming that Mark's dependence on Matthew will simply be obvious from his analysis, which simply takes Matthean priority as its presupposition (*Voraussetzung*).[34] For Hilgenfeld Mark stands in the *middle* position: its source is the Gospel of Matthew, its utilization driven by a particular *Tendenz*.

30. Baur, *Kritische Untersuchungen*, 581–82.

31. Hilgenfeld, *Evangelien*, 20–23, 27, 41.

32. Adolf Hilgenfeld, *Das Markus-Evangelium nach seiner Composition, seiner Stellung in der Evangelien-Literatur, seinem Ursprung und Charakter* (Leipzig: Breitkopf & Härtel, 1850), 4–8, 29, 44–47, 59–60.

33. Hilgenfeld, *Evangelien*, 11, 18–19; *Markus-Evangelium*, 107–8.

34. Hilgenfeld, *Markus-Evangelium*, 3, 87.

Luke uses the Gospel of Mark. Under the influence of a pro-Petrine *Tendenz* that shifts Jesus's first public appearance to Peter's hometown, Mark swaps out Matthew's Sermon for Jesus's public debut in the Capernaum synagogue (Mark 1:21–22), retaining of Matthew only the sensation that Jesus's teaching made: ἐξεπλήσσοντο ἐπὶ τῇ διδαχῇ (Matt 7:29–30//Mark 1:22).[35] Matthew's and Mark's striking divergence in the order of the narratives between Matthew 8–13 is a matter of Mark transposing Matthean episodes under the influence of a *Tendenz*: to alternate between *favorable* reactions to Jesus's ministry (e.g., Mark 2–3) and *unfavorable* reactions (e.g., Mark 4–5) (43–49, 83). We note that this alleged alternation has little connection with any dogmatic *Tendenz*; rather it is a literary (*malerische*) interest that Hilgenfeld invokes here to explain Mark's operations on the Matthew 8–13 materials.[36]

In Hilgenfeld's schema Matthew is mediated to Luke indirectly, through Luke's source Mark—this explains, for example, why Luke follows Mark's episode order in the Galilean ministry. But Hilgenfeld notes that Luke's overall disposition of the Synoptic tradition, which differs significantly from Matthew's, and materials like the Sermon that he uniquely shares with Matthew, cannot be explained on the grounds of his use of canonical Mark. Canonical Mark, so curiously deficient in essential elements, must therefore be a truncation of an earlier, more copious gospel, a "Petrine gospel" (in effect an Urmarkus) used by Luke. This copious gospel is the intermediating link between Matthew and Luke. It is the source of much of Luke's double tradition. Its Sermon evinces the transitional *Tendenz* that stands between Matthew's particularistic Jewish-Christian Sermon and its universalizing rendition in Luke as a pure, natural morality. The abrupt break after the Choosing of the Twelve in Mark 3:13–19a likely marks a lacuna where it stood in the Petrine gospel. Between the present Mark 9:50 and 10:1 it also contained a travel section.[37]

This Petrine gospel is Hilgenfeld's response to the difficulty of explaining Luke's use of Matthew. Its *Tendenz* is likewise transitional: an antithetical reaction to the Jewish particularism of the Gospel of Matthew. It moves in the direction of the free humanistic universalism, the natural morality, of the Gospel of Luke. Canonical Mark, on the other hand, is a post-Lukan redaction. Its drastic reduction of the Petrine gospel is driven by an irenic *Tendenz* that eliminates pronounced Jewish-Christian and universalizing passages from its

---

35. Hilgenfeld, *Markus-Evangelium*, 13–15.
36. Hilgenfeld, *Markus-Evangelium*, 50.
37. Hilgenfeld, *Markus-Evangelium*, 2–3, 92–98, 102–8.

copious *Vorlage* (in effect the return of the Griesbach Mark).[38] Its surplus in passages and in casual details—e.g., the fleeing youth (14:51–52), that Levi was the son of Alphaeus (2:14), that the blind man's name was Bartimaeus (10:46), the specification of Dalmanutha (8:10), that Simon was the father of Alexander and Rufus (15:21)—indicates, however, that the redactor drew in addition upon a historically valuable tradition of the Roman church.[39]

Hilgenfeld's Source History, 1854

The unwieldiness of this source schema is evident; it drew criticism from Köstlin in particular. The postulated Petrine gospel is a hybrid monstrosity. Moreover, other than a vague appeal to a transitional *Tendenz* Hilgenfeld does not explain why the Petrine gospel evangelist rearranged Matthew the way that he did. In 1854 he published a significantly modified version of his source history, from which the Petrine gospel of 1850 has disappeared. Baur's *Tendenzkritik* erred, he said, in starting from later, catholicizing works and working backward toward the origins of gospel writing. Hilgenfeld proposes to begin from *Tendenz*-history's point of departure in the Jewish Christianity of primitive Palestinian community—which stands in immediate continuity with the historical Jesus himself—and to move forward, using these findings to gauge the historicity levels of subsequent gospels.[40]

The point of departure for Synoptic writing was a proto-Matthean *Grundschrift*, a gospel, originating in the primitive community. It was composed in Greek by the apostle Matthew but subsequently expanded by a Hellenistic redactor to the present, more universalizing Gospel of Matthew. Its existence is corroborated by the Jewish-Christian Gospels of the Nazarenes and the Ebionites, like the Gospel of Matthew redactions of the *Grundschrift*. It began with the genealogy and continued directly into the Baptism and Temptation. Not surprisingly, given its incubation in a community living within the traditional frameworks of Palestinian Judaism, its *Tendenz* complexion was a strict Jewish-Christianity—with a polemical edge, evident in the sharp reactions to the Pauline mission found in the Sermon on the Mount, elements that stand in some tension with a core of authentic sayings (*geschichtlicher Kern*). The Sermon was not part of any instructional source (*Redenquelle*) but an

---

38. Hilgenfeld, *Markus-Evangelium*, 94, 123–32.
39. Hilgenfeld, *Markus-Evangelium*, 121.
40. Hilgenfeld, *Evangelien*, 23–28, 42 (hereafter page references to *Evangelien* will be in the text).

element of the primitive gospel *Grundschrift*, albeit not where the canonical redactor awkwardly placed it, delivered inexplicably to just four disciples. The *Grundschrift* was likely composed in the aftermath of the Pauline opening to the Gentiles; in its polemical elements in the Sermon it registers the outlook of the Jerusalem apostles.

The canonical redaction, however, was driven by a more universalizing Jewish-Christian *Tendenz* prompted by the receptivity of the Gentiles, a shift evident, for example, in the contrast between the Syrophoenician Woman (*Grundschrift*) and the Healing of the Centurion's Servant (redaction), the insertion of which has disturbed the original report of Jesus's entrance into Capernaum. The *Tendenz* of the canonical redaction is instrumentalized to build out the Gospel of Matthew from the *Grundschrift* (116–17). The Gospel is in turn the source for the Gospel of Mark. The *Tendenz* of the Markan redaction marks a qualitative step away from particularistic Jewish Christianity toward a full-blown universalism. It amounts to a "mild" Petrine universalism, the effect of which is to position the second gospel midway between Matthew's pronounced Jewish-Christianity and the radical Pauline universalism of the Gospel of Luke. Under its impulse the Markan evangelist purges his source of its particularistic Jewish-Christian elements (124, 145–54). However, Hilgenfeld must also invoke Mark's literary intentions, particularly evident in the Gospel's narrative layout that has initial enthusiastic reception of Jesus giving way to growing hostility (likely Hilgenfeld's attempt to account for Mark's different narrative order for the Galilean ministry). The numerous unique, often vivid details that give the Gospel the appearance of primitivity Hilgenfeld explains by positing the evangelist's use of a separate Petrine-Roman tradition mediated orally or in pre-Synoptic collections (145–48). Notable here is his all-but-complete abandonment of his earlier Urmarkus (*Petrusevangelium*)/ Marcan truncation hypothesis. The evangelist's *Tendenz* and literary intentionality account for his divergences from Matthew.

The Gospel of Luke still occupies the third place in this modified source schema, with the Gospel of Mark as its principal source. How does Hilgenfeld construe Luke, especially since his discarded Urmarkus had served to explain Luke's divergences from Matthew? He now conceives Luke using Matthew in addition to Mark, his source utilization influenced by a sharp Pauline *Tendenz*. He rejects Baur's theory that canonical Luke is an irenic redaction of a radically Pauline proto-Luke. Instead, equating Paulinism with stringent anti-Judaism, he imputes this antithetical *Tendenz* to the Gospel of Luke: Judaism stands in darkness and the shadow of death (1:79); it is blind and legalistic (6:39–42), the domain of demons (11:24–26) and spiritual darkness (11:33); the Jewish people are the fig tree that does not bear fruit (13:6–9). Jewish Christianity and the twelve apostles are amalgamated to Judaism: they are those who say "Lord, Lord but do not do the things that I say" (6:46). Luke rewrites Matthew's Nativity to accord with Paulinism: Jesus is born under the law, born of a woman (154, 163–68, 220–23). Luke eliminates from Matthew's Sermon the connection of Jesus's moral teaching to the law, and by importing sayings like "the blind leading the blind" (Matt 15:14//Luke 6:39–40) gives it an anti-Judaism coloration—though Hilgenfeld does not explain why Luke has transposed so much material out of it (173).

How does Hilgenfeld now handle Luke's travel section, the bane of source schemas that have Luke using Matthew? It likewise is the artifact of the evangelist's anti-Judaistic *Tendenz* operating on his sources, of the antithesis (*Gegensatz*) between particularistic, narrow-minded (*Engherzigkeit*) Judaism and the open universalism of the mission to the Gentile world, between *Judenthum* and *Christenthum*, law and gospel, works righteousness and faith righteousness (i.e., Martha versus Mary). The reading of 16:17 preserved in Marcion's gospel—"it is easier for heaven and earth to pass away than for one jot *of my words* (τῶν λόγων μου) to fall away"—is more primitive than the current reading (186–89, 200–201). And so forth: elements of the travel section are pulled into this binary schema, with Hilgenfeld blurring Luke's "judenfeindliche" attack on Judaism with his polemic against the Twelve, symbols of Jewish Christianity (196). The Sending of the Seventy is calibrated as a deliberate marginalization of the Jewish apostles (Hilgenfeld follows Baur). The evangelist pulls the Matthew 8:18–22 call stories over to Luke 9:57–62 to signify the formation of a new group of disciples.

Luke's *Tendenz* serves as the omni-explanation for utilization questions and operations. But even this flexible instrument runs up against limits: Hilgenfeld can give no *Tendenz* account, for example, of why Luke has transposed the Do Not Be Anxious passage from Matthew's Sermon (Matt 6:25–33) to the travel section (Luke 12:22–36). He therefore posits Luke's use of *an additional source*, an "old travel report," of Jewish-Christian complexion, of Jesus's travels in the boundary area of Samaria and Galilee, which perhaps even had the proportions of a primitive gospel. In addition to many Lukan special materials it contained numerous double-tradition parallels: e.g., the discipleship and salt sayings (14:25–35), Offenses (17:1–4), Faith as a Mustard Seed (17:5–6), Sign of Son of Man (13:20–37), Treasures in Heaven (12:33–34), likely the baseline (*Grundlage*) of the Luke 10 Commissioning—indeed, possibly of the entire sequence 9:51–13:9 (193, 208–10). In this "old travel report" Hilgenfeld's 1850 *Petrusevangelium*, the expedient propounded to deal with the problem of Luke's overlaps with and divergences from Matthew, makes a ghostly reappearance (218). Functionally it amounts to a phantom Q: Luke does not take all or even perhaps very much of the double tradition in the travel section from Matthew.

Hilgenfeld's *Tendenzkritik* amounts to little more than stratifying Synoptic materials into layers that correspond to a dogma-history schema. Hilgenfeld distinguishes his *Grundschrift* (his Matthean Urgospel) from the canonical redaction on the grounds that a "strict Jewish Christianity closed off to the Gentile world" is the point of departure for dogmatic developments in early Christianity (116). *Tendenzkritik* is his principal reason for rejecting the theory of an instructional source (*Redenquelle*): the dividing line between layers demarcated by the *Tendenz* runs through the middle of sayings sequences and the narrative sequences alike (113).

Oral Tradition and Writing in Hilgenfeld's Source History

What media assumptions inform Hilgenfeld's analysis? Tradition exists principally in the written medium: Hilgenfeld's source history is a matter of an array of evangelists and redactors operating upon written texts. How *Tendenz*-driven redactional actions upon source texts actually generate the observable patterns of variation and agreement never gets explored in any depth. Oral tradition is an occasional accessory to Synoptic writing, adduced ad hoc to get around some utilization difficulty—e.g., the source for Mark's unique details despite being dependent upon Matthew, and for some of the Matthean redactor's additions to the Matthean Urgospel. Hilgenfeld in the main imagines the tradition to be present to the evangelists in raw, provisional written collections (*zusammenhangslose, vereinzelte Aufzeichnungen*) not ontologically distinct from oral tradition (48, 146).

Hilgenfeld's Grundschift: The Authentic Source

Hilgenfeld's source history is a quest to identify the authentic grounds of the tradition. *Tendenzkritik* is instrumental to this quest. If the evangelists and redactors are controlled by dogmatic *Tendenz* viewpoints and are operating upon similarly *Tendenz*-formed sources (*Tendenzschriften*), it follows that the earliest evangelist, notwithstanding his own historically conditioned *Tendenz*, will stand in closest proximity to the life of Jesus. The purity of the materials in this Urgospel would be the highest. This in turn would supply the measure for gauging the historicity of subsequent gospels (42).

Hilgenfeld strengthens the connection by identifying the apostle Matthew as the Urevangelist. Hilgenfeld grounds this attribution in the patristic testimony, but also in the claim that the Urgospel is colored by the Jewish-Christian outlook of the Jerusalem apostles circa AD 50–60, attested in Galatians 2. The apostolic *Grundschrift*, that is, is the artifact of a particularistic Jewish-Christian *Tendenz* reflecting, on the one hand, the averse response of the Palestinian community to the law-free Pauline mission and, on the other, its reactive affirmation of the eternal validity of the law and of an exclusively Jewish mission (115–16). But thanks to *Tendenzkritik* these alloying elements of community theology can be distinguished and separated out (e.g., Matt 5:17–18; 7:6; 10:5–6) from historically authentic base materials (*der Kern*), a de-layering operation that also demarcates the primitive Palestinian *Grundschrift* from its subsequent universalizing, Hellenizing redaction (48–51, 65, 73–74, 114). Once these critical operations are carried out, the *Grundschrift* yields up authentic history *not affected by dogma*.

Though denying that the Markan evangelist is an eyewitness, Hilgenfeld nevertheless connects the unique details of his gospel to a primitive Roman "Petrine" tradition, circulating in primitive collections (*Aufzeichnungen*) of Peter's preaching that have descended to the evangelist and that he uses to supplement his Matthew utilization (146–48). In this way Hilgenfeld manages to connect both the Gospel of Matthew (the *Grundschrift*) and Mark (the "Petrine tradition") directly to eyewitness memory. This allows him to seal off the base gospel materials from mythicizing oral saga.

Hilgenfeld's Phantom 2DH

Hilgenfeld runs into difficulties explaining Mark as a utilization of Matthew. He marvels at the autonomous narrative arrangement and coherence of Mark's Galilean ministry sequence, commenting—in a swipe at the Griesbach hypothesis—that such could hardly be the product of someone slavishly dependent on sources.[41] One would think that the observation would apply equally well to Mark's dependence on Matthew: Hilgenfeld's explication of Mark's autonomous narrative intentionality in his different arrangement of Matthew's Galilean sequences does not really require the tacked-on assumption of Matthean priority at all.[42] Here and elsewhere we see a kind of phantom Markan priority lurking in Hilgenfeld's ad hoc explanations of Mark's use of Matthew, which basically amount to his arguing that Mark did use Matthew *despite appearances*. In 1850 he explained Mark's shortness in comparison to Matthew by identifying canonical Mark as a truncation of a copious Urmarkus. By 1854 he has abandoned this expedient, but he offers no alternative explanation. *De*

41. Hilgenfeld, *Markus-Evangelium*, 88.
42. Hilgenfeld, *Markus-Evangelium*, 47–49.

facto Markan priority effectively turns *de jure* when Hilgenfeld, to explain the numerous little details unique to Mark, proposes that in addition to Matthew the evangelist used a primitive Petrine source (146–48).[43]

What about the double tradition? Hilgenfeld readily acknowledges that Luke's divergences from Matthew are difficult to square with dependence on Matthew. In 1850 he got around this problem by having Luke access the Matthean double tradition indirectly through a non-Matthean source, a copious Urmarkus. In 1854, with Urmarkus out of the picture, he falls back on Luke's Pauline *Tendenz* and autonomous literary intentions to dispense with a number of the difficulties raised by his Matthew utilization. But in the face of the voluminous double-tradition parallels dispersed throughout the travel section Hilgenfeld abandons this approach and proposes that Luke used a non-Matthean source that among other things contained most of this double tradition—a phantom Q (142, 218). Moreover, he observes that the fit of certain major double-tradition sequences (the Sermon, the Commissioning, John the Baptist sequence, Beelzebul sequence) in canonical Matthew to their narrative settings sometimes appears awkward—the Sermon for example when Jesus has chosen just four disciples. The canonical redactor therefore must have rearranged the order in which these sequences appeared in the proto-Matthean *Grundschrift* (66, 81, 109). In other words, Hilgenfeld's Matthean redactor inserts double-tradition sequences at points of his own choosing in the narrative sequence of the *Grundschrift*, which by and large corresponds to the Markan narrative sequence! Why does Hilgenfeld not just embrace the *Redenquelle* hypothesis? His stated reasons—narrative elements appear among the sayings materials; the sayings frequently assume narrative knowledge—are predicated on a genre purity assumption (113). His unstated reason is that this would call into question the postulate of Matthean priority, and with it the dogma-history orthodoxy of *Tendenzkritik*.

KARL REINHOLD KÖSTLIN

Echoing Hilgenfeld and Baur, Karl Reinhold Köstlin identifies *Tendenzkritik* as the approach that will break the source-critical logjam.[44] But he acknowledges at the outset that identifying the *Tendenzen* of the evangelists alone cannot solve the problem of Synoptic relationships.[45]

---

43. Hilgenfeld, *Markus-Evangelium*, 121.

44. Karl Reinhold Köstlin, *Der Ursprung und die Komposition der synoptischen Evangelien* (Stuttgart: Carl Mäcken, 1853), 1–2.

45. Köstlin, *Ursprung*, 2 (hereafter page references will be in the text).

Köstlin and the Sources of the Gospel of Matthew

Köstlin follows Hilgenfeld in making the Gospel of Matthew the starting point in his source history. A first edition of the gospel originated within Palestinian Judaism, in the primitive "Nazarene" movement, remnants of which survived into Jewish-Christian sects of the sort attested by the Gospel of the Nazarenes. Notably, this first edition of the gospel issued from a primitive *Galilean* Jesus community (*die älteste galiläischen Christengemeinde*). Composed immediately following the Jewish War by a Galilean Jesus follower, it contains a Galilean stream of primitive oral tradition grounded in the living memory of Jesus's activity in the region. In its anti-Pharisaic, *antijüdischen* elements, it expresses the opposition of a regional Galilean piety to the elite scribal Judaism centered in remote Jerusalem and Judea (32–34, 112–13). Its biblical citations point to its being composed in Greek. Some time later it underwent a light redaction at the hands of a catholicizing Jewish-Christian redactor who added passages of a universalizing complexion such as Matthew 28:16–20 (43–45, 130).

The Galilean evangelist composed his gospel using two sources: on the one hand an instructional source (*Redenquelle*; Logia), preserved in its original form in the discourses found in Matthew 5–7, 10, 11, 12, 13, 19, 20–25 (Köstlin nods to Schleiermacher), and on the other a provisional collection of narrative materials. The existence of the instructional source is to be inferred from the similar complexion of the instructional discourses, their awkward compositional fit with the narrative blocks, the anomalousness of discourses compiled of sayings obviously from different times in Jesus ministry being positioned within a narrative that follows a precise chronology, and likewise the clash of the respective representations of Jesus—the Sermon on the Mount featuring Jesus in his full messianic dignity in open conflict with Pharisaic piety, in contrast to Jesus's just incipiently developed messianic identity and still low-conflict ministry depicted in the foregoing narrative materials. Its narrative elements are the minimum needed to make the didactic sequences intelligible. Even in the Beelzebul episode, narrative recedes in favor of the didactic. The gospel history, Köstlin observes, was well known, and the Logia source's recipients could supply narrative contextualizations (45–53, 57–62).

There is no reason, he continues, not to identify this source with Papias's λόγια work that unanimous patristic testimony identifies as the starting point of gospel writing, or to doubt the patristic attribution to the apostle Matthew. Like the first edition of the Matthean gospel, the Logia source originated in Galilee, where it is probable that the apostle Matthew was active (among the "Nazarenes"). Just like the proto-Matthew for which it is a principal source, the Logia reflects Galilean regional aversion to the elite scribal Judaism of Judea and Jerusalem (113). Though of Jewish-Christian origins, it is free of any pronounced antithetical *Tendenz*. In it the viewpoint of a primitive Galilean Jesus community comes to expression. The Matthean evangelist, likely also a Galilean Jesus follower, takes this Logia source as the basis for his own gospel-writing project, which amounted to supplementing it with materials from his narrative sources. Nevertheless, the divergences of Luke's double tradition from Matthew's preclude the proto-Matthean Logia from being their common source. The fragmentation (*Zerstücklung*) of the double tradition in Luke and its quite different ordering point to Luke's drawing upon a distinct source for these common materials (55–57, 65–69, 113).

What about the Gospel of Matthew's narrative (triple-tradition) materials? The Matthean evangelist's first and principal source was a provisional collection of episodic materials from the Galilean ministry and the journey to Jerusalem, as well as some of the Passion and Resurrection sequences. The source had not brought its constituent episodes into any firm chronological order. The Matthean evangelist uses it for episodic raw material that he arranges in a chronological order determined by the topical structure of his instructional source. This primitive narrative source therefore was not a fully realized gospel with a connected-up chronology, notwithstanding that it had some longer connected sequences that the Matthean evangelist takes over from it intact (*eine schon vorliegende Ordnung*), and notwithstanding that it overlaps significantly with the Gospel of Mark.[46] In fact, canonical Mark is to be understood as a redaction of the same source, like the Matthean evangelist improving the coherence and connectivity of its narrative order. This source likely originated outside of Palestine, where the frameworks for memory such as they existed in Palestine could not be easily transferred. Probably it is to be identified with the inchoately ordered collection of Peter's teachings that Papias refers to (71–74, 88–89, 98–105). The Matthean evangelist's second narrative source was a primitive Galilean collection, hardly distinguishable from oral tradition, with materials reflecting a glorifying Jewish-Christian messianic Christology (here Ewald's influence; see below), such as the Nativity, Baptism, the Temptation, and the Transfiguration, as well as a number of apologetic episodes, e.g., Pilate's wife, the Opening of the Tombs, the Grave Watch (85–88, 92–95).

---

46. These connected sequences include the Sea Storm/Gerasene Demoniacs sequence (Matt 8:18–34) and the Jairus's Daughter/Woman with the Flow/Jairus's Daughter sequence (Matt 9:18–26), as well as the controversies in Matt 12:1–15 and some of the triple-tradition sequences in Matthew 14.

Köstlin and Luke's Matthew Utilization

On the standard *Tendenzkritik* grounds, Köstlin tags the Gospel of Luke a Paulinist reaction to the Jewish-Christian Gospel of Matthew, declaring with typical *Tendenzkritik* assuredness that "almost all its individual features of selection, arrangement, and overall conception of the material are to be traced back to this *Tendenz*" (182). But abandoning a key *Tendenzkritik* tenet, Köstlin does not position Luke in *antithesis* to the Jewish-Christian Matthew. For all his appealing to *Tendenzkritik* to hold that Luke is dependent upon Matthew, Köstlin in truth adduces it only rarely in his analysis of Luke's Matthew utilization, the chief difficulty of which is Luke's dramatically different disposition (*so ganz entgegengesetzt*) of the Matthean materials (138).

How then to explain Luke's drastic fragmentation (*zum Extrem fragmentarische Zerstücklung*) of the Matthean discourses? Köstlin experiments with different explanations. Luke wants to give each aspect of Jesus's teaching separate presentation; accordingly he assigns the elements of Matthew's composite speeches to different contexts and occasions. Köstlin converts the patterns of Matthean double tradition found dispersed in Luke into Lukan editorial intentions. He tries to anchor this in the Prologue: assigning each element of Matthew's discourses its own historical context accords with presenting things ἀκριβῶς καθεξῆς. That is, though ostensibly prompted by a Pauline *Tendenz*, Luke in fact takes exception to Matthew's uneven and inaccurate chronological arrangement. But are not his secondary historical contextualizations contrived? How does this square with his claim to give an accurate account? Köstlin is aware of the difficulty. Luke's historiographical scruples, he ventures, were overridden by his polemical *Tendenz*: because of the prestige of the Jewish-Christian Gospel of Matthew, Luke resolves to give his Pauline gospel a starkly different layout (138–39). But the Matthean evangelist used the Galilean instructional source (the Logia). Might Luke have made direct use of that? No, Köstlin says, for Luke's agreements with Matthew are in Greek, whereas the instructional source is in Aramaic, and in any case Matthew's discourse arrangement conserves its format (140).

He admits, however, that the patterns of variation in certain double-tradition parallels, in the travel section especially, are such as to elude explanation on editorial or *Tendenz* grounds. These cases suggest that Luke has access to a *second* double-tradition source (or sources), albeit one that itself utilized Matthew (140–41). The wording of his Lord's Prayer (11:1–4) departs so markedly from Matthew's that he must have taken it from another source. Elements of Luke's Woes (11:39–42) appear to be more primitive than their

Matthean counterparts. Luke's Keep Your Lamps Burning (12:35–38) can hardly be explained on the basis of the Matthew 25:1–13 parallel. These and other parallels, particularly those falling between 14:1 and 18:14, suggest that in this segment of the travel section Luke is using a source that contained double tradition and parables (146–70).

Köstlin handles Luke's triple tradition in the same way: per *Tendenzkritik* Luke's source must be Matthew. But in high-variation parallels, or where Luke's parallel appears to be the more primitive, he is making subsidiary use of the same proto-Markan narrative collection that Matthew does. Or as Köstlin puts it, straining to maintain *Tendenzkritik* orthodoxy, Luke's relationship to Matthew in cases of this sort is "mediated" (*vermittelt*) by the proto-Markan source (139–40, 164, 170–80, 195).

Many of Luke's special traditions come from a special proto-Ebionite Judean source (246). This Judean source was in fact a coherently ordered narrative gospel that in addition to Luke's special materials contained numerous triple- and double-tradition parallels. Like Hilgenfeld's 1850 Urmarkus (his Petrine gospel), Köstlin's Judean gospel mediates between Matthew and Luke, serving to explain Luke's different arrangements of triple tradition and double tradition and high-variation versions of the same. It is Luke's source for certain triple-tradition parallels, including the first Capernaum exorcism, the Healing of the Paralytic, the Gerasene Demoniac, the Raising of Jairus's Daughter, the Healing of the Epileptic Boy, the Healing of the Blind Man at Jericho, and others. Luke follows its order for the Galilean ministry, and in fact it is a principal source (*Hauptquelle*) for his narrative. This unknown Judean evangelist has himself drawn principally upon the proto-Markan source, such that it comes to share its Petrine complexion. This Judean gospel is also the source for quite a bit of Luke's double tradition, including the Healing of the Centurion's Servant, the Sermon on the Plain (6:21b–49), the Luke 17 Apocalypse; it contained a shorter version of Luke's travel section that combined L^S and double tradition, such as the Mustard Seed and the Leaven (13:18–21), the opening call stories (9:58–62), the Lord's Prayer (11:1–8), the Woes (11:39–52), Enter through the Narrow Gate (13:23–30), and the like. These double-tradition parallels, mediated to Matthew in the Galilean Logia source, come to Luke through this Judean gospel, though Köstlin thinks that the Judean evangelist also used Matthew (222–23, 245, 254–66). As noted, it functions to explain Luke's divergences from Matthew in triple-tradition and double-tradition sequences. Bare appeal to Luke's *Tendenz*, Köstlin concludes, is not up to this task (233–37).

And yet this is not yet the entire source-critical story for the Gospel of Luke. Appropriating elements of Ewald's theory, Köstlin thinks that the Judean evangelist, in addition to the proto-Mark collection, used an instructional source (*Redensammlung*), parallel to but divergent from Matthew's, and in form more in the nature of a sayings collection, a gnomologium. Its existence is to be inferred behind the Lukan travel section, the sequence and contents of which cannot be derived from the Matthean source. It is a Judean reworking of Matthew's Galilean Logia source (so effectively a Q^{Luke}), which also involved supplementing it with L^S sayings and parables. The Judean evangelist used this gnomologium selectively. But Luke also had access to it, and he appropriated the elements that the Judean evangelist had passed over. When all is said and done, therefore, Luke's source array, hinted at in his Prologue, includes the proto-Markan source, a Judean redaction of the Galilean Logia, the Gospel of Matthew, and the Judean gospel (269–83).

Köstlin and Mark

Köstlin dispenses quickly with canonical Mark. Luke's divergences from Mark are inexplicable on the theory he is dependent on Mark. The short and long omissions, divergences in order, the high variation in numerous parallels, Luke's different renderings of transitional elements of their common episodes, additions to common material, and his copious non-Markan content indicate instead Luke's reliance on other sources. And if Mark were their common source, surely Matthew and Luke would agree more closely than they do. That Mark clearly signals acquaintance with the larger body of Jesus's teaching while including just pieces and hints of it indicates that his gospel instead is an epitome of Matthew and Luke. Its vivid realism is a matter of authorial style (283–85, 311–12, 324–31). But anomalies such as Mark's surplus of innocuous and sometimes divergent details, parallels that would entail complex cross-source utilization operations (e.g., Raising of Jairus's Daughter; Healing of Woman with the Flow), and that he sometimes has the more primitive version of a parallel, are difficult to explain on this Griesbach scenario. They therefore indicate that he also has access to a separate source, in fact the proto-Markan Petrine collection also used by Matthew and Luke (336–44).

Canonical Mark's consultation with this work, indeed, his use of it as his chief source (*Hauptquelle*), neatly explains the phenomena above. All but abandoning Griesbach, Köstlin says that canonical Mark is best understood as a redaction (*Umarbeitung*) of this primitive proto-Mark, just like Matthew did impressing a literary, narrative order upon the materials of a provisional collection under the aegis of a mediating *Tendenz*. For all practical purposes canonical Mark is a second version of the "original Mark"; the form of the latter is to be inferred from the former (98–99, 107–9, 355–58, 373).

Media Assumptions in Köstlin's Source History

This account of canonical Mark is an artifact of Köstlin's *Tendenzkritik* dogma-history schema: priority simply *cannot* be a property of a non-Jewish-Christian gospel like Mark. Köstlin's entire source history is an attempt to force refractory Synoptic realities into the standard *Tendenzkritik* framework. This difficulty is exacerbated because more so than Baur and Hilgenfeld, who were inclined to invoke evangelist *Tendenz* as the all-purpose solution to source-utilization puzzles, Köstlin pays attention to the actual patterns of Synoptic variation and agreement, making only rare appeals to *Tendenz*. He recognizes that notwithstanding their divergences, close verbal agreements among the Synoptics indicate written-source relationships. But his media assumptions allow only limited margins for variation in written-source utilization. This is a key operational premise in his source history. The outcome is his array of sources. Variation in order and wording that exceeds a limited range is parsed out amongst plural sources. Owing to the doctrinaire *Tendenzkritik* postulate of Matthean priority, these sources tend to form a nimbus around the Gospel of Luke—Köstlin must chart a way from Matthew to Luke.

In his efforts to maintain *Tendenzkritik* orthodoxy on Matthean priority Köstlin makes a number of observations about the oral tradition and its shift to written transmission. He concedes the indicators of primitivity in the Markan tradition, but he conceives the triple-tradition source as a subliterary collection (*Aufzeichnung*) of narrative leavened with some didactic materials, with little that distinguishes it, that is, from its predecessor body of variant oral tradition. He does this on the grounds that subliterary collections must have formed a transitional step from oral tradition to the gospels. Gospel writing is a matter of impressing an overall narrative order and literary conception on this still inchoate written tradition. This, he says, first truly begins with the Matthean evangelist who aligned narrative materials from this extempore proto-Markan triple-tradition collection to the chronology of his instructional source. Source copying does not permit much variation, and evangelist *Tendenzen* can only take us so far. A significant amount of verbal and sequential variation among Synoptic parallels, therefore, is due to subsequent evangelists (the Judean evangelist; Luke; Mark) also referencing this primitive triple-tradition collection as well as parallel collections of didactic traditions. The narrative sequences of the Synoptic Gospels are contrivances of the evangelists to organize a fragmentary tradition. Synoptic gospel writing therefore is simply the culmination of tradition-formation processes already long at work (*eine bloße Ergänzung der mündliche Ueberlieferung und Belehrung*) (94–99, 282–90, quotation 283).

Köstlin's Quest for the Authentic Tradition

Dogmatic *Tendenzen* stain the unsullied historical tradition (*Geschichtstof-fes*) with a "subjective-ideological coloration." Of the Synoptics the Jewish-Christian, Palestinian Gospel of Matthew is least affected by a *Tendenz*. This is due in no small part to its being built up around the Galilean Logia source, which is the artifact of an apostolic eyewitness and the bedrock (*Grundlage*) of unsullied authenticity for the written tradition, setting the course of its de-velopment (398–400). In the nature of things, narrative can render historical events only indirectly and opaquely, and it is prone to infestation by dogma. In the sayings Jesus's teaching exists as it came "from the mouth of Jesus" (394). Jewish-Christian in complexion but with universalizing accents, the Galilean Logia is free of any pronounced Christology or antithetical *Tendenz*. Its ele-ments have not yet reacted with the historical catalysts that will precipitate dogmatic and apologetic *Tendenzen*. They supply the standard (*Maßstab*) for assessing historical authenticity in the narrative tradition (46–55, 394–98). We recall that quite a bit of Luke's double tradition was taken from a parallel instructional source, mediated to the Lukan evangelist via the Judean gospel, though in some instances he used it directly. It likewise has a direct memory connection to Jesus: it was compiled early enough that its materials could be gleaned directly from living eyewitnesses (222–23, 282). Living memory, and by extension oral tradition, is not a field of play for antithetical *Tendenzen*, which instead become manifest in the mode of intentional gospel writing.

Nevertheless, he says, mediation of memory by means of narrative repre-sentation complicates matters. Galilee and Judea were the geographical zones of living oral memory of Jesus's ministry. From them issued a Galilean and Judean narrative tradition that was channeled into the proto-Markan collec-tion and the proto-Lukan Judean gospel, respectively (390–97). The proto-Markan collection, being hardly distinguishable from oral tradition, would not have been much affected by any *Tendenz*. But though derived from Peter, it originated at one remove from direct eyewitness testimony (99, 105, 360). Fading historicity would also have been an inevitable consequence of the wid-ening distance of this narrative tradition from the events themselves and of the gradual expiry of direct eyewitness testimony. The collection's episodic materials already show some light effects of christological reflection. For its part the Judean gospel also has eyewitness credentials. Given its interest in the cult it likely had a priestly author with an ardent (*begeisterte*) memory of Jesus's Judean ministry and his tragic fate. The priestly author also made use of the proto-Markan collection and its Petrine, Galilean traditions as well as a parallel instructional source (260–77, 364). Accordingly, it has a mixed pedigree: composed by an immediate eyewitness to Judean events, but otherwise making tendential use of sources with eyewitness connections. And finally, while Köstlin identifies memory with unsullied historicity and authenticity (*klare und deutlich Erinnerung*), he sees the process of giving memory narrative forms—i.e., its externalization as *tradition*—as a process of distortion: narrativization obscures clear, direct remembering.

The outcome of the play of these various factors is that precise, wide-ranging memory of historical events (*Geschichtserinnerung*) gradually reduces down to a body of separate, emblematic stories (*Hauptereignisse*), no longer the direct recollections of eyewitnesses but "local tradition" (362–64). Köstlin's source history is a story of increasing distancing from the transparently historical authenticity of eyewitness memory—a property imputable without qualification only to the Galilean Logia source—to gospel composition driven by literary intentionality and dogmatic *Tendenzen*. Like so many nineteenth-century scholars Köstlin subordinates the episodic tradition (narratively mediated memory) to the sayings tradition (unmediated memory) and has trouble articulating its significance other than as a kind of penumbra around Jesus's teaching.

Köstlin's Phantom 2DH

Though he gives up on *Tendenzen* as the principal factor in Synoptic source utilization, Köstlin holds fast to the *Tendenzkritik* dogma that priority is to be assigned to the Jewish-Christian Gospel of Matthew. His source history is a tortured attempt to square contrary source-critical indicators with this *Tendenzkritik* position. The gravitational pull on his analysis is toward Markan priority, and toward a *de facto* 2DH. This forces him back on various contrivances to maintain Matthean priority. He infers that the evangelist is building his gospel around a Galilean instructional source. This requires, however, another source for the narrative materials. Köstlin's *Aufzeichnung* (provisional collection) theory of proto-Mark is therefore essential to his maintaining Matthean priority: the proto-Markan source lacks the properties of a gospel (45–52, 74–78, 96–99). Yet Köstlin acknowledges that the Matthean evangelist takes over triple-tradition sequences already connected in this source, such as the Sea Storm/Gerasene Demoniacs sequence; the Jairus's Daughter/Woman with the Flow/Jairus's Daughter sequence; similarly Matthew 9:27–32; the controversies in 12:1–15; the Matthew 14 sequences (80–82). He grants that there are indicators of Matthew altering an "already present order sequence" and making insertions "into a pre-existing context." At times he comes close to saying that the evangelist inserts materials of the Galilean Logia source into an already existing narrative sequence (97–98).

As an orthodox *Tendenzkritik* critic Köstlin must likewise claim that Luke is dependent upon the Gospel of Matthew. But in the face of the formidable source-utilization challenges he ends up having Matthew mediated to Luke by intermediating sources. The chief of these is a Judean gospel with a moderate universalizing *Tendenz*, thus to all intents and purposes a proto-Luke. This gospel had used the proto-Markan source as its principal source, in fact is just a redaction (*Bearbeitung*) thereof, reproducing its sequences more closely than Matthew did. The difficulty for Luke's dependence on Matthew is his double-tradition arrangements and his omission of so much Matthean didactic material. Köstlin in the first instance tries out the standard *Tendenz* and authorial-intentionality explanations (*subjektive Motiven des Schriftstellers*) (178). But he is driven by the sheer scale of the double-tradition divergences to the theory of a parallel instructional collection, in part mediated to Luke via the Judean gospel, in part referenced by him directly. That Luke might have utilized the Logia source of the Matthean evangelist is ruled out because the Matthean arrangement of five discourses, in Köstlin's view, represents the source's original form (thus it raises the same difficulties for Lukan utilization). Köstlin never really argues for this. It owes much to his *Tendenzkritik* commitment to Matthean priority, the latter shifted subtly onto the five discourses, and to his concern to impute apostolic authorship to the Matthean Logia source, thereby securing it as the authentic bedrock of the tradition.

The Lukan evangelist on occasion also references proto-Mark and the parallel instructional collection directly. He has some token recourse to Matthew. For all practical purposes, that is, Matthean priority is redundant to this source-history account. In Köstlin's own words, his analysis has shown "how Matthew's Logia and the proto-Markan collection are the sources for the Gospels" (395). Köstlin goes so far as to conclude that the proto-Markan source is more or less isomorphic with its canonical counterpart, though containing more sayings material (311, 358). As he progresses deeper into his analysis Köstlin actually begins to slip and to describe the proto-Markan source as a "gospel" (*Evangelium*). The "provisional collection" (*Aufzeichnung*) characterization, so indispensable to his effort to maintain Matthean priority, gets submerged by Synoptic realities (45–46, 111, 362, 367). What Köstlin ends up with is a *de facto* two document hypothesis, featuring an Urmarkus. The *Tendenzkritik* postulate of Matthean priority is otiose to his actual source history and only creates complications for it. Though Hilgenfeld a year later will give it another try, this marks the abandonment of *Tendenzkritik* as a comprehensive source-critical method.

HEINRICH EWALD

Heinrich Ewald's resistance to *Tendenzkritik* finds its outlet in two essays, published in 1848 and 1849, in which he tries to tighten the connection between the Synoptic tradition and living eyewitness testimony. He subsumes oral tradition to eyewitness recollection, noting that the tradition formed in an environment thick in living eyewitnesses.[47] This confronts him with the disparity between eyewitness testimony and the observable forms of the tradition. His response is that recollective activity (*Rückerinnerung*) was an *intentional* enterprise, one in which the apostles and eyewitnesses active as preaching evangelists, i.e., "living sources of gospel memory," took the lead.[48] This intentional activity, however, was a belated response to the increasing distance from foundational events. Owing to the time-lag, these eyewitness recollections were imprecise and disconnected; they took the form of individual episodes, variant and meagre in details.[49] Eventually these bits of memory tradition (*einzeln Stückchen von Erinnerung*) were gathered into loose provisional collections, followed as a matter of course by efforts to confer coherent arrangements upon them, a process that would create variant sequencing. In view of the instructional imperatives of the primitive communities the earliest of these would be a sayings collection (*Spruchsammlung*) formed around mnemonic topical arrangements. Episodic traditions would similarly receive initial topical groupings (1:122–29, 138).

The next phase would be working up these materials into connected narrative accounts, a task falling to the class of evangelists, among whom were John Mark and Luke. The first of these was an Urmarkus, of which the present canonical Mark is a redaction (1:141; 2:188–89). In addition to written collections and excerpting from the sayings collection (*Spruchsammlung*), the Urmarkus composer drew upon a work of "higher history," a source that contained christologically infused episodes expressed in an elevated style, for example the Baptism, the Temptation, and the Transfiguration (and embryonically the birth narratives, as well as certain L^S materials and Passion episodes) (1:149–54; 2:192–95). This source is a contrivance of Ewald's to separate out the more christological, mythically colored, and highly authorial (*dichterische*) elements in the Synoptic tradition from the more down-to-earth, realistic

47. Heinrich Ewald, "Ursprung und Wesen der Evangelien," *Jahrbücher der biblischen Wissenschaft* 1 (1848): 113–54 (125–27).
48. Heinrich Ewald, "Ursprung und Wesen der Evangelien," *Jahrbücher der biblischen Wissenschaft* 2 (1849): 180–224 (181–83).
49. Ewald, "Ursprung und Wesen," 1:119–20 (hereafter page citations will be in the text).

elements. Urmarkus drew upon collections of topically arranged narrative materials, the contours of which are still visible in the gospel. The Markan episodes in their lifelike freshness retain the qualities of primitive eyewitness memories (*Urerinnerungen der Augenzeugen*). Canonical Mark, though written third and occasionally referencing Matthew and Luke, made such close use of Urmarkus that the primitive eyewitness qualities of this tradition have passed into it (2:203–7).[50]

For Ewald the patristic tradition of a Matthean Urgospel is not to be given presumptive deference (2:188). As it did for other critics, this frees his vision for recognition of Markan priority. It also brings the problem of the double tradition into the foreground. On the grounds of its didactic profile Ewald connects the double tradition to the sayings collection, excerpted, he says, by all three evangelists, but in its arrangement and contents closest to Matthew. In its utterances, he continues, one feels the very breath (*Anhauch*) of Jesus. Its originator must have been an intimate eyewitness, a living beam (*Wiederstrahl*) of the originating light, hence one of the Twelve, composing in Aramaic. This nicely lines up with Papias's testimony (2:196–202).

From Ewald's analysis emerge the elements of a two source hypothesis, or counting the ad hoc christological source, three. The Matthean evangelist primarily consolidates (*bloße Sammeln*) his sources—Urmarkus, the sayings collection, and an expanded version of the christological source. His project is a matter of combining his two principal sources, Urmarkus and the sayings collection, which he manages by fitting the sayings collection elements into the narrative frameworking provided by Urmarkus. This explains the curious transpositions of Markan sequences in Matthew 8–9, triggered by the need to accommodate the Markan narrative order to the order of the sayings collection, in particular its forward location of its inaugural Sermon (2:208–15).[51]

The Lukan evangelist is likewise a compiler and editor (*Verarbeiter*) of received sources (Ewald's push-back against *Tendenzkritik* is palpable here). Indeed, much more than Matthew the gospel is a "mere collection of sources," with less effort toward compositional integration (2:223). For his triple tradition the evangelist is dependent on Urmarkus. His double tradition derives ultimately from the sayings collection, but to explain the sharp divergence

---

50. Ewald's observations about an oral prehistory of the Markan tradition and then in written collections conflict with his attribution of eyewitness status to the evangelist, which comes from his desire for Papias's imprimatur. He squares this by claiming the evangelist used the collections as "Hülfsmittel" for his memory (2:205).

51. This account of the Markan transpositions was first bruited by Lachmann.

from its arrangement (preserved in the Gospel of Matthew) Ewald resorts to the expedient of intermediating sources. Luke takes the double tradition of the first half of his gospel from Urmarkus, which had excerpted from the sayings collection. Double tradition in the second half of his gospel (i.e., the travel section) comes from an epitomizing redaction of the sayings collection. Luke subjected his received double tradition to edits, shortening its long speeches and distributing their elements (2:220–23).

Like others, Ewald's source history is an effort to establish the authentic grounds of the tradition, in his case in reaction to the reduction of Synoptic source relations to the play of antithetical *Tendenzen*. It is in his effort to counter this that Ewald comes to grips with the tradition-memory nexus problematic. His approach is to subsume the tradition completely to eyewitness testimony. But why do the observable forms of the tradition not correspond to the profile of eyewitness testimony? For Ewald this is a matter of memory fallibility: the project of intentional recollection was belated, hence the large-scale loss of detail and the breakdown of historical continuity into disconnected episodes. Variation among parallels is due to differential recollection. Though crude, this is an early attempt to come up with a cognitive account of tradition formation, one that takes seriously the reality that the tradition formed in the matrix of early Christian memory practices.

Ewald's concern for a *Tendenz*-free source history also explains why he reduces the evangelists to mere compilers of sources. He plots an uninterrupted line from the pure historicity of eyewitness memories, to the oral tradition, to the pre-Synoptic collections, to the Synoptic Gospels. Via intermediary written collections oral transmission gives way to strictly written-source transmission, understood as compilation. In his effort to limit the play of interpretative forces in the history of the tradition he does not give the evangelists much leeway for redactional operations upon their sources.

We noted that Ewald decouples his source criticism from the reflexive deference to Papias—hence from *a priori* commitment to Matthean priority. Whenever this occurs it opens up space for recognition of Markan priority. Matthew's and Luke's dependence on Mark (or an Urmarkus) makes a source-critical reckoning with the double tradition and its divergent arrangements even more urgent. A sayings-source theory is not logically entailed by the postulate of Markan priority, but we are seeing that whenever Markan priority is granted, some permutation of a two source hypothesis seems to follow. Possible source-critical explanations for the double tradition are finite: either the Matthean evangelist composed the double tradition himself, or he took it from a source or sources. Ewald finds the Papias testimonial convenient to the extent that he can exploit it to impute Matthean origins and apostolic memory credentials to the sayings collection. But this residual adherence to Papias induces him to identify the Matthean double-tradition arrangement with that of the sayings collection. This means that like Hilgenfeld and Köstlin (and for that matter Baur), he must chart a complicated source-critical route for the double tradition from Matthew to Luke: through a copious Urmarkus that had excerpted freely from the *Spruchsammlung*, and for the travel section, a shortened redaction of the source (2:222).

HEINRICH MEYER

Meyer's Two-Source Theory

In the third edition (1853) of his commentary on the Gospel of Matthew, Heinrich Meyer dismisses out of hand the *Tendenzkritik* source schema that assigns priority to the Gospel of Matthew.[52] The evidence points instead to simple Markan priority.[53] Meyer takes the patristic testimony about the apostle Matthew authoring a primitive Aramaic work to be correct. He needs to reconcile this not only with the evidence of Markan priority but also with the fact that the Matthean evangelist could not have been an eyewitness, that is, not the apostle Matthew. Establishing the eyewitness credentials of the primitive tradition is important for Meyer. So how does he manage this? He argues that our Greek Matthew is a translation of an Aramaic narrative gospel that nucleated around an Aramaic instructional source (*Redensammlung*), the work composed by the apostle. Schleiermacher, says Meyer, correctly identified the Matthean didactic discourses with the λόγια work that Papias attributed to Matthew. The objection that λόγια refers to a narrative gospel, an Aramaic Urmatthew, fails because Papias has just described the narrative gospel Mark as τὰ ὑπὸ τοῦ Χριστοῦ λεχθέντα καὶ *πραχθέντα* (see also Acts 1:1); moreover, Papias describes Matthew as making an *arrangement* (i.e., a σύνταξις: τὰ λόγια συνετάξετο), not an *account* (that is, an ἐξήγησις) (2–4, 10). From the instructional source's sparse narrative notices grew the narrative gospel as over time the Aramaic believers attached additional narrative materials to it. This expanded work then underwent a final redaction and then a Greek translation (19). How does Meyer bring Markan priority into this picture? Because Mark bore Petrine authority (so Papias), it exerted influence on the formation

---

52. Heinrich A. W. Meyer, *Kritisch exegetisches Handbuch über das Evangelium des Matthäus*, 3rd ed. (Göttingen: Vandenhoeck & Ruprecht, 1853), 18.

53. Meyer, *Handbuch*, 28–30 (hereafter page citations will be in the text).

of the Matthean gospel—its content and narrative ordering—and on its final redaction, and then its translation into Greek. This is also Meyer's ingenious explanation of variation in wording and order: Greek Mark *influences* the formation of Aramaic Matthew, it *influences* its final redaction, and it *influences* its translation into Greek. It is never a direct literary source (29–30).

Luke likewise is dependent upon the Gospel of Mark. This explains the medial patterns displayed by the latter, which Griesbach critics have badly misinterpreted, "inflicting an egregious injustice on the Gospel of Mark" (30). The Lukan double tradition stems ultimately from the instructional source, but its divergences from the Matthean arrangement indicate that it has come to him via a "diverging tradition." The Gospel of Matthew's arrangement is closest to the original instructional source, because the Gospel develops directly from the apostolic source (168–70).

Meyer's Two-Source Theory as an Authenticity Strategy

Again we observe the emergence of a *de facto* 2DH. For Meyer this doubles as an authenticity strategy—with the aid of Papias's testimony he identifies the primordially authentic grounds of the tradition in the didactic source (*Redensammlung*), the artifact of an apostle's memory. The Gospel of Mark likewise has apostolic eyewitness credentials: it is Petrine, and it reproduces the form of the primitive Christian παράδοσις with the greatest immediacy (29). But the narrative tradition rates below the sayings tradition on the authenticity scale. The Markan tradition is Petrine but secondarily mediated by an evangelist. Further, narrative is susceptible to mythologizing, saga-forming forces. The didactic source was in fact the principal work of the primitive Palestinian community; narrative materials subsequently accrued to it.

Though Meyer associates the primitive didactic source and the Gospel of Mark to apostolic memory, his two-source theory is not itself the product of his authenticity agenda. It serves that agenda through its extraneous alignment with the patristic tradition of an apostolic Matthean Ursource and Mark's association with Peter. Once again we see that Schleiermacher's interpretation of Papias's λόγια reference is not so much responsible for the rise of the sayings-source theory as it is for the rise of Markan priority. Sayings collection theories are a knock-on effect of Markan priority.

Meyer has no particular theory of oral tradition. He takes the sayings tradition and the Markan narrative tradition as the efflux of individual apostolic memory: the apostle Matthew's in the one case, Peter's in the other. Like most of his contemporaries Meyer has difficulty conceiving how the tradition is cultivated other than in the written medium once it gets shifted into it. The tradition has first to find its way into written provisional collections (*Aufzeichnungen*) before it can even be used as raw material for the evangelists.

EDUARD REUSS

Eduard Reuss is another Tübinger who by 1853 had rejected the source-critical utility of *Tendenzkritik* and with it the Griesbach hypothesis in favor of Markan priority, though like his contemporaries he is unsure what to do with the double tradition.[54]

Markan Priority and Sayings Collections: Reuss's Source Hypothesis

Reuss locates the origins of Synoptic variation in the oral tradition, which is mediated to the evangelists in provisional written collections (*Aufzeichnungen*). Synoptic patterns of variation and agreement are due to the evangelists copying from an array of these collections, which frequently overlap in both content and order. The materials in these collections had received rudimentary organization around particular topics and rubrics, and were aggregated by catchword and analogy. This process of growing, intersecting collections continued, reaching its terminus in the projects of the three evangelists.[55] Just like the written collections emerge organically from oral tradition, the Synoptic Gospels emerge organically (*erwachsen*) from these collections (174).

The Gospel of Mark is a revision (*Umarbeitung*) of one of these expanded provisional collections. The reworking was perfunctory: the Second Gospel retains the character of a loosely connected sequence of episodes, and with its abrupt beginning and abrupt ending it still lacks the form of a complete gospel and certainly any theological aim. As Papias reliably informs us, the Matthean evangelist had at his disposal an Aramaic sayings collection (*Spruchsammlung*) originating with the apostle Matthew. The alternation of sayings discourses and narrative sequences in the Gospel of Matthew is artificial, which suggests that the evangelist takes up the Aramaic sayings collection into his gospel in more or less its original form. The gospel is therefore a skilled consolidation of written collections (171–82).

This brings Reuss to the Gospel of Luke. The Gospel of Matthew cannot be the source of Luke's narrative tradition, which is instead the Gospel of Mark (180–81, 190–91). But Matthew cannot be the source of Luke's double tradition

---

54. Eduard Reuss, *Die Geschichte der heiligen Schrift: Neuen Testaments*, 2nd ed. (Braunschweig: Schwetschke, 1853).
55. Reuss, *Geschichte*, 157–62 (hereafter page citations will be in the text).

either. This is ruled out, Reuss says, by its very different disposition in Luke, and by the difficulty of coming up with a rationale for Luke proceeding with these Matthean discourses in this way. But on exactly the same grounds Reuss rules out Luke's independent use of the sayings collection. Because the five Matthean discourses approximate to the arrangement of the original collection, Luke's use of this source presents the same difficulties as his use of Matthew (179, 191). In Reuss's media framework, moreover, the evangelists are mainly reworking earlier written collections. This explains why Reuss can declare without argument that "the first evangelist has not taken his closely connected instructional speeches from a source in which their elements were found separated and dispersed" (179). Given this scenario, Luke's double tradition must come from provisional collections that overlap in content with the Matthean source. The travel section is a loose aggregate of speech elements from indeterminate sources, to which Luke gives a perfunctory chronological organization (154, 190–95).

Reuss on Memory and the Oral Tradition

Reuss develops a sophisticated account of the origins of the oral tradition in primitive Christian memory that anticipates contemporary cognitive and cultural-identity formation approaches. The tradition originates in memory: in the first instance in the deep impression made by Jesus's teaching and personality on witnesses; in the second instance in the elicitation of these memories by the demands of instruction in the primitive community and by the pressing need, in threatening environs, to limn a Christian identity centered on Jesus's person. Eyewitness memories of events converged on the most extraordinary and the most salient, and particularly those events that occasioned striking sayings of Jesus. This is how Reuss explains the distillation of the tradition down to a delimited common content. In frequent repetition these narratives took on a resilient consistency (*einen gewissen Charakter der Festigkeit*) that nevertheless remained open to variation according to the preferences of a given narrator. Thus denuded of all but the barest time and place indicators and basic details, the narratives and sayings came to circulate in the fragmentary and variant episodic forms (*nackte Anekdote*), attested in the ad hoc written collections that feed into the Synoptic Gospels. Reuss interprets these observable features of the tradition, including its property of variability, in terms of a gradual loss over time and distance of the vividness and precision of eyewitness testimony, as a deterioration (*Abschwächung*) of the tradition's original memory qualities. Gathering it into written collections helped hedge the tradition against further deterioration, though even these collections circulated uncontrolled and vulnerable to corruption (151–57).

CARL WEIZSÄCKER

Carl Weizsäcker was a student of F. C. Baur and successor to Baur's professorship at Tübingen in 1861, but his source-critical work, *Untersuchungen über die evangelische Geschichte* (1864), seals the demise of Baur's *Tendenzkritik* as a source-critical method.[56] Weizsäcker's analysis leads him toward what amounts to the two document hypothesis, though Holtzmann had stolen a march on him with the 1863 publication of *Die synoptischen Evangelien.*[57]

Weizsäcker on Markan Priority

Weizsäcker is alert to the media dimension of the Synoptic problem. The Synoptic profile, he notes, attests to the origins of the tradition in a common enterprise of tradition formation, to the emergence of a common stock of normative baseline materials that served as the authorizing grist for missionary proclamation. In this sense this body of material was certainly "the gospel," the antecedent to the Synoptics and accounting for their common texturing. But the same profile—the striking verbal and sequential variation in particular, and its episodic forms—shows that it did not take the form of a uniform, cohering body of teaching (i.e., the oral gospel hypothesis). It was not the controlled product of a closed circle, transmitted intact by special memory practices. Rather, from the outset and in fact deep into the second century it was a matter of free enactment by individual proclaimers. The hypothesis of a written Urgospel is likewise undone by the patterns of Synoptic variation. The solution to the puzzle must lie in the source relationships among Synoptics.[58]

Weizsäcker's association with *Tendenzkritik* has primed him to accord significant redactional scope to the evangelists in their source utilization. He takes this as the leading factor that has generated the agreement and variation patterns among parallels. Analysis of the triple tradition free of the assumption that the earliest source will be the one with the most Jewish-Christian complexion shows that the base layer (*Grundlage*) of the Gospel of Matthew roughly corresponds to Mark. But this source is not canonical Mark but an Urmarkus. Some of the minor agreements against Mark point to this (especially in omission), as do some seemingly more primitive triple-tradition parallels in Luke (or Matthew) (vi, 11).

---

56. Carl Weizsäcker, *Untersuchungen über die evangelische Geschichte: Ihre Quellen und den Gang ihrer Entwicklung* (1864; repr., Tübingen: J. C. B. Mohr [Paul Siebeck], 1901).

57. Weizsäcker cites Holtzmann occasionally (around eight times) but his adoption of Markan priority does not appear to owe anything to Holtzmann's influence.

58. Weizsäcker, *Untersuchungen*, 7-8 (hereafter page citations will be in the text).

But Weizsäcker does not stuff his Urmarkus with double tradition and turn his canonical Mark into a maimed and lacunose truncation (*Verstümmelung und Verkürzung*), unlike Hilgenfeld, Ewald, and others driven to this extremity by the difficulty of the double tradition's divergent arrangements. The gospel as it stands is manifestly narrative in its literary execution and layout, a coherently integrated narrative *Gestalt*. Its sayings elements are smoothly aligned to the narrative ductus of the *bios*. Its two discourses of some length—the parable discourse of Mark 4 and the Mark 13 Apocalypse—register momentous turning points in the narrative itself. The parable discourse is not so much an instruction as it is a description of Jesus's cryptic mode of teaching. Similarly, the Urmarkus narrative contains numerous references to Jesus's teaching *activities*. Urmarkus is a calculated realization of narrative genre that everywhere flashes its awareness of another genre, the purpose of which is to present Jesus's words of instruction (*Lehrworte*)—one might say the *logos* counterpart to its *bios* (72). Notable is Weizsäcker's according independent weight to the narrative dimension of the Jesus tradition, against the usual tendency to subordinate the narrative tradition to the sayings tradition.

Weizsäcker and the Problem of the Double Tradition

This parallel body of didactic material is attested by the Matthean and Lukan double tradition, in drastically divergent arrangements. No compelling account has been forthcoming of Luke's derivation of these by redaction of Matthew or vice versa; all such accounts have been "highly forced" (85). Indications are that Matthew and Luke are working from a source, using different strategies to integrate it with their Urmarkus narrative. Matthew works the narrative and instructional materials into organic wholes; Luke fits the segments of his instructional source into his narrative source at different points. Luke 9:51–18:14 entire is manifestly an insertion from another source into the narrative, whether the entire section as a unit or an extended source sequence that Luke has supplemented with additional materials. Major component elements of the sequence fall into methodical groupings of materials that Luke does not particularly highlight and so likely did not himself compose (83–84).

But how to bridge the gulf between the respective Matthean and Lukan dispositions of the double-tradition materials? Clearly the double tradition has unity of origin. That the advanced arrangement in Matthew reflects the original *Gestalt* of the source is implausible not least because no one can stipulate an economical procedure for Luke's utilization of Matthew or an instructional source (*Redenquelle*) in this form. This leaves two possibilities: either Matthew and Luke took initiative in reworking the source, or the source has undergone significant versional developments prior to reaching them. While not treating these as mutually exclusive, Weizsäcker thinks it likely that versional development is the leading factor in the divergent Matthean and Lukan arrangements (85–86).

Compared superficially with Matthew, the version used by Luke looks primitive, even subliterary, but this inference is mistaken. Closer inspection shows that its materials are intelligibly organized around didactic *topoi* (*bestimmte Lehrzwecke*) and that Luke's historical contextualizations are artificial. The version coming to Luke appears to be a pragmatic redaction responsive to instructional exigencies of the apostolic era. Matthew's double tradition on the other hand lacks this orientation of Jesus's sayings to the practical needs of the apostolic period. It still retains the memory of the living historical settings, of the living declamations, in the ministry of Jesus. Consequently the redaction of the instructional source preserved in Matthew remains closer to the original. The layout of the original source is still visible behind the Matthean and Lukan versions, residues of an original sequence of instructions (Weizsäcker is likely referring to agreements in relative order) (88–92, 104–5, 130).[59] The format of Luke's version in some respects preserves this original layout more closely, for example Matthew's Commissioning is obviously a combination of two shorter sequences, and unlike the Matthew 24 parallel the Luke 17:23–37 Apocalypse hews to the paraenetic concerns of a didactic source. The Lukan special materials in double-tradition contexts (mainly between 9:51 and 18:44) are functionally adjunct to the double-tradition elements and therefore supplements appended somewhere along the way to the core source redaction that has descended to Luke (104–7, 115–16). Likewise for a number of the special materials found in Matthew (122).

The original instructional source therefore had an intelligible layout (*Anlage*), inaugurated by the Sermon setting out Jesus's programmatic teaching, and concluding appropriately with an eschatological discourse. Between these great summations lie historically indexed didactic encounters of the sort emblematic of Jesus's ministry, among the principal components the address to the disciples (Commissioning) in its turn followed by an address to his opponents (Beelzebul Accusation and sequel). This overall arrangement enacts the gospel proclamation: the center of gravity is the announcement of the messi-

---

59. For example, Weizsäcker says that the Commissioning of the Seventy in Luke 10 corresponds to the missionary situation in the apostolic period; the Commissioning of the Twelve in Matthew 10 to the historical setting in the life of Jesus (134). Weizsäcker offers some insightful commentary on the intelligible, sophisticated connections within the Lukan instructional sequences, recognizing, for example, that the Request for a Sign and the Lamp on a Lampstand/Eye the Lamp of the Body constitute a unified elaboration standing, moreover, in close connection to the Beelzebul Accusation (see e.g., 92–99).

anic kingdom, and the didactic contents, pragmatically arranged around instructional *topoi*, are broadly aligned to the sequence of the historical ministry. The didactic source is thus no mere catechism but itself a sort of gospel (*Evangelium*). Its horizon is Palestinian and Jewish-Christian (117–18, 123–25).

We see again that Weizsäcker, quite unusually, does not subordinate the narrative tradition to the sayings tradition but views the instructional source and Urmarkus as symbiotic genres. He does not take this view on *a priori* grounds but arrives at it from his source-critical analysis. He says that it is easy to see why this is the case. Were Jesus's significance to lie principally in his teaching, were he basically another great Jewish teacher, the didactic source would have been enough, or at most a work comprising sayings and chreias (*Anekdote*). But for his followers Jesus was God's Messiah, attested by mighty deeds. This dual conviction took expression along didactic and narrative lines in the corresponding genres, with the didactic tradition functioning to inculcate the ethos-dimension of the community identity that is forming around a master narrative of Jesus's life and death. The Passion narrative itself served as the narrative nucleation point for the eventual formation of Urmarkus, pulling the diverse elements of the episodic tradition of the Galilean ministry into its narrative gravitational alignment (73, 129–32).

Weizsäcker's Quest for the Authentic Memory Source

For Weizsäcker as for his contemporaries, source criticism is a matter of distinguishing layers (*verschiedene Schichten*) of the tradition to identify the base layer, where one comes into unfiltered contact with the living Jesus (iv–vii, 2). Weizsäcker's own route back to the historical Jesus is charted chiefly through his theory of a dual redaction of the didactic source. The redaction used by Luke with its topical organization is oriented to the pragmatic instructional tasks of the apostolic era; it adopts the standpoint of this later period. Thus it is historically inferior to the redaction used by Matthew, which retains memories (*Erinnerungen*) of the historical occasions on which Jesus delivered his teachings and thus is closer to the original instructional source (92–109). This prototype of the source originated in the primitive Palestinian community. It breathes the spirit of the *urapostolische* circle, and it is the direct expression of apostolic memory (125–27).

For its part Urmarkus is no transcription of the preaching of Peter but manifestly the product of literary reflection and narrative artifice. But its origins certainly must go back to a collection (*Aufzeichnung*) of primitive apostolic materials taken down to serve as an aid in gospel proclamation, for it still retains something of that profile: independent tradition episodes, some aggregated topically, have been brought together into a contingent narrative unity by the evangelist (40, 68, 132). Like the instructional source, Urmarkus was composed in Jerusalem or at least in Palestine, but its materials have come to its composer not through contact with apostolic circles but *vermittelt*, "through the medium of the tradition." Nevertheless, primitive memories are germinally (*kernhafte*) present in its narrative traditions. Though by no means naïve historical representation, Urmarkus is a witness to apostolic faith and an indispensable source for authentic knowledge of Jesus (75–81).

We see that Weizsäcker makes a simple identification of the most primitive layer of the tradition with apostolic memory. Apostolic memory is the unfiltered (*unmittelbare*) channel for the teaching of Jesus, collected into a didactic source likely composed by the apostle Matthew (118). The memory qualities of the earliest stratum secure its historical authenticity by definition, though to be sure, our access to that pristine source is indirect, filtered through a redaction used by the Matthean evangelist. Deterioration in authenticity is a function of increasing distance from the immediacy of memory that is uniquely the privilege of the primitive community (92). Memory, when it migrates out of the *urapostolische* eyewitness circle, enters the sphere of "tradition" (*paradosis*). Weizsäcker regards traditioning activity—*vermittelte Überlieferung*: passing through different hands (*durch verschiedene Hände*)—as *per se* a process of degeneration of the pristine historical qualities of apostolic memory (75–76). Non-memory elements supervene upon the memory elements once they move out of the range of eyewitness testimony.

Weizsäcker struggles with the problem of the memory-tradition nexus. He settles on speaking of it in terms of a tradition-memory binary: memory comes to exist as a distinct, authentic element within a husk—inauthentic— of tradition. In the main this affects the narrative tradition, i.e., Urmarkus. The Passion narrative, for example, has formed in the confluence of memory and prophecy interpretation. Elsewhere it is evident that memory gaps have been filled under the influence of contemporary events and viewpoints—the Mark 13 Apocalypse is a case in point. But though mainly constituted of "tradition," Urmarkus originated in Palestine and thus not far removed from apostolic circles, and the authentic memory elements can without too much difficulty be distinguished within its tradition (75–81). In any case, secondary elements in the tradition for the most part are interpretative, contemporizing extensions of core materials, bringing new things out of the old (102–3, 132).

Weizsäcker and the Two Document Hypothesis

Weizsäcker marks the endpoint of the twenty-five-year trek back not just to Markan priority but to the two document hypothesis. As we have seen, he offers a particularly thoughtful case for the 2DH that shows no dependence upon Holtzmann's defense of it the year prior (in certain respects his is superior to Holtzmann's). A large part of his analysis he devotes to the didactic source (*Redenquelle*). Luke's double-tradition source, he observes, is no primitive aggregate of sayings, no "random alluvial deposit of the free-flowing tradition" (88). Rather, its materials are gathered around ethical *topoi* and arranged in intelligible didactic sequences. It has a pragmatic orientation to particular instructional ends (*Lehrzwecke*). It has a thorough-going didactic complexion; even the Apocalypse in Luke 17 is paraenetic. Intelligible organization is evident at the macro level as well: it commences with an inaugural Sermon, proceeds through emblematic instructional situations in Jesus's ministry, and winds up with an outlook on the future.

To deal with the vexed problem of divergent double-tradition arrangements, however, Weizsäcker advances a two-redactions theory (i.e., a Q^{Matt}/Q^{Luke} expedient). One reason is that notwithstanding the redactional scope that he allows the evangelists, he still has the nineteenth-century tendency to take significant variation back to earlier redactional levels and intermediating sources. His deeper motive is that he needs to identify the redaction used by the evangelist Matthew as the earliest in order to connect the original instructional source to apostolic memory.

With Weizsäcker, successor to F. C. Baur, the Tübingen school completes its surprisingly quick journey from *Tendenzkritik* source criticism and its prop, the Griesbach hypothesis, to *de facto* commitment to Markan priority, usually in incipient two-source hypotheses. This happens not because of some enchantment cast by Schleiermacher but from hard-nosed analysis of Synoptic realities. Though Weizsäcker published his study one year after Holtzmann's *Die synoptischen Evangelien*, it is clear that he reasons his way to two-source conclusions independently. They coincide in their views, but Holtzmann's would have the greater impact.

Finding Jesus in the Two Document Hypothesis: Holtzmann to Wernle

T HE 1840S AND 1850S SAW the main lines of source criticism tack back toward source theories with various levels of affinity to the two document hypothesis. From Weizsäcker and Holtzmann forward, opinion started to gel around the 2DH.

H. J. HOLTZMANN

We will reconstruct the source-critical schema that H. J. Holtzmann worked out in 1863 in *Die synoptischen Evangelien*, paying particular attention to the roles he assigns to tradition and apostolic memory, and then follow its development in the 1886/1892 editions of his *Einleitung*, his *Hand-Commentar* of 1901, and through to his *Lehrbuch der neutestamentlichen Theologie* published posthumously in 1911.[1] Source criticism, Holtzmann says, is the objective and scientifically autonomous method for recovering the historical grounds of the tradition.[2]

Holtzmann: Memory, Oral Tradition, and Synoptic Sources

In *Die synoptischen Evangelien* Holtzmann imagines the oral tradition as a loose aggregate of individual episodes and sayings. Written sources emerged very early alongside its continuing oral circulation. These primitive written sources were not qualitatively distinct from the oral tradition. They were provisional drafts, *Auf-*

---

1. For a more detailed analysis of Holtzmann, see Alan Kirk, "Memory, Tradition, and Synoptic Sources: The Quest of Holtzmann and Wernle for a Pre-Dogma Jesus," in *Theological and Theoretical Issues in the Synoptic Problem*, ed. John S. Kloppenborg and Joseph Verheyden, LNTS 618 (London: Bloomsbury/T&T Clark, 2020), 53–70.

2. H. J. Holtzmann, *Die synoptischen Evangelien: ihr Ursprung und geschichtlicher Charakter* (Leipzig: Engelmann, 1863), 6.

zeichnungen, written aggregates, giving the materials little more than perfunctory organization. They arose as *aide-mémoires* for evangelists and teachers without first-hand memory of events and to cope with the expansion of the movement beyond Jewish Palestine.[3] In these circumstances these pre-Synoptic sources proliferated. Their residues can still be identified in the gospels, in Matthew and Luke especially.[4] The oral tradition continued to circulate freely even after the bulk of it passed into written sources. But these numerous pre-Synoptic written sources, among which are Holtzmann's Logia source and his Source A (Urmarkus), were the principal means by which the primordial tradition was mediated to the evangelists. Leftovers in Matthew and Luke difficult to assign to a pre-Synoptic source Holtzmann consigns to the still freely circulating oral tradition.[5]

The primordial oral tradition has immanent connections to apostolic memory: it is constituted of memorable (*denkwürdige*) episodes and sayings.[6] In the disconnected, unstable, episodic forms in which it circulates it corresponds closely to the form of individual recollections (*Einzelerinnerungen*).[7] Holtzmann grounds this model for the primordial oral tradition in the Lukan Prologue: the παράδοσις proceeds direct from the αὐτόπται, the eyewitnesses.[8] Its qualities of vividness and immediacy likewise attest to derivation from eyewitness memory, as do elements that make precise reference to Galilean geographic features and other local details.[9] Some Synoptic variation is due to differential recollection. Holtzmann attributes the "confused" version of the Anointing at Bethany of Mark 14:3–9 found in the Sinful Woman episode of Luke 7:35–50 to a less well-informed eyewitness report (*Nachricht*).[10] The Holtzmann of 1863 copes with dogmatic and miraculous elements in the tradition by identifying within traditions such as the sea-crossing miracles and the feeding stories a kernel of eyewitness memory, at the same time acknowledging, echoing Strauss, that these episodes have developed into symbolic vehicles for "ideal truths."[11] The problem of dogmatic, mythical, and miraculous elements in the tradition will loom larger for the later Holtzmann.

3. Holtzmann, *Evangelien*, 25, 244; *Hand-Commentar zum Neuen Testament*, vol. 1: *Die Synoptiker*, 3rd ed. (Tübingen: J. C. B. Mohr [Paul Siebeck], 1901), 25.
4. Holtzmann, *Evangelien*, 161–63, 211.
5. Holtzmann, *Evangelien*, 104, 161–63.
6. Holtzmann, *Evangelien*, 52–53.
7. Holtzmann, *Hand-Commentar*, 20–21.
8. Holtzmann, *Evangelien*, 244–45.
9. Holtzmann, *Evangelien*, 423, 449, 479–87.
10. Holtzmann, *Evangelien*, 220–21.
11. Holtzmann, *Evangelien*, 499.

Like many of his predecessors, Holtzmann sees an immediacy of relationship of the primitive oral tradition with the memories of the primitive Jerusalem community. In the very episodic and disconnected forms in which it circulates the oral tradition embodies naïve eyewitness recollection; it is a "conglomeration" (*Ansammlung*) of individual recollections.[12] Crucially, the written aggregates of the tradition that circulated in pre-Synoptic sources (*Aufzeichnungen*) share these memory qualities. But with one noteworthy exception these pre-Synoptic sources are artifacts of individuals that stand outside the circle of direct apostolic memory and thus need these written collections as *aide-mémoires*.[13] We see that Holtzmann makes a distinction between *memory*, understood as apostolic eyewitness recollection directly precipitated out in the primitive oral tradition, and the *history of the tradition*, understood as a process of steadily increasing distance from the privileged circle of apostolic memory in the primitive Jerusalem community. He makes a much more categorical distinction between the tradition circulating orally and in these collections and the literary artificing (*schriftstellerische*) activities of the evangelists working upon the received oral and written sources of the tradition. Holtzmann again finds the warrants for this schema in the connection the Lukan Prologue makes between the παράδοσις of the "eyewitnesses and servants of the word" and the ἀνατάξασθαι διήγησιν—"setting down of an orderly account"—where Luke places himself.[14]

Holtzmann's Urmarkus and the Logia: Memory Sources

Recognizing this schema with its gradations is essential to grasping the role Holtzmann assigns to his Logia source and (in 1863) to Urmarkus (Source A). He positions the Logia source, and—though more ambiguously—Urmarkus, among the pre-Synoptic sources. He assigns them, that is, to the simple, artless παράδοσις, to his primitive apostolic memory zone. The Logia source is a direct expression of apostolic memory: Holtzmann attributes it to the apostle Matthew.[15] It has the same qualities as the primordial oral tradition of the Jerusalem community. Therefore, it is the authentic source *par excellence*; it merits unreserved credence (*Glaubwürdigkeit*). It serves as the criterion (*Maßstab*) of authenticity for all the rest of the tradition; it sheds the most direct light

12. Holtzmann, *Hand-Commentar*, 20–21, 25; see *Evangelien*, 244, 418.
13. Holtzmann, *Hand-Commentar*, 25.
14. Holtzmann, *Evangelien*, 244–45.
15. Holtzmann, *Evangelien*, 450–51, 503–4.

on the historical Jesus.[16] The connection of Urmarkus to apostolic memory, on the other hand, is at one degree of separation.[17] Its nonapostolic composer stands outside the privileged circle of apostolic memory. Urmarkus nevertheless has the advantage of connections to the apostle Peter and hence to a direct channel of apostolic memory.[18] The Logia source and Urmarkus, along with other pre-Synoptic sources, oral and written, supply the raw materials for the literary artificing activities of the evangelists.

One sees that Holtzmann makes the simple correlation of apostolic memory to historical authenticity. Urmarkus and the Logia are neutral, naïve historical precipitates of the memory tradition, subsequently worked over and distorted by the literary and dogmatic agendas of Matthew and Luke. Positing an Urmarkus behind the Gospel of Mark pushes the triple-tradition source back into the παράδοσις zone of Holtzmann's schema—that is, into direct proximity to apostolic memory. But Urmarkus presents difficulties for this maneuver: Holtzmann concedes that it is clearly more than an *Aufzeichnung*, a subliterary collocation of tradition. It is manifestly a διήγησις, an effort to put the tradition into literary order. He tries to resolve this anomaly by conceiving it as a hybrid, straddling the παράδοσις/διήγησις boundary. Constituted directly from oral tradition, Urmarkus belongs among the pre-Synoptic sources; on the other hand it is the "first manifestation" of the διήγησις enterprise.[19] Its διήγησις character notwithstanding, Urmarkus stands qualitatively above Matthew and Luke, whose literary and dogmatic artificing has disarranged and degraded Urmarkus's naturalist presentation of Jesus's ministry.[20] Holtzmann observes unhistorical (e.g., the doubled Feeding stories), mythical, and dogmatic elements in Urmarkus episodes and puts these down to the writer's pious christological enthusiasm occasionally overflowing from his heart and flooding his rational faculties, leaving behind a mythical, dogmatic sediment upon the base memory materials of the tradition. But he downplays the effects: in Urmarkus these elements are just a slight residue that is not able to obscure the vivid reality of Jesus.[21] The immediacy of Urmarkus's connection to Petrine memory constrains mythical, dogmatizing tendencies.[22] Nevertheless the presence of

16. Holtzmann, *Evangelien*, 451.
17. Holtzmann toys with positing a distinction between αὐτόπται and ὑπηρέται τοῦ λόγου, assigning the Logia to the former, Urmarkus to the latter (*Evangelien*, 245).
18. Holtzmann, *Evangelien*, 449–50, 504.
19. Holtzmann, *Evangelien*, 244–46.
20. Holtzmann, *Evangelien*, 423, 434–37, 475.
21. Holtzmann, *Evangelien*, 446–47, 504.
22. Holtzmann, *Evangelien*, 504.

CHAPTER 3

these elements renders it just a *comparatively* sound historical source. The Logia, on the other hand, compiled "without any dogmatic tendency, but only for
the sake of its contents," is much the more authentic source.[23] The Urmarkus
narrative plays a supportive role: clarifying the precise historical contexts and
moments in which Jesus's sayings had their origins.[24]

It is in this connection that Holtzmann's curious insistence that the Logia
source is *primitive* and *subliterary* becomes intelligible. The source, he says,
is a rough aggregate of sayings, fragmentary and with little cohesion beyond
the most rudimentary topical and catchword connections.[25] That is to say, the
Logia source is a virtually unmediated manifestation of oral tradition.[26] In
Holtzmann's schema this means that it is the virtually unmediated expression
of apostolic memory. A more literarily formed Logia source would disrupt this
neat schema. To support this claim Holtzmann appeals to the much different,
seemingly much simpler disposition of the Logia materials in Luke compared
to Matthew and argues that Luke better preserves the double tradition in its
primitive, quasi-oral state. He takes a reasonable supporting argument for a
sayings source—why would Luke have disassembled and rearranged the finely
wrought Matthean double-tradition sequences?—and in a *non sequitur* posits
the *unordered* state of the double tradition in Luke.[27] Also, the seemingly simpler configuration of the double-tradition materials in Luke attests to a more
primitive evolutionary stage of the tradition.[28]

What is the payoff of a subliterary Logia source for Holtzmann? Holtzmann holds that in its very inchoate, primitive form (attested by Luke) the
Logia source presents the apostolic memory tradition in its virgin state, all
but untouched by literary and dogmatic artifice.[29] In effect Holtzmann asserts the priority of the sayings tradition over the narrative tradition and a
logia Christology over narrative Christology in the history of the tradition.
The logia tradition constitutes "the true [*eigentlich*] treasure of the primitive
community"; it forms "the deepest grounds of its religious consciousness."[30]
The narrative tradition gathered in Urmarkus arose rapidly but nevertheless
belatedly.[31] In 1901, in the *Hand-Commentar*, Holtzmann is prepared to ac-

23. Holtzmann, *Evangelien*, 401.
24. Holtzmann, *Evangelien*, 452.
25. Holtzmann, *Evangelien*, 134–35, 149–56; *Hand-Commentar*, 22, 34.
26. Holtzmann, *Hand-Commentar*, 22.
27. Holtzmann, *Evangelien*, 130–31; similarly, *Hand-Commentar*, 13.
28. Holtzmann, *Evangelien*, 130 ("in a more primitive literary state").
29. Holtzmann, *Evangelien*, 401, 421, 450–51; also *Hand-Commentar*, 20.
30. Holtzmann, *Hand-Commentar*, 22.
31. Holtzmann, *Hand-Commentar*, 23, 34.

knowledge that the Logia source was organized around primitive messianic Christology; the narrative interest, on the other hand, was generated by the dogmatic conviction that the Messiah died "for us," rose again, and will come in glory.[32] Accordingly, its generative core is the Passion narrative.

Anomalies appear in this impressive construction that Holtzmann puts on things. The intelligible connections among the elements of Luke 12:2–12 that Holtzmann elucidates seem at odds with his insistence upon the primitive, aggregative nature of the Logia source.[33] Holtzmann deals with this anomaly by attributing this and other intelligibly organized sequences of the Lukan double tradition like the Prayer instruction (Luke 11:2–13) to "the hand of Luke."[34] A more stubborn anomaly, however, is that though Holtzmann attributes the Logia source to the apostle Matthew, and to reinforce this argues for a close connection between the Logia and the Gospel of Matthew,[35] he identifies the most primitive form of the source in the double tradition of the Gospel of Luke—on the basis of its sharp contrast with the highly artificed arrangement of the Logia materials in the Gospel of Matthew!

Another difficulty is that though Holtzmann identifies oral tradition with almost unfiltered apostolic memory, and as such quintessentially authentic, in line with general views of oral tradition at the time (viewed since Herder as a specimen of oral saga), he imputes to it an innate proneness to dogmatic and mythical distortion.[36] It is at this point that problems in Holtzmann's direct association of memory and oral tradition become evident. It explains his concern to proliferate written pre-Synoptic collections of the tradition and his consigning oral tradition to a transitional role of being an initial stand-in, a token, for apostolic memory: writing, he thinks, fixes the tradition and arrests its free development.[37] The earlier the act of inscription, the greater the authenticity of the tradition; the later, the greater its colonization by mythical elements.[38] This is evident in a number of the legendary episodes in Matthew's and Luke's special materials, taken direct from the oral tradition as it circulated in their time.[39] In short, for Holtzmann oral tradition is significant insofar as it serves as a placeholder for primitive apostolic memory, and insofar as it finds its way very early into written collections. As regards the two major

---

32. Holtzmann, *Hand-Commentar*, 23.
33. Holtzmann, *Hand-Commentar*, 229.
34. Holtzmann, *Hand-Commentar*, 22; also *Evangelien*, 149–50.
35. Holtzmann, *Evangelien*, 365.
36. Holtzmann, *Evangelien*, 49–50, 444, and elsewhere.
37. Holtzmann, *Evangelien*, 162–63.
38. Holtzmann, *Evangelien*, 50, 444.
39. Holtzmann, *Evangelien*, 162–63, 425.

pre-Synoptic sources, it is the later Urmarkus that shows the incipient effects of mythological development and the presence of unhistorical elements in its episodes and in its narrative line.[40] Narrative tradition, Holtzmann believes, is congenitally susceptible to mythicizing forces. This helps explains why he scrupulously excludes the Preaching of John the Baptist and the Temptation from the Logia and puts them into Urmarkus: their traces of a narrative construction would contaminate the authenticity of the Logia.[41]

We have seen that Holtzmann draws a privileged circle of apostolic memory, at the center of which he places the Logia source and, at its periphery, Urmarkus. In his further identification of Galilee and Judea as the places of origin of the tradition Holtzmann attaches memory to geography: Galilee and Judea are the privileged zones of memory. Urmarkus originated outside of Palestine, but its narrative traditions show local connections to Galilee; hence its reports, originating "in the very aboriginal land of Christianity," carry the presumption of historical authenticity.[42] The Logia source has close connections to both Galilee and Judea. In assigning the geographical origins of Urmarkus to a location outside Palestine, the Logia source itself to Palestine, Holtzmann again privileges the sayings tradition over the narrative tradition. The conjunction of "primitive community" with "Palestine" privileges a particular history of the tradition, and a particular alignment of sources.

The Later Holtzmann on Memory and Synoptic Sources

Thus Holtzmann circa 1863. What about the Holtzmann of the 1892 (and 1886) *Lehrbuch der historisch-kritischen Einleitung*, the 1901 *Hand-Commentar*, and the 1911 *Lehrbuch der neutestamentlichen Theologie*? Most consequential is his abandonment of Urmarkus (Source A).[43] The Markan narrative tradition thereby loses its Urmarkus foothold in the privileged παράδοσις zone of direct apostolic memory on the other side of the schematic divide from the Synoptic Gospel authorships. Holtzmann now more forthrightly acknowledges that the symbolic world of Old Testament epic and christological tendencies are

40. Holtzmann, *Evangelien*, 411–12, 444–45.

41. He acknowledges that the sayings source (*Spruchsammlung*) contained such narrative notices as were required to understand the didactic elements, e.g., dialogic settings; see H. J. Holtzmann, "Die synoptischen Evangelien nach den Forschungen von Bernhard Weiss," *Protestantische Kirchenzeitung* 24 (1877): 820–27 (821).

42. Holtzmann, *Evangelien*, 443–45.

43. H. J. Holtzmann, *Lehrbuch der historisch-kritischen Einleitung in das Neue Testament*, 3rd ed. (Freiburg im Breisgau: J. C. B. Mohr [Paul Siebeck], 1892), 350 (hereafter, *Einleitung*).

operative within the tradition—the narrative tradition in particular—from its inception. The narrative tradition has nucleated around points of christological reflection which in turn shapes the total narrative representation of the public life of the Messiah. The effects of these forces, however, are differential. The merest traces of Old Testament epic are found in the Calling of the Disciples (the calling of Elisha by Elijah), whereas in the sea-crossing miracles and similar episodes it has penetrated the very core.[44]

Holtzmann now presses living apostolic memory into service as a temporary external restraint on these forces, which seize greater control of the tradition as the members of the apostolic college pass.[45] To further compensate for the disappearance of Urmarkus from the pre-Synoptic παράδοσις zone, Holtzmann puts a heavier accent on the Petrine eyewitness memory connections of the Gospel of Mark and upon the personal association of its author, the historical John Mark (now identified, on the basis of Mark 14:51–52, as an eyewitness in his own right), with Peter.[46] Citing Acts 13:5 he identifies Mark as one of the ὑπηρέται τοῦ λόγου of the Lukan Prologue.[47] In this scheme Peter's "eyewitness information" operates as a curb on mythicizing forces in the Markan tradition. Holtzmann therefore continues to insist on the just incipient dogmatic profile of the second gospel, as well as on the vivid naturalistic complexion of its episodes and the historical coherence of its narrative trajectory.[48]

Holtzmann further tries to mitigate the influence of Old Testament epic and christological reflection on the Markan narrative by softening the dualism, redescribing it as a matter of "conjunctions [*Übergange*] of historical memories and Old Testament epic," or as a "mixed relationship" (*Mischungsverhältnis*).[49] He is wrestling with questions presented by a tradition that has formed at the conjunction of memory with christological reflection exploiting the symbolic resources of the Old Testament.[50] He concedes that the Markan narrative sequence is not really so much on the face of it historical.[51] The high levels of

---

44. Holtzmann, *Hand-Commentar*, 26–28.

45. Holtzmann, *Hand-Commentar*, 27.

46. Holtzmann, *Einleitung*, 385; *Hand-Commentar*, 7, 10–12, 34–36; *Lehrbuch der neutestamentlichen Theologie*, ed. Adolf Jülicher and Walter Bauer, 2nd ed. (Freiburg im Breisgau: J. C. B. Mohr [Paul Siebeck], 1911), 1:491–93 (hereafter *Theologie*).

47. Holtzmann, *Einleitung*, 387.

48. Holtzmann, *Einleitung*, 359.

49. Holtzmann, *Hand-Commentar*, 27–28.

50. "The problem of historical research lies wholly in this virtually indissoluble combination of a trustworthy tradition with reflective religious cogitation" (*Hand-Commentar*, 26).

51. Holtzmann, *Einleitung*, 384.

the miraculous in Mark he again puts down to the overflow of enthusiastic piety into the tradition, while insisting that these elements stick out within the natural historical realism of the Markan episodes.[52] In what seems a departure from construing Mark as the personal channel for Peter's eyewitness memory, he also suggests that the Petrine memory materials were taken up as "community tradition" that has passed through a generation-long period of development, the course of which cannot be precisely reconstructed. Authentic memory materials therefore form the *fundament*, the *base layer* (*untersten Grundlagen*), of the Markan narrative tradition.[53] They are the original sprout from the authentic root (*wurzelechten Trieb*), which subsequently has undergone a "lush hothouse growth."[54] In consequence, the Gospel of Mark has just a "relative" historicity.[55]

The ever-firm ground of historical authenticity, the depository of primitive apostolic memory, therefore, is to be found in the Logia. Holtzmann's privileging of the sayings over the narrative tradition, with its generative core in the Passion narrative, accords with his concern to impute to Jesus the teaching that the relation to God was a purely ethical one, not mediated through temple and cult.[56] In the 1892 *Einleitung* Holtzmann reaffirms its immediate connection to apostolic memory, the Matthean authorship of its Aramaic original.[57] He repeats his claims about its subliterary form, from which in 1863 he had inferred its urapostolic memory qualities.[58] In his 1911 *Theologie*, however, his attribution of Matthean authorship is more tentative—he refers to it as the "sayings collection [*Spruchsammlung*], now customarily referred to as 'Q' (from Matthew?)."[59] The *Hand-Commentar* also appears to qualify his earlier claim that the Logia is virtually unmediated apostolic memory. "What we possess," he

52. Holtzmann, *Theologie*, 1:493–94.
53. Holtzmann, *Theologie*, 1:493; similarly, *Einleitung*, 385.
54. Holtzmann, *Theologie*, 1:494; also *Einleitung*, 384.
55. Holtzmann, *Theologie*, 1:495. One wonders about effects of Wrede's *Das Messiasgeheimnis*, published in 1901, upon the development of Holtzmann's views of the Markan tradition. In *Das messianische Bewusstsein Jesu: Ein Beitrag zur Leben-Jesu-Forschung* (Tübingen: Mohr Siebeck, 1907), Holtzmann argues that messianic elements are pervasive in the tradition, and that there could be no causal connection between resurrection faith and the origins of messianic belief. The Messianic Secret originates in Jesus's association, in his own consciousness, of his messianic identity with the coming Son of Man.
56. H. J. Holtzmann, "Zur synoptischen Frage," *Jahrbücher für protestantische Theologie* 4 (1878): 328–82, 533–68 (355–56).
57. Holtzmann, *Einleitung*, 376, 378, 387.
58. Holtzmann, *Einleitung*, 363.
59. Holtzmann, *Theologie*, 1:179.

says, "are words of Jesus, interfused with the reflections, extrapolations, and convictions of the first generation that these sayings have generated."[60] Perhaps to offset this, in the *Theologie* he dwells at length on the Logia tradition having the ring of authenticity: in it we hear neither the apostles, nor the evangelists, nor the primitive community, but the voice of a historical personality.[61]

Holtzmann further insists that the christological dynamic issues from the *commemorative* life of the early communities.[62] The powerful cultural symbols of the Jewish *Messiasideal* and the historical reality of Jesus (in particular his suffering) have reacted upon one another semantically. One detects here an incipient cultural memory account of the formation of the tradition and its history. What he does not recognize is that these symbolic associations are themselves memorializing operations; he never overcomes this basic dualism of the tradition. In the final analysis he regards its symbolic, mythicizing elements as proliferations of the "oriental" poeticizing religious consciousness that like rank growth have wound around the primitive memory element in the tradition. These exist side by side in the tradition as mutually alien elements, or, alternatively, primitive memories get transmuted into symbols of ideal types and truths.[63]

Holtzmann's Recantation of Urmarkus

Holtzmann is frequently credited with giving the 2DH its prominence, but this is hard to square with his actual theories. In the classic 1863 study he puts a large block of double tradition—Preaching of John the Baptist; the Temptation; Sermon; the Healing of the Centurion's Servant—into an Urmarkus (Source A), his Logia source proper commencing with Jesus's discourse on John the Baptist (Luke 7:18–35//Matt 11:2–19). But when in 1877 he abandons Urmarkus, he is reluctant to reassign these sequences to the Logia.[64] Rather, he now has Luke "influenced" by Matthew, including in these double-tradition materials.

Why is this? Urmarkus functioned for Holtzmann (as Urmarkus theories typically do) in 1863 to explain a range of smaller Matthew/Luke agreements

---

60. Holtzmann, *Hand-Commentar*, 34.
61. Holtzmann, *Theologie*, 1:180–81.
62. Holtzmann, *Hand-Commentar*, 21: "All the creating and fashioning that goes on in the community stems from a constant remembering, from a conscious adhesion to that indelible impression, from an uninterrupted renewal of the memory of Jesus."
63. Holtzmann, *Hand-Commentar*, 28–29.
64. On his abandoning Urmarkus see "Forschungen von Bernhard Weiss," 820.

against Mark. With the Urmarkus expedient gone, and with a media model of closed textual circuits, influence now can only be flowing direct from Matthew to Luke. But why also for these large blocks of double-tradition materials? One reason is Holtzmann's genre purity assumption: narrative episodes and narrative frameworks are anomalous for a sayings collection. The Temptation is therefore excluded from the Logia source by definition; the Preaching of John the Baptist is likewise "alien to a sayings collection," and it is Matthew who has added the Healing of the Centurion's Servant.[65] Luke must therefore be taking these materials direct from Matthew. The double-tradition Sermon does not suffer from this disability, but Holtzmann's position on whether Matthew or the Logia is the source of Luke's Sermon is quite nebulous. This is not so odd: once Matthew is accorded a measure of influence (Holtzmann's term) on Luke, there is little to stop that influence from seeping out into the entire double tradition.

This explains why Holtzmann can continue to think of Matthew (which simply steps into Urmarkus's place) as the principal influence on the Luke 6 Sermon and the Lukan parallels to Matthew's Sermon elsewhere in the gospel, and to some extent their source. In 1877 he rejects Bernhard Weiss's claim that the Sermon + the Healing of the Centurion's Servant sequence is a *Grundschrift* sequence (Weiss's *Grundschrift* is kind of proto-gospel made up predominantly of double tradition but containing a number of narrative episodes) that Matthew and Luke have inserted in the same Markan narrative context.[66] In an 1878 essay on Jesus's view of the law he states that "the relationship between Luke and Matthew [in the Sermon] is not at all clear."[67] He agrees with Weiss that Luke is abbreviating a longer Sermon. Accordingly, he argues that Luke in 16:16–18 is drawing from Matthew 5:18–21. He goes on to say that Luke has dropped the Antitheses.[68] Holtzmann's diffidence on the question of source relationships is the consequence of his positing Matthean "influence" on Luke. Because Holtzmann previously assigned the Sermon to Urmarkus, there is no compelling reason to reassign it to the Logia when he recants his Urmarkus theory. If Luke could take it from Urmarkus, he could just as easily get it now from Matthew. But since there is no longer an Urmarkus source for Matthew's and Luke's Sermons, perhaps it comes to both from the Logia. Hence Holtzmann's equivocation.

---

65. Holtzmann, *Hand-Commentar*, 17; *Einleitung*, 357.
66. Holtzmann, "Forschungen von Bernhard Weiss," 821.
67. Holtzmann, "Zur synoptischen Frage," 553.
68. Holtzmann, "Zur synoptischen Frage," 553–54, 561–62.

Matthean influence of course must perforce extend to the rest of the Lukan double tradition. Lukan parallels, Holtzmann argues, are not only generally secondary to their Matthean counterparts but in a number of cases influenced by them.[69] In other words, Luke is making subsidiary use of Matthew throughout his gospel. Holtzmann therefore runs into the difficulty on which theories of Lukan dependency on Matthew notoriously come to grief: giving an intelligible account of Luke's patterns of Matthean utilization. Does making Luke's Matthew utilization subsidiary to his use of the Logia alter things? Holtzmann's utilization account ends up being completely ad hoc. He gamely tries to turn this into an editorial policy: Luke "knew" but did not "use" Matthew; his use of Matthew is "unsystematic and unmediated"; it is a "supplementary source" (*Nebenquelle*).[70] Matthew 3–4 is the direct source for the double tradition in Luke 3–4. In the Markan block in Luke 4:31–6:19, however, Matthean influence "breaks through only in details of expression." Luke's Sermon, on the other hand, shows the "strong influence" of Matthew's Sermon, whereas the Healing of the Centurion's Servant marks Luke's return to Matthew as his direct source. Then to Luke 9:50 Matthew's influence is just by occasional "reminiscence." But in the travel section Luke takes certain double-tradition items directly from Matthew (10:13–15, 25–27; 11:14–32; 12:10–12; 13:24–30; 16:16–18; 17:1–2), some of which are from the Sermon on the Mount (which in Luke 6 was just a "strong influence").[71] But then, faced with the reality that the ἀδικία of Luke 13:26–27 is more primitive than the ἀνομία of Matthew 7:21–23, Holtzmann suddenly shifts to something like Bernhard Weiss's *Urschrift* theory: Luke draws here "on the same source from which Matthew drew material for the Sermon on the Mount."[72] When Luke continues with the Markan thread again at 18:15 (Mark 10:13), "knowledge of the Matthean report is evident at every turn."[73] Holtzmann ends up attributing at least four different utilization policies to Luke, including independent ad hoc use of Matthew's "source" for the Sermon (which is not the Logia). In his 1901 *Hand-Commentar* the Luke 6:21b-49 Sermon is now described as "a shorter counterpart to Matt 5:3–7:27" that Luke has inserted. But finally, in 1911 (published posthumously) he comes around to imputing a version of the Sermon to the Logia, which in accord with what had become the standard usage he now calls "Q."[74]

---

69. Holtzmann, "Forschungen von Bernhard Weiss," 825–26.

70. Holtzmann, *Einleitung*, 350, 356. Here he is quoting Eduard Simons; see below.

71. Holtzmann, *Einleitung*, 356–57.

72. Holtzmann, *Einleitung*, 366.

73. Holtzmann, *Einleitung*, 357.

74. Holtzmann, *Hand-Commentar*, 17–18; also *Einleitung*, 366; *Theologie*, 504.

CHAPTER 3

EDUARD SIMONS

Eduard Simons's *Hat der dritte Evangelist den kanonischen Matthäus benutzt?*—a dissertation written under Holtzmann's direction—influenced Holtzmann in his shift toward Luke's subsidiary use of Matthew.[75] Simons's analysis is notable as the first thoroughgoing attempt to pair Luke's dependence on Matthew with Markan priority. But in Simons's view it is impossible to dispense with the sayings source (*Spruchsammlung*) hypothesis. Attempts to derive Luke's double tradition exclusively from Matthew are unable to explain its divergent disposition. But this is neatly explained by a sayings collection.[76]

Simons's tidy source schema obliges him to find rationales for Luke's Matthew utilization. In addition, he must come up with explanations for why Luke opts for sayings source renderings over Matthean, and vice versa. His analysis becomes a welter of ad hoc rationales. In the Nativity Luke eliminates Matthew's adoration of the Magi because he regards it as a duplicate to the Simeon and Hannah episode, and Luke is averse to duplications. Because typological exegesis is alien to him, he rejects the flight to Egypt. Luke discards Matthew's Nativity and substitutes one from a source of his own. Nevertheless, in prefacing his gospel with a Nativity he is influenced by Matthew. Luke replaces Matthew's genealogy with one he considers more historically accurate. As a Paulinist, a genealogy back to Adam had more cachet than one with its terminus in Abraham. But that he even has a genealogy attests to Matthean influence (6–7). In sum three distinct rationales.

Simons comes up with various rationales for why Luke passes over Matthean additions to Markan contexts. We give just a few examples. As a Paulinist, Luke has absorbed Paul's Romans 9 predestination doctrine and prefers the Mark 4:12 rendering (ἵνα βλέποντες βλέπωσιν καὶ μὴ ἴδωσιν κ.τ.λ.) of Isaiah 6:9 to the Matthew 13:13b rendering (ἵνα βλέποντες οὐ βλέπουσιν κ.τ.λ.). And he prefers the original sayings source location of "Blessed are your eyes . . ." (Luke 10:23–24) to Matthew's placement of it here (Matt 13:16–17) (9). Luke omits the Matthew 8:17 citation (αὐτὸς τὰς ἀσθενείας ἡμῶν ἔλαβεν καὶ τὰς νόσους ἐβάστασεν) "because the connection of Isaiah 53:4 to the healing instead of suffering Messiah either was not intelligible or did not seem fitting to him [*nicht angemessen schien*]" (28). In this same vein, Matthew's interpretation of the "leaven of the scribes and Sadducees" saying was "not pleasing"

---

75. Eduard Simons, *Hat der dritte Evangelist den kanonischen Matthäus benutzt?* (Bonn: Universitäts-Buchdruckerei von Carl Georgi, 1880).
76. Simons, *Evangelist*, 2–8 (hereafter page citations will be in the text).

[*ungenügend*] to Luke (11). Numerous cases of Luke's omission of Matthean additions to Markan passages are simply a matter of Luke preferring to follow Mark, as the older, more habituated, more authoritative source. Similarly, cases of Luke's placement and contextualization of double tradition diverging markedly from Matthew's (e.g., Matt 8:11–12//Luke 13:28–29) are due to Luke following the sayings collection instead of Matthew: as the oldest source it held greater authority for him than the "secondary" Matthew (8, 11). Simons argues that because Luke was composed in the second century—allegedly he is familiar with Josephus—he must have known Matthew, which already by the end of the first century had achieved not only wide circulation but universal prestige. But if it had such prestige, why does Luke treat it as a secondary, less familiar, less authoritative source? Simons's claims cancel each other out. If he shifts Luke's origins to the first century, the chances that Luke knows Matthew fade. If he holds to its second-century origins, he loses his principal rationale for why Luke ignores Matthean additions to Markan contexts (13).

The venerable antiquity of the sayings collection is also a reason for Luke's different contextualization of a number of the Sermon on the Mount materials. The irrelevance of the conflict with Pharisaic righteousness to his Gentile audience explains his outright omission of other Sermon elements. Likewise, the divergence of Luke's Love Your Enemies sequence from its Antitheses parallels: Luke recasts these elements into a general paraenetic form to serve the ethical instruction of his Gentile community (36–38). But is Luke following the Sermon of the sayings source (thus the distribution of Matthean Sermon elements elsewhere in his gospel)? Or is he following but adapting the Matthean version of the Sermon and drastically altering the Matthean arrangements? Simons has him doing both. Having Luke use both Matthew and the sayings source gets him into this fix.

Simons's source schema puts him on the horns of a dilemma. He is nothing if not inventive in coming up with explanations for Luke's Matthew-utilization actions. Why not just have Luke adapting the double tradition entirely from Matthew? Simons is conscious of the plausibility limits that such an approach will run up against, whereas something like the sayings collection hypothesis gives a neat, simple account of Luke's divergent disposition of the double tradition. Why then not embrace a simple sayings source utilization theory? Because for Simons, Matthean influence on Luke is necessary to explain other patterns of Matt/Luke agreement. But once Matthean utilization is embraced in principle, it inevitably encroaches into the double tradition, for a theory of even limited Lukan use of Matthew cannot do without ingenious—and proliferating—rationales to explain Luke's utilization patterns. Once granted limited writ, there is no reason these explanatory measures should not be extended to all the double tradition. The problem becomes particularly evident when he faces the question of why Luke remains uninfluenced by Matthew's overall arrangement, by Matthew's solution to the technical problem of combining the sayings collection with the Markan narrative. The expedient of the older, more authoritative sayings collection, which Simons wheeled out to account for Luke omitting Matthean additions to Markan contexts, is inadequate here. He is forced to claim that Luke's opting for the block method was an act of contrariness (*gegensätzlich*) to Matthew—under what motivation, he does not say (105).

In Simons's own view his chief source-critical contribution lies in having secured Markan priority *simpliciter* and rendered the Urmarkus hypothesis redundant. This, he notes, is no small thing: treating Urmarkus as the convenient receptacle for the variety of Matt/Luke agreements against canonical Mark can have as its unintended consequence the "self-dissolution" of Markan priority and open the door to source theories like Bernhard Weiss's (a narratively expanded instructional source used by all three evangelists) (111–12). This leaves the triple-tradition agreements against Mark. To account for these, Simons posits secondary Matthean influence on Luke. This is the corollary of his exclusion of John's Preaching and the Temptation from the sayings source. In the absence of Urmarkus, these materials can only come to Luke from Matthew. If Simons were to assign John's Preaching and the Temptation to the sayings source, all bets are off whether he would nevertheless propose Luke's dependence on Matthew, with its viper's nest of source-utilization difficulties.

The outcome is a source-utilization shambles. Simons is unable to be clear about the source from case to case of Luke's double-tradition materials, shifting back and forth ad hoc between Matthew and the sayings collection. The source-utilization operations his schema entails are convoluted. He ends up with all the problems that attend the standard claim for Luke's dependence on Matthew: uncontrollably proliferating ad hoc rationales for why Luke passes over this or that Matthean passage and forced to take frequent recourse to Luke's subjective intentions.

BERNHARD WEISS

Weiss first set out his source theory in 1861 in "Zur Entstehungsgeschichte der drei synoptischen Evangelien." With modifications he was still arguing for it in his 1908 *Die Quellen der synoptischen Überlieferung*. Weiss's complicated theory was not fated to survive. Nevertheless, it serves as an instructive example of how particular media assumptions and the desire to find the authentic memory source drive source-critical solutions.

Weiss 1861: *Triple Tradition, Double Tradition, and the* Urschrift

In 1861 the Griesbach hypothesis still had some purchase. Weiss rejects it vigorously. But his more proximate target is Urmarkus theories. Such are superfluous, he argues, if one imputes to Matthew a measure of compositional freedom rather than wooden use of his sources.[77] But Weiss holds that canonical Mark nevertheless contains elements that are less primitive than their Matthean parallels. The intermingling (*Mischung*) of primitive and secondary elements frequently runs right through pericopes.[78] How to explain Matthew's evident dependence upon the narrative sequence of the Gospel of Mark yet his alternation with Mark in the primitivity of the parallels themselves?

In addition to Mark, Weiss explains, Matthew uses a primitive subliterary work, an *Urschrift* that Weiss also refers to as the *Matthäusquelle* ("Matthew-source"). This source consisted primarily of sayings sequences (*Reden und Aussprüchen Christi*), intermingled, however, with a number of narrative episodes not connected up into any coherent narrative depiction of the life of Jesus. The existence of a loose collection of sayings and narrative traditions of this sort, Weiss avers, is an *a priori* certainty: such would surely have been the most primitive expression of gospel writing. The Matthean evangelist takes the Gospel of Mark's coherently connected-up narrative sequence as his own narrative baseline. But owing to its greater antiquity and apostolic origins he chiefly consults the *Matthäusquelle* in the actual pericopes. This explains the mingling of primitive and secondary elements in these Matthean parallels, for the Markan evangelist also draws directly upon the primitive source, though with a bias toward its narrative over its didactic materials.[79] The just approximate agreement between Mark and Matthew in their overlap instructional passages is due to Mark relying on "reminiscence" to utilize these particular *Matthäusquelle* sequences.[80] Mark, for example, takes his Mission Instruction (Mark 6:7–13) from the *Matthäusquelle* by reminiscence, whereas Matthew and Luke (who like Matthew uses both Mark and the *Matthäusquelle*) draw more directly upon the *Matthäusquelle* for their versions (Matt 10:1–42; Luke 10:1–16).[81]

---

77. Bernhard Weiss, "Zur Entstehungsgeschichte der drei synoptischen Evangelien," *TSK* 34 (1861): 29–100, 646–713 (45–46).

78. Weiss, "Zur Entstehungsgeschichte," 59–67.

79. Weiss, "Zur Entstehungsgeschichte," 68–69.

80. Bernhard Weiss, *Die Quellen des Lukasevangeliums* (Stuttgart & Berlin: J. G. Cotta, 1907), 125.

81. Weiss, *Quellen des Lukasevangeliums*, 115–19; also "Zur Entstehungsgeschichte," 43, 74. Luke draws his Mission of the Twelve directly from Mark.

The *Matthäusquelle* is the Matthean evangelist's source for much of his double tradition. It is his effort to integrate this predominantly didactic source at various points into the Markan narrative that has scrambled the order of his Markan baseline.[82] The evangelist compiled his instructional discourses from the didactic materials of the source, where they existed disconnected and dispersed in short, topically aggregated sequences. Though preponderantly (*überwiegend; vorherrschend*) sayings, as noted it also contained numerous though unconnected Synoptic narrative episodes. Thus it was not a "sayings collection" (*Spruchsammlung*) but a "collection of materials" (*Stoffsammlung*).[83] That it collected together narratives alongside sayings is indicated by the Temptation, the Healing of the Centurion's Servant, the exorcism that inaugurates the Beelzebul controversy, the discipleship chreias in Luke 9:57–60, and chreiic elements such as the Luke 11:1 introduction to the Our Father and Luke 17:20. If it contained these, Weiss reasons, there is no obstacle to its containing triple-tradition narratives. That the source was a pure sayings collection is ruled out by its nature as a subliterary collection (*Aufzeichnung*) of raw oral tradition: such a project would scarcely have distinguished sayings from narratives, which circulated undifferentiated in the oral tradition.[84]

There is little to be said, Weiss says, for Luke's being to any degree dependent on Matthew. Divergent nativities, genealogies, different audiences for John's preaching, and the like are difficult to square with such a theory. Luke shows no awareness of Matthew's operations on Markan pericopes. It is difficult to stipulate a plausible rationale for his recycling of the Matthean compositions into his rather nondescript arrangements.[85] The pattern of their agreements against Mark is not such as to indicate that Luke has even a secondary awareness of Matthew. Luke's agreements with Matthew against Mark in a given pericope cannot be correlated with knowledge of the larger pattern of Matthew's redaction of the Markan parallel in question. In such passages it can be seen that they have independent redactional motives in their respective modifications of the Markan parallel.[86]

Therefore, just like Matthew, Luke uses the *Matthäusquelle* for his double-tradition materials. The detached distribution of these materials in Luke and the artificiality of the historical settings that he creates for them indicate that Luke preserves not only the subliterary profile but also the original order of the source

82. Weiss, "Zur Entstehungsgeschichte," 40, 70.
83. Weiss, "Zur Entstehungsgeschichte," 75–78, 703; *Quellen des Lukasevangeliums*, 277.
84. Weiss, "Zur Entstehungsgeschichte," 76–77; *Quellen des Lukasevangeliums*, 98–99; *Die Quellen der synoptischen Überlieferung* (Leipzig: Hinrichs, 1908), 76–78, 106–10.
85. Weiss, "Zur Entstehungsgeschichte," 78–79.
86. Weiss, *Quellen des Lukasevangeliums*, 18–19, 42.

and positioning of its material. The order of materials in the primitive *Matthäusquelle* was disturbed by Matthew's compiling project. On balance the wording of these materials in Luke also more closely approximates to the source.[87]

The Markan evangelist was the first to work up the narrative materials of the *Matthäusquelle* into a narratively cohering life of Jesus. To this end he passed over most of its sayings materials.[88] But he was also a privileged tradent of the Petrine oral tradition, which in composing his gospel he combined with the narrative elements of the *Matthäusquelle* (thus his two feeding stories).[89] The connected narrative of the Markan evangelist explains why Matthew uses the gospel for his narrative baseline. Luke likewise takes over the Markan narrative sequence as his own, bringing it over in blocks, separated by sequences from the *Matthäusquelle*. The *Matthäusquelle* is the main source for the first half of his travel section (Luke 9:5–13:35), which for the most part simply follows the order of the source. From 14:1–18:14, however, Luke appears to be following a different source that featured parables along with topically grouped sayings.[90]

The Later Weiss: Matthean and Lukan Urgospels

Thus Weiss circa 1861. Between 1861 and 1907/1908, when he publishes his last thoughts on the subject, he shifts his position considerably, while maintaining his basic source-history schema. Matthew's sharp divergence from Mark's narrative order in chapters 8–9 continues to vex him. In 1861 he argued that Matthew rearranges the Markan order to create a collection of miracles and to accommodate the early insertion of the *Matthäusquelle* Sermon in Matthew 5–7. But he now holds that Matthew's divergent order of these Matthew 8–9 episodes is the order of these narrative episodes in the *Matthäusquelle*.[91] In 1861 Weiss has Matthew following Mark for his narrative baseline, while using the *Matthäusquelle* for the pericopes themselves. Not only is this a quite cumbersome procedure but also a rather tenuous constraint on Matthew's utilization: why should the first evangelist not at some junctures also just opt for the *Matthäusquelle* narrative sequence? Weiss follows through on this logic.

---

87. Weiss, "Zur Entstehungsgeschichte," 80–83; *Quellen des Lukasevangeliums*, 69, 91, 104, 283, 295.

88. Weiss, "Zur Entstehungsgeschichte," 671–72.

89. Weiss, "Zur Entstehungsgeschichte," 696; *Quellen der synoptischen Überlieferung*, 201–9.

90. Weiss, "Zur Entstehungsgeschichte," 696–702.

91. Weiss, *Quellen der synoptischen Überlieferung*, 206–7, 225–27; *Quellen des Lukasevangeliums*, 20, 99.

The effect is to create worse problems for his source history. It requires abandoning the premise that the narrative order of the primitive source is incoherent. Is the source the disarranged provisional collection of oral tradition that Weiss claimed it is or not? If its narrative order is coherent, why does Mark abandon it? Weiss now says that unlike Matthew and Luke, Mark "knew" but did not "use" the primitive *Matthäusquelle* as a source, he was merely "influenced" by it, at any rate enough to explain his verbal agreements with Matthew and Luke.[92] But why then does Matthew return to Markan order at Mark 6:1? Why not follow the *Matthäusquelle* narrative order elsewhere? Is the *Matthäusquelle* order the same as Markan order from Mark 6:1 forward? Is the Matthew 8–9 miracle collection the Matthean evangelist's idea or the conception of the primitive *Matthäusquelle*? Is Weiss not drifting back toward an Urgospel theory? His original theory—Matthew rearranges Markan narrative order to accommodate materials from the source—was simpler and more coherent.

Though Weiss insists that the primitive *Matthäusquelle* is chiefly a collection of didactic materials (*Redenquelle*), in fact it turns out to be a quite copious collection of triple-tradition parallels, double tradition, and Matthean special materials.[93] Frequently Weiss infers that a given pericope was in the *Matthäusquelle* from its coherent connections with a previous pericope; this further undermines his claim that it was a primitive collection. What emerges, in other words, is a kind of shadow gospel, a proto-Matthew, that begins with John the Baptist and progresses through the ministry of Jesus toward the Passion narrative. However, Weiss has it ending abruptly with the Anointing at Bethany (Matt 26:6–13//Mark 14:3–9). To explain this, he falls back on the source being "essentially" a didactic collection whose narrative pericopes, moreover, had not been worked up into any narrative continuity.[94] Because the Anointing at Bethany refers to Jesus's interment, it effectively substitutes for the Passion narrative. Thus the source, though lacking narrative continuity, was "no formless collection of traditions."[95]

In 1861 Weiss has Luke drawing upon the *Matthäusquelle* and Mark, though he ventures that in the latter half of the travel section Luke makes use of a separate source. Sometime between 1861 and 1907/1908 Weiss abandons this scenario and shifts to having Luke use a comprehensive L source that con-

92. Weiss, *Quellen der synoptischen Überlieferung*, 253–55.
93. See Weiss, *Quellen der synoptischen Überlieferung*, 23–69; also *Quellen des Lukasevangeliums*, 157–79.
94. Weiss, *Quellen des Lukasevangeliums*, 157–59.
95. Weiss, *Quellen der synoptischen Überlieferung*, 88.

tained a parallel tradition to the *Matthäusquelle* double tradition, numerous triple-tradition parallels, and Luke's special materials. Weiss now believes that the divergences of Luke's Sermon from the Matthean Sermon are too great to be explained by Luke's utilization of the *Matthäusquelle*. That level of variation can only arise in oral tradition. Accordingly, an L Sermon and the *Matthäusquelle* Sermon developed separately in the oral tradition. The two sources, *Matthäusquelle* and L, which emerged organically and independently out of the oral tradition (*hervorgewachsen*), gave the variant traditions textual fixation.[96] The evangelist Luke, though working principally from L, is familiar with the primitive *Matthäusquelle*. What he does is weave elements of the *Matthäusquelle* version of double tradition into the L version before him. Luke has a harmonization tendency, the effect of which is to create additional verbal agreements.

Like the *Matthäusquelle*, the L source is no didactic collection of sayings but contains copious amounts of narrative material: quite a few triple-tradition parallels as well as most of the Lukan special materials. In fact, unlike the *Matthäusquelle*—which Weiss continues to characterize as an ad hoc collection—L is a proto-gospel, a cohering narrative of Jesus's life. It begins with the Lukan Nativity, it contains John's ethical instruction to various social classes, the genealogy, the Luke 4 Nazareth episode, the Luke 5 Call of the Fishermen, the Lukan apostle list, a version of Fasting and Wineskins, the L Sermon in Luke 6, Healing of the Centurion's Servant, the Nain miracle, the Healings in the Sight of John's Messengers, Anointing by the Sinful Woman, Women Disciples Follow Jesus, significant amounts of the travel section, Zacchaeus, Parable of the Talents, Triumphal Entry, Paying Taxes to Caesar, and the L versions of the Passion and Resurrection narratives.[97] Certain double-tradition sequences—the discourse about the Baptist; Return of the Unclean Spirit/Demand for a Sign; Do Not Be Anxious; Mustard Seed/Leaven—are high agreement. Luke therefore is taking these direct from the *Matthäusquelle*.[98] The Gospel of Luke is the artifact of the harmonizing evangelist weaving L together with the *Matthäusquelle* and the Gospel of Mark. Luke uses Mark for his narrative ductus and to supplement L: these are the close-agreement triple-tradition parallels.[99]

Notwithstanding his continued insistence that it is a provisional collection, the primitive *Matthäusquelle* too emerges as a kind of proto-gospel. Though

96. Weiss, *Quellen der synoptischen Überlieferung*, 113–14; *Quellen des Lukasevangeliums*, 259–61.

97. Weiss, *Quellen der synoptischen Überlieferung*, 104–49.

98. Weiss, *Quellen des Lukasevangeliums*, 213–14, 295; *Quellen der synoptischen Überlieferung*, iii.

99. Weiss, *Quellen der synoptischen Überlieferung*, 250.

containing the double tradition and their respective special materials, the L source and *Matthäusquelle* more or less shadow the Markan narrative. This is the consequence of Weiss's procedure and media assumptions: variant triple-tradition parallels get distributed out to three sources: *Matthäusquelle*, Mark, and L. This entails that the Markan narrative sequence will simply replicate itself in the L and *Matthäusquelle* narrative sequences. The Matthean and Lukan evangelists fill in the narrative gaps in these sources direct from the Gospel of Mark (the close-agreement triple-tradition passages).

Weiss: Matthäusquelle *and L as Authentic Memory Sources*

In the *Matthäusquelle* and L, Weiss finds a Jesus as yet undistorted by dogmatic interests.[100] There is nothing in their Christology that goes beyond traditional Jewish messianic beliefs that simply reflect Jesus's own convictions about his identity. Jesus's declarations about the future fit within standard Jewish eschatology. His kingdom is a restoration of the earthly kingdom, where his disciples judge the twelve tribes of Israel. As Messiah he will not remain in death that impends, he will be raised. His messianic work will be completed at his return as the Son of Man.[101] These sources are comparatively thin in supernatural elements. In L the people press upon Jesus not to seek healings but to "hear his word" (Luke 5:1).[102] But even the Lukan and Matthean evangelists evince little trace of writing under the impetus of a dogmatic *Tendenz.* Their project rather is simply that of combining and harmonizing their sources: Matthew the *Matthäusquelle* and Mark; Luke the *Matthäusquelle*, L, and Mark.[103]

Weiss's two proto-gospel sources possess these qualities because they are grounded in apostolic memory, the *Matthäusquelle* in particular. Jesus's sayings uttered on various occasions would rapidly assimilate to memory. But a particularly unusual and striking event would likewise leave a lasting imprint upon the disciples' memories (*sich der Erinnerung einprägen*).[104] In the primitive Jerusalem community focused recollection occurred in apostolic circles, driven by various contemporary exigencies. In this engaged remembering there formed, as a matter of course, an emergent body of shared, formulaic tradition. Though constituted directly of memory, its elements were not naïve representations of historical events but artifacts shaped in pragmatic utiliza-

100. Weiss, *Quellen der synoptischen Überlieferung,* 89.
101. Weiss, *Quellen der synoptischen Überlieferung,* 92–93, 185–86.
102. Weiss, *Quellen der synoptischen Überlieferung,* 182.
103. Weiss, *Quellen der synoptischen Überlieferung,* 235, 251–53.
104. Weiss, *Quellen der synoptischen Überlieferung,* 83.

tion. The *Matthäusquelle* is a collection of materials taken directly from this working inventory of tradition. The *Matthäusquelle*, that is, is an apostolic memory dump. This accounts for why Weiss insists that the source, though predominantly a collection of didactic materials (*Redensammlung*), was an expansive text that also contained a quantity of narratives. The *Matthäusquelle* therefore is the authentic source *par excellence*. In Weiss's source scenario the evangelist Mark makes use of it; Mark's Gospel therefore stands at one remove from apostolic memory. For his additional narrative materials Mark had privileged access to an oral body of eyewitness materials from the mouth of the apostle Peter. Numerous Markan episodes bear indicators of Peter's eyewitness testimony and of other eyewitness sources. The anecdotal form in which the *Matthäusquelle* materials and this variegated eyewitness tradition was available to the second evangelist, and the topical way in which his materials are frequently arranged, preclude, however, taking Mark's narrative as a transparently historical account of Jesus's ministry, as a life of Jesus.[105]

Weiss's Media Assumptions and His Source History

This source history rests upon a sharp binary between the oral medium and the written medium. Though Weiss accords the evangelists some scope for redactional interventions, he thinks that the observable levels of Synoptic variation cannot be accounted for by redaction. Synoptic levels of variation can only have arisen during the oral phase of the tradition. The effect of the eventual shift of these parallel traditions into primitive written sources was to bring variation to a virtual standstill beyond the limited range that Weiss is prepared to allow for redactional modification. Weiss's dual-source scenario—a *Matthäusquelle* and an L source—is the reflex of this media model: any Matt/Luke parallel, be it double tradition or triple tradition, which displays significant variation is taken back to separate sources. Hence the dual sources, *Matthäusquelle* and L, that more or less track each other and Mark. These proto-gospels, however, are just shadows cast by divergent triple- and double-tradition parallels; they are artifacts of Weiss's media model. Weiss's oral tradition gets flash-frozen in two sources, the *Matthäusquelle* and L. The observable pattern of close verbal agreements mingled with higher variation double and triple parallels is the product of an enterprise of harmonizing parallel texts, intentionally or involuntarily by reminiscence.[106]

---

105. Weiss, *Quellen der synoptischen Überlieferung*, 201–6, 220–22; "Zur Entstehungsgeschichte," 706, 675, 696.

106. Weiss, *Quellen der synoptischen Evangelien*, 131 n. 24.

Matthew and Luke's close interweaving of source strands within individual pericopes raises practical source-utilization problems. Weiss recognizes that the harmonizing evangelist, Luke or Matthew, could have only one source before him at a time.[107] He recognizes that an evangelist would not have gone hunting around in the parallel sources retrieving phrases, sentences, and sequences, as it were "thumbing around [*umherblättern*] in the book . . . trying to find the passage in question."[108] On the other hand, he does not impute variation dynamics to written tradition. He therefore adverts almost exclusively to evangelist reminiscence, voluntary and involuntary, of the parallel source or sources, to explain cross-source verbal agreements, exact and inexact. The sources (*Matthäusquelle*, L, Mark, as the case may be) were familiarized and had left some impression on the evangelists' memories.[109] Reminiscence is the all-purpose expedient in Weiss's schema: not only does it explain agreements but—paradoxically—also variation. Weiss floats the theory that variation level is a function of whether the evangelist has the source in front of him or is dependent on memory to access it. Exact agreement correlates to direct visual contact with the source (*vor Augen*).[110] Then he notes instances where this theory breaks down (e.g., Luke 13:24–25//Matt 23:37–39), in which case, he says, the evangelist must have had the passage securely in memory.[111] His source-utilization account descends into incoherence. His media straitjacket prevents him from coming up with a schema able to cope with the complex profile of the tradition.

Weiss's Source Theory and the 2DH

Weiss's source history has affinities to the 2DH: it posits Matthew's and Luke's dependence on the Gospel of Mark on the one hand and on a predominantly didactic *Matthäusquelle* (by 1907/1908 Weiss is simply calling it "Q") and parallel L source on the other. He diverges by imputing narrative as well as sayings to the parallel double-tradition sources. Though agreeing that it remains principally an instructional source, he characterizes the *Matthäusquelle* not as a sayings collection but as a "collection of materials," the more narrative-dense L as a kind of proto-gospel. We have seen that this position rests in the

---

107. Weiss, *Quellen des Lukasevangeliums*, 278.
108. Weiss, "Zur Entstehungsgeschichte," 706.
109. Weiss, "Zur Entstehungsgeschichte," 706–7.
110. Weiss, *Quellen des Lukasevangeliums*, 87, 282.
111. Weiss, *Quellen des Lukasevangeliums*, 98.

first instance on a genre purity fallacy: Weiss assumes that a sayings collection cannot contain any narrative elements. The presence of the Temptation, two healing stories, and the two discipleship chreias means that the double-tradition source, though chiefly instructional in profile, could not have been a sayings collection. In turn this gives Weiss license to import narrative (i.e., triple tradition) on a large scale into both the *Matthäusquelle* and L.

It also depends on a media model that assigns higher-variation parallels to parallel written sources. It follows that the *Matthäusquelle* and L will include double-tradition *and* triple-tradition parallels. In this scheme of things the double tradition becomes irrelevant as a source-delimiting criterion (it takes its revenge by forcing Weiss to posit *two* double-tradition sources, though with similarly ordered triple-tradition pericopes). Further, with many of his contemporaries Weiss assumes that gospel writing must have been preceded by provisional written collections (*Aufzeichnungen*) of raw oral tradition. Sayings and narrative tradition would be included in such collections indiscriminately. The *Matthäusquelle*, he avers, is just such a collection. Weiss has a stake in this claim. Because he identifies raw oral tradition directly with apostolic-memory materials, he can identify the *Matthäusquelle* as the apostolic-memory source. It ranks higher in authenticity than the L source, which is a first attempt at gospel writing.

There are no grounds to hold to the existence of Weiss's primitive *Matthäusquelle*, conceived as a provisional mixed collection of sayings and narrative. We find ourselves back therefore at the problem of the double tradition. What about his claim that Mark uses the *Matthäusquelle*? Weiss tacitly acknowledges that Markan overlap passages and their double-tradition parallels are more like oral variants than editorial variants, more like overlapping traditions than overlapping written sources. Moreover, Mark's usage of the *Matthäusquelle* is consistently by reminiscence, which for Weiss means consistently high variation.[112] Alternatively (and at odds with the reminiscence scenario), he occasionally experiments with the claim that Mark rewrites the source. Further, Weiss does not explain why Mark uses relatively little of the *Matthäusquelle* didactic material—beyond arguing in a circle that the evangelist was biased toward the narrative elements. Eventually Weiss gives the game away: Mark "knew" and was "influenced by," but did not "use" the older source.[113]

Weiss gives good reasons for holding that the order and disposition of the double tradition in Luke more closely approximates to its disposition in the original *Matthäusquelle*. He does not square this with his claim that the *Mat-*

112. E.g., *Quellen des Lukasevangeliums*, 115–16, also 147–48.
113. Weiss, *Quellen der synoptischen Überlieferung*, 253–54.

thäusquelle and L source represent parallel but separate streams of tradition. Given these origins why would they approximate to each other in sequence at all? Double-tradition agreements in order, such as they are, would seem rather to indicate derivation from a single source. When all is said and done, we find ourselves back at a simple form of the 2DH.

Paul Wernle

In Paul Wernle's *Die synoptische Frage*, published in 1899, the two document hypothesis is now operating as a premise, the soundness of which is demonstrated by its explanatory efficiency. Wernle's 1899 volume and his 1906 *Die Quellen des Lebens Jesu* are barometers of the sea change occurring in source criticism around the turn of the twentieth century: the 1906 work registers the effects of Wrede's *Das Messiasgeheimnis* (1901).

The Gospel of Mark and the sayings collection (*Spruchsammlung*) originate directly out of oral tradition; as such they form the most primitive layer of the tradition that is available.[114] Wernle posits indeterminate pre-Synoptic written sources for Luke's special materials.[115] Matthew's special materials likewise stem from indeterminate written and oral sources, more or less heavily reworked by Matthew.[116] Wernle's utilization account is dominated by written sources and writing. Oral tradition serves as a placeholder for the obscure early phase of the tradition and as a parallel source for Matthean and Lukan special materials.

Wernle's principal interest is in the sayings source and Mark, the sayings source in particular. Like Holtzmann's Logia, the source—more precisely, its earliest layer, which Wernle labels "Q"—has apostolic qualities. It is a Greek translation of an Aramaic original. This single translation is the origin of the versions that have descended to Matthew and Luke.[117] In its primitive version it appeared in the 60s, so barely within the lifetime of most of the apostles. Nevertheless, it was pulled together "by a man of the primitive apostolic orientation." It comprises the "legacy of Jesus to the community."[118] As it is for Holtzmann (and for Weiss's *Matthäusquelle*) so also for Wernle: Q is the authentic source beyond compare; its primitive layer—the *Grundstock*—mediates

114. Paul Wernle, *Die synoptische Frage* (Tübingen: J. C. B. Mohr [Paul Siebeck], 1899), 132–33, 209–11.
115. Paul Wernle, *Die Quellen des Lebens Jesu*, 3rd ed. (Tübingen: J. C. B. Mohr [Paul Siebeck], 1906), 79–80; *Synoptische Frage*, 38–39, 93, 107.
116. Wernle, *Synoptische Frage*, 189–93.
117. Wernle, *Quellen*, 52.
118. Wernle, *Synoptische Frage*, 231–33.

Jesus and his preaching with little distortion, "the essence of the gospel in its unadulterated clarity and its freedom."[119] Its materials are organized intelligibly under topical rubrics: the work owes its origin to the instructional needs of the community.[120] It is the unique witness to the primitive theology of the primitive Palestinian community, its materials lightly tinctured by an implicit and sometimes explicit messianic Christology.[121]

In Wernle's view, variation in the double tradition and its divergent arrangements in Matthew and Luke indicate that the source passed through a complex history of written transmission, undergoing redactions and supplementations prior to coming to the evangelists. Between the original "Q" and the final versions Q^{Matt} and Q^{Luke} lie intermediate redactions Q^1, Q^2, and Q^3, as well as, at some early point, a Q^{Jud} redaction that added Judaizing glosses.[122] Because it is incompatible with the early Judaizing redaction the Centurion episode belongs to a later redaction. Elements of a pronounced dogmatic complexion, such as Luke 10:21–24 with its advanced Christology, belong to later redactions. Wernle admits that precise demarcations of these various layers is a futile enterprise. The point is that pluralization of redactions is his way of explaining the rise of variants and the divergent arrangements of the materials in the evangelists.[123] Wernle assigns quite a bit of M material to Q^{Matt}, including the Antitheses, the M Beatitudes, possibly the Cult Didache, some of the M parables in Matthew 13.[124] The different locations of certain common materials—e.g., the Q 9:54–58 Call Stories; Love Your Enemies; the Woes; I Thank Thee, Father; Blessed Are the Eyes—indicate that these materials were added in subsequent redactions.

What about the Gospel of Mark? Here we must distinguish the pre-Wrede Wernle of 1899 from the Wernle of 1906. The earlier Wernle attributes the gospel to the historical Mark, the fleeing youth of Mark 14:51, companion of Peter and Paul. It is replete with indicators of Peter's eyewitness memories.[125] Its mediation of eyewitness memory is evident in its naïve historical realism, its vivid and realistic depiction of Jesus, its innocent joy in the miraculous, its eschatological enthusiasm, its historically realistic description of the course of Jesus's ministry, its completely nontheological complexion, especially the

---

119. Wernle, *Quellen*, 73.
120. Wernle, *Synoptische Frage*, 227–28; also *Quellen*, 71.
121. Wernle, *Synoptische Frage*, 228.
122. Wernle, *Synoptische Frage*, 231; also *Quellen*, 73–74.
123. Wernle, *Synoptische Frage*, 231–32.
124. Wernle, *Synoptische Frage*, 186–87.
125. Wernle, *Synoptische Frage*, 136.

absence in it of atonement interpretations of Jesus's suffering.[126] Like the sayings source, Mark has primitive apostolic qualities: direct connection to Jesus through the medium of Peter's eyewitness testimony. It communicates the simple, joyful piety of Peter and his fellow disciples; a lay Galilean piety of simple trust in God and instinctive moral response to God's will; a piety untrammeled by the legalism, purity codes, and ceremonialism of the religious elites of Judea; a piety "learned in the school of Jesus."[127] As for Holtzmann, so also for Wernle, memory is the channel for this predogmatic Jesus of the primitive community.

A big shift is evident in 1906. Mark's connection to Peter is no longer immediate; rather, the gospel is secondary, a conduit for Petrine *traditions*. Its narrative framework is a Markan contrivance, a literary expedient for bringing the fragmentary elements of the tradition into a coherent arrangement. The narrative is an amassment (*eine . . . stoffliche Anhäufung*) of self-contained individual episodes; it has little verifiable connection to the actual historical course of Jesus's ministry.[128] No biography of Jesus can be derived from it. Mark is "just a collector of individual pieces of tradition, which he unites into a whole on the basis of his own conjectures."[129] To be sure, the narrative framework and Mark's connective editorial tissue are not wholly invented: they preserve memories of Jesus's itineracy, of trips across the sea, the names of villages and regions where events took place. But with these Mark's knowledge of the course of Jesus's ministry is exhausted. These materials express Markan christological *Tendenzen*. Historical inquiry must therefore bypass the narrative frameworking and connective editorial elements and deal directly with the units of the tradition.[130]

Mark's memory connection is evident in its focused account beginning at the point Peter and his companions begin to follow Jesus. But the disciples were only concerned to communicate Jesus's words and deeds, not a narrative account of the course of his ministry. Moreover, these primitive memory traditions have been shaped over a forty-year period of oral transmission, during which they interacted with the faith and contemporary concerns of the early communities. Unhistorical elements reflecting contemporary community contexts have filtered into the tradition. Sayings have in some instances

---

126. Wernle, *Synoptische Frage*, 197–206.
127. Wernle, *Synoptische Frage*, 202–3.
128. Wernle, *Quellen*, 63–64.
129. Wernle, *Quellen*, 82.
130. Wernle, *Quellen*, 60–68.

generated narrative scenery. Diverse motifs and materials have been artificially combined. The narrative tradition, that is to say, has come to express in the first instance the faith of the primitive community.[131] Mark has himself heightened the miraculous elements in the tradition, at the expense of Jesus's teachings, in the dogmatic interest of proving Jesus to be the Son of God.[132] In consequence the Markan tradition transmits memory—and with it elements of authentic history—only fragmentarily.

Nevertheless, because Wernle affirms that authentic memories exist as kernels within the tradition, even in nature miracles such as the sea-crossing episodes, he urges that the historical worth of the Markan tradition continue to be rated highly. He holds that the tradition has been transmitted by eyewitnesses. Mark therefore remains for him an important conduit for memory. The evangelist has interfered very little in the tradition; he gives clear voice to the tradition as it has come to him from eyewitness informants.[133] But a dichotomy between authentic memory elements and unhistorical faith elements runs raggedly right through the tradition.

As it does for Holtzmann the burden of mediating the primitive memory of the predogmatic Jesus of history and the simple messianic Christology of the primitive community therefore falls chiefly upon the sayings source— its earliest layer, that is. But this burden it is eminently able to bear. In the "numerous memory glimpses" (*zahlreiche Augenblickserinnerungen*) that the source affords us, Jesus speaks as though he were our contemporary clearly and directly of simple trust in God, of yearning after purity of heart, mercy, and humility. Other than occasional light tincturing from the simple messianic faith of the primitive community, not wholly ungrounded in Jesus himself, the source presents a human Jesus, not yet distorted by christological development and dogmatizing faith.[134] It comes into its own here as the authentic source for a predogma Jesus of the word, tailored for modernity, giving insight into existence. In Wernle one observes with particular clarity how the powerful liberal aversion to the Christ of ecclesiastical dogma gets reflected in the sharpness of the dichotomy between what gets labeled authentic or inauthentic elements in the tradition. "The nearer we approach to Jesus in the tradition, the more everything dogmatic and theological recedes into the background.

---

131. Wernle, *Quellen*, 80–83.
132. Wernle, *Quellen*, 60–62. Wernle seems to suggest that the messianic secret is Markan, though to account for the Jews not accepting Jesus as the Son of God (so for apologetic motives), not to import messianic Christology into a nonmessianic tradition (83).
133. Wernle, *Quellen*, 69–70.
134. Wernle, *Quellen*, 86–87.

We behold a man whose words give us clear understanding of ourselves, our world, and—above all—God."[135] Source criticism becomes the outlet for this aversion, a way of hypostasizing it in a source history.

SUMMING UP

Source criticism took the lead role in nineteenth- and early twentieth-century debates about the historical Jesus and Christian origins. On one front, critics wielded it as a weapon against the dogmatic Jesus of orthodoxy, on another front against radical historical skepticism. Explicit or implicit notions of the nexus of memory with the tradition were at work in their attempts to identify a historically authentic stratum of the tradition, which for them meant a stratum lacking or light in dogmatic elements. Apostolic memory and historical authenticity were regarded as two sides of the same coin, primitive oral tradition as the effusion of apostolic memory. Precipitated out in pre-Synoptic written collections, it provided the raw material for the literary and theological (i.e., dogmatizing) activities of the evangelists. Nineteenth-century source criticism assigned a key role to memory at the incipient stage of the tradition, where it served to ground the tradition in the historical Jesus.

But nineteenth-century critics never successfully closed the gap between eyewitness testimony and the observable forms of the tradition. Deficient, nonrobust models for oral tradition were the rule. "Oral tradition" for many was a nominal placeholder for the tradition prior to its rapid movement into pre-Synoptic written sources. The analogy to oral saga was regulative for many. The narrative tradition was viewed as innately mythicizing and prone to being commandeered by dogmatic forces, the paradigm case being the formation of the Passion narrative. There was increasing cognizance—accelerated by Wrede—of the degree to which the faith of the early communities had affected the tradition. Authenticity, therefore, is most securely to be vested in the sayings tradition.

This gap between memory and the tradition that nineteenth-century criticism failed to close will be exploited by form criticism. Form criticism will all but completely sever memory from the Synoptic tradition.

---

135. Wernle, *Quellen*, 87.

Form Criticism: A Copernican Revolution?

THE PRINCIPAL ISSUE RAISED for Synoptic critics by Wrede's *The Messianic Secret* (1899) was not his undermining of confidence in the Markan narrative as a historical basis for a life of Jesus. Before and even after Holtzmann, source critics were quite prepared to allow that the Markan narrative was a literary contrivance, a contingent arrangement of traditions. Rather, it was Wrede's inference to historical skepticism. Some embraced this inference, regarding *The Messianic Secret* as inaugurating a new dispensation in gospel scholarship. Others rejected it, at least in its strong form, while nevertheless accepting that Mark was shot through with early Christian theology and so, taken as a source, could not be accepted at face value as a reliable narrative representation of the ministry of the historical Jesus. Their response was two pronged. On the one hand, they mounted critiques of Wrede's analysis of the Markan secrecy motif. On the other they took up afresh the longstanding project of finding a Jesus to liberal Protestant tastes in a primitive source. But Wrede, it seemed, had written the epitaph to this as a *source history* project. The whole enterprise therefore shifted, with scarcely a bump, to *tradition history*: the quest to identify the impeccably authentic primitive source became the quest to identify the impeccably authentic stratum of the tradition buried under layers of community dogma. The alternative did not bear thinking about: to accept Schweitzer's damning of the entire enterprise, declare the search for the liberal Jesus a dead end, and follow Schweitzer in reframing analysis of the Jesus tradition—and of Jesus—within the historical, cultural, and social realities of first-century Jewish Palestine. For these interpreters, trained as theologians, tradition history was a history of christological development, not what it in fact is—a project of cultural formation. This line of analysis in its modified, tradition-history manifestation reaches its apex in form criticism. Source history remains a leading factor in this enterprise, inasmuch as opinion gelled (though never completely solidifying) around the 2DH, which therefore provided the the source-critical baseline for the new tradition-history quest. For our media-analysis line of inquiry, what is of particular interest is how both Q and Mark, as written sources, come themselves to be assimilated to tradition-history forces.

THE POST-WREDE PROLOGUE TO FORM CRITICISM

Johannes Weiss

For Weiss the two document hypothesis is no longer something to be argued but "a secure source-critical result."[1] Against Wrede he points out that Jesus's messianic identity pervades the Markan tradition; it is no theological overlay but its foundational assumption. The explicit secrecy motif is certainly a Markan theological device, but Mark deploys it to align this messianic faith theologically to the cross.[2] Weiss therefore agrees with Wrede that the evangelist is not so much writing a biography as he is advancing certain dogmatic conceptions.[3]

Weiss: Markan Tradition and Memory

To vindicate the gospel against Wrede's claim that of the historical Jesus in Mark only "pale residues" remain, Weiss pivots to the oral tradition.[4] The contrast between the liveliness and pointed detail of the Markan episodes and the bland uniformity of the transitional connections between them shows, he says, that the evangelist is bearer of a "community tradition" that he is bequeathing to the next generation.[5] The local coloration and incidental detail are residues of the eyewitness origins of Mark's narrative tradition. The prominence of Peter points to his being the proximate source of this memory tradition.[6]

---

1. Johannes Weiss, *Das älteste Evangelium: Ein Beitrag zum Verständnis des Markusevangeliums und der ältesten evangelischen Überlieferung* (Göttingen: Vandenhoeck & Ruprecht, 1903), 1; also "Die drei älteren Evangelien," in *Die Schriften des Neuen Testaments*, ed. Johannes Weiss, 2nd ed. (Göttingen: Vandenhoeck & Ruprecht, 1907), 31–525 (35).

2. Weiss, *Evangelium*, 56–58, 143–44. Resurrection, he says, is the vindication of this messianic faith, not its source.

3. Weiss, "Evangelien," 34, 40; *Evangelium*, 2–3, 19–21.

4. William Wrede, *The Messianic Secret*, trans. J. C. G. Greig (London: James Clarke & Co., 1971 [1901]), 131.

5. Weiss, *Evangelium*, 111–12, 119, 169.

6. Weiss, *Evangelium*, 56, 63–65, 140, 178, 193; "Evangelien," 42–43.

But there are additional eyewitness sources as well: Simon of Cyrene, father of Alexander and Rufus, who were members of the Roman church, and the women of Galilee that witness the crucifixion. In naming these persons Mark identifies them as his eyewitness sources for these episodes.[7] Another tributary is a "school tradition," comprising the disputes and controversies. These lack the local coloration and Petrine perspectival angle that distinguish the other narrative materials.[8] That is, they lack eyewitness credentials, and are therefore of little interest to Weiss, for it is in the eyewitness memory tradition that he finds what he is looking for: "the most primitive layer [*die älteste Schicht*] of the gospel tradition," which is at the same time the most historically authentic layer (*geschichtlich unanfechtbar*).[9] This discovery reinforces Weiss's Wrede critique, for messianic belief pervades this layer of the tradition.[10]

To be sure, he says, this layer is not without supernatural elements: eyewitnesses remembered Jesus's healings and other extraordinary occurrences against the horizon of their prescientific mindset.[11] Though affected to some extent by Old Testament narratives, these episodes have an irreducible surplus of nonderivative elements. It is a matter of authentic memories being *shaped* by Old Testament narrative patterns.[12]

Nevertheless, inauthentic traditions have indeed overlaid and extruded into this bedrock memory stratum. As a specimen of oral saga, Weiss says, the oral tradition was prone to mythicization and folkloristic legend-building. This operated as "a law [*ein allgemeines Gesetz*] of the development of a tradition" that in concert with the naïve religious enthusiasm of the community was bound to overmaster the memory elements.[13] Dogmatic forces were likewise freely at play in the tradition. Christological interpretation of the Hebrew Bible stimulated vigorous narrative growth that grafted itself onto the simple messianic faith of the memory traditions. The gospels are not so much historical sources as they are witnesses to the faith and religious enthusiasm of the community. Yet, though supervening upon the historical tradition, these forces are far from having overcome it. To the contrary, what the tradition attests to is a concern

---

7. Weiss, *Evangelium*, 333, 340.

8. Weiss, *Evangelium*, 368.

9. Weiss, "Evangelien," 43.

10. Weiss, *Evangelium*, 362.

11. Weiss, *Evangelium*, 212–14, 364; "Evangelien," 48–50.

12. Weiss, *Evangelium*, 243–44, 320–26; "Evangelien," 46.

13. Weiss, *Evangelium*, 204, 333; "Evangelien," 39, 45–50 (quotation 45), 231. The manifestation of these traits in the apocryphal gospels confirms the operation of these tendencies in the early tradition (45–46).

to ground faith in the risen Christ in his historical person. But given this state of affairs, the task of the historian is like the geologist's: to drill down through the strata of the tradition to the authentic memory bedrock, there to find, at least in outline, the historical Jesus.[14]

Weiss: The Sayings Source as a Memory Deposit

What does Weiss say about Matthew and Luke, and their common sayings materials? Matthew and Luke are first and foremost mediators of a received tradition. In both gospels the identity and personality of the evangelist recedes behind the tradition. The evangelists take over the narrative tradition with a few modifications in its received Markan form. Though skilled in Greek composition, Luke only very partially works over his Markan materials, diverging conspicuously from the practice of Greco-Roman historians and biographers. The profile and complexion of the triple tradition in all three remains remarkably uniform.[15]

But in addition to Mark, Matthew and Luke make independent use of an instructional source, a *Redenquelle*. The formation of the sayings tradition, Weiss says, lies in the primitive Palestinian community's concern for moral transformation in anticipation of the impending kingdom of God. To this end they engaged in the work of remembering and cultivating Jesus's teachings. Since in Weiss's view the primitive community had no independent cultus, its chief orientation would be to Jesus's teachings. Many had heard Jesus's words (*Ohrenzeugen*), and this group was essential to the enterprise of establishing the didactic tradition. Quite early this body of tradition was shifted to a written format. The Gospel of Luke best conserves the original form and sequence of this source: the shorter-length, separate speech arrangement of the double tradition in Luke corresponds to the less artificed form this body of materials would take in an oral, memory-based tradition.[16] Again we see the profile of the double tradition in Luke being used to impute subliterary, oral qualities to the sayings source, and then on those grounds to claim that it is the sediment of the original theological thinking of the primitive Palestinian community.

As he was with Mark, Weiss is not so much interested in this didactic source as a written work as in the history of its tradition, which, he says, was not static but dynamic. Cognate sayings circulating in the ambient Jewish

---

14. Weiss, "Evangelien," 32, 39–40, 45–53.
15. Weiss, *Evangelium*, 9, 23–24; "Evangelien," 36–38, 230–31, 407.
16. Weiss, "Evangelien," 256–57, 408.

cultural register likely entered the tradition secondarily, attracted by analogy to authentic sayings.[17] On the other hand, Weiss finds the notion that the early communities created new sayings risible on the face of it. That the sayings tradition underwent transformations in dynamic adaptation to contingent community environments is another matter: this is what has generated patterns of variation (e.g., the Lord's Prayer), interpretive elaborations and expansions (e.g., the Beatitudes; the divorce saying), and the like.[18]

It follows that the sayings tradition requires the same critical sifting as the narrative tradition. It is in the primitive layer of the sayings tradition, Weiss says, that one finds the historical Jesus: a Jesus opposed to rigid Jewish legalism and purity codes, a Jesus who teaches a joyful piety founded in simple trust in God as heavenly father, a trust founded upon God's providential goodness manifest everywhere in the beauty of the natural world. For us today, Weiss says, God's existence is likewise revealed in the regularities of the natural world. The sensational wonderworker of the later tradition will always be foreign to us, but the authentic Jesus of the oldest tradition is a Jesus to whom we can relate.[19]

Weiss: The Tradition/Memory Nexus

Weiss wrestles with the memory-tradition nexus problem: trying to reconcile the observable profile of the tradition with his claim for its direct eyewitness derivation—more precisely, of its primitive layer. The tradition lacks the autobiographical point of view, the "clarity and definiteness of personal recollection."[20] On the other hand, one finds countervailing indicators: elements of local color and inessential detail in a sizeable subset of the Markan episodic tradition.[21] The call of Peter, Andrew, James, and John (Mark 1:16–20) is a case in point. Weiss notes its condensed narrative configuration, its concentration on a single action, the unusual suddenness of Peter's response, the rhythmic qualities of the narrative, and its patterning after the Elijah/Elisha story. Yet its details in all their sparseness are saturated in local color and contextual, even technically accurate realism. How to resolve this conundrum? Weiss acknowledges that "what we have here is far from the first recounting of the event but a highly developed, stylized depiction." The condensed narrative

---

17. Weiss, "Evangelien," 58.
18. Weiss, "Evangelien," 60–66.
19. Weiss, "Evangelien," 51, 64–65.
20. Weiss, *Evangelium*, 159, also 360.
21. E.g., Weiss, *Evangelium*, 178, 193.

configuration of the tradition approximates the form in which the eyewitness himself came to recount the event in his preaching. Like Paul's account of his conversion in Galatians 1:13–17, Peter's retellings in his preaching converged on the salient elements of his experience, whereas any nonsalient details rapidly faded from memory.[22]

Because of the correlation he makes of eyewitness testimony to historical authenticity, Weiss needs to establish the eyewitness credentials of these Petrine traditions. He therefore makes a categorical distinction between this bedrock layer of the tradition, constituted of authentic eyewitness accounts, and later inauthentic strata generated by mythicizing and dogmatic forces. The difficulty is that it is hard to see any differences in the form and complexion of the *memory* materials that Weiss assigns to the bedrock layer and the *tradition* materials of later strata. His core argument therefore is that the bedrock materials, in addition to their explicit connections to Peter (or some other named eyewitness), are more realistic and less supernaturalistic. But he acknowledges passages where these criteria do not hold, such as the Feeding of the Five Thousand (realistic details), the sensational evening healings and exorcisms in Capernaum (in the middle of a Petrine section). The distinction he tries to make between realistic Petrine episodes and stereotyped controversy episodes ("school tradition") is also precarious: he must explain away the fact that the Feasting and Fasting controversies of Mark 2:13–22 are connected to a meal hosted by a named disciple.[23] Weiss therefore is not successful in demarcating a body of memory materials vis-à-vis the rest of the tradition. Impasses like this will give form criticism its pretext to eliminate the memory factor completely and to find the origins of the tradition in community *Sitze im Leben*.

Adolf Jülicher

The successive editions of Jülicher's *Einleitung in das Neue Testament* fall into the pre-Wrede and the post-Wrede period. They register the paradigm shift from the source-history approach to a tradition-history approach. We will use the 1900, 1906, and 1931 editions as our reference points for the shifts in Jülicher's views (the 1919 edition does not differ significantly from the 1906 edition). He also gives a quite helpful statement of his views in *Neue Linien in der Kritik der evangelischen Überlieferung*, published in 1906.[24]

22. Weiss, *Evangelium*, 138–39.
23. Weiss, *Evangelium*, 159–60.
24. Adolf Jülicher, *Neue Linien in der Kritik der evangelischen Überlieferung* (Giessen: Topelmann, 1906).

For Jülicher likewise the 2DH is not something to be argued for but a point of departure.[25] In the 1900 *Einleitung* Jülicher describes Mark and Q much in the manner of a nineteenth-century source critic. Q is a selection of Jesus's most important sayings that were circulating in the primitive Palestinian community. They were written down "with all possible fidelity." In form the work is subliterary, "composed without any exercise of conscious art"; its composer gave just a perfunctory topical organization to the collection, which in genre resembles the sayings of the wise in Greek literature. Shortly after, this Aramaic work was translated into Greek. From this archetype other Greek versions were made; hence Matt/Luke variants in their otherwise close verbal agreement in Greek.[26] As regards the Gospel of Mark, Jülicher holds that "broadly speaking, the life of Jesus did unfold itself in the way in which Mark describes it."[27] The evangelist's baseline tradition has its origins in Petrine memory. The tradition that the evangelist was the Jerusalemite John Mark coheres with the profile of the Gospel.[28]

The 1906 *Einleitung* more or less repeats these claims.[29] A more accurate guide to the shift in Jülicher's views at the time is his *Neue Linien*. A ditch (*Graben*), Jülicher says, separates the Synoptics' story of Jesus from the actual story (*wirkliche Geschichte*) of Jesus. The Markan evangelist's intent is not to deliver a historical biography of Jesus; rather, he conveys Jesus as he lives in the faith of the primitive community. The evangelist is not a proxy for those who still remembered Jesus; theological reflection has overwhelmed memory. Source-criticism has led us back to Mark, but it has not led us back to the historical Jesus. The primitive source turns out to have a thoroughly dogmatic complexion.[30]

We see that Jülicher in principle accepts Wrede's verdict on Mark. But he declines to jump onto the skeptical bandwagon. Instead, he says, we have commenced upon a "new epoch in historical Jesus research," albeit one whose results will be not so secure as those source history hoped to deliver.[31] Jülicher

---

25. Adolf Jülicher, *An Introduction to the New Testament*, trans. Janet Penrose Ward (London: Smith and Elder, 1904; German edition 1900), 348–55; *Einleitung in das Neue Testament*, 5th ed. (Tübingen: J. C. B. Mohr [Paul Siebeck], 1906), 306–23.

26. Jülicher, *Introduction* (1900), 306–7, 356–59 (second quotation 356), 378 (first quotation).

27. Jülicher, *Introduction* (1900), 318.

28. Jülicher, *Introduction* (1900), 318–19.

29. Jülicher, *Einleitung* (1906), 276–79.

30. Jülicher, *Neue Linien*, 70–76; also Adolf Jülicher and Erich Fascher, *Einleitung in das Neue Testament*, 7th ed. (Tübingen: J. C. B. Mohr [Paul Siebeck], 1931), 352.

31. Jülicher, *Neue Linien*, 76.

finds Wrede's take on the messianic secret motif in Mark to be rather less than compelling. Markan messianic elements, he observes, cannot be so cleanly separated out from the narrative tradition. How can the Passion predictions be bracketed without qualification as unhistorical, when the motif is integrally formative of the Anointing at Bethany? One must either hold that the entire episode in all its elements is fabricated or concede that it—and the suffering motif in the tradition—is grounded in primitive memory. And this is no isolated case. In effect Jülicher takes Wrede's argument *ad absurdum*: removing the elements of messianic faith from the tradition leaves one without an intact tradition. By the same token, he points out, the sharpness of the wedge that Wrede drives between a nonmessianic tradition of a prophet and a messianic overlay leaves him at a loss to explain the rise of the community's messianic faith. Wrede tries to claim that it was resurrection faith, but "being resurrected and being Messiah are two different things."[32]

Jülicher is therefore more confident about the potential of the Synoptic tradition to yield up results to critical historiographical analysis. But the old, source-critical approach led to a dead end. The way forward is through reconstructing the history of the tradition, understood as a process of organic growth (*Wachstum*), and the evaluation of each little bit (*Stücklein*) of the tradition to distinguish the primitive and authentic elements from the copious secondary growth that is generated by the faith and the needs of the community.[33]

Mark and Q are tradition-history entities that lie at the far end of this gradual process of growth (*zu [seinen] jetzigen Umfang erst allmählich angewachsen*). One sees here the striking tendency to make *written works* the product of *tradition history* forces, to subsume literary history to tradition history. Jülicher's grounds for this are that primitive and secondary traditions can be seen to stand side by side in Mark. And if Mark, a unitary authorial artifact, so much more Q, a "loose collection" of sayings.[34] For Mark and Q the time span for secondary growth of their tradition is just thirty to forty years, a period that corresponds to the generational cycle of the founding cohorts of believers in Palestine, both Galilee and Jerusalem. The odds therefore are good that deposits of authentic traditions are to be found in both, though like the nineteenth-century source critics, Jülicher is particularly interested in the sayings tradition.[35]

32. Jülicher, *Neue Linien*, 23 (quotation), 27–30.
33. Jülicher, *Neue Linien*, 75.
34. Jülicher, *Neue Linien*, 46.
35. Jülicher, *Neue Linien*, 54–55.

In the earlier edition of the *Einleitung* Q *simpliciter* is a sayings collection with eyewitness credentials.[36] In the 1906 *Einleitung* this property is imputed just to its "primitive core" (*der älteste Kern*).[37] The source is now reconceived as the outcome of "gradual growth." This is also Jülicher's explanation of its narrative elements: the primitive sayings collection, originating "long before Mark," has evolved toward the form of a narrative gospel such that it amounts to a defective gospel (*Halbevangelium*), a gospel *manqué*.[38] In the 1931 (seventh) edition of the *Einleitung*, Jülicher and Fascher describe Q as a "growing layer of oral tradition" (*eine . . . in mündlicher Tradition wachsenden Schicht*) that eventually underwent a redaction that gave it a written hypostasis.[39] This has affinities to the form-critical account, but in its essentials Jülicher expresses it already in 1906. In fact, it simply registers a further development out of the long practice, going far back in nineteenth-century source criticism, of imputing subliterary qualities to the sayings source and pushing it under the *Aufzeichnung* rubric, the provisional collections that under the prevailing media assumptions were assumed to have formed a necessary transitional link between the oral tradition of the "primitive community" and the literary activity of Synoptic writing.

The Synoptic tradition as it presents itself to the critic in Mark and Q exists in multiple layers (*Schichten*). The task at hand is to the distinguish authentic, historical layer of the sayings tradition and the narrative tradition from the layers of community theology, to separate Jesus "as he actually was" (*wie er wirklich gewesen war*) from the Christ "that lived in the hearts of his community."[40] The bedrock authentic layer will be the memory layer. The most high-yield vein for mining authentic materials will be the sayings tradition. It stands closest to the simple messianic Christology of the primitive community, which had not decisively broken with the frameworks of Palestinian Judaism. That it was the Palestinian community that shaped the tradition, undertook its provisional collection, and bequeathed it, all before the passing of the first generation, likewise precludes our succumbing to historical skepticism. For this community was geographically centered in the "native land" of the early memory of Jesus, in local continuity with Jesus himself.[41]

---

36. The corresponding pages in the 1901 German edition translated by Janet Penrose Smith are 298–99.
37. Jülicher, *Einleitung* (1906), 322–23, 335.
38. Jülicher, *Einleitung* (1906), 322.
39. Jülicher & Fascher, *Einleitung*, 348–49.
40. Jülicher, *Neue Linien*, 6; *Einleitung* (1906), 327.
41. Jülicher, *Neue Linien*, 72–73.

It also precludes driving a wedge between the historically authentic base layer of the tradition and the inauthentic layers reflecting the Christ of community dogma. Whatever creativity is to be attributed to the primitive community, Jülicher says, is catalyzed by the memory of Jesus's words and deeds. Inauthentic elements in the tradition are derivative of the authentic memory elements; they are outgrowths from the kernels of memory. A nondescript, "many-headed" sociological entity, "the community," is manifestly incapable of creating the striking materials of the tradition whole cloth out of its own theological impulses. The evangelists exercised little creativity in generating new tradition: how can a creative energy so obviously lacking to the Synoptic authors be attributed to a vague community? The faith of the community may have generated the evangelical portrayal of Jesus, but it is the historical Jesus who birthed the community and its faith, a faith that expresses the significance of the historical Jesus in a way that a critical historian never can.[42] The forces driving the development of the tradition must therefore lie in the memory-based elements themselves.

The first step toward gospel writing, Jülicher continues, was the early appearance of modest provisional collections (*Aufzeichnungen*) of traditions. The next step was taken by the Markan evangelist; he fashioned a narrative framework for the gospel materials that became normative.[43] Though the Markan evangelist is cognizant of a teaching tradition, narrative tradition is more apropos to the missionary purpose he conceives for the gospel.[44] The subsequent consolidation of the narrative tradition and the sayings tradition in Matthew and Luke is the predictable effect of a consolidating impulse, itself triggered by altered exigencies.[45] In 1931 Jülicher adds that the sayings source would have been connected with the *Sitz im Leben* of paraenesis (*Lehrbetrieb*). "Consequently the integration of sayings tradition and narrative tradition would initially not have been self-evident."[46]

Julius Wellhausen

Julius Wellhausen's account likewise reacts to Wrede, whose theory of a non-messianic tradition, he says, is wrong. In his lifetime Jesus must have excited

---

42. Jülicher, *Neue Linien*, 27, 55–56; *Einleitung* (1906), 329–31, 341.
43. Jülicher, *Einleitung* (1906), 342.
44. Jülicher, *Introduction* (1900), 326–27, 357–58; *Einleitung* (1906), 286; *Neue Linien*, 50–52; Jülicher and Fascher, *Einleitung*, 348.
45. Jülicher, *Einleitung* (1906), 342, 386; *Neue Linien*, 52–53.
46. Jülicher and Fascher, *Einleitung*, 348.

belief that he was the Messiah of Jewish expectations. For if he was not crucified on those grounds, the rise of the Christian belief in his messiahship and
his proclamation as such by the community is scarcely explicable.[47] Wellhausen agrees, however, that the Markan evangelist has foisted the Christian
dogma of the Messiah on the base tradition to such an extent that the hope,
cherished since C. H. Weisse, that the gospel could serve as the historical basis
for the life of Jesus must be given up.[48]

For Wellhausen, therefore, analysis shifts to the Markan *tradition*. In what
can only be exasperating for the historian this tradition is not at all like historical reportage but much more like folklore, shaped to satisfy the popular
taste for the extraordinary and the sensational. Papias's testimony that Mark
gets his materials from eyewitness informants is manifestly worthless. The
tradition as it stands is remote from any origins it may have in eyewitness
testimony. It has undergone drastic reformulation in the direction of saga,
with a correspondingly precipitous reduction in historical clarity (8, 37–48,
155–56). In Wellhausen's view, that is, the base tradition itself is compromised;
it has become opaque to the originating historical events. This is not due to
dogmatic distortion but the consequence of the transmutation of memory
(which for Wellhausen equates to historicity) into folklore and saga, that is,
into the forms of the tradition itself.

The Markan tradition, Wellhausen further claims, constitutes the near
comprehensive deposit of this primitive Christian tradition, narrative *and*
sayings. The evangelist's project was the gather up all the tradition. Non-
Markan materials in Matthew and Luke have little claim to authenticity. The
Markan tradition, that is, constitutes the primitive layer of the tradition (61,
75, 156–57). The Q tradition likewise is secondary to the Markan tradition. The
conventional view that Q is more primitive than Mark, Wellhausen says, is
just a vestige of Papias's claim that the earliest composition was by the apostle
Matthew (158). As regards the work itself it is the Lukan double tradition that
best represents Q's original format. And contrary to the habituated scholarly
prejudice that Q is subliterary, Wellhausen observes that the sayings sequences
preserved in Luke are in fact finely wrought didactic arrangements (69–70,
162). All one needs to do, he says, is to compare these with Mark's scattershot
sayings tradition, little more than raw oral tradition, to see that Q registers
a more advanced stage of tradition-history development (75, 161). Further,
in Mark the dogmatic overlay on the primitive tradition is superficial. In Q,

---

47. Wellhausen, *Einleitung*, 82.
48. Wellhausen, *Einleitung*, 154 (hereafter page citations will be in the text).

christological dogma has had time to infuse the materials more deeply: tradition and dogma have converged. The Q speeches unfold under the aegis of Jesus's messianic authority right from the beginning. In Luke 10:22//Matt 11:27 Q even comes close to evolved Johannine Christology. Accordingly, much of the Q tradition is inauthentic (166–68).

No pristinely authentic layer of tradition, therefore, is to be found in Mark and Q no matter how far down one drills. But Wellhausen demurs from a hard skepticism. Instead he affirms what amounts to a reception approach. The tradition permits "inferences from the effect to the cause, from the stream to the source," though the historian must be reconciled to the reality that secure historical results are out of reach. Though both Mark and Q issue from the primitive Jerusalem community (*Urgemeinde*), Mark is the more promising source, for though its base tradition is the product of folkloric transformation, the Markan Jesus has escaped significant dogmatic distortion. Not so the Q tradition, though the spirit of Jesus still breathes in its teachings (169–70). The Christ of Christian faith, Wellhausen says, is the effect (*Nachwirkung*) of the historical Jesus who excited Jewish messianic hopes. The ethics of the Christian community are the effect of Jesus's teaching, an effect that his martyrdom could only intensify. The historical Jesus is the condition of Christian faith, not its antithesis (103–4).

Wellhausen refers to the primitive Markan tradition as "memories" (*Erinnerungen*), as "the old memory tradition" (*die alte gedächtnismäßige Tradition*). Its base substance is eyewitness memories that have undergone rapid distortion not only in folkloric transmutation but in the religious enthusiasm of the eyewitnesses themselves. Its eyewitness basis nevertheless ensured that the primitive tradition took its color from the deeds and teachings of the historical Jesus. This notwithstanding the sharp contraction of what would have been a mass of memory materials to a circumscribed, cramped deposit of fragmented sayings and folkloric narratives adapted to the popular taste for the sensational and miraculous, a species of popular remembrances of Jesus. Then, as this restraint fell away with the decline in influence of eyewitnesses, the early phase of *contraction* of the primitive tradition gave way to a phase of its unrestrained *expansion* with inauthentic materials generated by the faith of the community. The evangelist Mark has no connection with eyewitnesses, but he worked up his gospel not long after this shift got underway and thus remains grounded in the primitive tradition (45, 156–57, 168–69, 174).

Like Jülicher, Wellhausen supposes quite reasonably that the tradition must have had a substantive starting point in memory, and that inauthentic materials could hardly spring *ex nihilo* from community faith. They must be interpretative growths upon this living core of traditional materials. But he never closes the gap between eyewitness testimony and the observable forms of the tradition, never describes precisely how the memory materials undergo transmutation into the popular folkloric forms of the tradition. By the same token the popular folklore, oral saga analogy, doubtless applied by Wellhausen with good effect to the Hebrew Bible materials, gets rather crudely applied to the Synoptic tradition.

Adolf von Harnack

The post-Wrede collapse in the Gospel of Mark's status is starkly evident in Harnack's 1907 monograph on Q. Harnack's disparagement of the Second Gospel borders on vehemence. Mark is "chock full of contradictions, inconsistencies, and incredible elements which drive the critical scholar to despair." The evangelist "cannot distinguish between the original and the secondary, the reliable and the dubious; in his intemperate apocalypticism he throws the door open to anything."[49] Harnack privileges the sayings source as the primitive, authentic grounds of the tradition. But he intensifies this to the point of positioning it in *antithesis* to the Gospel of Mark and its Passion and Resurrection narrative.

Harnack has not signed on to reimaging Q as the product of tradition-history processes. Like the nineteenth-century source critics he approaches the sayings source as a premeditated composition, textually uniform and integral. Harnack views double-tradition variation patterns through the spectacles of a text critic— that is, as versional variants that develop in the natural course of things in the diverging lines of written transmission of the original Greek translation. For this same reason he decides that the Q-status of low-agreement parallels, such as the Parable of the Pounds and the Parable of the Banquet, is dubious.[50]

Though far from being the first source critic to have this interest, Harnack brings the sayings source into focus as a distinct work with its own textual profile. He argues that it has a linguistic, thematic, and stylistic texturing distinguishable from Matthew's and Luke's, and that it is textually more of single cloth than either of them, or Mark for that matter (111–18). Likewise, far from being a "formless" subliterary collection, its materials are designedly ordered in a sequence of moral topics (*Sachordnung*). The work has an intelligible, even chrono-

---

49. Adolf von Harnack, *Sprüche und Reden Jesu*, Beiträge zur Einleitung in das Neue Testament 2 (Leipzig: J. C. Hinrichs, 1907), 173.

50. Harnack, *Sprüche*, 32, 80–81 (hereafter page citations will be in the text).

logical metastructure; it begins with the Preaching of John the Baptist, and it concludes with an outlook on the eschatological future. Its genre affinities are to "sayings of wise," a genre common in Judaism, and this also accounts for why it does not incorporate a Passion narrative. That a specimen of this genre—a Λόγοι Ἰησοῦ—should emerge in primitive Christianity is hardly surprising given that the community construed Jesus's ministry under the conventional rubrics of his *teachings* and his *deeds*. The pragmatic orientation of the sayings source correlates to its genre: instruction of disciples (hence the prominent position of the Sermon). Its narrative elements, such as they are, are aligned to the work's instructional vector. It is not the healing that forms the climactic element of the Healing of the Centurion's Servant but Jesus's pronouncement on the centurion's exemplary trust in the power of Jesus's word (127–28, 136–48, 158–59).[51] It is unclear whether Harnack is current with the latest tradition-history approaches (though he takes a swipe at Wellhausen). He is an intellectual historian, not a journeyman gospel critic. But it is easy to see why he would disdain them as a viable account of the origins of the sayings source.

The Q instructional materials, Harnack continues, are infused with an understated messianic Christology that cannot be traced to a dogmatic or apologetic agenda. Its source is Jesus's own messianic consciousness, which has sprung from consciousness of his uniquely intimate sonship relation to God, not out of the febrile apocalyptic enthusiasms rampant in his time. The messianic profile of the Q materials, that is, is historically authentic (162–70, 209–10).

Here we come into touch with Harnack's strategy for salvaging the liberal Protestant project from the ruins of Mark: to identify Q in all of its elements as the uniquely authentic deposit of authentic Jesus tradition, to make it the sole basis for all true understanding of the historical Jesus. Q, he avers, is free of any theological or apologetic *Tendenz* of the sort rife in Matthew, Mark, and Luke. The work has only one agenda: to give a simple presentation of Jesus's preaching in its chief points (118–22, 162). Papias's testimony to its Matthean authorship cannot be validated, but the source clearly has an immanent connection to apostolic memory (146, 172).

Privileging the sayings tradition over the narrative tradition is not new; it is habitual in nineteenth-century criticism. But Harnack pushes the distinction to the point of an antithesis (*fundamentale Unterschied*) between the narrative gospel, Mark, with its materials aligned forward to the Passion and Resurrec-

---

51. Harnack thinks that, on balance, Matthew better preserves the original arrangement of the sayings source than Luke (127), but his description of Q's formal characteristics does not depend on that perspective.

tion narrative, and the sayings source Q, an ingenuous presentation of Jesus's sayings; between Mark, in the grip of apocalyptic fantasies and Paul's theology of the cross, and Q, wholly free of dogmatic distortion. So intent is Harnack on distancing the sayings source from the narrative gospel that he extends their polarization to *geography*, indeed as far as north is from south: between Q, whose geographical horizons are circumscribed by Galilee, and Mark, whose climactic passion narrative centers upon Judea and Jerusalem (118–19). Harnack can barely conceal his disgust for Mark and its apocalypticism, its crude Passion theology, its contradictions and discrepancies, its undiscriminating enthusiasm, its crass supernaturalism.

Elsewhere Harnack attributes the absence of a Passion narrative in Q to differences in genre; here he ratchets it up to a fundamental contrast in religious outlook: the sayings source is not theologically oriented to the Passion narrative. Harnack launders Q of any trace references to the Passion. The saying on taking up one's cross, he says, may not even be original to Q, and its reference to the Passion in any case is only indirect. So intent is he on distancing Q from even the scene of the Passion that he purges its Jerusalem references: the Announcement of Judgment Luke 11:49–51//Matt 23:34–36 is not a Jesus saying (118–21). The narrative interest in Jesus's crucifixion that generates the Passion narrative—in its turn the progenitor of the narrative gospel genre itself—is a belated development, the outcome of apologetic and dogmatic impulses in primitive Christianity that take the mild eschatological elements in Jesus's preaching to exaggerated extremes. (One need not waste time looking for Harnack's arguments for this staggered development, for he does not offer any.) The primitive eschatological outlook of the Palestinian community, and of Jesus himself, is preserved in Q's simple messianic Christology (162, 171–72). Matters do not end there, however. The projects of Matthew and Luke are attempts, driven by this *Tendenz*, to suppress (*verdrängen*) the authentic Jesus of Q, to suborn him to the dogmatic agenda of the Passion narrative gospel. But this machination "will always find its refutation" in the pure religious and moral preaching of the Jesus of Q, a work which likely bore just the simple incipit: Λόγοι τοῦ κυρίου Ἰησοῦ οὓς ἐλάλησεν διδάσκων—of the simple knowledge of God, of repentance and trust, of renunciation of the world and the gaining of heaven (173–74).

Harnack retrieves the nineteenth-century liberal project by substituting Q unqualifiedly for Mark as the basis for recovering the predogma Jesus of history. But one sees why he is hailed as a founder of modern Q studies. All the seeds of contemporary Q studies lie in his exposition. His sharp Q/Mark antithesis will find its reception in Bultmann, who will place the

Palestinian sayings source Q and the Hellenistic cult narrative Mark at the opposite extremities of a *religionsgeschichtliche* trajectory. Anticipating the form-critical postulate that the narrative interest (*bios*) is a later development on a tradition-history evolutionary trajectory, Harnack claims that Q forms "the preliminary stage [*Vorstufe*]" to the emergence of the narrative gospel (159). The geographical correlate that Harnack gives to his antithesis will in due course receive a sociological hypostasis in the Galilean Q community. Christologically autonomous Jesus movements are not far over the horizon. The effect of so decidedly cutting off the sayings from the larger body of early Christian tradition, however, is to make Q pliant to any theological schema whatever, a Rorschach test on which anyone can project any theological or social history of Christian origins whatever, an effect that becomes all the more pronounced once the form critics perfect the reconception of Q as a tradition-history entity.

Walther Haupt

Walther Haupt's idiosyncratic source history, published in 1913, found no traction. But it is a perfect case study for reconstructing the transition from nineteenth-century source criticism to form criticism. It confirms that form criticism is not so much a break with nineteenth-century source criticism as it is a continuation of its project and working assumptions. Haupt develops his history of the tradition from Wrede's sharp distinction between authentic nonmessianic material and inauthentic messianic materials. He attributes little historical worth to Mark as a work. In fact, authenticity is not to be imputed as a property to any particular written source. Rather, authenticity and inauthenticity exist blended and on a continuum within the tradition itself. This continuum maps to the overall historical trajectory of the tradition, imagined as a process of organic growth from buried seeds of memory, but it also exists at the small-scale level within each of its individual units. Unsullied authenticity, that is to say, is to be found nowhere in the tradition. On the other hand, Haupt's tradition history is a matter of gradually amalgamating, increasingly complex *written* sources. There is as yet no breakthrough to a new conception of the origins of the tradition and its history of development.

Haupt: Tradition History as Source History

For Haupt, giving up the dream of pristine authenticity does not mean abandoning the quest for authentic tradition, even if this is now to be understood only in relative terms. The project of "disentangling the various threads of the tradition, of distinguishing the older materials from the more recent and from the very recent, of tracing the development and growth [*Werden und Wachsen*] of the material" can proceed apace, in confident expectation of identifying a residue of "authentic words of Jesus," which in fact, he says, remains now as it always has been the object of the source-critical enterprise.[52]

Like other post-Wrede Synoptic critics Haupt shifts to a tradition-history approach, within the wide framework of the 2DH. But he construes *tradition history* as *written source history*—that is, as a series of stages from primitive written collections to intermediate written amalgamations of the latter, in turn redacted by the evangelists into their coherent gospel histories. His first priority, therefore, is to work out a redaction history for Q, in a schema featuring a Q^1, a Q^2, and a Q^3. His redaction history is an artifact of his stratum-differentiation criteria. The "Q" designator, he says, "refers not to a unitary collection of instructional speeches but to a historical sequence of three easily distinguishable enterprises of collection layered one upon another."[53] The first layer, Q^1, is a primitive discipleship instruction (*Jüngerrede*). It comprises the Mark/Q overlap passages (i.e., a layer shared by all three Synoptics), quite a bit of the Matt 10/Luke 10 Mission Instruction, Judaism-exclusive Matthean special materials from a primitive Palestinian stage of the Jesus movement, scattered elements from the Sermon on the Mount, the Parable of the Sower and some Matthean parables, and Matt 24/Luke 21 eschatological materials that betray a pre-70 outlook on an imminent parousia. The ethical-formation materials taken up in Q^1 are characterized by their intense eschatological motivation. The Mission Instruction gives the redaction its coherence. In due course a redactor incorporated a cycle of dispute stories (corresponding to Mark 2:1–3:6; 11:15–12:40) into this Q^1 source to create Q^2. This redactional initiative registers a further stage in the community's theological history, corresponding to the mission of Paul, when the status of the law has become a pressing issue. For this reason the Antitheses found in Matthew 5:21–32 also are to be assigned to this Q^2 redaction (11, 23, 35, 46–47, 155, 206–7).

Haupt assigns the bulk of the double tradition *per se* to Q^3. His reasons? Mark contains only the overlap passages, and he is unaware of double-tradition expansions of the Beelzebul Accusation, the Sign of Jonah, the Parable of the Leaven, and the like. Mark therefore knew the source only in its $Q^1 + Q^2$ per-

52. Walther Haupt, *Worte Jesu und Gemeindeüberlieferung: Eine Untersuchung zur Quellengeschichte der Synopse*, UNT 3 (Leipzig: Hinrichs, 1913), 1.

53. Haupt, *Worte Jesu*, 11 (hereafter page citations will be in the text).

mutation. Hence the Q^3 redaction is to be placed after the Gospel of Mark and before the appearance of the Gospels of Matthew and Luke (9–10). The double-tradition layer comprises the bulk of the source's instructional materials, and Haupt labels it *Didaskalia*. Its instructional sequences have a uniform literary profile, which indicates that the layer originated in a single compositional initiative, not through gradual accretion around nuclei of Jesus sayings (209). Its didactic sequences are grounded not in the authority of the law but in direct appeals to divine patterns. One also finds in these materials an openness to Gentiles along with a rejection of Judaism for its spurning of the proclamation. As such it stands in the sharpest tension with the Gentile-exclusionary Q^1 of the primitive Palestinian community and the preoccupation with the law that marks Q^2. Accordingly, though still of a Jewish-Christian complexion the Q^3 redaction registers a later stage of the community's theological and social trajectory. A law-free, universalistic outlook is coming to prevail; the community has broken with Judaism; its horizons are no longer the narrow confines of Jewish Palestine but the wide Hellenistic world (192–99, 206–7).

Haupt's three Q redactions plot out his history of the tradition. Other sources now get grafted to this trajectory at various junctures. Behind the triple-tradition patterns of agreement and variation Haupt sees the utilization of four sources. In addition to Q^2 Mark makes use of G (*Grundbericht*), a primitive collection of Jesus's deeds, combining it with a special source (*Sonderquelle*) that generally runs parallel with G. Matthew and Luke use Mark, but they similarly have at their disposal the older G source. Sometimes they independently opt for the G parallel, or select individual elements of a G parallel, over Mark. When they both do this, it generates agreements against Mark. Use of the G source also accounts for Luke's omission of Mark 6:44–8:27 (the G source lacked these materials that Mark has added from another source, and which Luke recognizes as duplicates) and for his divergences from Mark and Matthew in the Passion narrative (93–95, 123, 145). Mark, as noted, also has an episodic special source that runs parallel to a number of G sequences. Mark's supplementary use of his parallel *Sonderquelle* explains cases of three-way variation in the evangelists' common materials. Luke has his own parallel *Sonderquelle*, which explains his unique patterns of variation as well as his divergent narratives such as the Rejection at Nazareth and the Call of the Disciples. His Passion narrative is a combination of G and his *Sonderquelle* (54, 91, 230).

The number of large written sources that Haupt has feeding into the written Synoptics stands at four: G, Q, S^{Mk}, S^{Lk}, five if one counts separately $Q^{1,2}$, used by Mark, and Q^3, used by Matthew and Luke. But these sources themselves originate as amalgamations—in what is best described as hybrid collection-redaction operations—of an array of earlier written collections (*Sammlungen*; *Aufzeichnungen*; *Abschnitte*) (69–71, 164–65, 175). The formation of Q itself is understood by Haupt as a dynamic process, across its three redactions, of gradually expanding complexes of instructional sequences (*Redekomplexen*) that have nucleated around individual sayings of Jesus (155). The Synoptic narrative sources (G, and its near *Doppelgänger* S^{Mk} and S^{Lk}) originate in the combination of two written collections of oral traditions (*Erinnerungskomplexe*), one of Galilean episodic traditions from John the Baptist forward, and one of Jerusalem Passion traditions. These were subsequently attached to each other to form a basic episodic sequence (*Stammbericht*), which became the basis, the common spine (*Gerippe*) for the Synoptic narrative sources. But because this written *Stammbericht* circulated among communities of Palestinian believers in different locales, with different inventories of memory, and with different community interests, it came to exist in variant versions that then fed into and were fixed in the Synoptic sources. This is a chief cause, Haupt says, for the patterns of variation in Synoptic narrative parallels (148–49).

The picture that Haupt paints is that of successive source layering (*Schicht an Schicht gesetzt*). Its method is distinguishing of layers (*Quellenscheidung*). This is tradition history conceived as dynamic source history: primitive, simple written collections, gradually amalgamating into more complex collections, a process that finds a *telos* in the comprehensive redaction of these complex sources for the first time into a cohering, intelligible work by the evangelist Mark, emulated by Matthew and Luke (91–92, 183–91, 229, 249).

Haupt: Tradition History, Memory, and Authenticity

The oral tradition is nevertheless not quite a null factor. The consistency in the complexion of the Synoptic materials, which creates complications for demarcating its layers, is due to the "levelling effect" of the oral tradition (91–92). In addition, the oral tradition is the depository of memory. Its origins lie in eyewitness recollections; in fact, some of its variation arises from events being differently recalled (107, 148). The two earliest written collections of the narrative tradition that together formed the primitive *Stammbericht* Haupt refers to simply as memory-complexes (*Erinnerungskomplexe*). The speech-aggregate (*Redekomplexen*) profile of the Q^1 collection originates in the effort to fix individual sayings of the Lord in writing, which owing to their brevity and pithiness had been easily assimilated to memory (155). Taken in aggregate the bookrolls of large Synoptic sources G, Q, S^{Mk}, and S^{Lk} constituted "a first valuable body of *Memorabilien* from the life of Jesus, containing important memories that were still circulating in the contemporaneous [fourth to seventh decades AD] Jerusalem circles" (175).

Nevertheless, that the oral tradition is memory substance (*Erinnerungsstoff*) does not make it a bedrock layer of authenticity—though Haupt certainly identifies any residually authentic elements in the tradition with memory traces. Like normal human memories the memories of early Christians would have quickly faded in freshness and clarity and would have thinned out in number. But more to the point: memories of Jesus were filtered through the newborn messianic faith of community. They would have been immediately caught up in the community's urgent project of preaching, defending, and converting others to its messianic faith. Memories not apt for those ends would have fallen by the wayside. In short, Haupt says, the retroactive messianic coloration of the life of Jesus (Wrede's theory is Haupt's premise) began the moment that early Christian memory met early Christian faith (149–53).

Like his contemporaries Haupt thinks that the sayings tradition was less susceptible to these forces than the narrative tradition. Authentic elements will accordingly be found at greater concentrations in the sayings tradition. But he qualifies this significantly: sayings too were swept up in the messianic preaching, with the consequent loss of connection to their originating historical contexts. He holds, moreover, that it is the individual saying in its bare form that will constitute the authentic memory kernel of the tradition. Didactic sequences and narrative frameworks will be secondary and inauthentic.

What induces Haupt to make this claim so confidently, as if it were self-evident? It goes to his conception of the memory-tradition nexus. Because he directly associates early Christian memories to the primitive tradition, he imputes the imagined cognitive limitations of individual memory to the tradition and its transmission. Only the short, pithy saying (*einzelnes Diktum*), he says, is apt for easy assimilation to memory; longer sequences not at all. It follows that individual dominical sayings are the memory seeds of the tradition; their didactic and narrative elaborations are secondary expansions. Haupt points to the finely wrought didactic sequences of the double tradition. Suppose that Jesus did actually utter one of these speeches. Memory, he claims, would not have been capable of holding and transmitting it. The speeches and their elements are therefore mostly to be declared secondary and assigned to the late stratum Q^3. Indeed, in the course of time even Jesus's individual sayings would fade out in memory (167–71, 209, 250). Not even in the sayings tradition, therefore, does one encounter a firm ground of authenticity. The narrative frameworks for Jesus's sayings are likewise by and large secondary. The divorce saying appears in raw memory form in Matthew 5:32; in Mark 10:2–12 it is worked up into a narrative (*zu einem Erzählungsstück umgearbeitet*) fitted out with scriptural citations. But for this reason, he says, one can have a high level of confidence in the authenticity of the pronouncement elements of the Q^2 dispute stories (167–68).

Here let us pause to let the strangeness, even preposterousness of Haupt's assertions sink in. Is memory really only capable of remembering short, pithy sayings? Are humans, individually or corporately, incapable of remembering events, incapable of giving them narrative representation? Is it your cognitive experience, reader, that maxims and proverbs ineluctably fade from your memory? Haupt's extraordinary claims would be just a historical curiosity if they did not reappear in Bultmann and influence subsequent generations of scholars. Why would these claims even seem plausible to Haupt and his contemporaries? Given the scholarly tradition that Haupt stands in, they make perfect sense. They simply reprise the liberal Protestant trope: the privileging of Jesus's words over his deeds, the sayings tradition over the narrative tradition, albeit taken to a new level. The narrative tradition is now not just marginalized. It is erased from memory, made an epiphenomenon of dominical sayings.

Haupt: Identifying the Authentic Element of the Tradition

Though his account seems a throwback to nineteenth-century source criticism, we see that Haupt shares with his contemporaries the shift to an ostensibly tradition-history model for Synoptic gospel origins. Different from other critics that we have looked at, however, he takes Wrede's theory full strength—the bifurcation in the tradition between elements that express the messianic faith of the community on the one hand and authentic elements on the other (188). Likewise, the impulse driving the formation of the tradition is not orientation to the past but the contemporary community dynamics that pull authentic memory elements into their currents (250–51). Holtzmann, Weiss, Jülicher, and others pointed out in their critique of Wrede that the messianic element pervades the tradition. Haupt agrees. His response is simply to deny unqualified authenticity to any element of the tradition with messianic coloration. The outcome is predictable: a vanishingly small deposit of authentic tradition, mostly dominical sayings.

Haupt nevertheless adds a not unimportant qualification. Unalloyed authenticity, he says, is to be found nowhere in the tradition. Authenticity is a relative quality, not wholly absent even in traditions stemming from community theology. Sayings fabricated by community dogma may well have the color of Jesus's authentic teaching. Notwithstanding that the Antitheses (to take one example) reflect community preoccupation with the law some two decades after Jesus, they retain authentic accents of his new morality. The converse is also true: even authentic sayings cannot help but be colored by the dogmatic interests that they have been made to serve (162–67). Haupt likewise hesitates to impute blanket inauthenticity to the narrative tradition. Mark's narrative *Sonderquelle*, he says, is much less touched by dogmatic *Tendenzen* than the parallel *Grundbericht*. Some of its traditions still approximate to primordial memories (*Erinnerungsstücke*) not yet pulled very far into the dogmatic obscurity of messianic interpretation. Its version of John the Baptist's preaching has not yet become an explicit messianic announcement (176–78). Here Haupt shows a recidivistic tendency to attribute differential levels of authenticity to *sources*. This further confirms our suspicion that that the newfangled tradition-history approach is simply the older source-critical enterprise behind a tradition-history façade.

What the tradition-history perspective grants Haupt, however, is a way to visualize *continuity* between the authentic memory elements of the tradition on the one hand and inauthentic, community-generated elements on the other. The problem for a sharply dichotomous model of the tradition like Haupt's is to explain the workings behind the large-scale manufacture of community tradition. As Haupt himself puts it starkly in his sweeping classification of the Q^3 instructional speeches as inauthentic, "Either they are without exception uttered by Jesus, or they are the production of a later time" (209). What then is this so prolific production activity of a later time? Haupt singles out the authentic memory elements as the force driving the history of the tradition, as the leavening agent infusing it. Inauthentic tradition is profuse interpretative outgrowth, like sprigs and new buds, from the authentic memory elements, stimulated when these come into contact with the life of the community. Jesus's disputes with Pharisees that get incorporated into Q^2, for example, are narrative extensions of Jesus's authentic pronouncements about the law into the community's disputes with its contemporary opponents (168–69, 209).

Haupt and Form Criticism

A modicum of familiarity with nineteenth-century and then early twentieth-century scholarship is enough to call in question the view that form criticism amounts to a kind of Copernican revolution in Synoptic scholarship. Haupt may be a very minor luminary in the scholarly firmament, but his inability to conceive tradition history in any terms other than source history leads us to ask whether the form critics are really breaking free of the source-critical framework either. For Haupt the history of the tradition is a matter of a series of layers (*Schicht an Schicht gesetzt*), conceived as source criticism always has as a progression of written sources of decreasing authenticity. The whole model will get taken over in form criticism, which will substitute oral-tradition layers for written-source layers—little more than a relabeling exercise.

In Haupt's schema this is also a progression of written sources of increasing size and complexity, growing by combination into larger aggregates (*Komplexen*) of tradition, though in line with the general shift in scholarly perspective to tradition history he applies the metaphor of organic growth to this process. Form-critical tradition history will likewise be a matter of growing, increasingly complex aggregates of tradition. Haupt sets the evangelists' projects qualitatively apart from their sources as "redaction" (*Redaktion*) to "collection" (*Sammlung*) (165). This *Sammlung/Redaktion* binary reappears as an essential feature in form criticism. Haupt stands here in a long source-critical line that sees a lengthy phase of provisional written collections (*Aufzeichnungen*) preceding and feeding into Synoptic gospel writing. The form-critical *Sammlung/Redaktion* binary will be a permutation of this schema, with the difference that the "provisional collection" stage gets redesignated an oral phase. The form-critical account of the growth of the oral tradition in aggregating complexes is derivative of the *Aufzeichnung* model of provisional written collections that is itself symptomatic of defective nineteenth-century understandings of oral tradition.

Nevertheless, to leave matters there is to do form criticism an injustice. There must be something that accounts for its emergence and decades-long dominance as the cognitive framework for Synoptic criticism.

THE FORM-CRITICAL TURN

Hermann Gunkel and the Sitz im Leben

The form critics adapted a model worked out by Hermann Gunkel for Hebrew Bible form criticism. The literature of the Hebrew Bible, Gunkel observes, has a long oral prehistory. Oral tradition circulated in discrete genres, each of which was connected to a particular community *Sitz im Leben*: the law in the courts, victory songs at the return of victorious armies, prophetic oracles, laments, and hymns in their corresponding social settings, and so forth. Genres were also correlated to different groups: Torah with priests, prophets with oracles, and the like. This ensured the purity of the genre.[54] Narrative and poetic materials

---

54. Hermann Gunkel, "The Literature of Ancient Israel," in *Relating to the Text: Interdisciplinary and Form-Critical Insights on the Bible*, trans. Armin Siedlecki, ed. Timothy J.

belong under the rubric of oral saga. They may be variously classified under myth, folktale, fable, legend (religious legends and aetiological cult legends such as the Passover narrative), and novella, i.e., tales of the more developed sort. By definition oral saga is legendary, and popular; it is not "a sufficient medium for history." It contains historical elements only residually, recast as poetry and legend. The primitive cultural mind is mythopoeiic, not objective and rational. History writing is an elite, literary enterprise. Passing through many hands over long eras, generation upon generation, Israelite saga has long lost contact with authentic historical memory, which in Gunkel's view requires conceivable pathways for eyewitness transmission.[55]

The materials of oral tradition are the creation of the primitive Israelite community. The oral tradition is the immanent expression of its spirit and imagination. The Romantic schema of the primitive, saga-bound, enthusiastic community, situated at the beginning of a long cultural evolution toward cultural sophistication and rational artifice, controls Gunkel's history of Israelite oral tradition. A given oral tradition, Gunkel alleges, first circulates in its pure genre form, owing to its tight correlation to a particular *Sitz im Leben* and to a specific tradent group. Mixed genres therefore will be an effect of later literary refinement.[56] Gunkel's cultural evolution model becomes even more all-encompassing: cognitively people at this primitive cultural stage had only "limited attention span" and thus were incapable of transmitting more than short units of just one or two lines. Short aphorisms, for example, uttered in prophetic ecstasy are the most primitive units of prophecy. These gave way to longer speeches as prophets evolved the corresponding cultural and cognitive ability, but even these remained at a very primitive level of organization, asyndetic serializations of individual utterances loosely associated by topic.[57] As Gunkel sees it, the condensed forms and corporate characters (e.g., Joseph's brothers are simply "the eleven," or "the brothers") of oral tradition are not a cognitive strategy but symptomatic of primitive folk psychology, the "poverty of comprehension" of the primitive mind, its inability "to conceptualize and portray differences among people."[58]

To this cultural evolution corresponds a literary evolution. Simple units, at first circulating as isolates within discrete *Sitze im Leben*, began to aggregate into larger oral complexes, initially through like being attracted to like. The

---

Sandoval, Carleen Mandolfo, and Martin Buss; JSOTSup 384 (London: T&T Clark, 2003), 26–83 (30, 35–41).

55. Gunkel, "Literature," 30, 43–48; *Genesis*, trans. Mark E. Biddle (Macon, GA: Mercer University Press, 1997; German 3rd ed., 1910), vii–ix (quotation viii), xvi, xxvi–xxvii.

56. Gunkel, "Literature," 31; *Genesis*, xxvii–xxviii.

57. Gunkel, "Literature," 30, 61; *Genesis*, vii.

58. Gunkel, *Genesis*, xxx–xxxiii.

longer prophetic speech noted above is one instance of this evolution from simplicity to complexity. This oral process of collection continued seamlessly into written collections. But the written medium also opened up the opportunity for larger collocations of materials of different genres, and for increased redactional artifice, a process that eventually issued in the editorial combination of larger sources into the completed Pentateuch.[59]

Gunkel's cultural evolution schema is familiar to us from Herder forward. It is evidence of the remarkable staying power of the Romantic paradigm. Taking oral saga with its legend-building propensities as the paradigm for oral tradition is a long-familiar feature of this approach. The Romantic notion of evolutionary progress from primitive-simple through to advanced-complex stages of culture, however, is pronounced in Gunkel. Its presence reflects the influence of what James Turner describes as contemporary "theories of progress of civilization through universal stages." It owes something to the widespread concern at the time to connect humanistic lines of inquiry to the models and thus to the prestige of the natural sciences.[60]

Much of Gunkel's account in its specifics is simply taken over by Bultmann and Dibelius, not least his correlation of a genre to a specific *Sitz im Leben*, also his association of the primitive community with literary primitivity. Gunkel's seminal idea—that a genre arises from a typical sociological setting in life—"is largely mistaken."[61] That aside, Gunkel never argues that the sociological dynamics of a life setting *generate* the tradition. He explicitly denies that the relationship between the sociohistorical realities of a *Sitz* and a given tradition is homeostatic.[62] Both of these claims, however, are elements of Bultmann's history of the tradition. Another oddity is that Bultmann compresses the entire cultural evolution from primitive to advanced, which for Gunkel can only unfold over hundreds of years and multiple generations in ancient Israel, into the first Christian generation.

Richard Reitzenstein, Wilhelm Bousset, and the religionsgeschichtliche *Approach*

Another enabling development for Synoptic form criticism was the theory of the history of religions school (*religionsgeschichtliche Schule*) that Hellenistic

---

59. Gunkel, *Genesis*, lxix–lxxiv.

60. James Turner, *Philology: The Forgotten Origins of the Modern Humanities* (Princeton, NJ: Princeton University Press, 2014), 252.

61. Martin J. Buss, *The Changing Shape of Form Criticism: A Relational Approach* (Sheffield: Sheffield Academic, 2010), 58.

62. Gunkel, *Genesis*, lxxvi–lxxvii. Contemporary realities, he says, certainly shape the selection and use of a tradition, but the tradition cannot be reduced to those realities.

Christianity was a syncretistic *kyrios* cult like other Hellenistic mystery cults, a theory articulated by Richard Reitzenstein and others, and taken up by Bultmann most directly from Wilhelm Bousset's *Kyrios Christos*. Reitzenstein created a synthetic construct: *the* Hellenistic mystery cult, of which all the diverse cults—Osiris/Horus, Attis, Adonis, Mithras, the older Greek mysteries, and so forth—were simply variants. Mystery cults, he claimed, featured a dying and rising deity, cultic union with whom brought the initiate salvation, immortality, even divinity. All featured a sacred liturgy, sacraments of initiation, notions of a personal bond of initiate with the deity. They were salvation cults; one can even speak of a gospel (*Evangelium*) of Isis. They required faith (πίστις) in the deity. They featured preaching, thanksgivings, interpretation of sacred texts, miracle literature, and missionary outreach.[63] The apostle Paul was the radical Hellenizing agent who transformed the Palestinian Jesus movement into a Hellenistic mystery cult, a process already underway incipiently in the Hellenistic Christian communities.[64]

The Hellenistic mystery cult so understood has been discredited as a pseudo-construct, a forced synthesis (using Christian beliefs and practices as its template) of features of diverse cults that actually had few commonalities, one of which was decidedly not a dying and rising deity. Our interest, however, is in the influence of Wilhelm Bousset's account of the history of the tradition, which took this mystery-cult schema as its basis, on Bultmann.

Like his early twentieth-century contemporaries, Bousset construes tradition history as theological history, or better, as *Religionsgeschichte* (roughly, "religious-development history"). The oldest stratum of the tradition reflects the messianic faith of the primitive Palestinian community, filtered through the apocalyptic Son of Man concept. Jesus's crucifixion would have shattered the disciples' notions of an earthly Davidic Messiah. Understandably, therefore, the community's first interpretation of its Easter experience was that Jesus had been exalted to heaven (not resurrected). Its recharged messianic beliefs took the form of faith in Jesus as the transcendent, coming Son of Man. For Bousset this means that the apocalyptic Son of Man and cognate elements in the tradition are the "deposit of the theology of the primitive community."[65]

63. Richard Reitzenstein, *Die hellenistischen Mysterienreligionen: ihre Grundgedanken und Wirkungen*, 2nd ed. (Leipzig: B. G. Teubner, 1919), 7–10. In its essentials Bultmann reproduces this essentializing account in *Primitive Christianity in Its Contemporary Setting*, trans. Reginald H. Fuller (Philadelphia: Fortress, 1980), 157–60.
64. Reitzenstein, *Mysterienreligionen*, 66, 256–57.
65. Wilhelm Bousset, *Kyrios Christos*, trans. John E. Steely (Nashville: Abingdon, 1970), 33, 42 (quotation), 49, 73, 80.

Of the Palestinian tradition the materials of the Logia collection are the most primitive. This is evident, Bousset says, from its paucity in miraculous materials. In fact, it is likely a kind of "gospel of the Lord's words."[66] The Logia has fewer elements that are intrusions of community theology. The messianic announcement of Malachi 3:1 (Matt 11:10//Luke 7:27) and the apocalyptic Son of Man sayings are elements of the theology of the primitive community, whereas "all things have been handed over to me by my father" (Matt 11:27// Luke 10:22–23) is a late Hellenistic intrusion (83, 89). Things are quite otherwise with the narrative tradition. The miracle narratives are a secondary growth upon the authentic tradition that healing activities were part of Jesus's ministry. Miraculous legends of Jewish and Hellenistic provenance were attracted to this base tradition and attributed to Jesus (100–103, 108–9). The source of many of the Passion narrative episodes is interpretation of prophecy in the primitive community. "'Prophecy and miracle' therefore are the driving force in the expansion of the gospel narrative" (113). The interpretation of Christ's death as an atoning sacrifice that one finds in Paul is largely absent from this tradition of the Palestinian community (115).[67]

Thus it is the Logia collection that preserves the authentic gospel of Jesus: his joyful teaching of simple, daring trust in God, his battle for "simplicity and plainness in religion," of "the duty of fellowship in righteousness and love and mercy and reconciliation." This pure ethical gospel though was too austere for the religious imagination, and it is thanks to the primitive community's encasement of it in the narrative symbolism of the mythical, the apocalyptic, and the miraculous that it has been able to exert its powerful effects upon piety (116–17).

Bousset's tradition history is a progression of sharp disjunctions: between the historical Jesus and the Son of Man Christology of the primitive Palestinian community; between the Christology of the primitive Palestinian community and the syncretistic *kyrios* Christology of the Hellenistic churches. *Kyrios* Christology originates in Hellenistic mystery-cult piety: it was the form of

---

66. Bousset, *Kyrios Christos*, 98 (hereafter page citations will be in the text).

67. This claim is essential to the disjunction Bousset wants to maintain between Palestinian and Hellenistic Christianity, though he acknowledges, uncomfortably, that the idea was prominent in the Old Testament and central to the Jerusalem cult. The claim is also hard to square with the enterprise of Old Testament christological interpretation that he imputes to the primitive community. He tries to get around the difficulty by saying that the atonement theology "leads first of all to the tradition of the Hellenistic community" (which is question begging), and then suggesting that the primitive community derived "Christ died for our sins according to the Scriptures" from the Jewish martyr tradition.

address to the cult deities, such as Osiris, Isis, Serapis, Atargatis, and Hermes
(146–47). Hellenistic Christianity in fact displays all the accoutrements of a
Hellenistic mystery cult: baptismal initiations into the deity's dying and rising,
atonements, sacred meals in the presence of the cult hero, narratives of the
deity's miracles. To be sure, the Palestinian community had its sacred meal, the
Lord's Supper, but the meal did not have the cultic significance that it received
in the Hellenistic churches (131–37).

The Hellenistic *kyrios* cult is also the place of the emergence of divinity
Christology: Jesus is the cult *deity*, present in mystical union with his initiates. Old Testament monotheism was too entrenched to have been modified
by Palestinian believers, for whom Jesus remained the eschatological Son of
Man with messianic trappings. Only in Hellenistic mystery piety were the
conditions favorable for it. Hellenistic *kyrios* Christology all but submerges
Palestinian Christology, leaving it a residual, half-forgotten presence in the
tradition (147–52, 164–65). The simple Old Testament idea of God's gracious
forgiveness of sins in the preaching of Jesus and the Palestinian community is
turned into a redemption religion of the suffering and dying *kyrios Christos*.
To the simple interpretations of the symbols of the Palestinian Lord's Supper,
"this is my body . . . this is the covenant in my blood," were associated "given
for you . . . shed for the remission of sins" (182, 306).

It is on this *Religionsgeschichte* loom that Bultmann will weave his history
of the tradition, combining it with Harnack's antithesis of sayings tradition
to narrative tradition. Bousset never gets beyond a history of Christology,
which gratuitously doubles as a history of the tradition. He never explains
how *religionsgeschichtliche* and christological impulses, how the "faith of the
community," actually generates the tradition. A vague appeal to Easter faith is
his go-to rationale for all developments. He never reflects on how his proposed
religionsgeschichtliche stages in the history of the tradition can stand in such
sharp discontinuity from one another, how successive *religionsgeschichtliche*
developments in the tradition seem to get on with so few footholds in the
earlier tradition—in fact, he goes to pains to minimize any possible cross-
junctures. Like so many grand theories of Synoptic gospel origins, he rarely
engages with the actual materials of the tradition, with Synoptic minutiae.

Bousset's—and Bultmann's—procedure is intelligible, however, as a routine
application of the prevailing *religionsgeschichtliche* methodology. The scholars
of the *Religionsgeschichte* school abjured literary criticism. They construed
the text instead as a *religionsgeschichtliche* entity—as the end-product of a
dynamic history of a tradition accumulating layer upon layer of foreign ele-

ments as it passed through different religio-cultural spheres.[68] From its outset the *religionsgeschichtliche* school suffered from unclarity on the relationship between tradition history and *Religionsgeschichte*. Tradition history was subsumed to *Religionsgeschichte*—for Bousset the terms were interchangeable. Tradition history simply *was* syncretistic development along a *religionsgeschichtliche* trajectory. The corollary method was to peel off, one by one, the text's *religionsgeschichtliche* layers until one reached the authentic kernel of the tradition in the originating experience of a powerful religious personality, "the primevally primitive as the unadulterated" (*das Uranfängliche als das Unverfälschte*) as Paulsen aptly puts it. It follows that elements in the Synoptic tradition identified as *religionsgeschichtliche* layers around that nucleus will be foreign elements by definition, and the end form of the tradition will have only a tenuous genealogical connection to its beginnings in Jesus and the primitive Jerusalem community.[69] Conversely, authorial function in the work's genesis will be reduced to a vanishing point: the work is the end product of a community's social history.

This is Bultmann's method exactly. It is manifestly defective. Tradition cannot be reduced to a product of its *religionsgeschichtliche* contexts. A cultural tradition in fact is a potent entity that *reacts* with its cultural environment and *shapes* it reciprocally. Its defective premises make Bultmann's history of the tradition to all intents and purposes worthless. Its continued influence as a cognitive *episteme* in contemporary Christian origins scholarship is itself worthy of study. We will take a more microscopic view the specifics of Bultmann's history of the tradition, using the media/memory lenses of our study.

Rudolf Bultmann

The names of both Rudolf Bultmann and Martin Dibelius are associated with form criticism, but Bultmann's schema has been the more influential and consequently will engross our attention.[70] The two document hypothesis is the

68. Henning Paulsen, "Traditionsgeschichtliche Methode und religionsgeschichtliche Schule," *ZTK* 75 (1978): 20–55 (31–32).

69. Paulsen, "Traditionsgeschichtliche Methode," 24–26, 37–42; Gerd Lüdemann and Alf Özen, "Religionsgeschichtliche Schule," *TRE* 28 (1997): 618–24 (622).

70. K. L. Schmidt likewise prepared the ground for form criticism; see *Der Rahmen der Geschichte Jesu: Literarkritische Untersuchungen zur ältesten Jesusüberlieferung* (Berlin: Trowitzsch & Sohn, 1919); *The Place of the Gospels in the General History of Literature*, trans. Byron R. McCane (Columbia: University of South Carolina Press, 2002, German edition

framework for form criticism. The Synoptic problem itself has become (for a time) a peripheral issue. The focus of form criticism is the tradition. Erich Fascher points out that from Herder and Eichhorn forward the individual episode (*Einzelgeschichte*) was recognized to be the base unit of the tradition, but the success of the Markan hypothesis led to the marginalization of the oral tradition. Only with Wrede's attack on Mark's historical reliability did critics begin to examine the tradition apart from its written framework.[71]

But as we have observed, it is an error to view form criticism as a sort of Copernican revolution in Synoptic studies. Many nineteenth-century source critics had engaged with the tradition and its history, though to be sure, within constricted media horizons. And no different than it was for the source critics, for Bultmann analysis is a matter of working back through the "layers" (*Schichten*) of the tradition to the most primitive. For Bernhard Weiss the object of source history was "to distinguish sources as the layers of the tradition." Bultmann echoes this exactly: the object of form criticism is "to separate out the layers of Mark and to determine which comprises the old historical

---

1923). By showing that the Markan narrative framework is just an exogenous expedient Schmidt hopes to end to the misguided quest for an authentic source and direct attention what is truly of importance: the oral tradition. In their substance the units of the tradition converge on the christological and the ethical, effectively the timeless elements. Accompanying topographical and chronological information is perfunctory and indeterminate. Characters in the narratives are reduced to representational, sometimes moral types. A number of episodes have traces of eyewitness memory in their sparse situational details, which Schmidt regards as accidental residues. That is to say, memory and tradition are distinct phenomena. These individual narratives would begin to aggregate into larger oral complexes, connected by καί in primitive asyndetic sequences, some of which, he thinks, would have been written down. The Markan evangelist took these complexes (e.g., Mark 2:1–3:6) directly over into his compilation, throwing around them a loose redactional skein, knotting them together with transitional summaries that he composes out of elements of the tradition. The evangelist is principally a compiler of oral tradition—similarly Matthew and Luke, though they give their source some literary reworking. It is the tradent ethos that controls the work of the evangelists, not the authorial personality of the ancient literary biographer. Like the anonymous scribes of the Hebrew Bible the evangelists function principally as conduits of an authoritative tradition. The Gospel of Mark is *Kleinliteratur*, without close affinities to the genres of elite literary culture. It is a translucent window onto a sociological entity, the anonymous community that has created—and been created by—the tradition. Its existence as a written source is tangential to the sociological reality.

71. Erich Fascher, *Die formgeschichtliche Methode: eine Darstellung und Kritik, zugleich ein Beitrag zur Geschichte des synoptischen Problems* (Gießen: Töpelmann, 1924), 48–49.

tradition."[72] His history of the tradition remains lodged within the nineteenth-century source-critical paradigm.[73]

Bultmann: Sitz im Leben, *"Tendencies," and the History of the Tradition*

Form criticism's claim is to have identified the generative factor of the tradition: community *Sitze im Leben.* The forms or genres *(Gattungen)* of the tradition are immanent expressions of the sociological and theological forces definitive of community *Sitze im Leben.* The forms of the tradition are generated and shaped (Dibelius: *geschaffen, ausgebildet*; Bultmann: *hervortreiben, entspringt aus*) by these forces.[74] Though subsequently subject to folkloric laws of development, Dibelius says, the "ultimate origin" *(letzter Ursprung)* of the tradition—or as Bultmann puts it more uncompromisingly, the point of its genesis *(Entstehungsort)*—is the *Sitz.*[75]

From origins in the *Sitz* a whole history of the tradition commences that Bultmann undertakes to elaborate, along with a corollary methodology for isolating its most primitive layer. From the intimate correspondence of form to a particular *Sitz* it follows that the simple or pure form will be the most original; conversely, this allows identification of secondary expansions and formations.[76] But for all the professions about the *Sitz im Leben* as the matrix of the tradition's origins, one is hard put to find anywhere that Bultmann explains specifically how a given unit of tradition has been generated by a *Sitz.* In working out his history of the tradition he in fact appeals chiefly to certain lawlike "tendencies" *(Tendenzen; Gesetzmässigkeiten)* organic to the tradition that

72. Weiss, *Quellen der synoptischen Überlieferung*, 256; Rudolf Bultmann, *Die Geschichte der synoptischen Tradition*, 4th ed. (Göttingen: Vandenhoeck & Ruprecht, 1958), 1. Also: "The whole tradition about Jesus . . . is composed as a series of layers which can on the whole be clearly distinguished. . . . By means of this analysis an oldest layer can be determined, though it can be marked off with only relative exactness" (Rudolf Bultmann, *Jesus and the Word*, trans. Louise Pettibone Smith and Erminie Huntress Lantero [New York: Charles Scribner's Sons, 1958], 12–13).

73. A media confusion lucidly identified by Werner H. Kelber, *The Oral and the Written Gospel: The Hermeneutics of Speaking and Writing in the Synoptic Tradition, Mark, Paul, and Q* (1983; reprint, with a new introduction by Werner H. Kelber [Indianapolis: Indiana University Press, 1997], 6–8).

74. Martin Dibelius, *Die Formgeschichte des Evangeliums*, 6th ed. (Tübingen: Mohr Siebeck, 1971), 7–8; Bultmann, *Geschichte*, 4–5.

75. Dibelius, *Formgeschichte*, 1, 7–8 (quotation); Bultmann, *Geschichte*, 8, also 40.

76. Bultmann, *Geschichte*, 7 (hereafter page citations will be in the text).

drive its growth. These tendencies are to be extrapolated back from Matthew's and Luke's redactional operations on Mark and—as far as they can be determined—on Q. This is because there is no difference in principle between the oral tradition and its written manifestations; the shift in medium is a matter of indifference (*gleichgültig*). This follows from Mark, Q, and indeed Matthew and Luke being specimens of *Kleinliteratur*, manifestations of folk tradition, innocent of literary artifice. Innate tendencies of tradition therefore become manifest in its Markan, Q, Matthean, and Lukan appropriations, and on into scribal operations in the manuscript tradition and novelistic developments in the apocryphal gospels. Extrapolating these laws (*Gesetzen*) of development back into the oral tradition gives Bultmann his confidence that he can expose its hidden history of development (7).[77]

One such tendency is to attach specific names and labels to otherwise anonymous actors in the tradition. From this Bultmann determines that any case of τις or τινές in the Synoptic tradition is more primitive than any parallel that has an identifier. Luke 11:15 identifies Jesus's interlocutors as τινές; Matthew 12:24 has "the Pharisees"; Mark 3:22 "the scribes." Accordingly, the Lukan parallel (i.e., the Q version) is the more primitive (12). In most of the controversy stories Jesus's opponents were originally anonymous; only subsequently did they come to be characterized as "scribes" and "Pharisees" (71). It is on the basis of this tendency that Bultmann similarly designates "the Twelve" as a secondary development from an indeterminate μαθηταί (370). In Mark 4:10 the evangelist must have appended σὺν τοῖς δώδεκα to the οἱ περὶ αὐτόν of the tradition (Mark 4:10). That in the manuscript tradition D, W, and Θ read more simply οἱ μαθηταὶ αὐτοῦ seems to belie the tendency, but Bultmann is ready with an explanation: for this particular scribe "his disciples" and "the Twelve" are synonymous (70–71).

But particularly crucial to Bultmann's evolutionary history of the tradition is the tendency for *sayings* to generate *narrative settings*. It is this tendency, he says, that has formed the bulk of the apophthegms and controversy stories. The *idea* contained in a logion tends toward narrative expression in an *ideal scene* that gives symbolic representation to the social and theological dynamics of a particular *Sitz* (8–9, 24, 40). The setting in Mark 3:31–34 of Jesus's family attempting to get in to see him has been generated by the logion of 3:35: "Whoever does the will of God is my brother and sister and mother." The Rejection at Nazareth (Mark 6:1–6) is a paradigm example of an ideal scene, a "community formation" (*Gemeindebildung*) composed out of a logion: "No prophet is with-

---

77. Also Dibelius: "immanent laws" (*immanente Gesetzen*) (*Formgeschichte*, 1).

out honor except in his own country" (29–30). That Luke 17:20–21 is a secondary formation around the primitive saying, "The kingdom of God is in your midst," is confirmed by the fact that the apophthegm conforms to the form of the Greek philosophical apophthegm (ἐπερωτηθεὶς ὑπὸ . . . εἶπεν . . .) and thus is Hellenistic in origins (24). Mark 10:13–16, Jesus Blesses the Children, has not been generated by the Mark 10:15 saying ("Whosoever does not receive the kingdom of God as a little child shall in no wise enter therein") but is likely an ideal scene spun out of the Jewish practice of blessing and certain Old Testament narrative motifs. Nevertheless, the truth (*Wahrheit*) expressed by the saying finds apt symbolic representation (*symbolische Darstellung*) in the narrative (32). This is a Straussian view of the tradition—Synoptic narratives give symbolic representation to ideal truths—that reappears in Bultmann in the form of a tendency of the tradition from sayings to narrative. Bultmann identifies only a small set of apophthegms in which the narrative setting and the logion form a "unified conception"—that is, in which the saying only makes sense paired with the narrative (25–27). His canon is that if an apophthegm saying *can* be read in isolation, then it originally circulated in isolation and the narrative framework is secondary (*eine nachträgliche Bildung*) (48–51).

The sayings, therefore, are the seeds, the germs, of the narrative tradition. Thereby Bultmann declares most of the narrative tradition inauthentic. This holds for the dispute narratives as well. "One can speak," he says, "of a creative [*zeugenden*] power of the dispute story, of a tendency of the community to clothe its dominical sayings, its viewpoints, and its precepts in the form of a dispute" (53). The generative *Sitz* of the dispute tradition is the community's internal and external debates about the law. Jesus's dialogues with disciples are a variation on the genre, a means to transmit an otherwise situationless saying (42, 57–58). However, a dominical saying was not essential for a narrative to form. In its various *Sitze* the Palestinian community proliferated new Jesus traditions, created "in the spirit of Jesus," that authorized its emerging praxis and theology. The dispute (Mark 2:5b–10) interpolated into the simple Healing of the Paralytic story (Mark 2:1–5a, 11–12) originates (*ist entstanden*) to authorize the community's claim to the right to forgive sins (13). The ideal scenes of apophthegms and dispute stories as community formations are symbolic projections of community *Sitze*. This follows from the premise that *Sitze* generate tradition. For Bultmann the dead giveaway is that in a number of these narratives, opponents challenge Jesus about the practices of his *disciples*—e.g., the disputes about eating with sinners (Mark 2:15–17), fasting practices (Mark 2:18–20), plucking grain on the Sabbath (Mark 2:23–28), and eating with unwashed hands (Mark 7:1–8). The corporate "disciples" character in these disputes is a kind of cipher for the primitive Palestinian community that is creating these scenes (14–16).

Bultmann holds that the apophthegm and the dispute tradition formed chiefly in the Palestinian community. The issues addressed reflect Palestinian realities; they employ typical Jewish forms of argumentation, not Hellenistic; the ideal scenes draw mainly from Old Testament narrative motifs; and the form itself has its closest analogue in rabbinic genres. Bultmann grants the existence of a Greek apophthegm (chreia) tradition, but Synoptic apophthegms that conform more to Hellenistic type are relatively few (e.g., Mark 13:1–2; 14:3–9; Luke 10:38–42; Luke/Q 17:20–21) (49, 63–64). Quite a number of prophetic utterances attributed to Jesus originate in ecstatic utterances of early Christian prophets in the Palestinian congregation. Bultmann comes up with this expedient to deflect Erich Fascher's criticism that form criticism grossly exaggerates the productivity of the primitive community (40–41, 134–35, 176).

Bultmann: Formation of Q in the Primitive Palestinian Community

So far the primitive Palestinian tradition: sayings, plus the apophthegms and dispute stories, both a subset of the sayings tradition. Taking the sayings tradition as a proxy for the primitive Palestinian community (the *Urgemeinde*) is a scholarly habit that by now should be very familiar to us. This is Bultmann's cue to move to the formation of the Q source. The source is whole cloth the product of oral tradition processes (as Bultmann conceives them). Q is a microcosm of his history of the tradition, construed pseudo-scientifically as a process of organic evolution.[78] Its origins lie in a tendency for free logia to aggregate with similar logia to form lengthening catenae (14, 86). This tendency is accelerated by another—a saying engenders variants by analogy (*Analogiebildung*). The three Sabbath healings Mark 3:1–6, Luke 13:10–17, and 14:1–6 have formed from this tendency; likewise the three Call apophthegms of Mark 1:16–18, 19–20; 2:14, and the catena Luke 9:57–58, 59–60, 61–62 (65, 88). The logia clusters in Q gradually aggregated in layers around originating nuclei though primitive techniques of catchword connection and loose topical association. The Q Beelzebul Accusation expanded by stages from an original apophthegm (Luke 11:14–18//Matt 12:22–26), to which was later attached Luke 11:19–20//Matt 12:27–28 (Jewish Exorcists; Spirit/Finger of God), and

---

78. Combined with a physics *reductio* or, as Mary Midgley expresses it, an "atomistic pattern of explanation in terms of movements of ultimate, unsplittable particles" (*The Myths We Live By* [New York: Routledge, 2011], 53).

subsequently Luke 11:21–22//Matt 12:29 (Binding the Strong Man). Matthew preserves the last stage in the formation of the cluster: the redactional connection of Jewish Exorcists/Spirit of God (Matt 12:27–28) with the Sin against the Holy Spirit (Matt 12:31–32) by means of Whoever Is Not with Me (Matt 12:30// Luke 11:23) (11–12). Judge Not (Matt 7:1–5//Luke 6:37–42) grew organically (*in verschiedenen Stadien gewachsen*) from the logion "Judge not, that you be not judged. For by the measure of your judgment you will be judged" (7:1–2). Be Not Anxious (Matt 6:25–34//Luke 12:22–32) forms around the kernel of the opening admonition, originally a primitive independent saying: "Be not anxious for your life, what you shall eat" (Matt 6:25//Luke 12:22). Subsequently, "consider the ravens . . . consider the lilies" (Matt 6:26, 28–30//Luke 12:24, 27–28), whether themselves originally independent units or spun out from the original saying, were joined with the opening logion (Matt 6:25//Luke 12:22) to form a primitive cluster. To this then accrued Matt 6:27//Luke 12:25 ("which of you by being anxious can add a cubit to his lifespan?") and then the reiteration sayings Matt 6:31–33//Luke 12:29–31, which are likely a secondary formation from the primitive cluster (91–92). The apophthegm and dispute tradition of the primitive Palestinian community that eventually will be taken up into the Gospel of Mark aggregates and grows in a similar manner (35).

In addition, there was a massive influx of inauthentic sayings into the tradition from the wider Jewish cultural matrix. This sizeable enlargement of the tradition from external sources cannot be associated with an innate tendency of the tradition. Bultmann therefore suggests that it was precipitated by Jesus's practice of occasionally appropriating a Jewish maxim into his own teaching. This gave the community license to do so on a large scale. The inrush of Jewish and in some cases Hellenistic wisdom elements was such as to make any judgment that a saying or parable is authentic very uncertain. Relative confidence is possible only when such is not derivable from Judaism or the primitive community, and when it displays traits characteristic of Jesus's preaching: eschatological intensity, ethical radicalism, antithetical contrast to mundane Jewish piety and morality (107–10, 220–22).

Out of this first phase, tradition *formation*, develops a second phase, *collection*—that is, the combination of sayings clusters by means of the same primitive connective techniques into larger preredactional complexes (*Sammlungen*). Here we observe the reappearance of the *Aufzeichnungen*, the "provisional collections," of nineteenth-century scholarship. The only difference is that Bultmann relabels them a stage of the oral tradition. Bultmann acknowledges that the large Q collection is not totally without traces of intelligible compositional arrangements, and he even suggests genre parallels with apocalyptic paraenesis of the sort attested by *1 Enoch* and the *Didache*. But he insists that it never transcends the level of a provisional, ad hoc collection, the product of prolonged, simple-to-complex organic development (*Wachstum*), its materials loosely aggregated by catchword and topic. Any redaction entailed in the act of collection was perfunctory, nothing creating an "organic unity." Like Mark's apophthegma materials (*Erzählungsstoff*), the rough collection serves Matthew and Luke as a source of raw sayings materials (*Redenstoff*) for their redactional activity (119, 160–61, 348–51, 362, 378, 393, 399 [quotation 393]).[79] These are patented nineteenth-century source-critical conceptions.

The localization of the sayings tradition (and the apophthegm tradition, in Bultmann's schema a growth out of the sayings tradition) in the Palestinian congregation allows Bultmann to take Q as a proxy for the faith of the primitive community and, just thinly veiled by that faith, the authentic preaching of Jesus. Bultmann's Palestinian congregation is the original "Q community." Bultmann will combine Harnack's extreme Q/Mark polarization with Bousset's *religionsgeschichtliche* schema—with its categorical distinction between Palestinian and Hellenistic Christianity—to spectacularly widen the distance between Q with its sayings Christology and the cross and resurrection kerygma of Mark. By turning the episodic frameworks of the apophthegms into "ideal scenes" generated out of the sayings and assigning the healing stories to Hellenistic Christianity, he is able to all but eliminate narrative from the tradition of the primitive community. One marvels at the sheer genius of the scheme.

The sayings source, says Bultmann, "is nearest to the primitive community"; it "bring[s] one face to face with the subjectivity of the community."[80] This follows from the form-critical premise that the forms of the tradition are a "sociological construct," the precipitates of a *Sitz im Leben*. The expressions of the community's life condense out (*niederschlägt*) in its tradition (4–5). From Q's low quotient of healing stories and high quotient of eschatological-ethical exhortation it follows that the *Urgemeinde* remembered Jesus not primarily as healer and miracle worker but as eschatological preacher and lawgiver (256). The christological tincture of the sayings source—Jesus as Son of Man and Messiah—is the community's Easter kerygma: the resurrection signifies the exaltation of the crucified Jesus as Messiah and coming Son of Man. This Chris-

79. Also Rudolf Bultmann, "What the Sayings Source Reveals about the Early Church," in *The Shape of Q: Signal Essays on the Sayings Gospel*, ed. and trans. John S. Kloppenborg (Minneapolis: Fortress, 1994), 23–34 (30–31). This is a translation of "Was lässt die Spruchquelle über die Urgemeinde erkennen," *Oldenburgische Kirchenblatt* 19 (1913): 35–37, 41–44.

80. Bultmann, "Sayings Source," 23, 25; also "The New Approach to the Synoptic Problem," *JR* 6 (1926): 337–62 (341–42).

tology remains securely within traditional categories of Jewish eschatology. The community's identity is bounded by the horizons of Jewish sectarianism: Jesus's coming and his resurrection is the signal eschatological event; the community is the eschatological congregation of the last days.[81] Nevertheless, in the enthusiastic Easter faith of the primitive Palestinian congregation that rings throughout Q one can still hear the simple moral preaching of the historical Jesus: that God desires radical obedience rather than obedience regulated by codified law; that "excluded from the demands of God are all cultic and ritual regulation," so that "along with ethics Jesus sets free the purely religious relation to God in which man stands only as one who asks and receives, hopes and trusts."[82]

Certain passages in Q are anomalous on this model. Bultmann dispenses with these by identifying them as elements of a later, Hellenistic stratum, that is, in terms of his own *religionsgeschichtliche* schema. Though in genre the Temptation is Palestinian, its connection of the title υἱὸς τοῦ θεοῦ to miracle-working is Hellenistic: in Jewish tradition wonders were associated with the Messianic Age, but the Messiah was not necessarily expected to be a wonder-worker (275). Reception of the Spirit in baptism is an element of the mystery piety of the Hellenistic church. The Baptism of Jesus pericope therefore belongs to the Hellenistic layer. In any case, there is little indication that Q, if it even referenced Jesus's baptism by John, had it in its Hellenistic form (267–69). Luke 10:21//Matt 11:25–26 (ἐξομολογοῦμαί σοι πάτερ κ.τ.λ.) is Palestinian, but Luke 10:22//Matt 11:28 (πάντα μοι παρεδόθη κ.τ.λ.) is a Hellenistic "revelation word." Here and there in Q one can identify smaller Hellenistic growths upon the Palestinian materials (172, 179).

Bultmann: The Hellenistic Narrative Materials and the Gospel of Mark

This brings Bultmann to his Hellenistic stratum of tradition. If the sayings and apophthegm tradition is Palestinian, the healing and miracle stories (*Wundergeschichten*) are, on the whole, of Hellenistic origins—their sparseness in the Q tradition confirms this. Certainly, Bultmann says, Jesus performed deeds that "to his mind and to the minds of his contemporaries" were divine healings. A few traditions to this effect circulated in the Palestinian community,

81. Rudolf Bultmann, *Theology of the New Testament*, trans. Kendrick Grobel (New York: Charles Scribner's Sons, 1951), 37, 42–43, 53; "The Study of the Synoptic Gospels," in Rudolf Bultmann and Karl Kundsin, *Form Criticism*, trans. F. C. Grant (New York: Harper, 1962), 7–78 (17).

82. Bultmann, *Theology*, 13.

recognizable in being more like apophthegms than bona fide healing stories. But in form and motif the bulk of the Synoptic healing and miracle narratives find their parallels in the Hellenistic religious sphere, in myths attached to various heroes and deities (244–46, 255–56).[83] Bultmann dismisses Strauss's contention (it makes a poor fit with his *religionsgeschichtliche* schema) that Old Testament narrative was the principal formative influence on these Synoptic materials. The Synoptic Feeding stories are not reducible to the manna narratives of Exodus. It is doubtful that the Exodus 24 legend of Moses on the mountain is a parallel to the Transfiguration narrative: the two figures appearing with Jesus would originally have been anonymous, only later distinguished as Moses and Elijah (279). Similarly dismissed are Semiticisms in some miracle narratives: these expressions could have migrated into Koine Greek or are due to the later LXX influence on the tradition.

By this ingenious means Bultmann manages to rid the primitive Palestinian layer of the tradition of most elements with supernatural coloration, transposing these to the Hellenistic layer, at the same time preparing the ground to assign the Gospel of Mark—in contrast to Q replete with healing and miracle narratives—to the *kyrios* Christ cult of the Hellenistic church. His methodology is innovative, and he vacuums narrative out of the primitive tradition with an unprecedented efficiency, but assigning priority to the sayings over narrative in the history of the tradition is just standard procedure in liberal Protestant source criticism.

Bultmann senses the difficulty for his tradition-history scheme from the pragmatic directionality of the sayings source, which he himself acknowledges is paraenetic (373).[84] What if its low ingrediency in healing narratives is just a function of genre—or in Bultmann's terms, its *Sitz*? This would not bode well for his theory. Bultmann's answer? Healing and miracle stories would have been ideal for Q's paraenetic purposes. That it all but lacks them proves that they are not present in numbers in the Palestinian tradition (256). This answer makes sense, of sorts, within Bultmann's *Kleinliteratur*, growing-stratum-of-tradition conception of Q: the work (if it can even be called that) is untouched by the forces of genre. But one is pressed to ask: why then Q's thinness in apophthegms, on Bultmann's own telling not only Palestinian but little more than a narrative growth on the sayings? His supplementary argument relies on his *religionsgeschichtliche* schema: Mark's density in healing and miracle

83. Also Bultmann, *Jesus and the Word*, 173.

84. Bultmann had already associated Q with a catechetical pragmatic in 1913 ("Sayings Source," 30–31).

narratives is a function of its Hellenistic θεῖος ἄνθρωπος, divine-son Christology, in contrast to the eschatological preacher of Q, exalted in resurrection to coming Son of Man. It follows that the healing and miracle stories are of Hellenistic origins (256).

Another manufacturer of narrative tradition on an industrial scale is messianic prophecy. Here Bultmann splices his Wredian convictions into the *religionsgeschichtliche* operational apparatus. Obviously Jesus entered Jerusalem for Passover, but the Triumphal Entry (Mark 11:1–9) is almost whole cloth a legend, woven of prophecy interpretation (281). In fact, most of the Passion narrative is legend, its episodes generated out of prophecy. But at the same time it constitutes the cult narrative of the Hellenistic *kyrios* cult, which has overgrown and all but supplanted the traces of a simple narrative of Jesus's last supper with his disciples, a Passover meal, that in the Palestinian congregation served only to ground its continued observance of the Passover (284, 307–8). This primitive Passover meal story was likely connected up with a narrative of Jesus's crucifixion. But it was not enacted in the primitive community in connection with a cult meal: like other Jewish sects the community remained attached to the temple cult (Acts 2:46) (297–301).[85] Only subsequently has it been co-opted by the *kyrios* Christ cult of the Hellenistic church and turned into a cult liturgy of identification with the dying and rising the deity of the Pauline kerygma (307–8, 333).[86] Bultmann's theory—supported by the requisitely subtle tradition-history, *religionsgeschichtliche* distinctions—describes a Palestinian community with no cultic life of its own centered on the Eucharist. Such only emerges in the Hellenistic churches, under the impulse of Hellenistic mystery-cult piety and atonement theology. The Palestinian community is a community of proclamation, a community of the word, not of cult.

The Markan evangelist, working under the influence of the *kyrios* cult tendency, then makes his entrance to combine the Hellenistic *kyrios* cult narrative with the Palestinian apophthegm tradition and the Hellenistic healing and miracle stories, thereby inventing the narrative gospel. The effect of his project is to pull the Palestinian tradition into the orbit of the Hellenistic *kyrios* worship and its cross-and-resurrection cult narrative. Now the One speaking in the apophthegms, the disputes, and sayings, the One healing and exorcising, is the cult deity, journeying about Palestine incognito (334, 371–73).

But why, one might reasonably ask, should this convergence of such incommensurable outlooks occur? Why could the cult narrative not function

---

85. Also *Theology*, 53, 57.
86. Also "Synoptic Gospels," 17, 67.

alone, perhaps with a few satellite healing and miracle stories? Hellenistic cults certainly managed this well enough. Bultmann in fact claims elsewhere, trying to account for the sparseness of sayings in Mark, that it was not self-evident, in fact inappropriate (*unangemessen*) that sayings, collected for paraenetic ends, should be incorporated into a *kyrios*-cult narrative gospel (372–73). Bultmann's response, such as it is, is to claim, first, that elements of the Hellenistic kerygma such as the Lord's Supper narrative liturgy "invited expanded narrative depiction." Second, the "expanded kerygmatic summaries" of Acts 10:37–38 and 13:24–31 had already taken the step of bringing the historical ministry of Jesus into the purview of the kerygma. Third, a tradition grounded in a historical person like Jesus would "naturally" tend toward the form of a biographical narrative (395–96). One might ask: how does any such tendency lie latent in a Palestinian community for which "the idea of any unified, narratively connected life of Jesus was completely alien" (394)?

Cracks in Bultmann's religionsgeschichtliche *Edifice*

We have seen that breaches keep opening up in the Palestinian/Hellenistic binary that serves as the substructure of Bultmann's history of the tradition. Bultmann must plaster over these anomalies with various ad hoc expedients. Already in 1924 Fascher drew attention to the presence of so-called Hellenistic "cult legends" in the "tradition" that Bultmann claims Mark unites with the Hellenistic cult narrative. One of the main blocks of the "tradition" is the healing and miracle stories, on Bultmann's own telling largely of Hellenistic origins. For Fascher this comingling of "Hellenistic" and "Palestinian" materials in the "tradition" effectively falsifies Bultmann's account of Mark's project, "and the origins of the Gospel remains a riddle for us."[87] It is hard to disagree with him. The healing and miracle stories in particular give Bultmann headaches. He needs to move them out of the primitive Palestinian tradition to minimalize the presence in it of supernatural elements and to leave Q as the most authentic register of the primitive tradition and the Christology of the Palestinian community, the antipode to the Markan kerygma. Their origins therefore are mostly Hellenistic; they are artifacts of a Hellenistic θεῖος ἄνθρωπος Christology that bathes Jesus in mythical, divine light (256).

This is why Bultmann must discount the force of Strauss's analysis and deny that Old Testament narrative was a significant factor in their formation. But he is unable to sustain this. His critique of Strauss amounts to showing that

87. Fascher, *Methode*, 141.

the healing and miracle stories are not wholly derivatives of Old Testament narrative. He acknowledges that under the influence of messianic Christology "miracles of Jesus were narrated in the Palestinian community," and that "the Old Testament narrative motifs also made a few contributions" to some of these (245). Bultmann's account of the healing and miracle stories therefore ends up quite muddled. Fascher point out that it is odd that Bultmann assigns most of the healing and miracle stories to the Hellenistic stratum, but the dispute stories and "school discussions," which have close Hellenistic parallels, to the Palestinian stratum.[88] In the end Bultmann distributes some *Wundergeschichten* to the Palestinian stratum (the healing stories that are apophthegmatic in form), some to the Hellenistic, redrawing the *religionsgeschichtliche* line through the middle of this body of tradition, and doggedly presses on.

It is curious that Bultmann downplays the effects of Old Testament narrative on the healing and miracle stories, but then has little difficulty identifying messianic prophecy as the principal factor in the formation of Passion narrative episodes—in its Markan form the cult legend of the Hellenistic church. This anomaly seems to originate in an unresolved conflict between Bultmann's Wredian assumptions that make messianic dogma the leading generator of the tradition and his *religionsgeschichtliche* schema that associates Jewish cultural influences with the Palestinian layer. Bultmann can only equivocate: "doubtless" prophecy interpretation was an activity in the Hellenistic and the Palestinian churches (304). But even the apophthegm tradition, stipulated by Bultmann to be solidly Palestinian, does not fall neatly onto the Palestinian side of the ledger: a small subset conforms closely to the Hellenistic apophthegm form and thus "are presumably of Hellenistic origins" (64). The "I-sayings" (*Ich-Worte*) also originate in both the Palestinian and Hellenistic churches, albeit predominantly the latter (176).

Bultmann is not so obtuse as to not be aware of the difficulties for his tradition-history schema raised by leakages from his Hellenistic stratum into his Palestinian stratum. He is also cognizant that the artificial combination of two such cultural extremities and alien christological outlooks in Mark's Gospel is anything but a likely development, truth be told quite incredible. On its face it presents a "conundrum" (*Rätsel*) (330). He therefore embraces the expedient of *Hellenistic-Jewish* Christianity, a sort of *religionsgeschichtliche* mezzanine between primitive Palestinian Christianity and full-fledged Hellenistic Christianity. In this community Jesus is not yet a Hellenistic cult deity. Its Christology is messianic in an advanced expression, exemplified in the Nativities, which

88. Fascher, *Methode*, 128–29.

originate in this community. Hellenistic-Jewish Christianity allows Bultmann to explain the awkward presence of messianic prophecy interpretation in the Hellenistic cult narrative, to reconcile the Wredian and *religionsgeschichtliche* vectors in his analysis. The "messianic outlook" *per se* would have had little purchase (*keine Bedeutung*) in Hellenistic Christianity, the categories of which were cultic and mythic. Messianic Christology was therefore brought into Hellenistic Christianity by Hellenistic-Jewish converts in the Pauline communities. The Palestinian apophthegm and sayings tradition—and with it the notion of Jesus as διδάσκαλος—was likewise mediated by these circles (330, 394–95). Hellenistic-Jewish Christianity also neatly accounts for the Hellenistic elements in Q: doubtless Q underwent a redaction in this community. A case in point is the Temptation, an artifact of Hellenistic-Jewish scribality (331).

Notably, the appearance of scribal literacy in this redaction of the tradition-history entity Q indicates that Bultmann sees Hellenistic-Jewish Christianity marking a further (*fortgeschrittenere*) stage of cultural evolution. It shows that he correlates Q's rudimentary, subliterary profile to the "primitive"—that is, not just "early" but culturally *primitivistic* Palestinian community, a community that has never existed anywhere but in the Romantic imagination. Romantic primitivism controls Bultmann's notion of the early Palestinian community, which he positions at the beginning of a civilizational development trajectory that reaches its cosmopolitan apogee in the Hellenistic church (330–31, 373, 394–95).[89] Here it is aligned to the evolutionary paradigm of *Religionsgeschichte*, which conceives *religionsgeschichtliche* development in quasi-Darwinian terms as an advance from primitive enthusiasm (i.e., naïve religious experience; "Easter faith") through successive stages of increasing cultural sophistication.[90]

Bultmann concedes that this intermediary Hellenistic-Jewish Christianity with the role that he imagines for it is a speculative entity, wrapped in obscurity (*dunkel*), "heretofore little known," in need of much more investigation to bring its lineaments to light (330). This is not a project he undertakes in *Geschichte*, where it nakedly functions as a device to save his history of the tradition. The early chapters of Acts, on which Bultmann puts significant weight, locates Hellenistic Christianity already in Jerusalem. This complicates matters, to say the least. It accounts for why in contemporary Q scholarship

89. Because he recognizes scribal literary activity in Q's formation John Kloppenborg identifies a different basis for attributing the Q Temptation to a late redaction: he locates it late on a Q trajectory toward *bios* interest in Jesus; see *The Formation of Q: Trajectories in Ancient Wisdom Collections* (Philadelphia: Fortress, 1987), 261–62.
90. Lüdemann and Özen, "Religionsgeschichtliche Schule," 620, 622.

Bultmann's Palestinian congregation, reborn as the "Q community," gets relocated to Galilee.

A question Bultmann never explicitly addresses is how Q can be taken as the paradigm representative of the Palestinian community when it contains relatively few apophthegms and disputes. In Bultmann's schema these are likewise elements of the primitive tradition, subject to the same oral-aggregation processes, indeed simply a subset of the sayings tradition. One suspects that Bultmann is simply concerned to keep narrative tradition as far removed from the sayings tradition as possible. Or perhaps it is just the old source-critical habit reasserting itself of associating the sayings tradition with the Ursource and the primitive community. The genre factor—Q's paraenetic profile and pragmatic—intrudes perforce, destabilizing Bultmann's enabling *Kleinliteratur* framework.[91]

Breakdown of Bultmann's Sitz im Leben *Theory for Tradition Origins*

The question of genre brings us back to Bultmann's theory that the tradition originates in community *Sitze im Leben*. By and large the nineteenth-century source critics, while recognizing social and theological factors in its development, grounded the tradition in its origins in early Christian memory. But they were not able to crack the problem of the memory-tradition nexus. Bultmann stepped into the gap with his *Sitz im Leben* theory. There is no shortage of critiques of his theory—they begin as early as Fascher in 1924—but perhaps our media and memory approach can contribute something further.

When one drills down into the details, it is in fact unclear whether Bultmann is claiming that the tradition *incubates* or *originates* in the *Sitz*. On balance he appears to mean the latter while confusing it with the former. The various genres of the tradition are "precipitates" of the life of the community in its manifold expressions. The social forces constituting a particular *Sitz* generate (*hervortreiben*) a particular form. A given form is "not an aesthetic but sociological construct." The line between the form in question and the *Sitz im Leben* is all but invisible (4–5).[92] The "ideal scenes" of the apophthegms are symbolic narrative projections of the social-theological dynamics that constitute a particular *Sitz* (40, 393).

---

91. Dibelius is more prepared to recognize the genre factor in the Q profile, and as a force in the channeling of the tradition into sayings and narrative vectors (*Formgeschichte*, 25–26, 244–45).

92. He thinks this is entailed in *Kleinliteratur* definition of the Synoptic tradition.

In practice, however, Bultmann is unable to stipulate a one-to-one correlation of a given form to a particular *Sitz*. He says as much: "It is admittedly difficult to say from case to case in which concrete situations specific units of the tradition play a role," going on to observe that sayings likely functioned in at least three *Sitze*—preaching, instruction, and community discipline. He notes that in the Hellenistic congregations the disputes and apophthegms, which featured Palestinian concerns of little relevance, were transmitted apart from any *Sitz* at all, thus only by dint of their momentum (*Schwergewicht*) (395). With these admissions it is hard to see how he has not undermined his entire account of the origins of the tradition. Bultmann is never able to clarify the relationship between *Sitz* and tradition. That the tradition might shape the *Sitz* is of course not considered at all.

Bultmann makes a number of other observations about the tradition to similar effect. He identifies community paraenesis as the *Sitz* for the collection of sayings traditions (373). *Sitz*, that is, is the framework for the cultivation of tradition, and the form of a given genre has a functional appositeness within a given *Sitz*, indeed range of *Sitze* (as Bultmann acknowledges in the case of the Logia). But this is not an explanation of either its origins or contents. In describing the healing and miracle stories, he says that while some of their motifs are spontaneous manifestations of community realities, others, both central and peripheral, are folkloric or derive from analogous stories told of Greek heroes (244). Cultural forces external to the *Sitz*, in other words, are at work in the formation of these materials. In a similar vein he notes that the forms of the Synoptic tradition are drawn from a cultural repertoire of genres (393). As Fascher observes, this effectively severs the generative connection of form to *Sitz* essential to Bultmann's account of the origins of the tradition. This is underlined by the fact that a genre manifestly can function in diverse *Sitze*.[93] Bultmann's vacillation between the terms "form"—a sociological entity—and "genre" (*Gattung*)—a cultural entity—is likewise symptomatic of this unclarity.

In short, there is a disjunction between Bultmann's claims that the tradition originates in the *Sitz* and his actual observations about the tradition, which indicate rather that it exists independent of the *Sitz*, albeit in symbiotic relationship with it. It is in fact remarkable how seldom he explains inductively how a given unit of tradition is the manufacture of a particular *Sitz*. His reasoning simply runs in a circle. The "ideal scenes" of apophthegms are symbolic projections of a community situation; the *Streitgespräche* (dispute stories) represent narratively "internal and external discussions in the community over questions of the Law" (42). In practice it is the innate "tendencies" of the tradition that do

---

93. Fascher, *Methode*, 213–14.

all the heavy lifting in his account of the formation of the tradition, in concert with external factors such as *religionsgeschichtliche* forces and "Easter faith."

The origins of almost the entire apophthegm and *Streitgespräche* tradition, for example, lie in the "tendency" of sayings to generate ideal scenes. Dominical sayings and *meshalim* were spoken by Jesus, thus by definition are not the products of any *Sitz* that they function in. This explains why Bultmann takes them as generative seeds that contain the internal potencies that unfold in the lush, *religionsgeschichtliche* growth of the tradition. Dominical sayings generate the ideal scenes of apophthegms and analogous sayings, and they attract additional sayings from Jewish tradition. Much of the existing sayings tradition is in fact imported from external sources—a massive augmentation to the tradition driven by a cultural tendency for sayings to be attributed to famous teachers. *Sitz* is a factor in the sense that the imported sayings are apposite to instructional needs in community settings. Corollary to this is a tendency for community ethics to drift away from Jesus's radicalism toward alignment to common social norms (108–10). One of the most prolific generators of tradition is Easter faith. In Bultmann's view (following Wrede and Bousset), the experiences of Easter mark the origins of the primitive Christianity's messianic beliefs and the inversion of Jesus from the proclaimer to the Proclaimed. Any tradition bearing this dogmatic tendency is presumptively the artifact of that tendency.

The christological criterion is reinforced by hardline application of the double-dissimilarity criterion, and together they regulate Bultmann's classification of the elements of the tradition, sayings and narrative alike (222). They determine that the Triumphal Entry is almost without remainder the manufacture of messianic dogma in concert with cultural practices of prophecy interpretation, and that the elements of the Love Your Enemies sequence expressive of an everyday reciprocity ethic are secondary (106–8, 281). Identifying dogmatic tendencies as a principal source of the tradition of course is a practice that long predates Bultmann. But in his account, *religionsgeschichtliche* factors combine with messianic dogma to manufacture tradition on a large scale. Though intersecting with the cult *Sitz* of the Hellenistic churches, it is these forces of religious syncretism that in combination with folkloric tendencies generate healing and miracle stories, cult legends, the cult narrative, and the narrative gospel form itself.

Bultmann's Revived Oral Hypothesis

Bultmann's grand tradition-history edifice stands or falls with the media assumptions that it rests upon. Chief among these is his claim that the distinction between the oral medium and the written medium is a matter of indifference

(91, 347). Or more precisely, the shift to the *written* medium is of little significance: the processes at work in the formation of the oral tradition continue on without a hiccup into its written manifestations, including the writings of the evangelists, Mark in particular (64). This view of things is predicated on Bultmann's *Kleinliteratur* model for the Synoptics, which are not distinguished qualitatively from folk (i.e., oral) tradition.

We saw that Bultmann construes Q in particular as the outcome of oral processes (as he conceives these); it is little more than a growing stratum of tradition, as good as untouched by literary formation. Dibelius puts this pithily: "We are only justified in speaking of Q as a stratum [*Schicht*] of tradition, not as a written work [*Schrift*]."[94] Q is a microcosm of Bultmann's evolutionary history of the tradition, growing organically from individual logia by gradual aggregation into loose topical clusters in turn aggregating into larger complexes to the point of the present collection. But the Synoptic Gospels likewise are just terminal points of this development and its organic tendencies. They constitute no new point of departure in the history of the tradition. Their written fixation of the tradition was unliterary. Their significance lies in the *religionsgeschichtliche* stage that they mark (253–54, 347). Bultmann's entire tradition history, understood as an unbroken organic development through *religionsgeschichtliche* stages, is premised on this denial of media differences. A principled distinction, a break, between oral and written media would wreck the scheme beyond salvage.

On the other hand, Bultmann has put his finger on the reality that *oral practices persist into the written cultivation and transmission of the tradition.* As we would put it, the two media interface in complex ways. It is in this respect that Bultmann seems to represent a decisive break from the nineteenth-century media framework that associated Synoptic variation strictly with oral tradition and Synoptic agreements with writing, never being able to bring the two together. But like his nineteenth-century oral hypothesis predecessors, he only manages this at the cost of complete marginalization of the written medium. As Fascher notes, Bultmann's forerunner is Herder, and form criticism marks a return to the oral hypothesis.[95] The Synoptic Gospels (and Q) are simply outcomes of oral processes; they give perfunctory redaction to what is effectively an oral gospel.

What is distinctive about Bultmann's account, however, is that it amounts to a hybridization of the oral hypothesis with the two document hypothesis.

94. Dibelius, *Formgeschichte*, 236.
95. Fascher, *Methode*, 13–17.

He all but completely dissolves Synoptic writing, Q and Mark in particular, into oral processes. His *Kleinliteratur* assumptions allow him to turn Matthew's and Luke's redactional operations on Mark and Q into oral "tendencies." The elements of truth here (Q and Mark are nothing if not instantiations of tradition; oral utilization practices persist into written enactments of the tradition) get engulfed by this full assimilation of Synoptic writing to orality. But this is just ostensibly the case. In effect what Bultmann does is to take redactional operations enabled by the written medium and turn them into tendencies of oral tradition. His model for the history of the tradition is borrowed from source criticism: for succession of sources (*Schriften*) he substitutes succession of layers (*Schichten*), two of which correspond roughly to Q and Mark (97).

We saw that Bultmann's description of his growing aggregates of oral tradition is a permutation of the *Aufzeichnungen* theory of nineteenth-century scholars: provisional written collections of raw oral tradition, given perfunctory topical organization, that feed into Mark, Matthew, and Luke. Indeed, it is a matter of no import, Bultmann says, whether these tradition aggregates, which he also terms *Sammlungen* (collections) were written or oral. Q is one such primitive collection, and as such emblematic of the primitive Palestinian community. Bultmann's Mark is not so much different from Holtzmann's Urmarkus (Source A): half in, half out of the *Aufzeichnung* zone.

Nevertheless, the signal effects of the written medium perforce surface in his own analysis, in explicit or implicit acknowledgments that in various Synoptic pericopes one can see evidence of the meditated editorial operations that are enabled by the written medium. Already in Q, he says, one can observe authorial (*schriftstellerische*) composition, a case in point being the seven-fold Woes (Luke 11:39–48, 52), to which has been attached an Announcement of Judgment (Luke 11:49–51) to create an intelligible sequence (119). What about Mark? Bultmann puts Q and Mark on the same level: both are specimens of *Kleinliteratur*. But he cannot square this with his *religionsgeschichtliche* framework, which puts them at the extremities of a christological development. Like the Palestinian community itself, Q is inchoate and culturally primitive, whereas a "cohering, integrated portrayal of the life of Jesus, held together by a unified conception," i.e., the Gospel of Mark, can only be a creation (*Schöpfung*) of the Hellenistic church (393–94). It is difficult to see how an artifact such as he describes could originate in anything other than a meditated editorial undertaking.

Bultmann's account also assimilates Luke and Matthew to the *Kleinliteratur* conception, and from their redactional operations he infers "tendencies" of the tradition. Yet Bultmann characterizes Luke 6:27–36, Love Your Enemies, as an

editorial composition that by combining the two Q aggregates Matt 5:38–42//
Matt 5:43–48 and fetching over Matthew 7:12 (Luke 6:31) Luke has fashioned
"into a unified sequence on the theme of loving enemies" (100). In his discussion of the two Matthean clusters, however, he characterizes the Lukan parallel
as "a divergent tradition" (92). His media parameters simply cannot encompass
the Synoptic realities. Fascher points out that Bultmann never reconciles his
Formgeschichte with his source theory. That is, he never explains how Matthew,
Mark, and Luke (and Q for that matter) as identifiable *works* emerge from
undirected processes of tradition aggregation.[96] His erasure of the distinction
between redaction and oral tendencies, part and parcel of his denial of the
significance of the media distinction, is at the heart of the problem.[97]

Bultmann's Exclusion of Memory from Tradition Formation

It is on this point that Bultmann's exclusion of the memory factor from the
formation of the tradition claims our attention. We have noted that this exclusion is the consequence of nineteenth-century scholarship's failure to solve the
problem of the memory-tradition nexus, as Fascher grasped in his 1924 critique. Post-Strauss Synoptic source criticism marginalized the oral tradition,
because the oral hypothesis was associated with Strauss's radical skepticism.
The strategy was to identify Ursources that could be connected up directly to
apostolic eyewitness testimony. In due course these efforts converged on the
2DH: Mark, grounded in Peter's eyewitness testimony, and the sayings source,
if not composed by at least associated with the apostle Matthew.

This solution, however, was precarious. The oral tradition problematic was
suppressed, not resolved, waiting to burst out again and capsize it. There was
no place to fit oral tradition into this tight source schema. It was either marginalized or simply identified with eyewitness testimony. A few critics, conscious of the poor correlation of the tradition to eyewitness testimony, gave
some attention to the nexus problem, usually suggesting that the tradition
was a debased-currency form of primitive memory. But scholars almost never
doubted their intuition that the origins of the tradition must lie, somehow, in
early Christian memory. When Wrede finally gave this source-critical edifice a
push that toppled it, the problem of the oral tradition—and with it the question

---

96. Fascher, *Methode*, 142.

97. In the case of Q, Dieter Lührmann will try to deal with this by distinguishing the
intentional literary act of *Redaktion* from the contingent processes of *Sammlung*; see *Die
Redaktion der Logienquelle*, WMANT 33 (Neukirchen: Neukirchener Verlag, 1969).

of the memory-tradition nexus—came rushing back. Form criticism emerged out of the ensuing flux, professing to offer a robust theory of the oral tradition. Bultmann grasped the nettle of the memory-tradition problematic. The forms of the tradition bear little resemblance to eyewitness memories. The tradition must originate, therefore, not in memory but at the behest of other factors. These are the *Sitze im Leben*, and the organic "tendencies" of the tradition.[98]

Bultmann denies memory any agency in the formation of the tradition. He grants that "memories of Jesus, of his words and activity," played a role in the "literary" activities of the primitive community. But to see in the apophthegms and dispute stories, as some do, episodic memories of individual disciples, he says, is to ignore that the form corresponds to a literary genre, not to memories (50). Memory and tradition, that is to say, are alien entities. The *Individualisierung* tendency (names secondarily attached to originally anonymous actors and interlocutors) allows Bultmann to purge the tradition of possible eyewitness connections (228–30). Bultmann notes Mark's thrice mention of the women at the scenes of crucifixion, burial, and resurrection, but identifies them as elements in Mark's tradition, to fulfill the function of *Augenzeugen* (eyewitnesses) (298).[99]

To be sure, memories have not been completely occluded by tradition-forming forces. The depiction of Jesus as a teaching, disputing rabbi, for example, is still legible like a palimpsest under the dominant messianic conception and so must have some basis in memory, likewise Jesus's association with tax collectors. Occasionally traces of locales of Jesus's activity are to be found embedded in apophthegm settings. But these do not mean, Bultmann hastens to add, that the corresponding episode is historical. In the case of the "Who is my true family?" apophthegm (Mark 3:20, 31–35), a trace memory of the opposition of Jesus's family is simply being commandeered by tradition-forming forces (52). The only elements with odds of being reckoned authentic are therefore those that can survive strict application of double dissimilarity. In other words, Bultmann identifies the authentic elements of the tradition with surviving memory traces. Like the nineteenth-century critics, he makes the simple equation of *memory* with *historical authenticity*. When we recognize this, it becomes clear why he makes such a sharp distinction between authentic and inauthentic elements, why he places memory and tradition in such sharp contradistinction.

---

98. See Fascher, *Methode*, 7; also Dibelius, *Formgeschichte*, 56–57.

99. On the same page he posits the existence of a primitive "memory-based report" of the last Passover meal of Jesus with his disciples and events following.

The consequence of so deeply dichotomizing the tradition is that Bultmann, whose formidable mind runs in strong dualisms, cannot say what connection might exist between the authentic and inauthentic elements, what force of cohesion holds them together in a common body of tradition. His principled application of double dissimilarity is certainly a factor: authentic elements will stand in opposition (*Gegensatz*) to Jewish piety and ethics on the one hand and early Christian faith and practice on the other (222). But Bultmann has also ruled out memory as a force in the formation and history of the tradition. Authentic elements in the tradition are just inert residues. The complete inconsequence of memory in his account is illustrated by a functional role that he *does* assign to it: the influx of inauthentic sayings and parables into the tradition was facilitated by the memory that Jesus occasionally co-opted profane maxims. The efficient factor is the forces of the *Sitz* (108–10). In a similar vein, though the dispute-story scenes are through and through community formations, doubtless they correspond to the "historical recollection" (*geschichtliche Erinnerung*) of the "general character of Jesus's life and activity" (52). Bultmann's reasoning, that is to say, is that this representation of Jesus is so pervasive in the tradition that it must have some historical basis. But precisely *how* memory informs the formation of these scenes he does not say. He seems to view memory as a kind of residual inertial pull on the powers of community creativity in the Palestinian community.

Bultmann's enduring contribution is to have recognized the high interactivity between community exigencies and the tradition. The tradition does indeed give symbolic representation to community realities. It could hardly function as a normative tradition nourishing and sustaining the cultural identity of a tradent community if it did not. Table fellowship scenes like those in Mark 2:13–20 truly are functional symbols in which the community sees itself and by which it reproduces the constitutive norms of its own common life. Though acknowledging that historical elements doubtless have "precipitated out" in them, Bultmann rightly says that the apophthegms are not naively realistic descriptions of an event but a genre, a *Gattung*, that operates as an efficient vehicle for delivering a saying of Jesus. Its bare narrative essentials are calibrated to serve this end, not historical inquisitiveness (41, 66–67). The Synoptic tradition, that is, *is in the first instance a project of sustaining and reproducing a particular cultural identity*, or as Bultmann puts it, it serves "the needs of Christian faith and life."[100] The catch is that Bultmann opposes the

---

100. Bultmann, "Study of the Synoptic Gospels," 64; similarly Dibelius, *Formgeschichte*, 60.

"symbolic/ideal" to the historical. The "ideal scenes" of the apophthegms are "not direct reports of any historical event but [*sondern*] narrative expressions of an idea," an idea of existential significance (40). The Call of the Disciples (Mark 1:16–20) "reflects no historical situation . . . [but] sets forth symbolically and picturesquely the common experience of the disciples as they were raised by Jesus's wonderful power out of their previous spheres of life."[101]

We have seen that Bultmann lacks the conceptual apparatus for conceiving the relationship between memory and the tradition in anything other than binary terms. Nonetheless, on rare occasions he makes observations that point the way toward overcoming this binary. With regard to the Cleansing of the Temple (Mark 11:15–16) he says: "What in all likelihood is an historical event has been elevated [*erhoben*] to the level of an ideal scene" that exercises a symbolic function. Similarly, the Call of the Disciples (Mark 1:16–20) "condenses into one symbolic moment what in truth was the result of a process" (59–60). In Mark 3:20, 31–35 (Jesus's True Family) the historically authentic ambivalence of Jesus's family toward his ministry has been "fashioned" (*zurechtgemacht*) so as to make it a fitting vehicle for Jesus's pronouncement (29). What he describes, incipiently, is *the cultural process of distilling out from salient historical events their normative elements and fashioning them into durable tradition artifacts that function as formative cultural symbols for the tradent community— its cultural memory—and enable the transmissibility and reproduction of its cultural identity.* Memory, that is to say, is the principal force in the formation of the tradition.[102]

THE PERSISTENT SYNOPTIC PROBLEM

Fascher described form criticism as "the newest branch to sprout from the tree of the Synoptic Problem."[103] For the scholars who fill this chapter the Synoptic problem has been settled in favor of the two document hypothesis. For them, the debate is no longer over competing source theories but over the stubborn question of the historicity of the tradition. This issue, thought to have been resolved in the long source-critical debate, has been forced by Wrede. Now the question of historicity must be addressed within the parameters of the 2DH itself.

---

101. Bultmann, "Study of the Synoptic Gospels," 45; also *Geschichte*, 27.

102. Already intuited by Fascher, who refers to "the pathway from concrete event to gospel episode, which reveals to us the power of memory [*die Kraft der Erinnerung*]" (*Methode*, 144; similarly Dibelius, *Formgeschichte*, 12).

103. Fascher, *Methode*, 5.

This occasions the turn to the oral tradition, a redirection that culminates in form criticism. In Bultmann we find a hybridization of the 2DH with the oral hypothesis. Moreover, the practice of nineteenth-century scholarship of privileging of the sayings tradition over the narrative tradition, the logia over narrative gospel, is turned into a *religionsgeschichtliche* polarity, into alien kerygmas, represented by Q and Mark, respectively. The oralization of the sources finds its extreme in Q, which becomes a Palestinian layer of tradition, itself layered, and thus grist for tradition histories and redaction histories. The subliterary, *Aufzeichnung* characterization of Q, most forcibly expressed by Holtzmann, here finds its natural terminus in the conversion of Q into oral tradition. This is the Q bequeathed to contemporary Q scholarship. Contemporary Q scholarship is also where Bultmann's primitive Palestinian community (the *Urgemeinde*) and his *religionsgeschichtliche* schema both survive: in the "Q community" in Galilee, with a kerygma alien to the Markan Passion and Resurrection kerygma.

Even the best hypotheses are only more or less tentative. The two document hypothesis settlement was never universal in its own time. Inevitably challenges to it would emerge. And such is the case. Before our present inquiry takes us into contemporary Q scholarship, we must reckon with the Farrer juggernaut.

The Farrer Juggernaut: Is It Unstoppable?

CONSENSUS MAY HAVE GELLED around the two document hypothesis, but it never solidified. Resistance never completely disappeared, and to-day alternatives have reemerged advocated with considerable force of argu-ment. The Farrer hypothesis is the leading case in point. It marks a return of nineteenth-century approaches that postulate Luke's utilization of Matthew.[1] How does the Farrer hypothesis fare under a media analysis? Does it overcome the difficulties that doomed its nineteenth-century predecessors?

We saw that Herder weighed the likelihood of Luke's drawing his double tradition from the Gospel of the Hebrews, the Aramaic proto-Matthew. But in view of Luke's wide divergence from the Matthean arrangements he rejected this in favor of Luke's having separate access to the source of the Gospel of the Hebrews's double tradition, which he thought of as a loose body of oral tradition. Right at the outset of critical study of the Synoptics Herder iden-tifies the chief difficulty for any claim that Luke uses Matthew: coming up with a coherent, parsimonious explanation of Luke's procedures vis-à-vis the Matthean double tradition. In de Wette we encountered a Griesbacher and as such were obligated to square Luke's double tradition with derivation from Matthew, or as he sees it, a proto-Matthean Urgospel. He settled on Luke's use of an intermediary version of the Matthean Urgospel, one in which the double tradition was already rearranged.

De Wette labored under the debility that source criticism of the time took source utilization to be a somewhat wooden affair that allowed the evangelists little redactional agency. This changed with *Tendenzkritik*, which Baur applied

---

1. The Griesbach hypothesis is for all practical purposes a dead letter in the contem-porary debate. Matthean posteriority has found some new advocates, but it remains to be seen if it gets any traction.

to Luke's use of Matthew: the proto-Lukan evangelist's operations upon his source Matthew are explained by his radical Paulinist *Tendenz*. We recollect that Baur was forced constantly to have recourse to Luke's subjective intentions, his *Absichten*, and at the cost of attributing to the proto-Lukan evangelist and the canonical redactor an array of editorial motives so complex as to belie any claim to parsimony. Baur's fellow Tübinger Hilgenfeld tried the *Tendenz* approach, but defeated by the formidable difficulties that the travel section sequence presents for Luke's use of Matthew, he settled on a non-Matthean source that contained most of Luke's double tradition. Köstlin similarly tried the orthodox *Tendenz* approach at first. But as his efforts got dispersed into various ad hoc explanations and appeals to Luke's intentions he posited Luke's access to a parallel didactic source.

No less an eminence than Holtzmann came to think that Luke made subsidiary use Matthew in addition to the Logia source. He had no better luck than the *Tendenz* critics giving a coherent account of Luke's Matthew utilization. A major influence on Holtzmann was the work of Eduard Simons, notable as the first thorough-going attempt to pair Luke's dependence on Matthew with Markan priority. Simons put Luke's omissions of Matthean additions to Markan passages down to Luke preferring to follow Mark, the older, more habituated source, instead of the parvenu Matthew. He found it impossible to dispense with the sayings collection hypothesis because of the scale of Luke's divergent arrangements of the double tradition.

Pre-Farrer: Edward Lummis and H. J. Jameson

Austen Farrer's 1957 essay laid down the basic lines of the "Farrer hypothesis." But he was not without forerunners in twentieth-century scholarship. Edward Lummis was a true proto-Farrerist, pairing Markan priority with Luke's use of Matthew alone.[2] In his 1915 work he argued in a kind of inverse anticipation of Taylor's "multiple-scans" theory of Matthew's use of Q that Luke drew his double tradition directly from Matthew, rearranging it relative to Mark but largely taking the selections from their forward Matthean order.[3] Lummis

2. Edward W. Lummis, *How Luke Was Written* (Cambridge: Cambridge University Press, 1915). See Paul Foster, "The Rise and Development of the Farrer Hypothesis," in *The Q-Hypothesis Unveiled: Theological, Church-Political, Socio-Political, and Hermeneutical Issues Behind the Sayings Source*, ed. Markus Tiwald, BWA(N)T 225 (Stuttgart: Kohlhammer, 2020), 86–128.

3. Lummis, *How Luke Was Written*, 7–9, 21–22 (quotation 21); "A Case against 'Q,'" *HibJ* 24 (1925–1926): 755–65 (764).

claims Luke preferred Mark over Matthew because of Mark's "superior authority" as the "earlier of the two."[4] This has since become the go-to expedient in Farrer scholarship.

The challenge, however, is making sense of why Luke gives himself the trouble of rearranging Matthew's nonnarrative sequences. Luke's disposition of the Matthean materials, Lummis says, is determined by certain "fixed points" in Matthew, which are "in turn determined by Lk.'s treatment of Mk., viz. the breaks which Lk. makes in the Marcan narrative." These are Mark 3:19; 4:1; 9:40; and 10:13. That is to say, Mark 3:9 is where Luke leaves Mark to go over to the corresponding Matthean triple-tradition parallel to collate a block of "Matthean matter" (e.g., at Mark 3:19 the Sermon and additional double-tradition materials), and Mark 4:1 is where he rejoins Mark, job done. And similarly for Mark 9:40 and 10:13. In the one case the collated block of Matthean materials substitutes for the Markan sayings material between Mark 3:19 and 4:1, in the other for the Markan sayings material between 9:40 and 10:13. Luke's utilization of "Matthean matter," in other words, is determined by his "editorial work on Mark"—to replace two blocks of (in Luke's view) inferior Markan sayings material with two large blocks of superior Matthean sayings material, sweeping up in various passes Matthean matter that frequently though not always occurs prior to the parallel narrative passage in Matthew (38).[5] One notes, however, that forms of the allegedly inferior material between Mark 3:19 and 4:1 (Beelzebul Accusation; Blasphemy against the Holy Spirit) appear in the next block of collated Matthean materials, and Jesus's True Family (Mark 3:31–35) appears belatedly in Luke 8:19–21. Likewise for the Markan materials between 9:40 and 10:13.

Perhaps recognizing that this does not get him very far, Lummis appeals to the Prologue: by finding new settings and creating new connections Luke brought the quality of καθεξῆς to his Matthean source materials. This has the virtue, Lummis continues, of explaining a number of his omissions—a number of Matthean elements simply resisted accommodation into Luke's rearranged sequences—but at the same time Luke's "infelicitous" placements, such as Matthew 10:24, 25 (Disciple Not above the Teacher), inserted artificially between Luke 6:38 and 6:41 (39–40). Καθεξῆς is a versatile editorial principle that can even explain why Luke's own sequences are deficient in it. An additional editorial factor is Luke's redactional interests, for example, omission of materials not pertinent or unintelligible to Gentiles (52, 64). Luke omitted

4. Lummis, *How Luke Was Written*, 51 (hereafter page references will be in the text).
5. Also "Case against Q," 762–64.

Matthew 11:28–30 because the Paulinist in him "disliked" its use of ζυγός (84). He did not use Matthew 5:14b (City on a Hill) "because he did not value it," or alternatively, "found no place for it" (90–91).

Lummis has Luke visually collating Matthew and Mark, though he notes the difficulties of Luke's "work[ing] with crabbed rolls instead of with printed codices" (54–55). He is alert to the problem of how Luke managed the seemingly random relocation of various Matthean bits and pieces here and there into their new settings in his own large blocks, especially elements from the Sermon on the Mount. His solution is that Luke makes a compilation of extracts as he proceeds through Matthew (67–68, 90–93). The extract-collection theory marks a recurrence of the "phantom Q" phenomenon: a collection of sayings that Luke draws upon to compose a number of his double-tradition sequences.

H. J. Jameson was not like Lummis, a proto-Farrerist, but as an adherent of the Augustinian hypothesis he produced an account of Luke's use of Matthew that merits our attention because of its unusual alertness to the source-utilization problem. Jameson must get past the opening hurdle of why Luke chose Mark over Matthew for his narrative tradition when Matthew invitingly presents him with almost all the Markan triple tradition in mostly the same sequence and available without the compositional jujitsu that Luke must perform owing to some never-quite-explained preference for Mark in the triple tradition. In the Augustinian scenario Mark is not of greater antiquity. Jameson therefore appeals to Mark's Petrine authority.[6]

But how does Luke "use the two together without confusion and overlapping"? Luke first goes through Matthew, comparing it closely with Mark, distinguishing and "marking off" all the passages with Markan parallels. When afterward he is consulting Matthew, these Markan parallels are visible and he can avoid encroaching upon them.[7] But how did Luke manage the relocation and rearrangement of numerous Matthean double-tradition elements in his gospel? Very many of these "displaced" double-tradition passages, Jameson observes, fall in Matthew prior the point Luke has reached in his absolute progression through the main gospel sequence. When earlier he had traversed these parts of Matthew (such as the Sermon) he crossed out the Matthean passages he used at that time. The passed-over Matthean passages would therefore have stood out starkly from their crossed-out surroundings, readily identifiable "for possible future use." When subsequently he discovers that

6. H. G. Jameson, *Origins of the Synoptic Gospels: A Revision of the Synoptic Problem* (Oxford: Blackwell, 1922), 12–13, 27, 46.

7. Jameson, *Origins*, 50–51 (hereafter page citations will be in the text).

he has room for them after all, he goes back and picks them up. Hence the collocation of many of these passages in the travel section. Not only are these passages fresh in his mind from having recently been read, but his mark-up method allows him to go back from time to time and review them, keeping them "present in his mind" for possible use (84).

Quite a few of Luke's utilization movements within Matthew, however, appear rather less methodical. A case in point is the odd conjunction of Luke 6:39, Blind Leading the Blind, and Luke 6:40, Disciple Not above His Teacher. Because Matthew 15:14, Luke's source for Blind Leading the Blind, occurs in the middle of a long sequence of Mark-paralleled materials that Luke had crossed out at the start, it "caught [Luke's] attention" scrolling forward, and he carried it back to a new location his sermon in 6:39. His inexact rendering of Matthew 10:24, his source for Disciple Not above His Teacher (6:40), on the other hand, indicates that he retrieved it by memory (73).

Likewise, it is true that for 11:37–54 (Woes) Luke jumps forward to Matthew 23 from Matthew 12:38–42 (Sign of Jonah). But most of the intervening materials are Markan parallels that Luke had stroked off at the outset (80). Finding himself in Matthew 23 and having used it for his Woes, he continues forward to Matthew 24:9–14 and encounters the warnings on persecution. This triggers recollection of the doublet in Matthew 10:22, and he scrolls back there. This passage is a "cancelled one" (a parallel to Mark 13:13), and Matthew 10:24–25 has already been used (Luke 6:40). But this brings Luke to Matthew 10:26–33 (Nothing Hidden; Fear Not). Perceiving a natural link to the hypocrisy denounced in the Woes, he utilizes this material as Luke 12:2–9, though first inserting, from memory, Matthew 14:6 on the Leaven of the Pharisees. The passage on denying the Son of Man (Luke 12:8–9) triggered recollection of the passed-over parallel in Matthew 12:32 (Mark 3:28–29), Blasphemy against the Holy Spirit, which he now fits into the Luke 12 sequence. The mention of the Holy Spirit in turn cues a recollection of Matthew 10:19, 20, on the Holy Spirit's Aid, just a few verses back from the Matthew 24:9–14 doublet that had pulled him back to Matthew 10:22, setting off the cascade of these utilization moves. This sequence completed, he returns to the position he had left in Matthew 24:9–14, bringing the following passages on Faithful Servants over into his Luke 12:35–48, though "hark[ing] back again" to Matthew 10:34–36, which in approximate form he appropriates as Luke 12:49–59. "And why do you not judge yourselves what is right" (Luke 12:57) cues his memory of Matthew 5:25–26, on reconciling with one's opponent, which he uses for the concluding Luke 12:58–59 (82–83). Like Goulder will do fifty years later, Jameson describes Luke's rather unsystematic utilization movements around Matthew as a series of scrolling operations that not infrequently have been prompted by ad hoc memory cues. Absence of method is baked into the utilization.

Jameson's account also features a phantom Q. Luke has taken his copy of Matthew and preemptively struck out the Markan parallels. This conveniently highlights the materials from which he will take his double tradition. Luke's Matthew-source in point of fact is a copious Q+M (51). When Luke goes through Matthew's Sermon he "tick[s] off" passages selected for relocation and rearrangement, thereby "providing himself . . . with a small, manageable collection of passages" (72).[8]

These pre-Farrer efforts of Lummis and Jameson predated redaction criticism. Redaction criticism will grant much more editorial latitude and theological originality to Luke and to the other evangelists. Redaction critics will also imagine that redaction criticism has superseded source criticism as the principal approach to Synoptic relations. It can hardly be coincidence that the emergence of the Farrer hypothesis coincides with the rise of redaction criticism. On the other hand, in an environment newly attentive to ancient media realities and practices, the Farrer hypothesis has found itself pressed to address the utilization difficulties attendant upon any theory that has Luke dependent upon Matthew.

AUSTEN FARRER

While not using the term "redaction criticism," Austen Farrer notes that the obsolescence of the notion that Luke is "essentially an adapter and compiler" has now made it possible to make sense of his use of Matthew and with the same stroke consign the Q hypothesis to oblivion.[9] Farrer's 1957 essay is tendentious and uneven in the quality of its argumentation, more programmatic than definitive. While hailing it as their founding document, contemporary Farrer hypothesis (FH) scholars view it with some reserve and do not much

---

8. In his *Matthew, Mark, and Luke: A Study in the Order and Interrelation of the Synoptic Gospels* (New York: Longmans and Green, 1937), Jameson's fellow Augustinian John Chapman has an argument against the existence of a common source for Matthew and Luke that anticipates one that will be advanced by Mark Goodacre. Owing to their divergence, variant double-tradition parallels cannot derive from a common source. Luke has other sources for his variant double-tradition passages, which he corrects toward Matthew. But neither do the high agreement double-tradition parallels attest to a common source, for independent use of such a source must produce more variation. Luke therefore took high agreement parallels direct from Matthew (105–6, 155).

9. A. M. Farrer, "On Dispensing with Q," in *Studies in the Gospels: Essays in Honour of R. H. Lightfoot*, ed. D. E. Nineham (Oxford: Blackwell, 1957), 55–88 (56).

advert to its authority in specifics. Yet certain of Farrer's postulates will become fixed elements in subsequent FH theorizing.

Luke preferred Mark, Farrer says, as "the more ancient narrative."[10] It is not clear whether he means that Luke passed a historiographical judgment on Mark's superior authority or that the work possessed for Luke the aura of greater antiquity. Since Luke does not in either case handle the Markan tradition much differently than he handles the Matthean tradition and accords it no particular deference, the problem of why Luke opts for Mark over Matthew remains an open one that subsequent Farrer defenders will try to address. On alternating primitivity Farrer says that most cases can be explained redaction-critically. He concedes, however, that Luke may be substituting a version of the Lord's Prayer more familiar to the believers of the Achaean churches (64–65)—thereby allowing a small opening for a non-Matthean source for double tradition.

The crux problem has been coming up with intelligible rationales for the multitude of Luke's specific utilization operations upon Matthew. Like his predecessors Farrer retreats to the unassailable refuge of Luke's subjectivity. True, he says, it is difficult to make sense of Luke's dislocation and dispersal of Matthean materials in the travel section; the arrangements are indeed rather "awkward." But why should this matter? Luke "is not dividing and rearranging existing material, he is presenting his vision of the gospel according to his inspiration" (68). The elements that he selects from the copious Matthean materials on offer all have the quality of "Luke-pleasingness"; conversely, the materials left aside are those "he did not care for" (57). We do not need to give an account of Luke's choices and rearrangements. Rather, "all we need to show is that Luke's plan was capable of attracting St. Luke" (65).

This reasoning is so consummately circular that there must be a special logic at work that accounts for why Farrer and subsequent FH scholarship find it probative. Indeed there is. Farrer holds that the 2DH is predicated on the alleged "incredibility" of Luke's use of Matthew, in turn predicated on the old source-critical conception of Luke as an "adapter and compiler." Redaction criticism has shifted the ground under this debate. What was "incredible" is now credible. Source-utilization agency is now vested in the theological subjectivities of the evangelists. There are few limits to Luke's creativity. It follows that the 2DH is an offense against Occam's Razor.

This logic will function down to the present as a kind of basic cognitive programming within Farrerist discourse.[11] We can refer to it as "FH logics." On

---

10. Farrer, "Dispensing," 63, 65 (hereafter page citations will be in the text).

11. On this logical substructure of the FH see also Christopher Tuckett, "The Reception of Q Studies in the UK: No Room at the Inn?," in *The Q Hypothesis Unveiled: Theological, So-*

this view of things, even the demand for an accounting of Luke's procedures vis-à-vis Matthew is an impertinence. "Why Luke did what he did, rather than anything else, cannot be the question. He did what he was moved to do. It is enough if we can see what he did" (75). To defeat the 2DH the Farrer hypothesis only needs to be shown to be *possible*, whereas the 2DH must be shown to be *probable* (62). One might be tempted to question the critical credentials of a theory that finds its moment of triumph in reaching the threshold of the merely possible, but this follows from Farrer's logic above. To refute the alternatives all that the FH needs to do is to hit the possibility threshold—that is, Luke's use of Matthew is not "incredible." The FH can never be refuted, for it can never not meet that benchmark. Some subsequent Farrer defenders will be uncomfortable with pushing the logic that far (its effect is to preimmunize the FH against virtually any critique) and make the effort to show that notwithstanding its difficulties the hypothesis is probable or at least credible.

Farrer nevertheless feels some need to address the source-utilization difficulties. Luke manages his reverse source-critical task of disarticulating Matthean from Markan materials, he says, through a combination of visual discrimination and memory. Great chunks of these Matthean materials Luke finds in blocks that are only nominally connected with the Markan frameworks. It would be an easy matter for him to discriminate these visually, even more so since for most of them his just preceding use of Mark would have left the Markan parallels freshly impressed on his memory. No markup of the Matthean manuscript would even have been necessary. Luke simply takes over Matthew's Markan contextualizations of John's Preaching and the Sermon. For many elements in the travel section all Luke has to do is to scan back through Matthew "bear[ing] in mind" the Matthean materials that he had already utilized. Farrer acknowledges that these explanations will not work so well for materials for which Luke roves ahead into Matthew 19–25 which he "has not yet skimmed of [its] Marcan elements." Blocks such as the Woes and the Great Supper would present no insuperable difficulties. Farrer admits, however, that Luke's stripping of the Matthean elements out of Matthew's augmented version of the Mark 13 Apocalypse to create his Luke 17 Apocalypse is a more difficult task, which to manage Luke would have had to carry out a close side-by-side comparison of his Markan and Matthean manuscripts. But this would have been eased by his having the Markan Apocalypse "virtually by heart" (83–84).

---

ciological, and Hermeneutical Issues Behind the Sayings Source, ed. Marcus Tiwald, BWANT 225 (Stuttgart: Kohlhammer, 2020), 62–85 (72–75, 82).

One ought not to fault Farrer for this rather cursory treatment of the source-utilization challenges in what amounts to a concept essay. He passes over Luke's avoidance of Markan elements in the Matthean Beelzebul episode and the Mission Instruction. Luke's dual manipulation of Mark and Matthew in composing Luke 3–6 also receives no attention. Visually distinguishing the boundaries of non-Markan and Markan materials in his Matthew manuscript might present greater difficulties to Luke than Farrer supposes, similarly for Luke's intermittent scans back through Matthew, particularly when composing the travel section, to pick out Matthean materials that he had previously passed over. That Luke can appropriate significant sequences of Matthean materials in blocks still leaves some rather challenging operations, such as picking out Matthew 8:19–22 (Candidates for Discipleship) cleanly from its Markan environs, including from its Markan lead (Matt 8:18). Or Matthew 13:16–17 (Blessed Are the Eyes) from the middle of extensive blocks fore and aft of Markan materials, similarly Matthew 13:31–32 (Mustard Seed and Leaven), Matthew 15:14b (Blind Guides), Matthew 18:7 (Scandals), Matthew 19:28 (Twelve Thrones), by way of example. Jointly and severally none of these operations is impossible. The question rather is the cognitive expenditure required to carry them off, especially when a compelling reason for why Luke prefers Mark to Matthew for the narrative tradition has not yet been offered.

In reluctantly allowing that Luke took his Our Father from the tradition of the Achaean churches Farrer opens the door a crack to phantom Q—a non-Matthean source for double-tradition materials. Alert to this he immediately throws himself against the door to keep other elements of the double tradition from tumbling in after it, reassuring the reader that the concession "casts no light whatever on the literary relation of St. Luke and St. Matthew," and that it was Matthew's Lord's Prayer that triggered Luke's recollection of the alternate version (65).

In Farrer's media framework "living oral tradition" precedes Synoptic writing. Presumably oral tradition is Mark's principal source, and it is Matthew's for his M/double-tradition materials. Matthew uses "no other source" than the written Mark for the triple tradition (85). We can surmise that this is Farrer's rationale for holding that, analogously, Matthew is Luke's principal source for the double tradition, not a parallel oral tradition. The extensive relative agreements in order can be taken to support this. Source utilization itself a matter of visual scanning and copying of the manuscript script. Memory is a peripheral factor, invoked ad hoc to help manage certain utilization difficulties (83–84).

MICHAEL GOULDER

Goulder and FH Logics

Michael Goulder ratchets Farrer's "possible" threshold up a notch, holding that Luke's use of Matthew must be shown to be *plausible*. But channeling Farrer, he insists that if the FH achieves the "plausibility" threshold, it enjoys default privilege over the likewise plausible 2DH by virtue of Occam's Razor. For its part 2DH scholarship bears the burden of showing that the FH is positively *implausible*. Like Farrer, Goulder sets up the board to reduce the FH's burden of demonstration while increasing it for 2DH.[12] In any case, the gap between Farrer's "possible" and Goulder's "plausible" is vanishingly small. Again we ask, what critical theorist would be content aiming for plausibility rather than probability? Why might Farrer scholarship shrink from the probability test?

Goulder is too intelligent a critic, however, to think that a theory's being "plausible" is the same as its being correct, and he has allowed that the FH must now pass at least the plausibility test. Thus, despite asserting with all the optimism of the redaction critic that elucidating Luke's theological and literary interests suffices to explain his source utilization, Goulder makes a concerted effort to engage with the practicalities of Luke's use of Matthew. This includes giving unprecedented attention to the problem of Luke's scroll manipulation.

Goulder: Matthew and the Origins of the Double Tradition

Appealing to the analogy of Jewish midrash, Goulder has Matthew *composing* virtually all the non-Markan materials in his gospel out of the Markan textual matrix. The theological and literary profile of these materials, he points out, is Matthean. It follows that Matthew composed them.[13] Though Goulder will subsequently be obliged to concede that the analogy to Jewish midrashic activity is spurious, Matthean composition of the non-Markan materials remains an immutable element of his account. It is essential to his dispensing with Q:

---

12. Michael Goulder, "Luke's Compositional Options," *NTS* 38 (1993): 150–52 (151); "Luke's Knowledge of Matthew," in *Minor Agreements: Symposium Göttingen 1991* (Göttingen: Vandenhoeck & Ruprecht, 1993), 143–61 (159–60); "Michael Goulder Responds," in *The Gospels according to Michael Goulder: A North American Response*, ed. Christopher A. Rollston (Harrisburg, PA: Trinity Press International, 2002), 137–52 (141–42).

13. Michael D. Goulder, *Midrash and Lection in Matthew* (London: SPCK, 1974), 4–5, 32, 64, 151–52.

Matthew is the source of the double tradition.[14] Luke takes his double tradition from Matthew, impressing it with his redactional and stylistic distinctives, and like Matthew he creatively composes his own special materials out of the Markan and Matthean textual matrices, mostly the Matthean. There is no need to posit external sources, a "hypothetical tradition," either for Luke's double tradition or for his special materials.[15]

This plays into Goulder's take on the "alternating primitivity" problem: Matthew composed the double tradition, and Luke's parallels are easily explained as redactional derivatives.[16] The Lord's Prayer is Matthew's own composition from Markan motifs; Luke's version is his redaction of Matthew's. Any Prayer descending from Jesus would have been memorized and thus virtually identical in both.[17] Even a difficult case like the oracle of judgment over Jerusalem (Matt 23:34//Luke 11:49) can yield to redaction criticism. Luke alters Matthew's "therefore behold, I am sending them prophets and sages and scribes" to "therefore also the Wisdom of God said, 'I will send to them prophets and apostles.'" He does this because he interprets "prophets" as Old Testament prophets and therefore sent by God, identified as the Divine Wisdom not only on the basis of the σοφούς cue in Matthew but also because of the divine *foreknowledge* of Israel's rejection, a Romans theme familiar to the Paulinist Luke. Luke "does not fancy Matthew's Jewish-type" sages and scribes and alters them to "the more universal" ἀποστόλους.[18]

Goulder: Why Luke Prefers Mark

Like all defenders of the FH, Goulder must first identify a rationale for why Luke opts for Mark over Matthew for the triple tradition. This is the extra gear needed by the FH to make it work. The FH rides on this rationale: it is not clear why Luke should adopt this course, yet it is the master premise of the hypothesis. It is how the FH resolves the problem of the divergent disposition of the double tradition in Matthew and Luke. The choice encumbers Luke with discriminating the Markan parallels in Matthew, cleanly culling the Matthean

---

14. Michael D. Goulder, *Luke: A New Paradigm*, 2 vols., JSNTSup 20 (Sheffield: JSOT Press, 1989), 12–14, 22–23; "Michael Goulder Responds," 137–39.

15. Goulder, *Midrash and Lection*, 452; *Luke*, 22–23, 87–88 (quotation).

16. Goulder, "Luke's Knowledge of Matthew," 159; "On Putting Q to the Test," *NTS* 24 (1978): 218–34 (234).

17. Goulder, *Midrash and Lection*, 297.

18. Michael D. Goulder, "Is Q a Juggernaut?," *JBL* 115 (1996): 667–81 (673–74).

materials, and inventing for them new contexts, with the logic of the new arrangements not always immediately clear.

Goulder's sensitivity to the difficulty is evident in his piling up of rationales: Mark is habituated to Luke from a dozen years of exclusive use in his community; Mark bears the prestige of the Roman church of the martyred Peter and Paul; its traditions carry the authority of Peter himself; Mark was perhaps Luke's close friend (Col 4:10, 14); Luke sides with Paul over against the Jerusalem pillars and cannot share Matthew's enthusiasm for Peter and for the law; Luke thought that Matthew had shortcomings as a lectionary.[19] Whether these suffice to explain such things as Luke's scrubbing of Markan elements out of overlap passages can remain an open question for now. Manifestly Luke does not treat Mark with any particular deference. Goulder himself imagines Luke following not Mark but Matthew for the John the Baptist, Baptism, and Temptation sequence, with Mark exerting occasional memory influence.[20] In the sequence Luke 4:16a (Ναζαρά); 4:16b–30 (Rejection at Nazareth); 4:31–44 (Capernaum Healings); 5:1–11 (Call of Disciples), Goulder has Luke nimbly using Mark's *content* while following Matthew's *order* (i.e., in addition to the Ναζαρά agreement both Matthew and Luke place a Call of the Disciples *after* Jesus begins a Capernaum-based ministry).[21] He also has Luke subordinating both Mark and Matthew indifferently to his larger lectionary project; they are equivalently "rewritten . . . transcribed . . . quarried . . . transcribed" in its realization.[22] Elsewhere he can speak of Luke's concern being to *reconcile* his two sources.[23] His own analysis, that is, does not accord with the status of Mark that he imputes to Luke.

Goulder: Scrolls and Memory in Luke's Matthew Utilization

We can leave that question unresolved for now and turn to how Goulder makes sense of Luke's Matthew-utilization operations. "Luke-pleasingness" is his criterion for Luke's selection and omission of Matthean materials. Here Goulder is simply making standard redaction-critical judgments about Luke's guiding theological interests, such as his indifference to Matthew's intra-Jewish disputes.[24] But the classic difficulty confronting Goulder is to account for Luke's

19. Goulder, *Midrash and Lection*, 453–54; "Luke's Compositional Options," 151–52. See F. Gerald Downing, "A Paradigm Perplex: Luke, Matthew, and Mark," *NTS* 38 (1992): 15–36 (25).
20. Goulder, *Luke*, 282.
21. Goulder, *Luke*, 311.
22. Goulder, *Midrash and Lection*, 465.
23. E.g., Goulder, *Luke*, 340–41.
24. Goulder, *Midrash and Lection*, 454.

reordering of his Matthean source, to show that Luke was not a crank. In his first stab at the problem, in *Midrash and Lection*, Goulder proposed that Luke's project was to create a Sabbath-cycle lectionary arrangement out of Matthew's festal-cycle arrangement, which included ordering the Matthean materials in the travel section to accord with the topical progression of Deuteronomy.[25] Subsequently he retreats from the Lukan lectionary theory, without wholly abandoning it. He briefly proposes supplementing it by attributing to Luke a "topical" principle of arrangement but never develops the idea.[26] Failing to subsume Luke's rearrangement operations under a comprehensive rubric, Goulder effectively gives up and shifts to ad hoc explanations. His lectionary theory will survive as one among a number of such expedients.

Goulder stands out for the extent to which he tries to envision the realities of Luke's source-utilization operations. He was ahead of his time in recognizing that this is indispensable to making the Farrer hypothesis plausible. Goulder imagines Luke working at a table with one scroll open before him—be it Mark or Matthew—and the other on the floor, and the scrolls alternately exchanging positions. While Luke is using one source the other source on the floor can influence him by memory, or as Goulder puts it, "from reminiscence of a familiar parallel text." This explains such things as overlaps and the triple-tradition minor agreements.[27] The Markan elements in Luke's opening sequence that runs from John the Baptist through to the Temptation, where Luke "still has Matthew open on the table before him," are a case in point.[28] It is more likely that Luke composed with a given scroll on his knees, not spread out on a table, but it is hard to see that this affects Goulder's account in any way. His imagined scene remains correct in its basics.

Goulder's working conception is that Luke's source-utilization mode is visual, with memory operating in the background in the form of Luke's "reminiscence" of his sources, frequently ad hoc and unpremeditated. Memory is not a compositional competence for enacting a normative tradition but a highly volatile factor impinging on visual source utilization. In a similar vein Goulder sometimes envisions Luke reading over the passage in the source at hand and then retaining it in unstable short-term memory as he turns to his destination scroll. This aids Goulder in explaining changes that occur between

25. Goulder, *Midrash and Lection*, 470–71.

26. Michael Goulder, "The Order of a Crank," in *Synoptic Studies: The Ampleforth Conferences of 1982 and 1983*, ed. C. M. Tuckett, JSNTSup 7 (Sheffield: JSOT Press, 1984), 111–30 (115, 128); see Mark S. Goodacre, *Goulder and the Gospels: An Examination of a New Paradigm*, JSNTSup 133 (Sheffield: Sheffield Academic, 1996), 300.

27. Goulder, "Order of a Crank," 113.

28. Goulder, *Luke*, 282, 291.

Mark and Luke, for example Luke's transposition of certain phrases within the long pericope of Mark's Healing of Jairus's Daughter/Woman with the Flow (Mark 5:25–43//Luke 8:40–55). These include the transposition of ἦν γαρ ἐτῶν δώδεκα from the end to the beginning of the story (Mark 5:42//Luke 8:42), as well as transpositions of a few other phrases. The rapid decay of short-term memory accounts in the same passage for the much weaker reminiscence—as a memory intrusion—of the Matthean version of the same pericope that generated the important minor agreement προσελθοῦσα . . . τοῦ κρασπέδου (Luke 8:44//Matt 9:22b). Having been read earlier, the Matthean passage is not so fresh in Luke's memory as Mark's version is.[29] Memory for Goulder is always ancillary to Luke's visual-utilization access to his sources. As often as not it serves simply to prompt Luke's scrolling action backward or forward to the memory-cued passage. Only where such scrolling action would become too furious and random does Goulder hold that Luke retrieves a particular passage from the remote context by memory.

How successful is Goulder at producing a "plausible" account of Luke's use of Matthew, where previous attempts have failed? We have already seen that for the sequence Luke 4:16a (Ναζαρά); 4:16b–30 (Rejection at Nazareth); 4:31–44 (Capernaum Healings); 5:1–11 (Call of Disciples), Goulder has Luke using Mark's content while "for the present" preferring Matthew's order. But then Luke begins to follow the Markan order rather than the Matthew 8–9 order of healings because he "takes the view that the order and detail are better preserved in Mark."[30] Goulder, that is, finds himself here and elsewhere quickly resorting to ad hoc rationalizations of Luke's utilization actions that rest upon on-the-spot determinations about Luke's subjective intentionality and his literary imagination.[31] Explanations of this sort might clear the rather low bar of "plausibility," but their drawback is that any utilization hypothesis whatsoever can resolve its utilization problems this way.

Luke's travel section has been the graveyard of attempts to make coherent sense of Luke's Matthew utilization. Goulder's own effort converges with his keen interest in doing justice to the practicalities of scroll manipulation, which for him is a matter of visually based copying and secondary memory-cuing that is itself optically triggered by the visual script. Memory is invoked

---

29. Goulder, *Luke*, 425.

30. Goulder, *Luke*, 311. Incidentally, Luke places his Call of Disciples/Catch of Fish story after Mark 1:39; Matthew places his after Mark 1:15, so in fact Luke is not following Matthew's order. It is Matthew 4:23 that is Matthew's temporary substitute for the Markan day in Capernaum and Galilean preaching tour, not 4:15.

31. Goulder, "Luke's Compositional Options," 151.

ad hoc as "reminiscence" to deal with anomalies, mostly anomalies of order, that arise in optically centered literary-utilization scenarios. Goulder's usual protocol for explaining Luke's departures from Matthew's order is to claim that eye-catching motifs and key words on the page before Luke trigger recollection, often quite spontaneous, of fitting passages from remote and hence out-of-sequence Matthean locations. While copying Matthew 7:1–5 (Judge Not; Luke 6:38–42), for example, "a text from Matthew *comes to [Luke's] mind*: 'A disciple is not above his teacher . . .' ([Matt] 10.24f.)," that Luke thereupon inserts (6:40).[32]

Ad hoc appeals to memory of this sort spike in Goulder's treatment of the travel section, where double tradition is concentrated but a common absolute sequence with Matthew all but disappears. Here it becomes extraordinarily difficult to correlate Luke's actual ordering of the double tradition with his scrolling usage of Matthew. Goulder must posit for Luke a complex combination of scrolling and copying operations—for example, forward (Matt 9 to Matt 16), skipping forward (to Matt 23–25), then backward (from Matt 25 to Matt 17), then forward again (to Matt 24 for the Luke 17 Apocalypse). Memory is called upon for the numerous passages that still cannot be resolved into sequence by these maneuvers.[33] Goulder has Luke scrolling ahead from Matthew 16 to Matthew 24–25 to locate and copy the Servant Parable (Luke 12:41–48), but for the next unit, "I have come to cast fire . . ." (Luke 12:49–53), "cast[ing] his mind back" to Matthew 10:34–35.[34] While Luke's scroll is again open to Matthew 25, the conclusion of the Bridesmaids Parable (Matt 25:10–13), "'and the door was shut,' *recalls* an earlier Matthean charge to enter through the narrow gate (7.13). . . . Luke accordingly adapts the gate of Matthew 7 to the door of Matthew 25," the result being the sequence Luke 13:24–27.[35] Three chapters previously in his composition Luke had jumped ahead by memory (". . . and there comes to mind . . .") from his position in Matthew 11 to Matthew 13:16–17 to retrieve Blessed Are the Eyes (Luke 10:23–24) for placement after I Thank Thee, Father (Luke 10:21–22).[36]

32. Goulder, *Luke*, 370, emphasis added.
33. Goulder, *Luke*, 581–82. Goulder attributes to Luke additional irregular scrolling movements, as when Luke scrolls from Matthew 12 to Matthew 15:1–20 (Hand-Washing Controversy) from which Luke infers a meal setting for his Woes (11:37–38, 54), and then forward to Matthew 23 for the Woes material, then back to Matthew 15 and 16:5–6 (Beware the Leaven of the Pharisees).
34. Goulder, *Luke*, 552.
35. Goulder, *Luke*, 572, emphasis added.
36. Goulder, *Luke*, 480. One cannot but be impressed that Luke's spontaneous, topic-

The strains upon this line of explanation become especially evident in Goulder's account of Luke's scrolling usage of Matthew 16 for the composition of his Luke 12:1–49 sequences. Though open to Matthew 16, Luke actually copies very little of it as it mostly duplicates triple tradition already picked up (from Mark) in Luke 8–9. Instead, Matthew 16 affects Luke's composition as a sort of virtual sequence, providing a set of often quite vague memory cues, the "thread under the embroidery," for recollecting double-tradition materials, often with impressive accuracy, from remote locations in Matthew 6, 10, 12 (passages passed over when Luke's Matthew scroll was actually open to them), and 24:43–25:13 (for Luke 12:35–40).[37] After this effortless roving by memory, however, Goulder has Luke suddenly scroll forward from Matthew 16 to Matthew 24 virtually mid-pericope (his present *memory* location being Matt 24:43–44) to copy the Servant Parable (Luke 12:41–46//Matt 24:45–51). Goulder's grounds for Luke's sudden switch from memory to scrolling and copying is the close agreement of the parallels.[38] But this is curious in view of Luke's closely preceding, virtually verbatim reproduction from memory of Do Not Be Anxious (Matt 6:25–34; Luke 12:22–32). The truth is that Goulder can no longer plausibly maintain that Luke actually has his scroll open to Matthew 16 (in 12:1–40 Luke has been everywhere except Matthew 16), and at any rate Goulder needs to get Luke physically to Matthew 24–25 to set up (after Luke 13:23) the reverse scrolling operation back to Matthew 17. However, this in turn requires that for 12:54–56 (Signs of the Times) Luke reach back by memory to Matthew 16:2–3, passed over (but "kept in mind") when he had just had it before his eyes.[39]

This ad hoc jumble of scrolling-copying and memory operations makes little sense of Luke's use of Matthew.[40] Goulder's commendable attention to scrolling maneuvers has not served so much to lessen the utilization problem for the FH as to make it more acute.

---

cued reminiscences, particularly of passages in Matthew 23–25, correspond unerringly to Matthew's additions to Mark.

37. Goulder, *Luke*, 529–35.

38. Goulder, *Luke*, 549.

39. Goulder, *Luke*, 557.

40. For fine-grained analysis of the breakdown of coherence in Goulder's utilization account see Robert A. Derrenbacker Jr., *Ancient Compositional Practices and the Synoptic Problem*, BETL 186 (Leuven: Leuven University Press; Peeters, 2005), 195–200; "Greco-Roman Writing Practices and Luke's Gospel: Revisiting 'The Order of a Crank,'" in Rollston, *Gospels according to Michael Goulder*, 61–83 (78–79).

Goulder: Luke's "Unpicking" of Matthew

"Unpicking" refers to FH Luke's surgical separation of M from Markan materials when they appear in common contexts in his Matthean source. The unpicking issue surfaces frequently in critiques of the FH. Goulder points out that much of the M material in Matthew occurs in large, self-contained segments—such as the Sermon on the Mount—that Luke, given his familiarity with Mark, can easily distinguish from neighboring Markan materials in the Matthean context. Luke moreover composes from his sources in blocks: he follows Mark for an extended sequence (Luke 4:31 to 6:19; 8:4 to 9:50; 18:14 to the end), and then, putting Mark down and picking up his copy of Matthew, selects the M additions to the just-copied Markan parallels that he wishes to use. Memory plays a role in this operation: the Markan passages are fresh in Luke's mind, and this makes the procedure even less difficult.[41]

This takes Goulder only so far. The "unpicking" problem in fact arises in connection with the not infrequent cases in which the admixture of Markan and M elements is closer. These include passages where short M elements are embedded in Markan contexts and vice versa, some examples being Mark 11:25 in the Prayer instruction in the Sermon on the Mount (Matt 6:14), Luke 6:39 (Blind Guides) from Matthew 15:14, Luke 10:21–22 (Blessed Are the Eyes) from Matthew 13:16–17, Luke 22:28–30 (Twelve Thrones) from Matthew 19:28. They also include the overlap passages, and Luke's scavenging of M elements from the Matthew 24 Apocalypse to build his own Luke 17 travel-section Apocalypse. How does Luke manage to comb the Mark 6 Mission elements out of Matthew 10, and the Markan elements out of the Matthean Beelzebul episode? How does he avoid the Markan elements in the controversy itself, e.g., τὸν σατανᾶν ἐκβάλλω (Mark 3:23b//Matt 12:26a) and cleanly pick out just the Matthean expansion of the Markan Blasphemy against the Holy Spirit (Luke 12:10// Matt 12:32//Mark 3:28)? What method does Luke use when scanning back through Matthew's Sermon for travel-section materials to distinguish these from passages that he has already used?

Here Goulder becomes less certain. He experiments with different expedients, each connected to his visual-utilization model. His initial tack is to suggest that Luke can easily reinforce his memory if needed. The just-copied Markan Mission Instruction is still fresh in Luke's mind when he comes to the Matthew 10 Instruction. If he still finds himself in any uncertainty, he can

---

41. Goulder, *Luke*, 39, 610–11; "Is Q a Juggernaut?," 676.

pick up his copy of Mark and review the Mark 6 Mission Instruction.[42] The situation though is different for the Blasphemy against the Holy Spirit in the Matthew 12 Beelzebul episode. Does Luke scroll back and study the Mark 3 parallel, which he had passed over completely, so that he can make a clean incision around and extract the expansion (Matt 12:31b–32) that Matthew inserted between Mark 3:28 and 29?

Goulder's appeal to memory itself raises complications. Elsewhere Luke's "reminiscence" of one of his sources intrudes—frequently unbidden—into his use of the other source. This is the stock FH explanation of the minor agreements: the Matthean parallel memory-leaks into Luke's utilization of the Markan passage. The effect is also bidirectional. Goulder holds that in following Matthew 18:6–7 in composing 17:1–2 (Scandals), Luke transposes Matthew 18:7 to the first position. Then, "with these changes in order . . . he takes his eye off the scroll, and in creep some phrases from the ever more familiar Mark, εἰ, περίκειται [περὶ τὸν τράχηλον] . . . for Matthew's κρεμασθῇ / '(thrown) into the sea' for Matthew's 'drowned in (its) depth.'"[43] Luke no sooner takes his eyes off his copy of Matthew than Markan elements rush in from memory. In composing 6:44 (Trees and Fruit), although visually fastened on Matthew 7:16a, Luke is drawing the wording by reminiscence from Matthew 12:33—involuntarily and unconsciously, for it is Matthew 7:16a "which was in Luke's conscious mind," because he proceeds immediately to Matthew 7:16b.[44]

If Luke's memory is confounding Markan and Matthean elements, how is he able to so cleanly, consistently, and without confusion distinguish and separate M from Markan materials in already close admixture elsewhere? Why are elements of the often seamlessly adjoining Markan or M materials not memory-bleeding into each other when Luke is using the one source or the other? After all, he must put down his immediate source to copy out by memory what he has just read. How does he so rarely confuse close M continuations or M prefaces with the Markan passage? Luke's reverse engineering project of disarticulating source elements from each other in Matthew turns out to pose formidable practical difficulties.[45]

---

42. Goulder, *Luke*, 39.

43. Goulder, *Luke*, 639–40.

44. Goulder, *Luke*, 371.

45. There is some resonance here with F. Gerald Downing's concern that in phrases of 30+ characters in non-sayings and non-Scripture quotations, Farrer Luke frequently agrees verbatim or close to verbatim with *either* Matthew *or* Mark when they diverge from each other, but consistently diverges from *both* when they closely agree in wording. Downing comments on the sheer editorial anomalousness of the pattern. See "Disagreements of Each

It is not surprising therefore that Goulder falls back on the expedient that "to discriminate Marcan from non-Marcan sentences in Matthew" Luke has "simply marked his copy of Matthew with his pen!"[46] There are a couple of difficulties that arise for this scenario, the first being the visual presentation of the source script itself, the second being the robust instrumental role of memory in ancient source utilization. To illustrate the first, we can follow the visualizing approach used to good effect by Downing, using a segment of the Matthew 10 Mission Instruction, 10:7–16, that is Luke's source for his Mission Instruction.

ΠΟΡΕΥΟΜΕΝΟΙΔΕΚΨΡΥΣΣΕΤΕΛΕΓΟΝΤΕΣΟΤΙΗΓΓΙΚΕΝΗΒΑΣΙΛ
ΕΙΑΤΩΝΟΥΡΑΝΩΝΑΣΘΕΝΟΥΝΤΑΣΘΕΡΑΠΕΥΕΤΕΝΕΚΡΟΥΣΕΓΕΙ
ΡΕΤΕΛΕΠΡΟΥΣΚΑΘΑΡΙΘΕΤΕΔΑΙΜΟΝΙΑΕΚΒΑΛΛΕΤΕΔΩΟΡΕΑΝΕ
ΛΑΒΕΤΕΔΩΡΕΑΝΔΟΤΕΜΗΚΤΗΣΗΣΘΕΧΡΥΣΟΝΜΗΔΕΑΡΓΥΡΟΝΜ
ΗΔΕΧΑΛΚΟΝΕΙΣΤΑΣΖΩΝΑΣΗΥΜΩΝΜΗΠΗΡΑΝΕΙΣΟΔΟΝΜΗΔ
ΕΔΥΟΧΙΤΩΝΑΣ ΜΗΔΕΥΠΟΔΗΜΑΤΑΜΗΔΕΡΑΒΔΟΝΑΞΙΟΣΓΑΡΗ
ΟΕΡΓΑΤΗΣΤΗΣΤΡΟΦΗΣΑΥΤΟΕΙΣΗΝΔΕΑΝΠΟΛΙΝΗΚΩΜΗΝΕΙΣ
ΕΛΘΗΤΕΕΞΕΤΑΣΑΤΕΤΙΣΕΝΑΥΤΗΑΞΙΟΣΕΣΤΙΝΚΑΚΕΙΜΕΙΝΑΤΕΕΩ
ΣΑΝΕΞΕΛΘΗΤΕΕΙΣΕΡΧΟΜΕΝΟΙΔΕΕΙΣΤΗΝΟΙΚΙΑΝΑΣΠΑΣΑΣΤΗ
ΕΑΥΤΗΝΚΑΙΕΑΝΜΕΝΗΙΟΙΚΙΑΑΞΙΑΕΛΘΑΤΩΗΕΙΡΗΝΗΥΜΩΝΕΠΑ
ΥΤΗΝΕΑΝΔΕΜΗΗΑΞΙΑΗ ΕΙΡΗΝΗΥΜΩΝΠΡΟΣΥΜΑΣΕΠΙΣΤΡΑΦ
ΗΤΩΚΑΙΟΣΑΝΜΗΔΕΞΗΤΑΙΥΜΑΣΜΗΔΕΑΚΟΥΣΗΤΟΥΣΛΟΓΟΥΣ
ΥΜΩΝΕΞΕΡΧΟΜΕΝΟΙΕΞΩΤΗΣΟΙΚΙΑΣΗΤΗΣΠΟΛΕΩΣΕΚΕΙΝΗΣΕ
ΚΤΙΝΑΞΑΤΕΤΟΝΚΟΝΙΟΡΤΟΝΤΩΝΠΟΔΩΝΥΜΩΝΑΜΗΝΛΕΓΩΥ

Evangelist with the Minor Close Agreements of the Other Two," *ETL* 80 (2004): 445–69; "Plausibility, Probability, and Synoptic Hypotheses," *ETL* 93 (2017): 313–37. Not all the cases that Downing gives of Luke's refusal of longer Mark/Matt verbal agreements are equally compelling, and he may not always allow Lukan redaction adequate scope. Further, as Ken Olson riposted, Luke's preference for Mark in the triple tradition on the FH means that he is not comparing Mark with Matthew looking for agreements (or vice versa), hence the practice of ancient authors to embrace the common witness of their sources is irrelevant (Ken Olson, "Unpicking on the Farrer Theory," in *Questioning Q: A Multidimensional Critique*, ed. Mark Goodacre and Nicholas Perrin [Downers Grove, IL: InterVarsity Press, 2004], 127–50 [132]). Nevertheless, if (as Goulder holds) Luke's memory of his Matthean source is prone to interfere in his use of Mark, and on occasion his memory of his Markan source in his use of Matthew, it seems to follow that Luke would tend to converge on Matthew's and Mark's readings where they reinforce each other.

46. Goulder, *Luke*, 40; "Is Q a Juggernaut?," 677 n. 30. Elsewhere he suggests that in Luke's copy of Matthew pericope beginnings were indicated by *ektheses*—the beginning of the first line of a pericope protruding slightly into the margin as an aid to lectors ("Michael Goulder Responds," 146).

ΜΙΝΑΝΕΚΤΟΤΕΡΟΝΕΣΤΑΙΓΗΣΟΔΟΜΩΝΚΑΙΓΟΜΟΡΡΩΝΕΝΗΜ
ΕΡΚΡΙΣΕΩΣΗΤΗΠΟΛΕΙΕΚΕΙΝΗΙΔΟΥΕΓΩΑΠΟΣΤΕΛΛΟΩΥΜΑΣΩ
ΣΠΡΟΒΑΤΑΕΝΜΕΣΩΛΥΚΩΝΓΙΝΕΣΘΕΟΥΝΦΡΟΝΙΜΟΙΩΣΗΟΟΦ
ΕΙΣΚΑΙΑΚΕΡΑΙΟΙΩΣΑΙΠΕΡΙΣΤΕΡΑΙ.

Let it be stipulated that an ancient author like Luke would have enjoyed a high level of facility in reading continuous script like the above, and also that Luke was well versed in both of his sources. The difficulties that would attend discriminating and bracketing out the Markan equipment elements embedded in the Matthean sequence are nevertheless considerable. That it would not have been easy for Luke to cross-check Matthew with the Markan parallel—to which can be added the source-confounding factor of "reminiscence" in Luke's utilization—makes the scarcity of three-way agreements in the Luke 10 Instruction even more impressive. That the operation was not impossible can be granted. One might take the three-way agreement in the equipment list, μὴ πήραν (Luke 10:4//Matt 10:10//Mark 6:8), as indicating that Luke's clearing the Matthean Mission Instruction of Markan elements was incomplete, or selective. But it is not obvious for what end Luke was prepared to make the requisite level of cognitive expenditure.

There appear therefore to be problems with the optical utilization model—with "reminiscence" a subsidiary and volatile factor—that is the basis of Goulder's analysis. That memory in fact played not a peripheral role as "reminiscence" but an instrumental role in the manuscript-utilization practices of ancient scholars and writers exacerbates the problem. We will have more to say about this in due course, but for now it can be said that it is considerably more difficult for Luke's unmixing of Markan and M elements from one another in closely contiguous contexts to occur in the medium of memory. The difficulty is compounded when one recognizes that ancient writers engaged with their source texts orally and aurally, and that Luke is re-actualizing the tradition of his sources.

In sum: notwithstanding a virtuoso display of ingenuity, Goulder remains unable to identify a consistent set of editorial policies guiding Luke's utilization of Matthew. In his earliest publications he argues that Luke has "liturgical reasons for rearranging Matthew": Luke's gospel is a revised lectionary project.[47] "It is in light of this," he suggests, "that the riddle of Luke's order is to be

---

47. Goulder, "On Putting Q to the Test," 534; *Midrash and Lection*, 470–71; "Order of a Crank," 128. See Goodacre, *Goulder and the Gospels*, 300.

resolved."[48] In his 1989 *Luke: A New Paradigm* Goulder continues to apply this rationale to Luke's use of Matthew—to begin with. He claims, for example, that Luke suddenly jumps ahead to Matthew 11:2–19 to pull forward Jesus's John the Baptist discourse (Luke 7:18–35) because he needs a reading for New Year's Sunday, which Luke's church "has been used to celebrating with thoughts of John the Baptist."[49] The Sinful Woman (Luke 7:36–50) follows naturally for Atonement Sunday, and then the Parable of the Sower (8:4–8) appropriately for the harvest festival Tabernacles. This explains Luke's move from Matthew 9 over to Mark 4 at this point.[50] The revised-lectionary hypothesis mires down in the travel section, however, where Goulder adverts to it only occasionally as one of an array of ad hoc rationales: Luke is composing in triads (e.g., three discipleship candidates in Luke 9:56–62; three controversies in 11:14–54, pulled together from various Matthean locations, including roving ahead to the Matthew 23 Woes); Luke wants to create a topical catechetical progression; Luke is following a policy of utilizing Mark and Matthew in separate blocks.[51] But we have seen that Goulder's attempts to make sense of Luke's utilization patterns in the travel section unravel into a series of random scrolling movements, frequently precipitated by chance reminiscences, chance encounters with eye-catching Matthean motifs, and on-the-spot inspiration, maneuvers that do not so much as explain as they merely describe Luke's various movements around Matthew.

Goulder eventually abandons the effort to identify the editorial policies guiding Luke's Matthew utilization in favor of appealing like Farrer did to the inscrutability of Luke's creative mind. "Master jewelers," he says, take responsibility only for producing works of art."[52] He adopts the "evasive tactics" described by philosopher of science Karl Popper, the point of which is to immunize a hypothesis against refutation. He makes his theory "compatible with everything that could happen."[53] As it did Goulder's nineteenth-century predecessors, the travel section defeats his efforts to explain Luke's Matthew utilization.

48. Goulder, *Midrash and Lection*, 455.

49. Goulder, *Luke*, 387.

50. Goulder *Luke*, 407.

51. Goulder, *Luke*, 39, 170–72, 255, 517–18.

52. Goulder, "Is Q a Juggernaut?," 680, in response to Christopher Tuckett's enumeration of anomalies in Goulder's backward scrolling expedient (Christopher M. Tuckett, "The Existence of Q," in *Q and the History of Early Christianity* [Edinburgh: T&T Clark, 1996], 1–41 [16–31]).

53. Karl Popper, "The Problem of Demarcation," in *Popper Selections*, ed. David Miller (Princeton, NJ: Princeton University Press, 1985), 118–30 (125–26).

Goulder: Double-Tradition Origins and Authorial Agency

A lead argument of our study is that defective media models are the principal cause of the difficulties that various utilization hypotheses run into and indeed of the impasse in the Synoptic problem. What are Goulder's governing media assumptions? Utilization is strictly through the optical sensorium; Luke is visually fastened on his source manuscripts. Memory is a peripheral and random factor, an involuntary reflex, a matter of "reminiscence." It serves ad hoc to resolve anomalies in Luke's source utilization. It is a weak faculty incapable of exactitude and responsible for producing variant versions of memory-retrieved passages.

This leads us to Goulder's model for the history of the early Christian tradition in *Midrash and Lection*, reiterated in *Luke: A New Paradigm*. He thinks of the tradition as a static consolidation of apostolic memories. This body of tradition, which formed in the Jerusalem community, is inert; it undergoes no development beyond some "erosions" and "amplifications."[54] This static memory formation then received textual incarnation in the Gospel of Mark. Mark therefore preserves the bulk of the primitive Christian oral tradition. But more to the point, because the tradition is inert, lacking any internal dynamic of development, *individual authorial agency* becomes the solo force driving its growth and evolution, which accordingly can only begin after the tradition takes written form in Mark. Matthew rewrites the Markan tradition and composes expansions from the textual matrices of Mark and the Old Testament; Luke creatively rewrites Mark and the Matthean expansions, likewise with inspiration from Old Testament texts.[55]

These media assumptions explain Goulder's curious self-assuredness that the double tradition is composed by Matthew on the basis of the Markan text. It explains his disinclination to concede that there is any Lukan double-tradition parallel that can be definitely shown to be more primitive than its Matthean counterpart. Both Luke's double tradition and his special materials can be comprehended as artistically inspired rewritings and elaborations of the M materials in his own style. Thus "it is hard to see that there is a need for a further hypothetical tradition."[56]

All utilization actions in Goulder's account occur in a sealed textual world, along closed circuits of written works. Luke's closed textual circuit is consti-

54. Goulder, *Luke*, 22–23.
55. Goulder, *Midrash and Lection*, 7–8, 32, 91, 138–41, 151–52; *Luke*, 22–23, 543.
56. Goulder, *Luke*, 87–88.

tuted of Matthew, Mark, the Old Testament, and Paul.[57] All the non-Markan tradition is the invention of authorial writing. No wider matrix of tradition is impinging upon Matthew and Luke in their writing activity, with the exception that Matthew on occasion draws on Oral Torah.[58] The so-called Q materials, Goulder points out, everywhere reference a narrative background: John's ascetic diet and clothing; Jesus's call of disciples, association with tax collectors, his rejection by Galilean towns, and the like. On his media assumptions it follows that they could not have existed anywhere apart from their Markan narrative contextualizations in Matthew.[59] Minor agreements are dispositive against the 2DH because such could only have come to Luke from Matthew. Oral tradition for Goulder is little more than a placeholder until it finds written incarnation in Mark. There is something strategic in this: Goulder needs to rule out other sources for the double tradition that might turn into a phantom Q. He fears, justifiably, that conceding *any* case of alternating primitivity would be the thin edge of the wedge for an additional source or sources for the double tradition.

Goulder nevertheless must make a small concession to the existence of a wider field of tradition. Given the evidence of such in the Pauline epistles he grants that Matthew will have at his disposal "a modicum" of non-Marcan material, very little though.[60] Elsewhere he says that even if Luke did have access to a more primitive version of a Matthean double-tradition parallel (which he does not concede), this would not in any way rule out that he is taking the rest direct from Matthew.[61] Goulder is able to come very close indeed to completely cutting off the possibility of alternative sources for any elements of the double tradition.

Critique of his application of the midrash analogy to Matthew's expansions of Mark, however, forced Goulder to abandon it.[62] This left him without a viable cultural mechanism for Matthew's creation of the bulk of the double tradition. Nevertheless, he just continued to assert Matthew's authorship for it. Post-Goulder FH scholarship understandably has abandoned this plank of his theory. But this comes with consequences: it draws attention afresh to the problem of double-tradition origins.

---

57. On this point see Goodacre, *Goulder and the Gospels*, 18.
58. Goulder, *Midrash and Lection*, 17.
59. Goulder, *Luke*, 69.
60. Goulder, *Midrash and Lection*, 4.
61. Goulder, "On Putting Q to the Test," 234.
62. Goodacre, *Goulder and the Gospels*, 21.

Goulder and Contemporary FH Scholarship

Among contemporary Farrer defenders there is a palpable reluctance to have the hypothesis too closely associated with Goulder. This has to do with his untenable theory of double-tradition origins, his lectionary proposal, and his elaborate scrolling schema. These are regarded as Goulder's regrettable idiosyncrasies and distanced from the Farrer enterprise. Perhaps this is not so easily done. These elements of Goulder's theory are essential to his effort to overcome what he recognized to be real hazards for the FH. The difficulties to which they constitute a response do not so conveniently disappear.

In fact, Goulder has not been completely exorcised from contemporary Farrer scholarship. His recourse to *creative authorial rewriting* continues as a recurrent feature of Farrer hypothesizing, invoked as Goulder did in the face of the formidable explanatory challenges presented by Luke's Matthew utilization. Goulder's identification of creative writing as the main force driving developments in the tradition was predicated on some doubtful media assumptions. His "creative genius" writer Luke is the logical corollary of his model for the tradition as a static, inert entity needing the touch of the creative author to bring it to life.[63] This raises the question as to the extent the FH as a theory is the product of those assumptions, and whether it can be made viable without them.

MARK GOODACRE

The Farrer hypothesis owes much of its present cachet to Mark Goodacre's intellectual vigor and to the nuanced argumentation that he has brought to bear on its behalf. Our approach, here as before, is to study the media conceptions that inform his analysis.

Goodacre and FH Logics

One hears nothing from Goodacre about Austen Farrer's low threshold of "possible" that the FH needs to hit in order to prevail. However, he repeats the standard Farrer claim that Occam's Razor inherently advantages the FH by virtue of its making do with extant sources, and that to overcome this presumption in its favor Matthew and Luke must be shown to be "demonstrably

---

63. The "creative genius" characterization of Goulder's Luke is Goodacre's (*Goulder and the Gospels*, 135).

independent of each other."[64] It follows for him, as it did for Goulder, that what the FH needs to aim at to succeed is to deliver an account of Luke's use of Matthew that meets the "plausibility" benchmark.[65] The "plausibility" rhetoric aside, it is clear that Goodacre's herculean efforts, just as Goulder's were, are in fact directed toward giving an account that makes Luke's use of Matthew *probable*, particularly since he combines the enterprise with an exposition of the "fallacies" on which the 2DH is predicated.

Goodacre on Why Luke Prefers Mark in the Triple Tradition

As a Farrer defender Goodacre must offer reasons for why Luke opted to use Mark for the narrative tradition. He could have used Matthew. The utilization difficulties and editorial questions connected with his selection and rearrangement of double-tradition materials would remain, but it would have saved him the trouble of managing two scrolls instead of one. Similarly, the work of disengaging M materials from Markan materials in Matthew is created by his choice to take Mark for the narrative tradition. Luke needs to pick out Matthean additions from contiguous Markan contexts and on occasion comb Markan elements out of what he judges to be principally Matthean pericopes (e.g., the Beelzebul Accusation). Given manuscript realities these are quite difficult operations, even more so since they involve the juggling and comparison of two manuscripts to keep the Markan and M source strands separate during utilization. Without a compelling motivation for Luke's procedure the FH has difficulty getting off the ground.

Like his predecessors Goodacre manages this by converting the postulate of Markan priority into a set of Lukan preferences. Luke was more habituated to Mark; it had "fixed itself in his mind"; through reading it and preaching from it he had been "steadily getting Mark by heart"; it had "entered into his bloodstream." It is not the parvenu Matthew but Mark that has shaped "his understanding of the Jesus story." Matthew's theological appropriation of it could only appear to Luke as a "contamination" and Matthew's reordering of it experienced as a disruption of a familiarized narrative. Many of the M materials, on the other hand, are welcome additions, and they have the added

---

64. Mark Goodacre, "Farrer Hypothesis Response," in *The Synoptic Problem: Four Views*, ed. Stanley E. Porter and Bryan R. Dyer (Grand Rapids: Baker, 2016), 127–38 (132–33); also *The Case against Q: Studies in Markan Priority and the Synoptic Problem* (Harrisburg, PA: Trinity Press International, 2002), 77.

65. Mark Goodacre, *The Synoptic Problem: A Way through the Maze* (London: T&T Clark, 2001), 160.

advantage that as sayings they lend themselves to easy rearrangement relative to the primary Markan narrative that Luke maintains.[66]

These rationales align awkwardly with claims that Goodacre makes elsewhere. He indeed holds that Matthew has "radically restructured Mark" in chapters 3–11.[67] This is a leading reason for Luke's abjuring Matthew and taking Mark as his narrative source, with weighty consequences for Luke's disposition of the double tradition found in the radically reordered Matthew 3–11.[68] Elsewhere, however, reacting to the 2DH argument that because Luke has not significantly altered the order of Mark it is not likely that he altered the order of the double tradition, Goodacre avers that "the extent of Matthew's reordering of Mark . . . is not as radical as is sometimes claimed." Luke himself, he continues, occasionally alters Mark's order, indeed omits an extensive Markan sequence, "and so the most balanced statement of the evidence would be that Matthew and Luke both depart, at times, from Mark's order, though in different ways."[69] It turns out that Luke is not so devoted to Mark's order after all, and Matthew's reordering of Mark is not so much greater than Luke's.

Also, when the point requires it, Goodacre holds that Luke treats Mark and Matthew equivalently. Luke shortens Matthew's discourses; he shortens Mark's discourses.[70] Luke's treatment of the wording and internal order of Markan pericopes differs little from his treatment of the wording and internal order of Matthean pericopes. Luke regards Matthew's theological coloration of Mark as a "contamination" of a familiarized narrative, yet he refashions Markan passages to his own redactional interests and stylistic preferences. No privileging of Mark over Matthew, no particular affective attachment to the former over the latter, is actually evident.[71] It gives reason for thinking that, were both sources in front of him, Luke likely would have taken Matthew and Mark to be simply variant instantiations of the same normative tradition.

Until FH scholarship can supply cogent reasons for Luke to prefer Mark over Matthew in the triple tradition, reasons that hold up, it is hard to see how the hypothesis gets going. Humans are what experimental psychologists refer to as "cognitive misers," referring to the wired-in efficiency strategy to achieve

---

66. Goodacre, *Case against Q*, 89–91.

67. Goodacre, *Case against Q*, 180.

68. Goodacre, *Case against Q*, 104.

69. Goodacre, *Case against Q*, 88.

70. Goodacre, *Case against Q*, 92.

71. A point made by Paul Foster, "Is It Possible to Dispense with Q?," *NovT* 45 (2003): 313–37 (318).

a desired end with an economy of cognitive expenditure.[72] Luke's option for Mark over Matthew for the triple tradition comes with a considerably higher cognitive expenditure than the alternative. Compelling reasons must be supplied for why he makes this choice.

Luke in fact does not stick with what is supposed to be his cardinal practice of following Mark in the triple tradition for the reasons that Goodacre gives. In the triple-tradition passages John the Baptist's Preaching and Announcement (Mark 1:2–6//Matt 3:1–12//Luke 3:1–18), the Temptation (Mark 1:12–13//Matt 4:1–11//Luke 4:1–13), the Mustard Seed (Mark 4:30–32//Matt 13:31–32//Luke 13:18–19), and the Beelzebul Accusation (Mark 3:22–27//Matt 12:22–30//Luke 11:14–23), Luke agrees significantly more with Matthew than he does with Mark, and two of them (Mustard Seed; Beelzebul Accusation) he gives a different location vis-à-vis the Markan narrative outline. Goodacre has Luke switching from Mark to follow the fuller Matthean parallel, dismissing the idea that these constitute any problem for the FH: "If Luke is using Matthew as well as Mark, it is not surprising that on some occasions he will agree with Matthew far more than he does with Mark. . . . On the Farrer theory, the explanation is straightforward. On occasions like this . . . Luke is working with Matthew as his primary source and not Mark."[73]

But these are anomalous on the FH, for which it is axiomatic that Luke prefers Mark over Matthew for the narrative tradition and hence typically avoids Matthean expansions of Markan pericopes. Luke no sooner launches into the triple tradition in Luke 3 than he opts for Matthew over Mark. And if he has no principled objection to these Matthew-expanded Markan pericopes—indeed in the Beelzebul pericope he cleans out the significant Markan elements—why not spare himself a lot of trouble and just take Matthew as his source for his triple tradition as well as his double tradition? This is an instance of Goodacre asserting one thing about Luke's editorial procedures in one context (why does Luke opt for Mark over Matthew for the triple tradition?), and another thing in another context (how to explain the overlap passages on the FH?).[74] The old problem reasserts itself: difficulty stipulating consistent editorial policies for Luke.

---

72. The term "cognitive miser" was coined by Susan T. Fiske and Shelley E. Taylor, *Social Cognition* (New York: McGraw Hill, 1984), 11–12.

73. Mark Goodacre, "Taking Our Leave of Mark-Q Overlaps: Major Agreements and the Farrer Theory," in *Gospel Interpretation and the Q-Hypothesis*, ed. Mogens Müller and Heike Omerzu, LNTS 573 (London: T&T Clark, 2018), 201–22 (217).

74. In this connection Goodacre proposes a "spectrum" model for the pattern of Matt/Luke agreements that invites a brief analysis. Rather than clustering into the three distinct categories of minor agreements, "overlap" passage agreements, and double tradition—a

Goodacre: Triple Tradition Traces in Luke 3–7 Double Tradition

Goodacre points to the narrative traces that surface in the materials found in double tradition blocks in Luke 3–7: περίχωρον τοῦ Ἰορδάνου (Luke 3:3a// Matt 3:5b); the trace agreements in the Baptism narrative (Luke 3:21–22// Matt 3:16) and in the incipit to the Temptation (Luke 4:1//Matt 4:1); Ναζαρά

---

nomenclature obligated to 2DH assumptions—Matt/Luke agreements actually form a "spectrum," a "continuum," a "sliding scale" of Matthean influence on Luke. Pure triple-tradition passages with minor agreements are found at one end, major Matt/Luke-agreement-against-Mark passages at the other (the double tradition), and so-called "overlap" passages in the middle, but these all converge in continua of overlapping gradations of agreement. This pattern, Goodacre says, is just what one would expect were Luke using Matthew and Mark as his principal sources: Matthew would be exerting a range of influence on Luke (Goodacre, *Synoptic Problem*, 150; *Case against Q*, 163–64; "Taking Our Leave," 213, 222). The way that Goodacre works up his statistical analysis, however, elides what in fact persist as distinctive patterns of agreement. He collects five "overlap" passages, in four of them finds a range of Matt/Luke agreement from 27 percent to 56 percent, but then adds the disputed "Baptism of Jesus" pericope (Matt/Luke agreement 7 percent) to the group. This allows him to claim a 7–56 percent "spectrum" in the overlap passages, a 49 percent spread, though in 4/5 of the cases it is actually a 29 percent spread. Next, he selects three classic minor-agreement passages, finds a Matt/Luke agreement range of 5–6 percent, and declares that "the lower end of agreement in a Mark-Q overlap passage (7 percent) [i.e., the Baptism] is just above the level of agreement in these triple-tradition passages that feature minor agreements." *Ergo* his "sliding scale" of Matt/Luke agreement. He then adduces a second set of four minor-agreement passages that give a range of 7 to 9.5 percent Matt/Luke agreement but to this set adds a fifth, the Great Commandment (25 percent). This allows him to claim that the putatively distinct categories of Matt/Luke agreement in fact overlap and therefore form a spectrum, a "difference of degree and not a difference in kind" ("Taking Our Leave," 213–16). The argument therefore is rather less than compelling. In any case, it is not clear why Goodacre feels he needs this "spectrum" argument to defend the FH, which accommodates the three distinct categories of agreement as such, correlating them to *three distinct utilization modes* of Luke vis-à-vis his sources: the minor agreements are unbidden reminiscences of Matthew *while Luke is using Mark directly*; the double-tradition passages are when *Luke is using Matthew directly*; the "overlap" passages are where *Luke temporarily opts to use Matthew instead of Mark* in the triple tradition. In fact, the "spectrum" model, which homogenizes these patterns, seems at odds with that account. His target may be the 2DH category of "Mark-Q overlap," to label it as one of the 2DH "fallacies" (*Case against Q*, 52–54, 163–65). But on the 2DH the category is a reasonable inference grounded in the general absence in Luke of Markan pericopes that contain Matthean expansions. Goodacre's point therefore may be that the FH can explain the phenomenon without postulating a source. But the FH—and Goodacre explicitly—must postulate an exception to Luke's policy of following Mark in the triple tradition to explain the "overlap" passages. If one is not alert, the "spectrum" argument ("difference of degree, not of kind") can obscure that.

(Luke 4:16//Matt 4:13); the disciple circle narrative setting for the Sermon (Luke 6:20a//Matt 5:1); the entrance to Capernaum leading into the Centurion pericope εἰσελθόντος δὲ . . . εἰς Καφαρναούμ . . . ἑκατόνταρχος, which also creates a narrative link with the Sermon (Luke 7:1//Matt 8:5); the embassy from John the Baptist (Luke 7:18–19//Matt 11:2). These narrative markers, he says, are the consequence of Luke taking these materials from Matthew 3–11, a section in which Matthew has "radically restructured" Mark and, accordingly, given particularly Matthean narrative contextualizations to the M expansions that Luke takes over. That Luke is taking narrative markers over from Matthew is confirmed by the fact that these markers peter out in the double-tradition material in Luke 10 and following—which coincides with Matthew's sudden shift in Matthew 12 to following the Markan narrative. It also happens to be where Luke, embarking on his travel section, pauses following Mark until Luke 18:15. This curious pattern of Matt/Luke narrative traces—starting where Matthew has radically restructured Mark, ending where "Matthew settles [back] in to the Markan sequence"—is evidence that Luke draws his double tradition directly from Matthew.[75]

It is instructive to view the argument from the vantage point of media realities. Goodacre is less than explicit about how he conceives Luke actually utilizing Matthew for these Luke 3–7 materials, but let us reasonably conceive it as a visually assisted activation of a memory-internalized tradition that pulls in elements of the Matthean narrative contextualization along with the target passage. How then does Luke manage to not take over any traces of the Markan elements that in Matthew 3:5–6 closely compound with the Matthean narrative marker πᾶσα ἡ περίχωρος τοῦ Ἰορδάνου (Matt 3:5b//Luke 3:3a)? Ναζαρά (Luke 4:16//Matt 4:13) is the most meagre of agreements, and there is no real agreement in Matthew's and Luke's narrative deployment of it. More seriously for the argument: how does Luke manage to avoid taking over any hints of the Markan narrative contextualizations that Matthew gives to a number of the double-tradition sequences found in Luke 10:1–18:14; 19:11–27; 22:28–30? This is the substance of John Kloppenborg's criticism: "Luke betrays no awareness of the particular ways that Matthew attached these to Mark's framework."[76]

---

75. Goodacre, *Case for Q*, 175–76, 180–82, 185; *Synoptic Problem*, 152–53.

76. John S. Kloppenborg, "On Dispensing with Q? Goodacre on the Relation of Luke to Matthew," *NTS* 49 (2003): 210–36 (232–33), singling out the Woes (Luke 11:37–48//Matt 23:4–39), Oracle on Jerusalem (Luke 13:34–35//Matt 23:37–39), Luke's apocalyptic materials (Luke 12:39–59//Matt 24:42–51; Luke 17:23–37//Matt 24:23–28, 37–41), and the Parable of the Pounds (Luke 19:11–27//Matt 25:14–30).

Kloppenborg's point is further sharpened by what would have been the media and tradition-enactment factors impinging on Luke's Matthew utilization.

Goodacre's clinching argument is that these narrative-connective materials in the double tradition, and the itinerary and narrative metastructure that they mark out in Luke 3–7 (from the Jordan, to the wilderness, to Nazara, to Capernaum), are anomalous for a sayings collection. It follows that Luke can only have derived his double tradition from a narrative gospel—i.e., Matthew. Thus is refuted the argument for Q that appeals to its distinctiveness because of a supposed genre affinity with the *Gospel of Thomas*.[77]

This is an impressive take-down of that line of 2DH reasoning, turning *Thomas* against those who brandish it in defense of the Q hypothesis. Goodacre's critique, however, remains locked into the very genre-purity fallacy committed by these Q advocates. This fallacy—separating sayings and narrative traditions into mutually exclusive genres—has a long and agenda-driven history in Synoptic source criticism. Goodacre takes it over in the particularly egregious form advanced by Koester and Robinson that holds the *Gospel of Thomas* to be prototypical for the sayings genre, and that sets up an ensuing genre binary between sayings collection on the one hand and narrative gospel on the other.

For Goodacre, therefore, it follows from the double tradition's narrative traces that it can only have been embedded in the first instance in a narrative gospel, i.e., Matthew, from whose contexts Luke has extracted it, with narrative threads occasionally trailing along. This also explains why Goodacre holds narrative gospel to be the archetypal primitive Christian genre, which also gives him his grounds for his attack on Watson's L/M hypothesis. Early Christian sayings collections are derivatives of the narrative gospels, for any narrative trace can only have come from being embedded in a narrative context. That the sayings of the *Gospel of Thomas* themselves carry narrative "remnants" indicates that *Thomas* was created through excerpting sayings from Synoptic contexts.[78] In 2003, in *The Case against Q*, Goodacre claimed that the double tradition is unlike *Thomas* because it has narrative residues; in 2019 he bases his argument against Watson (who takes *Thomas* as the prototypical genre for pre-Matthean sayings collections) on narrative residues evident in *Thomas* sayings.

77. Goodacre, *Case against Q*, 178, 182–85; *Synoptic Problem*, 152, 184–85.

78. Mark Goodacre, "What Does *Thomas* Have to Do with Q? The Afterlife of a Sayings Gospel," in *Writing the Gospels: A Dialogue with Francis Watson*, ed. Catherine Sider Hamilton, LNTS 606 (London: T&T Clark, 2019), 81–89 (86–89).

From Goodacre's line of reasoning it further follows that the double tradition lacks any distinctive genre profile: the double tradition is nondescript, a contingent, Luke-pleasing assemblage of materials, "a source-critically extracted mongrel from Matthew's and Luke's non-Marcan material."[79] This is difficult to square with the double tradition's pronounced instructional profile and with Goodacre's own declarations to that effect. Narrative notices "dissipate" in the double tradition after Luke 3–7, for Luke is no longer following Matthew's unique narrative framing for the materials, nor is he aligning them to Mark's narrative framework. What can this mean except that the M materials Luke takes over are in the main sayings? In another context, needing to explain why Luke is so free with the double tradition while being so strict in maintaining narrative order, Goodacre declares that "the bulk of [the double tradition] is made up of sayings," which lend themselves to easy rearrangement.[80] This is another case of a shift in position depending on context: the double tradition is "a source-critically extracted mongrel"; the double tradition is "made up of sayings." In a departure from Goulder, Goodacre holds that Matthew took his M materials from the wider, undifferentiated body of primitive Christian oral tradition.[81] It is curious that from this undifferentiated body Matthew selected so many instructional traditions and so few narrative traditions. One senses a phantom Q lurking about. This conundrum will induce Watson to postulate a pre-Matthean sayings collection source for the double tradition.

Goodacre: Luke Influenced by Matthew or the Bios Genre?

Genre bears upon another of Goodacre's arguments, one that in *The Case against Q* he reckons to be of such force that he places it first among the fallacies upon which the Q hypothesis rests. He argues that the notion of revising Mark, expanding it with teaching material, adding a Nativity, and filling it out with appearance accounts could only have come to Luke from Matthew. It is just too much of a coincidence that such similar projects should emerge at about the same time in the last third of the first century independently of each other.[82] It is not clear that Goodacre still defends this argument; it is hard to find references to it in his post-2003 work. If he does not, understandably so:

79. Goodacre, "What Does *Thomas* Have to Do with Q?," 83.
80. Goodacre, *Case against Q*, 90–91.
81. Goodacre, "Farrer Hypothesis Response," 132.
82. Goodacre, *Case against Q*, 44–49, 90.

to the extent the Gospel of Mark has affinities to the Greco-Roman *bios* genre, expanding it with Nativity stories and additional teaching materials could indeed occur independently to Matthew and Luke. This would give a simple explanation for why their revisions—their Nativities, Resurrection accounts, their arrangements—are so very different from each other.

But to pursue the genre angle further: we see that Goodacre follows Goulder in regarding the evangelists more as individual authors conceiving literary works, and less as tradents—that is, agents in the urgent cultural formation enterprise of receiving, consolidating, and propagating a normative deposit of tradition. For Goodacre, Luke's conception of his compositional idea must germinate from an encounter with a work by another evangelist. But viewing the rise of gospel writing in the last third of the first century from the perspective of cultural-formation exigencies puts a different complexion on things. Mark struck the breakthrough solution to the pressing problem of generational change-over in primitive Christianity, experienced with particular urgency between AD 65 and 70. This generational shift disrupts the mode of living transmission of the normative tradition and precipitates a crisis of memory.[83] The challenge is to shift the mostly oral, diffuse tradition into the more durable cross-generational medium of writing. Mark's breakthrough—aligning a diffuse, chreia-like tradition narratively with primitive Christianity's master commemorative narrative, the Passion—is widely embraced, and it radiates around the eastern Mediterranean along Christian social networks. Mark's achievement becomes the point of departure for further developments of the cultural form.

Art historian George Kubler's analysis of the cultural trajectories of artistic and artisanal breakthroughs—new "entrances"—provides apposite analogies. With regard to the seventeenth-century innovation in chiaroscuro composition he comments, "This new organization of the surfaces rapidly spread throughout the visual arts. No province of Europe escaped the dominion of these forms: the contagion spread from city to court, or from city to city . . . and from thence to every cranny of the social structure, exempting only the most isolated communities."[84] The form itself—in our case Mark's work—and its genre affinities open out in certain finite directions of further development. But then why does one not find a profusion of gospel-writing initiatives

83. The analysis here is indebted to Jan Assmann, *Das kulturelle Gedächtnis: Schrift, Erinnerung und politische Identität in frühen Hochkulturen* (Munich: C. H. Beck, 1992).
84. George Kubler, *The Shape of Time: Remarks on the History of Things* (1962; repr., New Haven, CT: Yale University Press, 2008), 44.

prompted by the appearance of Mark? The reason is that the production of a gospel is not so much a literary pastime as it is a programmatic cultural project, a response to significant alterations in the social and historical conditions of a tradent community that call forth a fresh mobilization and further consolidation of the tradition. The generational transmission crisis, exacerbated by the traumas of the Roman persecution and the destruction of Jerusalem, brought forth the Markan response. It is not a surprise to see the other two Synoptics emerging twenty years on, when Mark is no longer experienced as adequate to contemporary conditions and developments.

Goodacre: Luke-Pleasing M Materials

We move on to Goodacre's effort to overcome what has been the most nettlesome challenge for theories that posit Luke's dependence on Matthew: making sense of his Matthew utilization. Redaction criticism gives Goodacre his key to accounting for Luke's selection and omission of M passages in a way that can avoid appeal to Luke's pure subjectivity. To be sure, Luke took over M elements that were "congenial" to him, that were "Luke pleasing." Conversely, the numerous M elements that he omitted were not "Luke pleasing." But frequently a case can be made that Luke's choices in M materials line up with what can be determined of his redactional interests. He omits the "Thou art Peter" declaration in Matthew 16:18–20 because he "is not as positive about Peter overall as Matthew."[85] Matthew's interest in the law in the Sermon likewise has little resonance for him. The not "Luke-pleasing" M units that Luke omits for Goodacre means that they are "characterized by particularly Matthean interests."[86] They have a "characteristically Matthaean stamp."[87] In this way Goodacre answers the charge that the significant quantities of omitted M material indicate that Luke did not know Matthew.

How though to explain the double-tradition materials that exhibit a distinctively non-Matthean theology and profile? 2DH scholars take this as evidence for a non-Matthean source. These materials, Goodacre counters, are the result of a "*'Luke-pleasing' reworking* of Matthew's non-Markan material," for example significantly reworking Matthew's Beatitudes to recenter them upon the poor.[88] This deflects the 2DH argument for the double tradition's non-

---

85. Goodacre, *Case against Q*, 51.
86. Goodacre, *Case against Q*, 59.
87. Goodacre, *Synoptic Problem*, 129.
88. Goodacre, *Case against Q*, 68–71, emphasis added.

Matthean distinctiveness, but at the cost of a certain tension with his earlier explanation of Luke's wholesale omission of M materials. Goodacre is caught between trying to answer two objections. Is Luke taking over "Luke-pleasing" material from Matthew (hence the many omitted M passages)? Or is he reworking M materials to render them Luke pleasing (hence the non-Matthean distinctives of double-tradition passages)? Why then he did not subject more M materials to a "reworking" to make them Luke-pleasing—especially given the redactional surgery he is prepared to perform on Matthew's Beatitudes? We see again Goodacre's tendency to shift positions depending on the particular objection to Luke's use of Matthew that he is dealing with. He is being pulled willy-nilly into the ad hoc-ism that has plagued previous attempts to explain Luke's Matthew utilization.

Goodacre: Luke's Narrative Artistry

Goodacre's principal challenge, however, is to explain Luke's rearrangement of the double-tradition materials and to make sense of the corresponding source-utilization actions. He seeks to avoid Goulder's fate by making a big bet on redaction criticism and its offspring, narrative criticism. The problems of Luke's source utilization dissolve in Luke's narrative artistry, in "the creative power of the religious imagination."[89] Luke "skillfully and creatively incorporated elements of Matthew and Mark into . . . a grand-scale, sequential narrative."[90] Source-criticism—pedestrian, wooden, and old-fashioned—is supplanted by aesthetics, by Luke's redactional and narrative art. For Goulder, authorial-literary creativity was the primary factor in the generation of much of the tradition. Goodacre abandons Goulder's claim that Matthew authored the double tradition (see below), but he holds firmly to authorial creativity to account for Luke's utilization of Matthew. To answer the question of Luke's source utilization, all one needs to do is give an account of his narrative vision. This is the grounds for Goodacre's analogizing of Luke's narrative construction to the creators of Jesus films who edit various elements of the Synoptics together to realize their own narrative concept.[91] Goulder, he says, erred in

89. Goodacre, *Case against Q*, 122–23; "The Synoptic Jesus and the Celluloid Christ: Solving the Synoptic Problem through Film," *JSNT* 80 (2000): 31–43 (32). Goodacre adopts the phrase from W. R. Telford, "The New Testament in Fiction and Film: A Biblical Scholar's Perspective," in *Words Remembered, Texts Renewed: Essays in Honour of John F. A. Sawyer*, ed. Jon Davies et al. (Sheffield: Sheffield Academic, 1995), 360–94 (388).
90. Goodacre, *Case against Q*, 104.
91. Goodacre, "Celluloid Christ," 40. He backpedals somewhat in "On Choosing and

letting himself get dragged into scrolling minutiae, owing to "his attachment to the old paradigm."[92]

Goodacre's conversion of Luke's Matthew utilization to a problem of narrative criticism is a manifestation of the confidence of redaction criticism that it can supply the answers to the questions of Synoptic relationships that eluded source criticism. That Luke's divergences from Matthew's order in the double tradition can even be regarded as a difficulty for the Farrer hypothesis is due to "failures in both the application of redaction criticism and the appreciation of Luke's literary ability or narrative agenda."[93] This ingeniously writes up the rules of the game such that the FH can never lose: how can one refute a utilization hypothesis that refers its emblematic features and its difficulties to authorial creativity and the literary imagination? There is nothing that cannot be explained this way.[94]

But bringing to light Luke's narrative design does not so much obviate as it sharpens the question of how he managed it practically, given ancient media conditions, not least because Goodacre does not think that Luke has deeply internalized Matthew, which is one of the reasons he gives for Luke's opting for Mark over Matthew in the first place. If he were in fact alleging no more than that a source-critical account of Luke's use of Matthew is incomplete if not correlated with an account of Luke's narrative design, as he on occasion intimates, it is hard to imagine anyone disagreeing with him.[95] But that is not his stance. A narrative-critical account of the consummate artistry of Luke's arrangement is a sufficient explanation of his Matthew utilization, full stop.

The assuredness with which Goodacre propounds this makes one suspect that something additional is driving his reasoning than just a high estimation of the competence range of narrative criticism. In fact, there is: an inference of sorts from the latter. He conflates two distinct issues, or better, collapses the second one into the first: (1) the supposedly inferior aesthetic qualities of Luke's ordering of the double tradition compared to Matthew's; (2) Luke's uti-

---

Using Appropriate Analogies: A Response to F. Gerald Downing," *JSNT* 26 (2003): 237–40 (238), but he invokes the analogy again in "Re-walking the 'Way of the Lord': Luke's Use of Mark and His Reaction to Matthew," in *Luke's Literary Creativity*, ed. Jesper Tang Nielsen and Mogens Müller, LNTS 550 (London: Bloomsbury/T&T Clark, 2016), 26–43 (28).

92. Goodacre, *Case against Q*, 118.

93. Goodacre, *Case against Q*, 61.

94. An observation also made by Stephen Hultgren, *Narrative Elements in the Double Tradition: A Study of Their Place within the Framework of the Gospel Narrative*, BZNW 113 (Berlin: de Gruyter, 2002), 232–33 n. 33.

95. Goodacre, *Case against Q*, 118–20.

lization procedures vis-à-vis his Matthean source. Put differently, he subsumes the perennial problem of Luke's *dramatic divergence in order* from Matthew's double tradition to the shopworn 2DH claim that compared to Matthew, Luke's double tradition is *disordered*, or *primitively ordered*. Narrative analysis is said to dispose peremptorily of this calumny, and so naturally for Goodacre the other problem vanishes with it.[96] This is to confuse the question of design with the question of execution, the literary conception of a composition with the media operations required for its realization. It is like discoursing on the beauteous proportions of the Parthenon but ignoring questions of how it was erected. To show the aesthetic qualities of Luke's arrangement is not to show how he managed the challenges of quarrying his sources and fitting the pieces together to bring it to realization. That Goodacre thinks that it does explains why he pays so little attention to the practicalities and mechanics of Luke's source utilization and indeed, chides Goulder for doing so.

Given the eggs that he puts in the narrative-critical basket, one is surprised to find that Goodacre carries out relatively little narrative analysis of Luke's actual arrangements, the travel section in particular, the nemesis of hypotheses asserting Luke's dependence on Matthew. In *The Case against Q* he assesses just two of these double-tradition sequences, 11:1–13 and 12:13–34, for their coherence. His analysis of 11:1–13 repays a closer look. He says, "Jesus is now enacting, in 11:1–13, that commission first revealed in 10:22: πάντα μοι παρεδόθη ὑπὸ τοῦ πατρός μου. Jesus [in 11:1–13] calls his disciples together and chooses to reveal to them what he has recently received from his father; and he teaches them appropriately about the mutual fictive kingship, and their relationship to God in prayer."[97] In making the case for the excellence of Luke's thematic connections between 10:21–22 and 11:2–13 he fails to note that in the hypothesized Q source these items follow on one another directly; that is, the connection is even clearer, and therefore even more excellent than in Luke, where they

96. E.g., *Case against Q*, 109–13; *Synoptic Problem*, 126; "Celluloid Christ," 109–10. Like Goulder before him, Goodacre is pushing back with understandable tetchiness on Streeter's claim that, if Luke were using Matthew, he would be shifting double-tradition passages from Matthean settings "where they are always exceedingly appropriate" to Markan settings in his own gospel of "no special appropriateness," and thus that his arrangements are those of a "crank" (Burnett Hillman Streeter, *Four Gospels: A Study of Origins* [London: Macmillan, 1924], 183). It ought to be noted, however, that in the passage in question Streeter equally, indeed more, has in mind Luke's challenging and not immediately comprehensible utilization operation: "He must have gone through both Matthew and Mark to discriminate with meticulous precision between Marcan and non-Marcan material," etc. Hence "we [would have] reason to believe he was a crank."

97. Goodacre, *Case against Q*, 112.

are separated by a block of unrelated material (Good Samaritan; Mary and Martha). The evidence seems to point rather to Luke having broken up the connections of a source by inserting other materials into its sequence.

More promisingly, Goodacre has recently proposed that Luke takes over Mark's Isaiah "Way of the Lord" narrative theology and makes it the principle of coherence for his collocation of Matthean materials in the travel section. His rearrangement of Matthean double tradition is a consequence of his settled admiration for the familiar Mark and his preferring Mark over Matthew for the narrative tradition. Matthew's large block discourses break up the Markan narrative and dissipate the force of its "Way of the Lord" narrative Christology. Not only does Luke follow Mark but he extends out his "Way of the Lord" into the travel section, a literary device that allows him to take numerous elements of Matthew's block discourses and align them to this Markan vector. This neatly explains why Luke would want to dismantle Matthew's discourses.[98]

Goodacre remains disinclined, however, to engage with Luke's actual source-utilization actions in Matthew in putting the travel section together.[99] But this is the nub of the matter. That Luke creates the travel section to accommodate materials from other sources, seizing upon Mark's "Way of the Lord" narrative motif to do so, is amenable to a number of Synoptic-problem solutions. It does not point unequivocally to Luke's dependence on Matthew, and in fact the complicated pattern of Luke's corresponding utilization movements leaves room for one to harbor positive doubts that it does.[100] Goulder recognized that if the FH was to hit the threshold of plausibility, not to say probability, it had to make sense of Luke's actual source utilization. Goodacre emphatically repudiates Goulder's scrolling account but is himself not particularly exercised by the question of ancient media constraints on Luke's use of his sources.

To be sure, with a few luminous exceptions (Downing especially), prior to Derrenbacker's breakthrough 2005 volume, Synoptic scholarship was not paying much attention to the issue. Goulder in fact is remarkable for his alertness to Luke's ancient media context and its import for the plausibility of the FH. But Goodacre does not wholly ignore the question. He points out that Luke's alternating use of Mark and Matthew in blocks "is . . . quite consonant" with

---

98. Goodacre, "Re-walking the Way of the Lord," 29–40.
99. See also Derrenbacker, *Ancient Compositional Practices*, 200 n. 26.
100. Perhaps "FH logics" has kicked in: Occam's Razor settles the question. A concrete source, Matthew, is present, and with enough ingenuity one can postulate that Luke used him.

what Downing says about ancient authors following one source at a time. Likewise in response to Downing he observes that just like Luke in his use of Matthew, Josephus collocates laws from the Torah out of order and from two different books (from Lev 12–14; Num 5:11–31; and Lev 20) to compose *Ant.* 3:258–275.[101] Elsewhere, pointing to the practiced dexterity of ancient authors in scroll manipulation, he suggests that concerns about Luke finding his way around Matthew to desired passages are overblown.[102] The principal issue, however, is that the scroll medium, unformatted script displays, and the oral-aural dimensions of source utilization are not conducive to search-and-location and to precise operations like the so-called "unpicking" of Matthean and Markan elements from each other in close contexts. Goodacre floats the idea that in line with a widespread practice of elite Greco-Roman authors, and of Paul, Luke might have dictated to a scribe.[103] But he does not enlarge on how this practice would dispel the difficulties arising in connection with Luke's proposed Matthew utilization, or how it might explain the Synoptic profile of variation and agreement.

The limited attention that Goodacre gives to these questions is to no small extent the consequence of the emphasis he places upon Luke's creative authorial agency, which he quite reasonably cautions is liable to be eclipsed by preoccupation with the "wooden" mechanics of source handling.[104] It nevertheless remains the case that Luke must realize his literary design within a certain set of media constraints and the corollary cultural practices of source utilization.

Goodacre on Luke's "Unpicking" of Matthew

In accord with his marginalizing of media factors Goodacre pays little attention to the so-called "unpicking" or "unscrambling" problem: Luke's separation of Markan and M strands from one another in their closely contiguous contexts in Matthew. In accordance with his redaction-critical outlook he asks only whether Matthew's additions to Mark are congenial or uncongenial to Luke's interests. Considered in light of ancient media-manuscript realities,

---

101. Goodacre, "Using Appropriate Analogies," 239–40.

102. Mark Goodacre, "Q, Memory, and Matthew: A Response to Alan Kirk," *JSHJ* 15 (2017): 224–33 (226–27).

103. Goodacre, "Q, Memory, and Matthew," 227; "Too Good to Be Q: High Verbatim Agreement in the Double Tradition," in *Marcan Priority without Q: Explorations in the Farrer Hypothesis*, ed. John C. Poirier and Jeffrey Peterson, LNTS 455 (London: Bloomsbury/T&T Clark, 2015), 82–100 (98).

104. Goodacre, "Q, Memory, and Matthew," 230.

this kind of visual discrimination and separation of materials is quite difficult and laborious, not to mention the awkwardness of any side-by-side consultation with Mark. It is axiomatic for the FH that Luke has a good memory grasp of Mark, and we can agree with Goodacre that this would aid Luke in discriminating M elements that he "sees" embedded within Markan contexts in Matthew.[105] This though is itself complicated by the fact that Matthew has often considerably reworked the Markan passages in question, and that the FH Luke's memory of the Matthean parallel is constantly prone to interfere with his rendering of a Markan passage.

One must also question the soundness of the visualist paradigm for source utilization that Goodacre relies upon. Luke as a competent tradent would have appropriated his written tradition generatively, in a confluence of oral and aural modes with visual cueing, which activates, moreover, the work as a memory-internalized entity. The memory factor further volatilizes the process. The visual script acts as an important control but not a determinant in Luke's reproduction of his written tradition. These dynamics go a long way toward elucidating Synoptic patterns of variation and agreement. They are characteristic of the stage of the tradition in front of our eyes in the Synoptics, that is, in which written transmission is not yet distinct from oral-utilization modes. None of this rules out the source-disentangling operation that the FH imputes to Luke, but one suspects FH scholarship of some naïveté about the obstacles to be overcome in pulling it off successfully and consistently. One also suspects that the FH is locked into a model that construes Luke as a kind of reverse-engineering Synoptic source critic or, in the mode of an Alexandrian critic, collating versions of Homer to identify and strike out corrupt passages.

Goodacre: FH Luke's Editorial Fatigue

Goodacre's 1998 "Fatigue in the Synoptics" piece opens a window onto his media conceptions. The phenomenon in question is the well-known continuity errors committed by Matthew and Luke in their reproduction of their sources. Matthew describes Jesus's mother and brothers "standing outside" (Matt 12:46) even though he has omitted the reference in Mark 3:20 to Jesus being in a house. In 14:1 Matthew corrects Herod's appellation to "tetrarch" but reverts to Mark's technically inaccurate "king" (Mark 6:14, 22, 25, 26, 27) in 14:9. Mark presents Herodias as the one with enmity toward John, and Herod as distressed at John's death (Mark 6:26), whereas in Matthew it is Herod who wants to

---

105. Goodacre, *Case against Q*, 51.

kill John, yet anomalously he is distressed by John's death (Matt 14:9). Luke begins the Parable of the Pounds with ten servants (Luke 19:13) in contrast to Matthew's three (Matt 25:15) but reverts to three servants in the accounting scene (Luke 19:16–20).[106] Goodacre puts this down to "editorial fatigue": difficulty maintaining close editorial attention to the details of the passage that the evangelists are copying, a deficiency in the requisite powers of concentration. Goodacre turns this against the 2DH, alleging that in the double tradition one finds *no* instances of Matthean editorial fatigue (in contrast to numerous cases of it in his use of Mark) whereas in Luke one finds three or four (e.g., the Parable of the Pounds). It follows that Luke's source for the double tradition must be Matthew, not a hypothetical document Q to which he and Matthew supposedly have independent access.[107]

One can reasonably doubt that Matthew and Luke would be deficient in the requisite powers of editorial concentration. Cases of so-called editorial fatigue might bear a different explanation. The enabling assumption in Goodacre's argument is that Matthew and Luke are appropriating Markan (and for FH Luke, Matthean) passages in a procedure of close visual editing, such that fatigue sets in and inattentiveness with it, leading to amusing continuity errors. Their flagging concentration is compounded by their apparent nonchalance about any review process to detect and correct these errors. Yet this is the same FH Luke who successfully executes, with unerring precision, the far more difficult task of separating out M elements from their Markan contexts in Matthew, and Markan elements from their Matthean expansions in the so-called overlap passages! Which is the real Luke? The exact source-critical

---

106. Mark Goodacre, "Fatigue in the Synoptics," *NTS* 44 (1998): 45–58 (43).

107. Goodacre, "Fatigue," 57–58; *Synoptic Problem*, 154–55. For a critique see Tobias Hägerland, "Editorial Fatigue and the Existence of Q," *NTS* 65 (2019): 190–206. Goodacre, he notes, does not take cognizance of the distinction between narrative and sayings—i.e., that continuity errors are more likely to be manifest, and be easier to detect, in narrative than in sayings (198–99). To this we can add that episodic pericopes have a delicate narrative logic that cannot be disrupted without generating narrative incongruities. Second, Hägerland identifies a case of Matthean "editorial fatigue" in the double tradition. In Matthew 3:7a the evangelist makes the proximate audience for John's preaching of judgment in 3:7b–10 the "many Pharisees and Sadducees who went out to where he was baptizing." This audience, "who neither have shown any sign of repentance thus far nor will do so throughout the Matthean narrative" (204–5), is incongruent, however, with the immediate sequel in 3:11–12: "I indeed baptize you with water for repentance. . . . He will baptize you with the Holy Spirit and fire." Luke's version on the other hand is "consistent" and "runs smoothly" (203). By staking his pro-FH argument to there being *no* cases of Matthean editorial fatigue in the double tradition, Goodacre has given hostages to fortune.

surgeon? Or the inattentive bumbler unable to sustain a narrative modification over the course of a single pericope and content to leave his work strewn with textual inconcinnities?

Alternatively—and in fidelity to actual source-utilization practices—we might propose that Matthew and Luke in fact are not appropriating their Markan passages in operations of close visual editing, such that they would experience editorial fatigue. Rather, they read over a target Markan passage carefully, lay aside their Markan scroll, and start copying out the passage in their destination scroll. This activates their habituated memory version of the passage, which asserts itself and begins overriding their redactional modifications. This is a more satisfactory explanation. It aligns with how Luke (and Matthew) would actually be handling his sources, and it takes into account the interaction of memory and manuscript in reenactments of a normative tradition. Nor is this utilization reality commensurable with an FH Luke who is closely examining and comparing his Matthean and Markan sources to discriminate M elements from Markan elements, and Markan elements from M passages. In the Beelzebul passage the deeply internalized Markan parallel would be interfering with Luke's attempt to give a rendering of the Matthean version from whatever refreshed memory impression he carries of the latter from his Matthew scroll, now lying by his side. The Matthean πόλιν . . . τῆς πόλεως ἐκείνης (Matt 10:11, 14) surfacing as ἀπὸ τῆς πόλεως ἐκείνης in Luke's rendering of the Mark 6 Mission Instruction (Luke 9:4–5) in fact shows how hard it is for Luke to keep Matthean elements from memory-intruding into Markan contexts.

We can leave the matter there but with one final remark. Why indeed no careful revision process to comb out inconcinnities, bring materials to stylistic uniformity, and the like? Such skillful writers as Matthew and Luke are not to be accused of carelessness or ineptitude. In fact, it is highly revealing of the nature of Matthew's and Luke's cultural project and its execution. The line between oral, memory-grounded enactment of the tradition and its written cultivation is still indistinct. Writing is their medium, with all the possibilities that the medium offers for conceiving and fashioning a coherent work, but the work is realized pericope by pericope in moments of active, living reactualization of the tradition of their sources. Those moments of enactment are ends in themselves. This accounts for the phenomenon in question, and it goes a long way toward explaining Synoptic patterns of variation and agreement, the evangelists' uneven digestion of their written traditions. It especially illuminates the patterns of variation *within* pericopes, which have something of the complexion of oral variants and (as Wilke conceded so long ago) resist reduction without remainder to a redactional logic.

CHAPTER 5

Goodacre on Double-Tradition Agreements: "Too Good to Be Q"

The spectrum of agreement in Synoptic parallels is in fact grist for another of Goodacre's arguments, which like the foregoing is informative of his operative media assumptions. He reprises with greater nuance John Chapman's argument: Matthew's and Luke's statistically higher levels of close verbal agreement in the double tradition is consistent with Luke taking his double tradition direct from Matthew, whereas their statistically lower level of agreement in the triple tradition is consistent with their redacting Mark independently. This pattern therefore is confirmatory of the Farrer hypothesis and a contraindication for the 2DH, for were Luke and Matthew independently redacting a double-tradition source, as they are with Mark, their higher agreement levels in the double tradition would instead be more like their lower agreement levels in the Markan tradition.[108]

A media model that makes close verbal agreement the criterion for direct utilization will have difficulty accommodating low-agreement parallels in the double tradition. If close agreement is the totem of direct copying, what do intermediate, low, or intermixed levels of agreement indicate? Goodacre needs a model that can account more robustly for the observable patterns of variation in written source utilization. His reasoning is that source utilization involves not wooden copying but redaction, that higher triple-tradition variation levels are a kind of arithmetic sum of Matthew's and Luke's independent redactions of Mark, whereas the lower double-tradition variation levels are the single quantity of Luke's redaction of Matthean passages. One doubts that this simple algorithm can capture the complex range of agreement and variation in both the triple and the double tradition. Also, if one relies on the premise that close verbal agreement is the criterion for direct utilization of a source, the more one must concede that there is no consistent pattern of close agreement in the double tradition, and the weaker the case for the FH becomes.

In fact, Goodacre works with overall statistical averages of agreement in the double and triple tradition, respectively. He cites Carlston and Norlin's study to the effect that Matthew and Luke's use of the hypothesized Q is 27 percent more conservative than their use of Mark.[109] Notably, this large spread per-

---

108. Goodacre, "Too Good to Be Q," 83; also Goodacre, "The Synoptic Problem: John the Baptist and Jesus," in *Method and Meaning: Essays on New Testament Introduction in Honor of Harold W. Attridge*, ed. Andrew B. McGowan (Atlanta: SBL Press, 2011), 177–92 (188).

109. Goodacre, "Too Good to Be Q," 93; see Charles E. Carlston and Dennis Norlin, "Statistics and Q—Some Further Observations," *NovT* 41 (1999): 108–23. Carlston and Norlin's argument is (1) written sources are evident in high verbatim ratios relative to oral

tains to the subcategory of Matt/Luke Triple-Tradition Miscellaneous Sayings (58.5 percent agreement); Matt/Luke Double-Tradition Miscellaneous Sayings (84.1 percent). The latter though comprises just 216 words in Matthew and 225 words in Luke.[110] The differential in the category "Words of Jesus" in the triple tradition is 65.8 percent, in the double tradition 71.5 percent, a rather less dramatic spread of 5.7 percent. Overall, in Markan sayings material Matthew and Luke agree with one another 64 percent of the time, in the double-tradition sayings material 72.7 percent of the time, an 8.7 percent spread.[111] When one factors in that Markan sayings frequently occur in narrative contexts solitarily, whereas double-tradition sayings mostly occur in close-knit sayings sequences, one is hard-pressed to see any significant statistical difference in agreement levels.[112]

This raises the question of the genre variable in the different agreement levels, which also might answer Goodacre's question. Goodacre does not control for genre. The profile of the double tradition is predominantly sayings, the triple tradition predominantly narrative. Sayings genres have greater baked-in resistance to variation than narrative genres. To use David Rubin's terms, oral genres can be understood as systems of "multiple constraints."[113] Sayings genres are tightly bound high-constraint systems, for excess variation would result in loss of meaning. Narrative genres are lower constraint, for variation (within limits) does not necessarily compromise the coherence of the narrative. The genre variable accounts economically for the variation spread between the triple tradition and the double tradition.

Though our purpose here is not to make a pitch for the two document hypothesis, it does no harm to point out that the higher genre stability of

---

sources; (2) Matt/Luke in double tradition are more conservative than in triple tradition; (3) Mark (triple tradition) was a written source; (4) therefore, double tradition (Q) was a written source. Goodacre cleverly turns this into an argument for the FH: Luke's direct use of Matthew for the double tradition.

110. Carlston and Norlin, "Statistics and Q," 115. To his credit Goodacre draws attention to the smallness of the "Miscellaneous Sayings" sample.

111. Carlston and Norlin, "Statistics and Q," 113–14.

112. John S. Kloppenborg, "The Farrer/Mark without Q Hypothesis: A Response," in Poirier and Peterson, *Marcan Priority without Q*, 226–44 (242). In his statistical analysis undertaken in his 2010 dissertation Joseph Weaks observes that Markan *sayings materials* frequently are preserved "more reliably"—i.e., verbatim—in the Matt/Luke parallels. See his "Mark without Mark: Problematizing the Reliability of a Reconstructed Text of Q" (PhD diss., Brite Divinity School, 2010), 237.

113. David C. Rubin, *Memory in Oral Traditions: The Cognitive Psychology of Epic, Ballads, and Counting Out Rhymes* (New York: Oxford University Press, 1995), 251.

sayings might explain, in Goodacre's own terms, the existence of a decent quantum of higher-variation double-tradition parallels—from Matthew and Luke independently redacting a double-tradition source. Or to turn the direction of the argument around: given the genre-grounded stability of sayings material, on the FH one would not expect to see so many high variation Matt/Luke parallels. In the end Goodacre retreats to the weaker claim that "the more examples there are of high verbatim agreement [in the double tradition], the more difficult it becomes to attribute these to Matthew's and Luke's independent use of Q, regardless of overall [statistical] figures." He faults the low-agreement double-tradition passages, "less clearly diagnostic of direct contact," for depressing the overall double-tradition agreement levels.[114] One understands his predicament, to which his "too good to be Q" argument is a characteristically bold response. Matt/Luke variation in the double tradition is roughly comparable to their variation in the triple tradition, *ergo*, since they are independently using Mark in the latter case, the data are at least consistent with their using a source in the former case. Goodacre gamely tries to fit these same data to the FH framework.

Goodacre and FH Luke's Closed Textual Universe

Notwithstanding that Goodacre will diverge sharply from Goulder by allowing Luke to graze in the field of oral tradition, like Goulder he conceives Luke operating within a self-contained textual universe. All Luke's non-Markan materials are either copied from or cued by elements of Matthew's text, and creative redaction is the versatile method for explaining his appropriation or his extension of them, as the case may be. Little happens in Luke's literary world apart from a prompt from Matthew; verbal agreements of the most negligible and formulaic kind indicate the influence of the Matthean text. Goodacre, for example, cannot conceive how Luke could have gotten the notion of prefacing Mark with "natal stories" apart from the "catalyst" of Matthew's Nativity.[115]

In part this is simply the corollary of his belief, the consequence of not controlling for genre, that it is impossible coincidence that Luke and Matthew should, at roughly the same time, embark upon a revision and expansion of the Markan gospel, and in similar ways. But it also owes something to his positioning Luke within a closed textual circuit constituted of Matthew and Mark rather than within a matrix of cultural tradition. Thus the single phrase

114. Goodacre, "Too Good to Be Q," 95.
115. Goodacre, *Case against Q*, 57.

τέξεται δὲ υἱόν καὶ καλέσεις τὸ ὄνομα αὐτοῦ Ἰησοῦν (Matt 1:21) // τέξῃ υἱὸν, καὶ καλέσεις τὸ ὄνομα αὐτοῦ Ἰησοῦν (Luke 1:31) becomes the textual basis for securing the literary dependency of Luke's Nativity upon Matthew's. Goodacre tries to reinforce this delicate thread of a connection, also text-internally, arguing that the phrase is more appropriate to the Matthean context, where καλέσεις is "addressed appropriately to Joseph who . . . will [later] name the child," than to the Lukan context, where it is "addressed less appropriately to Mary," for in Luke either the father alone (Zechariah in 1:13) or both the father and mother (2:21) name a child.[116] But beyond the formulaic nature of the shared phrase, locating Luke within the wider matrix of cultural tradition puts a rather different complexion on things. In Jewish birth stories it is just as frequently, if not more frequently, the mother who names the significant child (Gen 4:25; 21:6; 35:18; Exod 2:10; Judg 13:24; Ruth 4:16–17; 1 Sam 1:19). To all appearances Luke and Matthew take their cues from quite different narrative patterns in the cultural register: Matthew from Moses motifs and the Exodus, Luke from birth stories.

Similarly, for Goodacre Luke's κηρυχθῆναι ἐπὶ τῷ ὀνόματι αὐτοῦ μετάνοιαν . . . πάντα τὰ ἔθνη (Luke 24:47) can only come from his awareness of the text of Matthew's Great Commission: πάντα τὰ ἔθνη, βαπτίζοντες αὐτοὺς εἰς τὸ ὄνομα (Matt 28:19). Luke's dependence upon Matthew's text thereby secured, "redaction criticism" kicks in to take care of the rest—the striking divergence of Luke's Resurrection narrative from Matthew's.[117] With characteristic agility Goodacre again converts what one might normally take to be evidence against Luke's knowledge of Matthew—absence of substantive verbal agreements; sharp divergence in narrative content—into positive evidence for it. But the FH leaves him no other option. Luke must be dependent upon Matthew in the Nativity and Resurrection narratives or not be dependent upon Matthew at all. Like Goulder, therefore, Goodacre must take everything non-Markan in Luke back in some way or another to Matthew's text.

The reader might be puzzled why Goodacre should think that his rather perfunctory treatments of the Nativity and Resurrection narratives suffice to carry his point. One suspects that "FH logics" is operating here: one only need show that it is *possible* for Luke to have been dependent on Matthew in the narrative in question to defeat the 2DH (the FH fails only if Luke and Matthew are "demonstrably independent" of each other).[118] Once this threshold is met,

116. Goodacre, *Case against Q*, 56–57.
117. Goodacre, *Case against Q*, 58.
118. Goodacre, "Farrer Hypothesis Response," 132.

Occam's Razor kicks in and decides the question in favor of the FH. Simply to give a Farrer account of the textual phenomena in question, an account which naturally will make sense within its FH terms of reference, suffices to establish the FH.

Goodacre, Oral Tradition, and Phantom Q

Goodacre nevertheless opens the door to oral tradition to cope with two issues: first, the failure of Goulder's argument that Matthew authored the M/double tradition and Luke his special materials; second, alternating primitivity in the double tradition. On the first, Goodacre makes the simple point against Goulder that it does not follow from the Matthean stylistic imprint upon the M materials that Matthew authored these materials (similarly in Luke's case for the L^S materials). Tradition is receptive of different stylistic imprints.[119] It further follows that Matthew and Luke are "drawing . . . from sources unknown to us." Not unreasonably Goodacre conceives these sources as oral tradition. Luke's extensive roster of L^S parables is indicative that he is "interacting creatively with oral traditions" just like he "interacts with the traditions he finds in Matthew and Mark."[120]

This brings Goodacre to the appearances of "alternating primitivity" in the double tradition. Goulder took any concession to alternating primitivity to be fatal, the thin edge of the wedge for a Q-type hypothesis, and he went to considerable lengths to interpret allegedly more primitive Lukan parallels as redactions of the Matthean parallel. This concern doubtless was also a factor in his determination to derive the M/double tradition wholly from Matthean invention and L^S from Lukan invention. Goodacre, having shown that Goulder's arguments for Matthean and Lukan invention of their non-Markan materials fail, affirms the existence of oral tradition sources. Unflinchingly he draws the further inference that Luke's recourse to an overlapping oral tradition explains those "occasional signs of greater primitivity" in Luke's double tradition. Clearly Goodacre does not think that the strained attempts to derive passages such as the Lord's Prayer from Luke's redaction of the Matthean parallel are an asset to the Farrer hypothesis. On occasion there are indeed "solid grounds" for taking a Lukan form to be the more original.[121]

This amounts to acknowledging a non-Matthean source for some of Luke's double tradition. Understandably Goodacre bends his efforts toward its con-

---

119. Goodacre, *Goulder and the Gospels*, 168, 191, 201, 229.
120. Goodacre, *Goulder and the Gospels*, 289–90.
121. Goodacre, *Case against Q*, 64–66.

tainment, to forestalling its spreading to other elements of the double tradition, most of which not only likewise diverge to some degree or other from
the Matthean parallel but also (different from Matthew's and Luke's use of
Mark) vary quite drastically from Matthew in their patterns of arrangement.
He marshals several arguments to this end. One is to draw an analogy to
Luke's procedures with Mark. Just as Luke adverts occasionally to an alternate
version of a *Markan* pericope—e.g., the words of institution, attested also in
1 Corinthians 11:23–26—on occasion he selects an alternative to a passage of his
Matthew source.[122] The force of the Markan analogy is somewhat equivocal.
The profile of Matthew's and Luke's variation and agreement in their Markan
materials roughly approximates to the corresponding profile of their double
tradition. They are utilizing Mark independently, so one might reason by analogy that they are independently using a double-tradition source. Goodacre's
response likely would be that that this is to posit a hypothetical source, but the
similarity in variation profile is nevertheless such that he worked up his "too
good to be Q" argument to neutralize it.

Goodacre is careful to limit Luke's recourse to oral tradition strictly to that
tiny subset of double-tradition passages with regard to which he is prepared
to acknowledge that there are "solid grounds" for the greater primitivity of
the Lukan parallel, the Lord's Prayer being the emblematic instance.[123] His
recourse to oral tradition, in other words, is a temporary expedient to cope
with one potentially lethal anomaly in the FH—those parallels where Luke's
creative redaction of Matthew cannot plausibly be stretched to encompass
the divergence. Otherwise, oral tradition and oral practices play no role in his
account. All other variation in double-tradition parallels is generated by Luke's
redaction of Matthew. Luke's Beatitudes—as dramatic an instance of variation
as any—are a "Luke-pleasing reworking" of the Matthean Beatitudes.

Summoning oral tradition, otherwise a negligible entity consigned to
the fringes, to cover rough patches or fill gaps in utilization hypotheses is
a longstanding habit in Synoptic source criticism. Nevertheless, some FH-
pertinent questions arise in this connection. One might think that positing
a non-Matthean oral source for some of Luke's double tradition in place of a
non-Matthean written source is a distinction without a difference. One might
also think that the FH surrenders its claims to greater economy by needing to
posit two sources for Luke's double tradition rather than one. But not so and
not so, says Goodacre. It is more critically respectable, he says, to hold that

122. Goodacre, *Case against Q*, 65; *Synoptic Problem*, 138.
123. Goodacre, *Case against Q*, 64.

Luke's source for the alternating primitivity passages is oral tradition, rather than a written source. Why posit a hypothetical source to account for what can be explained by Luke's redaction of an extant source, Matthew, with occasional recourse to oral tradition? That the early Christian oral tradition existed is all but universally acknowledged, not so "this unseen, hypothetical text [Q]." Not only does the Farrer hypothesis give the more economical explanation of alternating primitivity, but also one far better attuned to the reality of the early Christian oral tradition than the 2DH, which by throwing these materials into a written source parades its ignorance of the important role played by oral tradition in Synoptic Gospel production.[124]

From these boasts one would never know that Goodacre limits the role of oral tradition in the FH to two or three controverted double-tradition passages. And that among Farrer defenders he is somewhat of an outlier in daring to go even that far.[125] It also bears pointing out that in opposing the "unseen, hypothetical text Q" to the living stream of oral tradition, the existence of which commands wide assent, Goodacre compares apples and oranges, or better, an apple with orange trees. The correct comparison would be between "genres of ancient sayings collections," and "the living stream of oral tradition." That ancient sayings collections existed likewise commands wide assent, also that in many cases such are codifications of oral traditions. This again helps explain why Goodacre is concerned to claim that narrative gospel is the archetypal primitive Christian genre.

That Matthew did not invent the double tradition raises the question of his sources for these materials. Goodacre himself exposed the linguistic fallacies in Goulder's arguments for Matthean invention, and he readily acknowledges that Matthew had "recourse to substantial extra-Markan sources." Though it is a safe bet, he thinks, that these sources are oral tradition, he declines to elaborate further, and indeed says in a discussion of the Beatitudes that though "the question of Matthew's source material . . . remains . . . for the purposes of discussing the Synoptic Problem this is a secondary issue, rather like the issues of the source material for Mark."[126] But perhaps the question is

124. Mark Goodacre, "A World without Q," in Goodacre and Perrin, *Questioning Q*, 174–79 (179); also *Case against Q*, 35–35, 64.

125. Goodacre's FH colleague Ken Olson is concerned enough about Goodacre's concession to non-Markan sources for Luke's double tradition that he works up a fresh argument that Luke's Lord's Prayer is a Lukan abridgment of Matthew's. See Olson, "The Lord's Prayer (Abridged Edition)," in Poirier and Peterson, *Marcan Priority without Q*, 101–18.

126. Goodacre, *Case against Q*, 70 n. 49. Ron Huggins explores some of the potential problems here for the FH in his unpublished paper, "Q Doesn't Go Away, It Only Changes

not so secondary, and perhaps Goulder's determined marginalization of oral tradition was actually not an oversight after all.[127] To account for alternating primitivity, Goodacre allows Luke access to the living stream of oral tradition. There is nothing unreasonable about a scheme that has Luke principally using Matthew with occasional recourse to oral tradition for some parallels. But once M/DT origins in "substantial extra-Markan sources" is granted, on what grounds are we to prefer Goodacre's explanation of the distinctive profile of the double tradition as being due to a "Luke-pleasing reworking" of Matthean materials? Why could the double tradition's distinctive profile not be due to Luke, like Matthew, taking his materials direct from the oral tradition (or however Goodacre conceives these "substantial extra-Markan sources")? After all, Goodacre has Luke reworking his L^S materials, which are taken from the tradition.[128] This alternative would eliminate Luke's labor-intensive manipulation of his Markan and Matthean sources to extract desired M = DT units and to rearrange them.

Goodacre understands the field of oral tradition open to Matthew and Luke to be generically diverse: "rich, dynamic, and expansive . . . spread far and wide across every stream of Gospel data, whether triple tradition, double tradition, Special Matthew, or Special Luke."[129] But conversely, he consents that the M = Double Tradition is principally sayings—that it displays a distinctive genre profile (which, incidentally, suggests a *work*).[130] These are incommensurable stances. One might try to reconcile them by claiming that Matthew selected mainly sayings from the tradition, but this amounts to positing a kind of subtle-body Q.[131]

Goodacre, Goulder, and Ancient Media

Goodacre is concerned to distance the Farrer hypothesis from Goulder and what he regards as his more idiosyncratic lines of analysis.[132] Yet when all is said and

---

Shape," presented at the Annual Meeting of the Society of Biblical Literature, San Diego, November 2014.

127. Goodacre complains that "Goulder does not take the question of oral traditions seriously" (*Goulder and the Gospels*, 284–85).

128. Goodacre, *Goulder and the Gospels*, 290.

129. Goodacre, "Farrer Hypothesis Response," 132.

130. Goodacre, *Case against Q*, 90–91; also "Farrer Hypothesis Response," 132.

131. Following out this logic, Francis Watson posits a Matthean "Sayings Collection"; see below.

132. Goodacre, *Case against Q*, 14–15.

done, it is Goulder who is the more attuned to ancient media realities, and more alert to their implications for the Farrer hypothesis. His scrolling account was a serious effort to come to grips with the media pragmatics of the utilization hypothesis. Goodacre reduces the source utilization issue to a problem for narrative criticism. For the same reason one finds in Goodacre little engagement with the "unpicking" problem: the latter becomes pressing only when one views the relevant passages in the light of source-utilization realities, and when one takes the measure of an environment in which oral practices were not cleanly separable from practices in connection with transmission of a written tradition.

Goodacre does have an incipient sense of the instrumental role played by memory in ancient source utilization practices, and he calls on it—ad hoc to be sure—to try to deal with certain difficulties in Luke's use of Matthew. He invokes it to explain the minor agreements (triple-tradition memory interference from Matthew) but also as a rationale for Luke's opting for Mark over Matthew in the triple tradition (Luke has Mark "by heart"). Memory for Goodacre is not a source and compositional competence, not even in the ancillary sense that Goulder allowed. Rather, it is simple habituation as a function of length of usage that serves to explain why Luke would for practical and affective reasons have chosen Mark over Matthew as his source for the triple tradition. *Ex hypothesi* he does not regard Luke as having significant memory control of Matthew. Memory, therefore, cannot provide Luke much assistance in finding his way around Matthew and in carrying out the various utilization operations that he must perform.

The risk that Goodacre's neglect of the media dimensions of the FH poses to the hypothesis has been recognized by a number of his FH colleagues, and one finds in more recent defenses of the FH renewed efforts to situate it within ancient media frameworks. Two of the more well-considered of these come from John Poirier and Ken Olson.

John Poirier and Ken Olson

Poirier: Wax Tablets and Luke's Matthew Utilization

John Poirier attributes wax-tablet usage to Luke to explain how he manages to rearrange his Matthean materials, given the practical difficulties of scroll manipulations.[133] Wax tablets were used in Greco-Roman authorial projects to

---

133. John C. Poirier, "The Roll, the Codex, the Wax Tablet, and the Synoptic Problem," *JSNT* 35 (2012): 3–30 (23–24).

facilitate collection and gestation of materials, subsequently worked up into a preliminary draft that was then literarily refined and transferred in clean copy to a papyrus roll. The theory runs into the difficulty, however, of the limited capacity of wax-tablet notebooks. After venturing that "he could have bought or borrowed enough tablets to do the job in one pass," Poirier opts to associate the three large divisions of Luke (3:1–9:50; 9:51–18:14; 18:15–24:53) with "three successive uses of wax tablets."[134] But Luke would need quite a bit more capacity to draft just one of these segments, Downing estimates, "at least 60–70 for each one-third successive section of his Gospel."[135] Poirier then modifies the scenario to having Luke use wax tablets in a more direct source-utilization mode: to excerpt passages from Matthew to facilitate their transfer into their new arrangement in the travel section. Luke's thorough memory habituation to Mark would make his discrimination and separation of these Matthean additions an easy matter. These could then be transported via wax tablets to various locations in his own composition.[136] Poirier's account operates within a visual-utilization model. In any case, it is not clear how a utilization scenario of copying, rearranging, and recopying excerpts coheres with the patterns of agreement and variation in the parallels.

Poirier on Luke's Reasons for Rearranging Matthean Materials

Other than this foray into ancient media practices Poirier's defense of the FH runs largely on the tracks laid down by Goulder and Goodacre—for example, accepting Goulder's reverse-scrolling account of Luke's Matthew utilization (in tension with his wax tablet scenario).[137] Wary of the opening Goodacre gave to oral tradition, he reverts to reading the "alternating primitivity passages" as Lukan redactions of the Matthean parallel—e.g., the "finger/Spirit of God" crux (Luke 11:20//Matt 12:28); the Sign of Jonah (Luke 11:29–32//Matt 12:38–42).[138]

---

134. Poirier, "The Roll," 23.

135. F. Gerald Downing, "Waxing Careless: Poirier, Derrenbacker, and Downing," *JSNT* 35 (2013): 388–93 (391). Downing points out that Diogenes Laertius treats the report ("some say") that Philippus of Opus (Plato's secretary) copied out Plato's *The Laws* (418 pages in the Teubner edition), which allegedly he found in a complete draft on wax tablets, as curious hearsay, and that there really is no evidence for the kind of usage Poirier attributes to Luke.

136. John C. Poirier, "Delbert Burkett's Defense of Q," in Poirier and Peterson, *Marcan Priority without Q*, 191–225 (208).

137. John C. Poirier, "The Composition of Luke in Source-Critical Perspective," in Foster et al., *New Studies in the Synoptic Problem*, 209–26 (225).

138. Poirier, "Burkett's Defense," 213–14.

The perennial question, however, is Luke's rationale for undertaking his rearrangements. Poirier experiments with three rationales. Like Lummis he finds the first in Luke's comment in the Prologue about concern for καθεξῆς: Luke did not think that the arrangement of the double tradition in his Matthew source, "arbitrarily inserted . . . at so many junctures," was the "correct order" of these materials relative to the Markan narrative sequence. It gave the false impression that those were the actual occasions on which Jesus had delivered those teachings. Accordingly, he "uproot[ed] the double tradition from its Matthean contexts," in Poirier's view "an easy enough task," and collated it in a "compendium" inserted at the Galilee/Judea junction in Mark's narrative and running from Luke 9:51 to 18:14. But would not Luke's readers have thought that Jesus delivered these teachings on various occasions in his journey from Galilee to Jerusalem? Though reluctant to concede the force of this objection, Poirier then adopts Goodacre's rationale, suggesting that Luke consolidated the double tradition in this central compendium "so as not to spoil the effect of the [Markan] gospel narrative as Matthew had done."[139] His third rationale, one that has become quite popular among FH defenders, is that Luke was critical of the Gospel of Matthew and wanted to supplant it. Once again the grounds are to be found in the Prologue: Luke is dissatisfied with the "others" who have attempted to write up an account. But to displace Matthew his gospel needed to look quite different from Matthew's so as not to be mistaken for just a revision of it. The advantage of this rationale is that it relieves the FH of having to give an account of Luke's rearrangements: no other explanation is needed than Luke's desire to differentiate his gospel from Matthew's.[140] A skeptic might take this instead as a tacit admission that the FH is unable to stipulate a plausible rationale for Luke's manner of proceeding with Matthew.

Mark would also be among the predecessors that Luke is dissatisfied with, yet for the FH it is axiomatic that Luke is devoted to the Gospel of Mark. The rationale also sits uncomfortably with Poirier's interpretation of passages such as the Beelzebul Accusation, where Luke exchanges his preference for Mark in the triple tradition for preference for Matthew. But why then does Luke go to lengths to avoid the Markan elements in the Beelzebul passage? Poirier says that Luke liked Matthew's wording better; after all, would not Matthew's literary superiority to

139. Poirier, "Burkett's Defense," 210; also "Composition of Luke," 220–21.
140. John C. Poirier, "Introduction: Why the Farrer Hypothesis? Why Now?," in Poirier and Peterson, *Marcan Priority without Q*, 1–15 (7–9); "Burkett's Defense," 208–9, 221; "Composition of Luke," 221.

Mark be one of the reasons for its popularity?[141] But Matthew has improved Mark across the board. Why not prefer his versions on more occasions? Poirier continues in this vein that Luke "favored shorter accounts" and eliminated the Markan elements from Matthew's "prolix" version of the Beelzebul pericope to shorten it.[142] In short: Luke temporarily abandons his loyalty to Mark in the triple tradition to follow Matthew's Beelzebul account, impressed by the superior literary qualities of the latter, but at the same time he finds it "prolix," which he rectifies by dropping out the Markan elements—while nevertheless replacing the Mark/Matthew Strong Man segment (Matt 12:29//Mark 3:27, twenty-seven words) with a longer version (Luke 11:21–22, thirty-three words).

Finally, Poirier's wax tablet collection of Matthean excerpts, Luke's "compendium," is an *ersatz* Q: a distinct collection of double-tradition sayings that Luke draws upon directly as his source for sayings materials. Once again Q stubbornly refuses to be dispensed with.

Olson: Media Realities and Luke's Unpicking of Matthew's Beelzebul Accusation

Ken Olson's commendably detailed engagement with the "unpicking" problem in the Beelzebul passage merits attention owing to its sensitivity to ancient source-utilization realities. Agreeing with his sparring partner, Downing, on the point, Olson stipulates that in accord with the practice of classical authors to follow "only one source at a time for any given episode and . . . occasionally influenced by the memory of other sources," Luke would be using Matthew, his lead source for the Beelzebul passage. He would do this "without keeping his eye on his other source to see what it has in the parallel passage."[143] That is, Luke would not be comparing Matthew and Mark to assist in picking out and eliminating Markan elements from the Matthean passage. Though he would likely have read over the versions in his two sources before proceeding, he is following Matthew alone. "Thus [he] does not know precisely where Matthew and Mark have similar materials, and where they do not."[144]

Olson does not much discuss Matthew's smaller agreements with Mark against Luke in Matthew 12:25–26, arguable ones being σταθήσεται/στα-

141. Poirier, "Burkett's Defense," 198–99, 218–22.

142. Poirier, "Burkett's Defense," 218.

143. Olson, "Unpicking," 132–33. Olson is countering Downing's claim that Luke would have sought out the common witness of Mark and Matthew.

144. Olson, "Unpicking," 141–42.

θῆναι (Matt 12:25c//Mark 3:25c); τὸν σατανᾶν ἐκβάλλει/σατανᾶν ἐκβάλ-
λειν (Matt 12:26a//Mark 3:23b); μερισθεῖσα καθ' ἑαυτῆς/ἐφ' ἑαυτὴν μερισθῇ
(Matt 12:25c//Mark 3:25a). Doubtless he would understand these as Matthew's
reminiscences of the Markan parallel. Luke's failure to agree with Matthew in
these Markan elements and the paucity of his agreements with Mark against
Matthew generally in this section are noteworthy, but we will content ourselves
with the observation that the first sequence Matthew 12:22–26 has not so much
the appearance of the core Markan pericope (3:22–26) with Matthean redactional additions and modifications but of a Matthean version of the Markan
pericope with some Markan elements entering via reminiscence. Given that on
the FH the Gospel of Mark is deeply memory habituated to Luke, it is notable
that there is comparatively little memory interference from Mark into Luke's
rendering of the less familiarized (on the FH) Matthean version, especially
since he is writing the Matthean version from memory of what he has just
read over in his Matthew scroll—and writing it quite freely.

One can nevertheless debate the import of the patterns of agreement and
disagreement in this opening sequence, and so here we concentrate on Olson's
explanation of Luke's major Markan omissions. Luke 11:21–22, he says, is Luke's
rewrite of the Matt/Mark Strong Man pericope (Matt 12:29//Mark 3:27). Luke is
not unpicking but rewriting a Markan element. That he does so precisely at the
point at which Matthew shifts from his own expansions back to Mark, and that
he then rejoins Matthew verbatim for the saying at Matt 11:30//Luke 12:23, "is,
apparently, entirely coincidental."[145] Given the almost complete lack of verbal
agreement, absent Goulder-level creative rewriting one is hard pressed to understand the Lukan Strong Man as Luke's redaction of the Matthean (Markan)
Strong Man. It might be better understood as a variant. It is nevertheless a
unit-for-unit substitution, and if one shares Olson's tolerance for coincidence
in Markan elements again going missing in Luke's Beelzebul, it is not out of the
question that Luke switched out the Matt/Mark Strong Man for his variant.

The "Blaspheming the Holy Spirit" saying in Matthew 12:31–32//Luke 12:10
presents a more difficult challenge for the FH: Luke has cleanly excised the
Matthean expansion from its embedment in the Mark 3:28–29 parallel and
relocated it to Luke 12:10. Olson himself stipulates that Luke would have had
to perform this unpicking operation without cross-consultation with Mark,
without "know[ing] precisely where Matthew and Mark have similar materials,

---

145. Olson, "Unpicking," 141.

and where they do not."[146] Accordingly, he must explain it solely in terms of Luke's contingent redactional decisions vis-à-vis the Matthew text. Matthew uses the core Markan saying (Mark 3:28–29), on the blasphemies and sins of the "sons of men" that will be forgiven them, as a frame for his expansion—the "word against the Son of Man" that will be forgiven the one who utters it. By doing so he has created a doublet. Luke is averse to doublets. He selects the Matthean addition (Matt 12:31b, 32a) over the original Markan saying *and* picks it out cleanly from the frame formed by the Markan saying (Matt 12:31a, 32b), likewise simply by the natural operation of his redactional interests: he prefers the christological reference "Son of Man" of Matthew's expansion, and its intimate pairing with the Holy Spirit, to the nonchristological τοῖς ἀνθρώ-ποις of the Markan framework saying (Matthew's alteration of Mark's τοῖς υἱοῖς τῶν ἀνθρώπων). The Matthean "Son of Man/Holy Spirit" thematic of the saying also makes a superior fit with the thematic configuration of sayings in Luke 12:8–12, on confessing the Son of Man, and on bold witness enabled by the Holy Spirit.[147]

This is a *tour de force* explanation of the seemingly impossible: an excision of a Matthean addition from its vice-like enclosure in its Markan frame—without any side consultation with Mark. In addition, because the exclusion of these Markan elements (and also of the Strong Man) is not meditated but rather a secondary effect of redactional decisions, Olson does not need to come up with reasons for Luke's strange avoidance of Mark (at least in the case of the Beelzebul Accusation).

How well does this explanation hold up? Luke in fact appears closer to Matthew 12:31b than to Matthew 12:32b. One will also notice that without the Markan frame (Matt 12:31a/32b) the sequence Matthew 12:31b, 32a is incoherent. What Luke has actually done is separate the Matthean apodosis from the Markan protasis in the first saying, and the Matthean protasis from the Markan apodosis in the second saying. One further observes that in Luke 12:10, the order of these clauses is inverted, the effect of which is a coherent, self-contained saying.

One might therefore imagine a different scenario. Luke has access to the saying in Luke 12:10. Matthew has access to the same saying. He conflates it with its variant Mark 3:28–29 by a simple reversal of its clauses and a redactional alteration of Mark's τοῖς υἱοῖς ἀνθώπων to τοῖς ἀνθρώποις. This combi-

---

146. Olson, "Unpicking," 141–42.
147. Olson, "Unpicking," 140–41.

native operation, easy enough for a scribe like Matthew, practiced in the arts of cultivating wisdom materials, is possible because the Markan saying and this saying are variants of each other. Interleaving the protasis of the one with the apodosis of the other, and vice versa, creates two sayings. Disliking doublets, Luke abjures the Mark 3 variant altogether.

Olson's is a media-aware and refreshingly in-depth examination of the "unpicking" problem from the Farrer perspective. It shows though that FH struggles with the problem of Luke's "unpicking" continue. The difficulties are further complicated by the fact that close cross-comparison of Matthew with Mark is now ruled out, that Luke is not writing visually from his Matthew source either but from the freshened memory of his preliminary read-over of the passage in question, and that oral practices manifestly remain operative in his rendering of his written tradition. Plus—and as Olson acknowledges—there is the volatile factor of memory interference from one or the other of his sources.[148]

Francis Watson

Francis Watson makes up the fourth member of the quartet of the most important Farrer theorists, other members being Farrer, Goulder, and Goodacre. His L/M utilization hypothesis posits a sayings collection (SC) as the source of Matthew's double tradition. Some might argue that this is a departure from Farrer orthodoxy—none less than Goodacre launched an attack on it. We will see, however, that this feature is simply a function of his media model, which assigns a less prominent role to oral tradition. In all other respects the L/M and the Farrer hypotheses run on the same tracks.

Watson and FH Logics

Watson views matters through the "FH logics" lens: the Q hypothesis is predicated on the *inconceivability*, the *implausibility*, of Luke's use of Matthew (Watson uses both terms). To defeat it one only need show that Luke's use of Matthew is conceivable and plausible. Watson follows Goulder in raising the benchmark from Farrer's "possible" to plausible.[149] On the other hand, he

---

148. Olson, "Unpicking," 147.

149. Francis Watson, *Gospel Writing: A Canonical Perspective* (Grand Rapids: Eerdmans, 2013), 185; also "Q as Hypothesis: A Study in Methodology," *NTS* 55 (2009): 397–415 (398, 405).

holds that the plausibility benchmark is attained if Luke's L/M compositional procedure can be shown to be "intelligible."[150] He appears not to share Goulder and Goodacre's concern that the FH be shown to be probable. This low bar may owe something to the credence he accords to Goodacre's "coincidences" argument as sufficient grounds for dispensing with the 2DH and "the Q edifice" (131, also 157–58).[151] Again one cannot but be puzzled that showing a hypothesis to be "plausible" and "intelligible" should be held up as its primary achievement. Any hypothesis is plausible and intelligible within its own terms of reference. To be sure, Watson says, the corresponding redactional account needs to be compared with the competing 2DH account for plausibility. But this is where Occam's Razor can be applied: the 2DH "generates . . . a double redactional process" (i.e., Matthew and Luke combine Mark and Q), the L/M "a single process, in which Luke edits Matthew."[152]

This line of FH logics reasoning explains Watson's dismissive attitude toward the persistent questions raised by Luke's Matthew utilization, questions that engrossed the likes of Goulder and Goodacre, to an extent even Farrer. Explanatory demands, such as *why* Luke reserves a number of passages in Matthew's Sermon for later use, or for accountings of some of Luke's omissions, are almost an impertinence. "The best answer is the one he himself gives: it seemed good to him to compose his own gospel in his own way, so as to address problems of order bequeathed by his predecessors (cf. Lk 1.1–4). Beyond that we cannot go" (169, also 174–75). The "alternating primitivity" question is a nitpicking distraction from the business of showing the plausibility and intelligibility of Luke's compositional procedures vis-à-vis Matthew, which a few "proof-texts" cannot affect (162–63). All this reduces the explanatory burden that Watson must bear, but the peremptory dismissal of not unreasonable questions raised by Luke's Matthew utilization dims the prospects of his L/M hypothesis from the outset. One must do more than describe what Luke has done, given the FH, and declare the Q hypothesis defeated.

Watson's logic, and FH logics in general, may be represented thus: (1) the Q hypothesis is predicated on the implausibility/incredibility of Luke's use of

150. Watson, *Gospel Writing*, 169 (hereafter page citations will be in the text).

151. Watson identifies Luke's and Matthew's independent—on the 2DH—conflation of the John the Baptist materials of Mark and the hypothesized Q as one of these remarkable coincidences (401). It only qualifies as a remarkable coincidence, however, if there were an open-ended number of ways to incorporate the hypothesized John the Baptist Q parallel coherently into the Markan narrative line.

152. Watson, "Q as Hypothesis," 399.

Matthew; (2) the plausibility of a hypothesis equates to the plausibility of the redactional account that hypothesis generates; (3) the FH generates a plausible redactional account of Luke's use of Matthew; (4) the Q hypothesis is defeated. The first two premises are both unsound: any redactional account is plausible within the terms of reference of the enabling hypothesis. Watson professes that it is important to weigh the relative plausibility of the redactional accounts generated by competing utilization hypotheses. The plausibility of the FH, however, is contingent on the answers it is able to give to the persistent utilization questions connected with Luke's use of Matthew. It is difficult to see that Watson's L/M version of the FH gets any traction if it refuses those questions.

Watson's Explanations of Luke's L/M Procedures

It accords with this view of matters that Watson offers little in the way of a rationale for Luke's preference for Mark over Matthew in the triple tradition, noting it simply as Luke's "redactional decision to differentiate Markan and Matthean material and to give precedence to Mark."[153] Similarly, to give "a clear and compelling account of [Luke's editorial] procedures" it suffices to enumerate those procedures: prioritizing Mark in the triple tradition, relocating many of Matthew's supplementary materials to later points in the Markan narrative, reserving other of these "for use in his own L sequence" (i.e., the travel section) (184). This is not the whole story, of course. Watson finds grounds for Luke's procedures in the Lukan Prologue. Luke's "it seemed good to me" is justification enough for not probing into why Luke proceeded as he did, beyond his own declaration that he is motivated by a concern to write his source materials "in order" (καθεξῆς σοι γράψαι) (148, 169). There are few of Luke's utilization actions that cannot be rationalized under this commodious rubric. But on occasion Watson goes further. He follows Goodacre in identifying a "concern to restore the original Markan sequence" as the reason Luke ends up placing a number of the Matthean supplements to be found among Matthew's Markan transpositions at later points in the Markan narrative sequence (215–16). Luke's genealogy with its "Solomonic lineage" is to be explained as a reaction against Matthew's genealogy (143). In a recent essay Watson floats the increasingly popular rationale that Luke may be critical of Matthew "and perhaps . . . wishes to supplant him."[154]

153. Watson, "Q as Hypothesis," 413.
154. Francis Watson, "The Archaeology of the Q Hypothesis: The Case of H. J. Holtz-

These are standard FH rationales for Luke's editorial actions. Where Watson innovates is in his characterization of Luke's utilization of Matthew as "creative interpretation," and, further, validating this utilization mode with reference to ancient media practices. Synoptic source utilization, he says, is an act of literary reception of the Jesus tradition, and reception is always an act of interpretation. Crucially, this is both an *oral* and a *written* operation, "for the texts are scripts to be read or performed." Accordingly, Luke's utilization of Matthew is a manifestation of the inner dynamism of the tradition itself; it presents to us a Luke who is a "creative interpreter of the tradition" received from Mark and Matthew. For Watson this translates to Luke's "interpretative freedom" with his sources (i.e., with Matthew) (118–19).

Watson therefore finds in ancient orality a novel, media-astute way to dissolve the difficulties in Luke's Matthew utilization, the latter based, ostensibly, in the "dynamism" of tradition cultivation and transmission. The classic utilization problems arising in connection with Luke's selections and rearrangements of his Matthean materials, Watson says, are relics of mechanical models of source utilization. Their relevance fades once Luke's project is properly understood as a creative reception and Luke himself as a creative interpreter of Matthew (158–66).

This echoes Goodacre's disparagement of "wooden" cut-and-paste models of source utilization, a caricature of source criticism that serves as a convenient foil to Luke's redactional freedom. One also encounters in Watson's "creative interpretation" a reprise of Goodacre's assimilation of Luke's Matthew utilization to Luke's "creative narrative artistry," the difference being that tradition dynamics rather than narrative criticism provides the validation. Both methods make a virtue of the necessity, endemic to the FH, to refer utilization problems to Luke's authorial prerogatives. Watson puts this candidly: "The grounds for Luke's editorial decisions do not always have to be equally obvious, but the principle that subsumes all of them is simply his intention to compose a new gospel rather than to copy out the old. Luke is an ambitious author (see Lk 1,1–4), and we need to assume for him a generous amount of editorial freedom."[155] The straw man here is the opposition between "composing" and "copying," a variation on the opposition between "author" and "copyist," both of which erase the intermediating points where we can plot Luke the tradent.

---

mann," in *Theological and Theoretical Issues in the Synoptic Problem*, ed. John S. Kloppenborg and Joseph Verheyden, LNTS 618 (London: T&T Clark, 2020), 37–52 (39).

155. Francis Watson, "Braucht Lukas Q? Ein Plädoyer für die L/M Hypothese," *ZNT* 22 (2019): 61–77 (69).

Watson's Accounting for Luke's Rearrangements

Luke's utilization of Matthew is an act of reception and an act of interpretation, and oral-utilization practices play a big role. But the constraints exercised by the written work upon utilization are not neutralized by references to the "dynamism of tradition" and "scripts to be performed." The term "script" itself supervenes here: a script is a determinant of its own enactment. The point does not escape Watson. From Herder forward the cardinal challenge to theories of Luke's use of Matthew has always been Luke's large-scale divergence from Matthew's arrangement of the double tradition. For Watson the καθεξῆς principle together with Luke's interpretative sovereignty suffices to explain *why* Luke carried out the rearrangement. Καθεξῆς and Luke's authorial prerogative prop each other up. Luke's reordering? Καθεξῆς. Luke's rationale for reordering as he does? "It seemed good to me." Be that as it may, the issue then is to explain *how* Luke managed it—particularly his mass collocation of Matthean materials into the travel section—and to do so without reprising Goulder's scrolling debacle. Watson proposes that as Luke passed through the Sermon on the Mount and other Matthean contexts he copied out passages that he wished to reserve for later use into a notebook collection of extracts. "The passages are then readily available to him and may be incorporated in any order" (170).[156] Reaching for the expedient of an intermediary source (which goes back as far as de Wette) is a tacit acknowledgement that Luke's direct utilization of Matthew is difficult to conceive.

The excerpting practice that Watson attributes to Luke naturally leads on to the "unpicking" question—in Watson's words, "Luke's identification of non-Markan elements within Matthew."[157] Watson is incredulous that this should even be an issue: it was a "simple procedure" of visual discrimination: many of these are "easily recognizable additions to their Markan context"; Matthew's additions embedded in Markan passages in the later chapters of Matthew "can easily be extracted"; "it does not take meticulous precision . . . to note the supplementary Matthean material."[158]

It is difficult to see that the unpicking operations and the close visual inspection of the text that the FH must attribute to Luke can be reconciled

---

156. Similarly, Watson, "Q as Hypothesis," 406; and "Seven Theses on the Synoptic Problem, in Disagreement with Christopher Tuckett," in Müller and Omerzu, *Gospel Interpretation*, 139–47 (145).

157. Watson, "Seven Theses," 144.

158. Watson, "Seven Theses," 144; *Gospel Writing*, 175, 186.

with Watson's descriptions of the dynamic interpenetration of orality with Luke's engagement with his Matthew source, his "script for performance," in the mode of oral interpretation (272). "Writing and orality," he says, "are interdependent and interact freely" (251). This commits Watson to a memory-based, oral-enacted source-utilization mode at odds with the meticulous text-discrimination operations that Luke must perform on Matthew. Watson's oral-interpretative utilization mode accords nicely with the Synoptic patterns of variation, less so with visual inspection, extraction, and copying-out operations that he attributes to Luke.

Watson: Sayings Collections and Double-Tradition Origins

Watson's sayings collection theory brings us to the heart of his media framework. The "primitive Sayings Collection" is, in Watson's words, an "archaic genre." The *Gospel of Thomas*, a relic of the genre, exemplifies its prototypical features (221). Sayings collections are the principal means for the transmission of Synoptic sayings and parable materials in the era prior to the appearance of the Synoptic Gospels. They fill the space scholarship typically assigns to that often vaguely defined entity "the oral tradition" (250–51).[159]

More to the point—and reprising F. C. Baur's and Köstlin's sayings-dense proto-Matthean source—Watson holds that "one or more" sayings collections are Matthew's principal source for the double tradition (284). This is usually regarded as a break with Farrer orthodoxy, but Watson is simply giving his answer to the very natural question also addressed by Goulder and Goodacre on the source of the M/DT materials. Goodacre posits the aggregate of oral tradition in the pre-Synoptic period, Watson a more mixed matrix of oral and written transmission modes, hardly an *outré* position to adopt. Because it accounts for the double tradition's instructional profile Watson's sayings collection theory is in fact more defensible than Goodacre's oral tradition theory. We saw that to controvert Watson, Goodacre is forced to claim that narrative gospel is the archetypal primitive Christian genre and that the elements of early Christian sayings collections are extracts from narrative gospels.

To be sure, for Watson pre-Synoptic transmission modes are heavily weighted away from oral tradition and toward primitive collections. In part this is owing to his not having a robust model for oral tradition. He assumes that oral tradition is not capable of durable transmission, absent "any obvious

---

159. Watson also posits primitive collections of narrative episodes (345–46), and thus countenances the streaming of the tradition into sayings and narrative genres, respectively.

institutional mechanism for controlling transmission."[160] Thus writing, in the form of these subliterary collections, very early becomes *the* means not only for the transmission but also for the cultivation of the tradition (251, 285). Watson's description of these "nonliterary" collections and their function reprises the *Aufzeichnungen* of the nineteenth-century source critics (e.g., 346–47). Their persistence into the second century is attested, Watson thinks, by vestiges such as the *Gospel of Thomas* and by variant patristic citations.[161]

Notwithstanding his promising declarations about the interpenetration of orality and writing, it turns out that Watson's history of the tradition from beginning to end is very much defined by the written medium. The history of the tradition is a matter of copying of sayings collections into successive sayings collections, in the reception mode of "interpretative rewriting." It is a serial regress of written texts connected up by interpretative rewriting (288, 342–43). There exists a parallel oral tradition, but it is itself "textually determined," an epiphenomenal "secondary orality" generated by the public reading of written sayings collections and related gospel-type works. To the extent that a text does not stand in a direct literary relationship with a precursor, it may still be dependent on it via secondary orality from its public performance (251, 272). Synoptic variation is generated by interpretative rewriting along the succession of sayings collections—similarly in the case of Luke's reception of Matthew. It follows that any variation must have a documentary source. The intermediating collections that Watson must theorize therefore proliferate uncontrollably (342–43). Watson finds himself in Eichhorn's predicament, and for the same reason: notwithstanding gestures to orality his history of the tradition is tightly bound to the modes of the written medium.

Watson's Matthean Sayings Collection: A Phantom Q?

One might think that in positing a pre-Synoptic sayings collection as the source of Matthew's double tradition, Watson has made a fatal concession to the two source hypothesis. Watson himself holds that his sayings collection theory forces a qualification of the FH logics axiom that by virtue of Occam's Razor a plausible account of Luke's redaction of Matthew *per se* defeats the Q hypothesis. This is because a "Q-like" source is needed to account for the transmission of this body of sayings over the decades intervening between Jesus and their incorporation in the Gospel of Matthew. Watson sees only two

---

160. Francis Watson, "Q and the *Logia*: On the Discovery and Marginalizing of P. Oxy. 1," in Müller and Omerzu, *Gospel Interpretation*, 97–113 (97–98).
161. Watson, "Q and the *Logia*," 107.

alternatives to his pre-Matthean sayings collection, both problematic: either a vague gesture toward an unstable, indeterminate oral tradition, or Goulder's Matthean authorship of the double tradition.[162]

But he insists that he has not let Q sneak in the back door, and that Luke remains dependent upon Matthew for his double tradition. He offers several arguments for this. In the Prologue Luke stipulates that his tradition stems from the "eyewitnesses." This, Watson claims, indicates that Luke is working primarily with a *narrative* tradition—i.e., what is "seen," and not a *sayings* tradition, what is "heard."[163] Second, he alleges *ad hominem* that the contemporary Q hypothesis is the product of the "deeply conservative" bias of the Oxford group toward deriving the double tradition intracanonically from Matthew and Luke and against conceding any role in explaining gospel origins to noncanonical sayings collections like *P. Oxy 1* and the *Gospel of Thomas*.[164] Third, on the grounds that *P. Oxy 1* and the *Gospel of Thomas* are normative exemplars of the sayings collection genre, he argues that narrative elements in Luke's double tradition and its speech format (that is, rather than individual sayings) rule out Luke's using Matthew's sayings collection or any sayings collection.[165] Fourth, he says that the Q hypothesis "stands or falls by its own merits."[166] His point is not precisely clear, but he seems to be saying that the Q hypothesis fails on its own terms. Perhaps he has Goodacre's "coincidences" critique of the hypothesis in mind, which he thinks is dispositive.

These arguments do not go far in allaying concerns that Watson's sayings collections theory is the Q hypothesis in another guise. As Watson himself points out, in extracting Matthean passages into a notebook as a utilization aid, Luke has effectively "compiled his own SC." Elsewhere Watson describes it as "Luke's Matthean sayings collection" (187, also 284). This is a two document hypothesis in all but name. Again Q refuses to go gentle into that good night (apologies to Dylan Thomas).

Watson on Memory, Source History, and Jesus

Uniquely among FH scholars Watson, in a considered analysis, works from his L/M source solution back to the tradition's origins in memories of Jesus. This is due to his foregrounding reception as the effective factor in Synoptic source

---

162. Watson, "Q and the *Logia*," 97–98.

163. Francis Watson, "Luke Rewriting and Rewritten," in Nielsen and Müller, *Luke's Literary Creativity*, 79–95 (83).

164. Watson, "Seven Theses," 146–47; also "Q and the *Logia*," 100–101.

165. Watson, "Q and the *Logia*," 108.

166. Francis Watson, "A Reply to My Critics," in Hamilton, *Writing the Gospels*, 227–48 (241).

history. The tradition's dominant orientation to the past points to its ultimate grounding in memory. The history of the tradition, he says, originates in early Christian recollection. Those closest to Jesus have a special position in the community as the authoritative memory links between Jesus and the present community. Their recollections fall under the rubrics of Jesus's sayings and his deeds. The recollections lose their individual imprint as they become the common currency of the early community: individual memories are transformed into the social memory of the communities in Judea and Galilee, subsequently also of the communities in Antioch, Asia Minor, Rome, and elsewhere. The various *Sitze im Leben* of community life—"teaching, worship, controversy, initiation, scriptural interpretation, mutual aid, and ethical formation," and mission—are the sites for the cultivation of memory (346).

On the question of the memory-tradition nexus, Watson takes his cue from Dibelius's characterization of the tradition as *geformte Erinnerung* (shaped memory). Whether in original forms as sayings or subsequently in the formation of the narrative tradition, memory avails itself of a range of genres to take on its stabilizing and abiding forms (351–52). But it is the all-important act of the inscription of the tradition in pre-Synoptic collections that secures the connection between the written gospel tradition, early Christian memory, and Jesus. Inscription of the tradition in sayings collections is the first stage of Watson's L/M source history, for with its existence in the written medium the tradition can become the object of interpretation and reception through rewriting (344–47).

Watson and the Tatian Analogy to FH Luke

Watson's rejoinder to critics who declare that Luke's utilization operations are prohibitively awkward and difficult is that Tatian's operations in weaving together strands from four gospels into a new unity provide an almost exact analogy to Luke's extracting, unpicking, and relocating operations vis-à-vis Matthew and Mark. Indeed, Tatian's project with four sources was considerably more daunting than Luke's, with two sources.[167] The Tatian analogy is enjoying a vogue in FH scholarship because it seems to answer the persistent questions about the feasibility of Luke's FH procedures.[168]

Debates continue about the *Diatessaron*'s reconstruction from commentaries and descendant gospel harmonies, and whether the Dura Europos papyrus

---

167. Watson, "Reply to My Critics," 243–45; "Seven Theses," 144.

168. E.g., James W. Barker, "Ancient Compositional Practices and the Gospels: A Reassessment," *JBL* 135 (2016): 109–21 (109, 117–19).

is a fragment of the *Diatessaron* or of some similar harmony.[169] Nevertheless, enough information is available to reconstruct Tatian's practices—and if the Dura fragment is not a specimen of Tatian's work it nevertheless is a good case study of the procedures required to harmonize the four gospels.

While Tatian provides a good analogy to conflation of sources, he offers no analogy to FH Luke's unpicking of his sources.[170] In fact, Tatian exacerbates the unpicking problem for the FH. Any reconstructed *Diatessaron* passage will show this—for example, this one: the Fuldensis version of Tatian's second Nazareth Rejection episode (*italics* = Matthew; **bold** = Luke; underline = Mark).[171]

> GMt 13.54 *And coming into his native town, he was teaching them in* **their synagogues** *so that they marveled and said, "Where did he get this wisdom and* GMk 6.2 <u>such miracles that are accomplished through his hands?</u>" GMt 13.55 *Is he not the son of a carpenter, is not his mother called Mary and his brothers James and Joseph and Simon and Judas?* GMt 13.56 *And are not all of his sisters with us? Therefore where did he get all these things?* GMt 13.57 *And they were offended at him.* GLk 4.23 **And he said to them, "Surely you will say to me this proverb, 'Physician, heal yourself! Whatever things we have heard were done in Capernaum, do also here in your native town.'** GLk 4.24 **Truly I say to you that no prophet is accepted in his native town** GMt 13.57/GMk 6.4 <u>and in his house.</u>" GMt 13.58 *And he did not do there many miracles on account of their unbelief,* GMk 6.5 <u>except that he did heal a few sick people by laying on his hands,</u> GMk 6.6 <u>and he marveled on account of their unbelief.</u> GLk 4.25 **"In truth I say to you, many widows were in Israel in the days of Elijah when heaven was closed for three years and six months, when a great famine came over all the land,** GLk 4.26 **and Elijah was sent to none of them except to Zarephath of Sidon, to a woman who was a widow.** GLk 4.27 **And there were many lepers in Israel under Elisha the prophet and not one of them**

169. See, e.g., D. C. Parker, D. G. K. Taylor, and M. S. Goodacre, "The Dura-Europos Gospel Harmony," *Studies in the Early Text of the Gospels and Acts,* ed. D. G. K. Taylor (Atlanta: SBL Press, 1999), 192–228 (199); Ulrich B. Schmid, "The Diatessaron of Tatian," in *The Text of the New Testament in Contemporary Research: Essays on the Status Quaestionis,* ed. B. D. Ehrman and M. W. Holmes, 2nd ed. (Leiden: Brill, 2013), 115–42 (124).

170. Downing has already criticized the analogy ("A Paradigm Perplex," 32).

171. From Matthew R. Crawford, "Rejection at Nazareth in the Gospels of *Mark, Matthew, Luke*—and Tatian," in *Connecting Gospels: Beyond the Canonical/Non-Canonical Divide,* ed. Francis Watson and Sarah Parkhouse (Oxford: Oxford University Press, 2018), 97–124 (113–14).

was cleansed except Naaman the Syrian." ᴳᴸᵏ ⁴·²⁸ And all those in the synagogue were filled with wrath as they heard these things, ᴳᴸᵏ ⁴·²⁹ and they rose up and cast him out of the town and led him to the brow of the hill on which their town was built, in order to throw him down. ᴳᴸᵏ ⁴·³⁰ But he, passing through their midst, went on his way.

Tatian is bringing together the pieces of the three Synoptic parallels. In Crawford's words, he "has attempted to include almost every scrap of text found in the canonical texts."[172] Of the Joseph of Arimathea pericope in the Dura Europos fragment Crawford comments, "Everything from his source texts is present."[173] FH Luke on the other hand is *disarticulating* the source threads from each another.[174] Luke in fact does little conflation of his sources, with the debatable exception of John's Preaching and Announcement of the Coming One. In regards to the above passage one might imagine an intrepid author after the fashion of FH Luke resolving to unpick, say, the "Lukan additions" (alternatively the Markan) to a basically Matthean account—keeping in mind that said author would not have the benefit of the word separation and typeface source coding of the above extract. The long Lukan block would not present too many difficulties, but this cannot be said of the others. Even if one were to grant that with some effort the remaining Lukan elements could be disentangled from the pericope, one must still ask what the point of the operation would be, the justification of the cognitive expenditure.

As with Luke's use of Matthew, Tatian must do a lot of scrolling around—or turning codex leaves—in his sources, and often back and forth. The signal difference is that it is easier to observe in Tatian a methodical pattern, whereas the pattern that FH Luke follows is rather more inscrutable. Tatian generally follows Matthew as his baseline text, collating elements from the parallel pericopes in the other gospels to the Matthean baseline passage.[175] In the Rejection at Nazareth he adopts the Matthew 13:54–58 position of the pericope, collating with it Markan and Lukan elements and, notably, the second half of the variant Luke 4 version (Tatian handles the divergent versions by creating a doublet, two Rejections, retaining the first half of the Lukan passage in the Mark 1:14–15//

172. Crawford, "Rejection at Nazareth," 114.
173. Matthew R. Crawford, "The Diatessaron, Canonical or Non-Canonical? Rereading the Dura Fragment," *NTS* 62 (2016): 253–77 (266).
174. John S. Kloppenborg, "Assimilation, Harmonization, Conflation: Comments on James Barker's 'Ancient Compositional Practices and the Gospels,'" paper presented at the Annual Meeting of the Society of Biblical Literature, San Diego, November 2014.
175. Crawford, "The Diatessaron," 268; Watson, "Reply to My Critics," 244.

Matt 4:17 position).[176] In effect Tatian is using a kind of "peg" system, collating elements of Markan, Lukan, and Johannine parallels to a Matthean peg passage. In the Dura fragment, "Joseph of Arimathea" provides the cue for the collocation of Matthean, Lukan, and Johannine descriptors of the man.[177] The point is that this method regulates Tatian's scrolling (or page-turning) operations. On the safe assumption that he has thorough memory control of his gospel source texts, he can rapidly scroll (or flip through the codices) to find the parallel passages. To be sure, it takes work to take the bits and put them together coherently—we ought not think Tatian's task was easy—but this is not even a tithe of the effort it would have taken to unpick the source threads. The cultural project justifying the cognitive expenditure is also intelligible.

Another indicator that Tatian's project is not analogous to Luke's is his low level of variation from his source texts. Besides the editing required to piece elements from disparate sources together coherently, Tatian makes redactional modifications and clarifying additions to his source texts.[178] But he generally hews closely to the wording of Matthew, Mark, Luke, and John, as Crawford grants: "For the most part Tatian probably followed the wording of his source."[179] The evangelists' source utilization generates difference; Tatian's irons it out. His cultural project is very different from theirs, and more to the point, from Luke's. Crawford downplays Tatian's close verbal agreement with the sources because it does not square with his claim that Tatian is an evangelist in his own right pursuing a project little different from the evangelists'. He puts some of the verbal agreement down to subsequent harmonization to the corresponding gospel passages.[180] But this can hardly explain the scale and consistency of the verbal agreement, which contrasts sharply to the Synoptic profile of variation and agreement. As Crawford acknowledges, this utilization

---

176. Crawford, "Rejection at Nazareth," 107–10, 119.

177. Neatly represented schematically by Watson: [GMt 27.57] *there came a [ ] man* [GLk 23.50] **being a member of the council** [GLk 23.51] **from Erinmathea, a city of [Jude]a** [GMt 27.57] *the name Joseph* [GLk 23.50] **g[o]od, ri[ghteous],** [GJn 19.38] being a disciple of Jesus, but se[cret]ly, for fear of the Jews [GMt 27.57] *and he was* [GLk 23.51] **looking for [the] k[ingdom] of God.** [GLk 23.51] **This man [had] not [con]sented to [their] p[urpose]** ("Reply to My Critics," 244).

178. For some cases see Parker, Taylor, and Goodacre, "Dura-Europos Gospel Harmony," 213–14; Crawford, "Rejection at Nazareth," 117; Watson, "Luke Rewriting," 89–90.

179. Crawford, "Rejection at Nazareth," 118; "The Diatessaron," 262–63; Parker, Taylor, and Goodacre, "Dura-Europos Gospel Harmony," 204–5; also Sharon Lea Mattila, "A Question Too Often Neglected," *NTS* 41 (1995): 199–217 (204–5): "The Gospel phrases . . . are for the most part intact, their vocabulary, syntax, and phraseology all preserved with remarkable fidelity."

180. Crawford, "Rejection at Nazareth," 100, 107–9, 121–22; "The Diatessaron," 255.

pattern is even more striking given that Tatian was a "well-trained rhetor." His rationalization—that the task of combining the sources was demanding enough without the additional task of a more engaged rendering—is ad hoc.[181]

Tatian's cultural project and the exigencies spurring it are very different from the those of the evangelists. As Goodacre and others point out, Tatian's comprehensive harmonization program is "an apologetically motivated response to the . . . emergence of four authoritative Gospels. Luke, and the churches of his day, have no such crisis." Tatian's program is to harmonize disparities, not generate them.[182] Tatian reinscribes his base texts with their increasingly fixed, normative wording, whereas the evangelists reenact their baseline tradition. Their gospels are artifacts of an era when gospel is still kerygma, oral proclamation. The evangelists straddle the boundary of the oral and the written medium; their source utilization remains significantly affected by oral practices. In 1796 Herder had already adumbrated this categorical difference in the cultural dynamics of the respective settings of Tatian and the evangelists:

> That afterwards Gospels were publicly read and expounded . . . that Gospel scrolls were laid upon the Chair of the Bishop, that oaths were taken over them—all these things do not belong in the time of gospel origins [*Evangeliogonie*], the time that written gospels were emerging from oral tradition. For in this later time the Gospels had already long existed in written form, had long been established in the churches as the holy scriptures of the new covenant. In the beginning things were not thus: this new entity was παράδοσις, tradition, oral proclamation.[183]

Tatian's close adherence to the wording of his gospel sources corresponds to the increasingly normative, authoritative status of gospel texts now *read* in the churches, with its corollary: the visual, graphic objectification of their written scripts.

Hence the remoteness of the Tatian analogy from any Lukan utilization procedure entailed by the Farrer hypothesis. Cambry Pardee points out that the close manuscript comparison of the sort observable in Tatian's project is

181. Crawford, "Rejection at Nazareth," 122.
182. Goodacre, *Case against Q*, 89; see also Kloppenborg, "Assimilation," 8–9; Mattila, "A Question," 205.
183. Herder, "Vom Erlöser," 685–86 n. 13.

unattested "in the fourth century or earlier. . . . This type of procedure was restricted to the creation of Gospel Harmonies."[184] It is an anachronism to impute this procedure to Luke. To the extent that Tatian's utilization practices are salient they accord with those the 2DH imputes to Matthew: a "peg" technique for collating sources; the creation of doublets; conflation of overlaps; following primarily one version of a pericope while inlaying or assimilating elements of the parallel.

Eric Eve

Eric Eve's publications between 2011 and 2021 are a thorough-going attempt—the first since Goulder—to find for the Farrer hypothesis a firm footing in ancient media practices.[185] Eve stands out among his Farrer contemporaries for his clear-eyed appraisal of the challenges that ancient media realities raise for the FH.

Eve and FH Logics

Eve is a conventional Farrerist in his full embrace of FH logics: the 2DH is predicated on the *implausibility* of Luke's use of Matthew. One therefore need do no more than make a case that Luke's use of Matthew is plausible to settle matters in favor of the Farrer hypothesis, by application of Occam's Razor.[186] This marks a retreat from the probability concerns of Goulder and Goodacre to a plausibility position that in fact drifts close to Farrer's low-threshold "possible" benchmark. In Eve's own words: "It is not necessary for the FH to demonstrate that Luke's transformation of Matthew is compelling in each case, but *merely* that it is not positively implausible."[187] In particular cases he is prepared to claim that Luke's use of Matthew is "reasonably plausible," "highly plausible," and in two or three instances boldly that it is "reasonably convincing" or even

---

184. Cambry G. Pardee, *Scribal Harmonization in the Synoptic Gospels*, NTTSD 60 (Leiden: Brill, 2019), 431.

185. Eric Eve, *Relating the Gospels: Memory, Imitation, and the Farrer Hypothesis*, LNTS 592 (London: T&T Clark, 2021).

186. E.g., Eve, *Relating the Gospels*, 3, 103–6, 121 n. 20, 124; "The Devil in the Detail: Exorcising Q from the Beelzebul Controversy," in Poirier and Peterson, *Marcan Priority without Q*, 16–43 (42).

187. Eve, *Relating the Gospels*, 126 (emphasis added), in reference to alternating primitivity passages.

"probable," but plausibility is his baseline for deciding matters for the FH.[188] In a twist on this standard FH approach, however, Eve further defines this benchmark as providing an explanation that is "at least as plausible as that offered by the 2DH." By this he means that whatever the explanatory difficulties for the FH in particular cases, the 2DH suffers from at least equivalent disabilities.[189] This modification of the FH schema appears to arise out of Eve's recognition that ancient media practices do create worries for the FH. His response is to put the 2DH in the same boat and then reapply Occam's Razor to secure the advantage for the FH, the "simpler explanation" (105–6).

The constancy with which the FH logics schema appears in all FH theorizing, from Farrer forward, indicates that it is not a quirk but essential to the hypothesis, a backhanded acknowledgment that the prospects for the FH hitting the probability threshold are dim. Its genius is to rig things such that the FH can always prevail—by applying FH terms of reference to the patterns of agreement and divergence in a given case, declaring the account plausible (or rather, "merely that it is not positively implausible"), and then bringing in Occam to settle the matter. Eve draws this defensive cordon even tighter: the FH only needs to show that its account in particular cases is plausible, whereas the 2DH, if it is to prevail, must demonstrate that the FH account is "positively implausible" (126). Again, one marvels at a hypothesis whose moment of triumph is its claim to be plausible, which has no aspiration to be compelling, and whose stance is perpetually defensive.

Be that as it may, the argumentation itself is defective. One cannot use the terms of one's own hypothesis—here the FH—to make a plausibility claim, and then adduce Occam's Razor to decide for the FH over the 2DH when the plausibility claim is predicated on the FH itself. FH logics confuses *coherence*, or *consistency*, with *plausibility*. FH accounts are by definition coherent—that is, consistent with the basic postulates of the hypothesis. This does not make the accounts plausible (though coherence will certainly be a property of a true hypothesis).

Our interest though is in examining the media foundations of the FH. Eve develops a number of substantive arguments that are nothing if not a serious effort to supply the FH what it lacks: a grounding in ancient media realities. This gives it its special salience for our study.

---

188. Eve, *Relating the Gospels*, 103, 121 n. 20, 194, 205; "Devil in the Detail," 42; "The Synoptic Problem without Q?," in Foster et al., *New Studies in the Synoptic Problem*, 551–70 (563).
189. Eve, *Relating the Gospels*, 3 (hereafter most page references will be in the text).

Eve on Luke's Preference for Mark in the Triple Tradition

Eve's effort includes throwing certain standard FH claims overboard, a prominent one being Goodacre's "coincidence" argument—it is unlikely Luke and Matthew would independently undertake to expand Mark identically with Nativities and extended Resurrection accounts. "Assuming Matthew and Luke were familiar with the conventions of the Graeco-Roman *bios*," Eve says, "it is not so much of a coincidence" (36). On the other hand Eve offers no explanation of why Luke opts to follow Mark rather than Matthew in the triple tradition, a question recognized by Goulder and Goodacre to be of critical importance. The reason for this striking omission is not far to seek: Eve's solution to the intractable problem of Luke's Matthew utilization will be that Luke takes Matthew as his object for *rhetorical emulation*. Among other things this entails, Eve says, that the Gospel of Matthew, far from coming comparatively recently to Luke's attention, must have exercised a large influence upon the conception of Jesus held by Luke's target audience (196–97). It is difficult to see how a preference for Mark can be squared with this. Eve therefore just sidesteps the question.

Eve's grasp of ancient authorial practices gives him further reason to quietly abandon the usual FH rationales offered for Luke's opting for Mark over Matthew. To account for the sequences where Luke's two sources run in parallel and where the Lukan rendering is dense in dual agreements, Eve imagines Luke following the well-attested practice of reviewing the respective versions of his two sources in preparation for composing his own (83, 104–5). This procedure is incommensurate with a systematic preference for Mark in the triple tradition. Eve further holds that as an ancient author and tradent Luke likely would have exercised an "equally good memory command" over both Matthew and Mark (82).[190] This means that Mark cannot have been more habituated to Luke and more memory engrained than Matthew, as Goodacre alleges. To explain why Luke fails to take over certain embedded Matthean additions to Mark (e.g., 3:14–15; 12:5–7; 13:14–15; 14:28–31; 16:16–19; 17:18–24), and also to explain the "overlap" passages, where Luke follows Matthew instead of Mark in the triple tradition, Eve again appeals to ancient source-utilization practices: Luke "sometimes follows Mark, sometimes follows Matthew, as his main source" (127). Eve judges that Luke does not even switch to Mark until 4:31 (Mark 1:21). Luke's resort to this customary pattern of source alternation

190. Also Eric Eve, *Writing the Gospels: Composition and Memory* (London: SPCK, 2016), 142.

is difficult to square with any particular devotion to the Markan narrative. Luke likewise accords Mark no special treatment vis-à-vis his treatment of Matthew. And as Eve observes, Luke and Matthew both "absorb Mark into narratives of their own design. . . . They effectively silence Mark's version of Jesus by incorporating it into their own" (131).

In short, Eve's very attention to ancient practices strands him without a rationale for FH Luke's adopting his trademark pattern of source utilization. It is hard to see that the FH can remain viable without such a rationale, not least in view of the considerable cognitive labor for FH Luke to separate out the Markan and M/DT source strands in Matthew. Eve himself expresses the problem with admirable forthrightness: "Why, if Luke knew and used Matthew from memory . . . should he have bothered with Mark at all? Since virtually the whole substance of Mark was contained in Matthew, it would surely have been easier for Luke to have worked from one source (Matthew) than to try to combine two sources that were very often similar." He speculates that Luke perhaps has in mind to reach two sorts of audience, those "more familiar with Mark and others [more familiar] with Matthew."[191] A variation on this appears fleetingly at the end of Eve's recent volume: Luke "emulate[s] his predecessors by choosing the best of each (roughly speaking Mark's narrative and Matthew's teaching material) and then seeking to improve on it." Rhetorical emulation does service here as a blanket explanation: "There were no set rules on how to imitate" (195). Luke is free to use his sources as he wishes.

The most recalcitrant problem for hypotheses that posit Luke's use of Matthew, however, has been accounting for Luke's large-scale rearrangements of his Matthean materials. Eve poses the problem again forthrightly: "The difficulty remains why Luke should have gone out of his way to extract material from Matthew and reorder it . . . in a manner that apparently makes only partial sense."[192] To an extent not seen since Goulder, Eve attempts to come to grips with the actual source-utilization operations that correspond to Luke's rearrangement of Matthew. Like Goulder, he recognizes that the viability of the FH is at stake. He launches an impressive effort to render these intelligible with reference to ancient media, memory, and writing practices.[193]

191. Eve, *Writing the Gospels*, 138–39.
192. Eve, "Synoptic Problem without Q?," 564.
193. There are some coherence issues for Eve's redaction-critical rationale for Luke's operations upon Matthew's Sermon on the Mount. He offers the familiar theological rationale that the Sermon's intra-Jewish debates were irrelevant to Luke's Gentile audience, adding that its preoccupation with the question of Torah-observance might well generate

Eve on Luke's Memory Control of His Sources

Eve seizes on the fact that like other ancient writers Matthew and Luke enjoyed "memory command" of Mark, and Luke memory command of Matthew. He conceives Luke and Matthew working less by visual contact with their sources and more from memory, consulting with the scrolls to refresh their memories (23, 27).[194] The evangelists acquired their memory competence from long practice of themselves being tradents, "authoritative performers," of the tradition as it was laid down in their written sources, and prior to that, performers of the tradition in its oral manifestation. This practice persists into their source utilization, and taken together with their facility in the wider field of oral tradition it is likewise a factor in generating variation among Synoptic parallels. This means, Eve says, that we should only refer to Matthew and Luke "redacting" or "editing" their written sources in quotation marks (23).[195] Memory-based source utilization was also a function of the scroll format of the sources and the unformatted continuous scripts inscribed therein. Taken together these made visual search-and-retrieval operations of a precision sort impractical, with the difficulties exacerbated by the awkwardness of consulting more than one scroll at a time. To be sure, skilled literates such as Matthew and Luke would have been adept at handling scrolls, and given their practiced familiarity with the texts the continuous script of their manuscripts would not have presented the level of difficulty it offers to modern readers. It nevertheless remains the case, Eve points out, that "ancient manuscripts were not particularly well suited for ready reference," hence the reliance on memory.[196]

It is from the vantage point of these ancient source-utilization realities that Eve addresses the question of Luke's rearrangement of Matthew and puts forward his thesis of *rhetorical emulation*. We will concentrate on his treatment of the travel section, where hypotheses featuring Lukan dependence on Matthew usually come to grief.

---

insecurity among Gentile believers about their salvation (*Relating the Gospels*, 19, 164). Elsewhere, however, he holds that Luke's target audience had been shaped by the Gospel of Matthew, which indeed is why Luke takes it as his basis for emulation (196–97). The Gospel of Matthew was in fact wildly popular in the Gentile churches. To parry this, Eve must argue ad hoc that Luke wrote "at a time when the new Gentile church was less sure of either its identity or its legitimacy" (19).

194. Also *Writing the Gospels*, xiii, 41–42, 93.
195. Also "Devil in the Detail," 18–19; *Writing the Gospels*, 9.
196. Eve, *Writing the Gospels*, 3–6.

Eve: Luke's Spontaneous Memory Cuing

One of Eve's virtues is his honest appraisal of the difficulties faced by the FH. In an early essay (2011) he acknowledges that Luke's travel section is not well ordered nor are his editorial rationales quite intelligible. It is not clear, he says, "why Luke should have gone out of his way to extract material from Matthew and reorder it . . . in a manner that apparently makes only partial sense." He experiments with a couple of solutions. The first is that the Matthean material that Luke was "anxious to use . . . defeated his best efforts to fit neatly into the alternative schema he had devised for it." The second is that Luke's reliance on memory to access Matthew rather than "frantically winding through a scroll" has brought about "a mental jumbling of Matthew's order."[197] These two suggestions laid down the basic lines of approach Eve will take to the problems of Luke's central section

Initially he experiments with the idea that Luke makes use of wax tablets to assist him in relocating M/DT elements into his own schema. He gets around the difficulty of the large number of tablets required to cope with the volume by having Luke take down not full extracts but abbreviated "memory prompts" (e.g., just the incipit of the Lord's Prayer, "Our Father"). He imagines Luke composing in the manner of Greco-Roman authors, with the help of notes rearranging Matthean materials over the course of several drafts.[198] As his thinking about ancient utilization practices continues to evolve, however, he shifts more decidedly toward Luke's utilization movements around Matthew being memory based, while maintaining that this would likely need some support from a papyrus notebook or wax tablets (152, 159–60).

At all costs Eve wants to avoid getting drawn into Goulder's scrolling debacle, which he finds implausible (145).[199] He hopes to manage this by substituting memory retrieval for Goulder's scrolling retrieval: Luke scrolls progressively forward through Matthew in its absolute order, but to fetch M/DT passages out of that order he reaches forward or backward in his Matthew source by memory. Goulder invoked memory very occasionally to get around utilization anomalies not amenable to scrolling scenarios. Eve greatly expands its remit, making it a leading feature of Luke's source utilization.

For instance, rather than scrolling forward to the Matthew 23 Woes and then rewinding to his absolute position at Matthew 12, Luke "reworked" the

197. Eve, "Synoptic Problem without Q?," 564, 568–69.
198. Eve, "Synoptic Problem without Q?," 568; *Writing the Gospels*, 144–45.
199. Also "Synoptic Problem without Q?," 569.

Matthean Woes by memory. Luke's low agreement with the Matthean Woes in wording and order is corroboration (179). Memory retains something of the ad hoc role it played in Goulder's account in that Eve adduces it mainly when Luke is using Matthean materials out of Matthew's absolute order. Conversely, to iron out small wrinkles in his utilization account, Eve is prepared on the rare occasion to have Luke scrolling backward in Matthew "a very short way" (188–89). In important respects Eve's account of Luke's use Matthew in the travel section is a rehabilitation of Goulder—quite a comeback for the old master, after years of being regarded in Farrer scholarship as somewhat of an embarrassment.

But to return to the matter at hand: the difficulty that Eve faces with his expanded memory expedient is the unsystematic nature of Luke's memory utilization of Matthew. If, as Eve holds, Luke had internalized Matthew through his long, active performance of it as a coherently ordered work, one might expect a greater correlation between his patterns of memory utilization and the cognitive patterns in which Matthew had come to exist in his memory. The layout and organization of a work doubles as a mnemonic network that facilitates its memory utilization. Eve recognizes the problem and circumvents it by adducing *associative memory cuing*, which he thinks delivers exactly what the FH needs: unsystematic cuing of Matthean materials. It would be no difficulty for Luke to pull M/DT sayings by memory spontaneously from anywhere in Matthew, cued by whatever associations might be triggered by the passage he might currently be working with (46, 151).

Eve's account of the two sayings that are found juxtaposed in Luke 6:39–40 illustrates Lukan memory processes as he conceives them. The first, Blind Leading the Blind (Luke 6:39//Matt 15:14), is found as a Matthean addition embedded in the Markan dispute with the Pharisees over hand-washing and ritual purity (Matt 15:1–20)—that is, in a narrative thematically alien to Matthew 7:1–5, Luke's scroll-based location in Matthew at the moment. The saying, Eve argues, gets associatively "prompted" in Luke's memory by the speck/log in the eye images in Matthew 7:3–5. In an associative cognitive cascade this saying in its turn stimulates recollection of the Disciple and Teacher (Matt 10:24–25), found in the Matthew 10 Mission segment on persecution, the associative trigger being that "a teacher is a better-sighted guide" (160–62). This solution is purchased at the considerable cost of allowing quite a bit of spontaneity if not outright disorganization (Eve thinks that the resulting sequence is somewhat muddled) into Luke's use of Matthew (though this, of course, is the point). Luke 6:39//Matt 15:14 is triggered by Matthew 7:3–5, and it in turn triggers Matthew 10:24–25, the outcome being (in Eve's opinion) an "intrusive" and "clumsy" Lukan insertion into a smoothly flowing Matthean sequence (Matt 7:1–5). That Luke's use of Matthew is spontaneously triggered by cues he encounters visually in Matthew's text is an explanation that was advanced by Goulder. Eve takes it up, now fitted out with associative memory theory.

Eve adverts to spontaneous memory cuing because he recognizes that Luke does not have a well-defined topical schema of his own to serve as his mnemonic for systematically searching out related Matthean materials.[200] But he also looks for ancient analogues to Luke's procedure of "occasional random access . . . [i.e., his] ability to pluck the odd piece of material from its original context and place it elsewhere" (54). Philo's source utilization in *Life of Moses* and the *Special Laws,* he thinks, fits the bill. In the *Life of Moses* Philo "ranges over the Pentateuch liberally . . . substantially reorder[ing] the materials he uses" around topics such as Moses as prophet and Moses as priest, the latter broken down topically into the construction of the sanctuary, the finishing of the sanctuary, the appointment of priests (48–50).

A closer look at both compositions shows, however, that Philo is composing following sharply defined topical schemas of his own devising that serve as his mnemonic coordinates for searching out and collating topically associated Pentateuchal materials. One observes (and Eve himself observes) that the central section of *Life of Moses* is closely organized around the three *topos* headings Moses as Ruler, Moses as Priest, Moses as Prophet, each of which Philo elaborates in a distinctly marked and intelligible progression of subordinate *topoi.* "Moses the Priest," for example, unfolds by means of the sub-*topoi* Building and Furnishing the Sanctuary, Consecration of Priests (pulling topically related materials from Leviticus), the Choosing and the Orders of the Levites, each of which supplies the mnemonic peg to collate the corresponding details and special laws drawn from the corollary passages of the Pentateuch. Among other things the Choosing of the Levites *topos* provides Philo the occasion to recount the narrative of the Golden Calf.[201]

For its part the *Special Laws* is tightly organized around the Decalogue. Each of the Commandments functions as a master *topos,* each of which Philo then unpacks in a sequence of subordinate *topoi.* In his own words: "I have followed the principal heads set out before us [the Ten Commandments] and

200. 2DH Matthew had already made the Pharisees his foil for the Sermon, so there is a motif link from the Matthew 15:1–20 Hand-Washing Controversy (Mark 7:1–23) back to Q/Luke 6:39.

201. Philo, *De Vita Mosis*, trans. F. A. Colson, LCL (Cambridge, MA: Harvard University Press, 1966).

the sequence of subjects demanded" (*Spec. Leg.* 37.223). Under the third Commandment, "Remember the Sabbath Day to keep it holy," he assembles associatively connected special laws using distinct sub-*topoi*—e.g., Sabbath/Jubilee Year release from debts; fallowing the land; the festival cycle (connection to the seven days of creation and the marking of the seasons), and so forth. Under "Thou Shalt Not Commit Adultery" he pulls together all the special laws on sex (prohibitions of incest; intermarriage; prostitution; laws pertaining to rape, and the like); under "Thou Shalt Not Kill" laws on degrees of intent and corresponding punishments, infanticide, cities of refuge, an ox goring a man, accidental deaths, negligence, and then further into laws on common bodily assaults, the *lex talionis*, compensations for bodily injuries.[202]

Clearly demarcated and intelligible *topoi* schemata provide Philo with his mnemonic coordinates to assemble specific laws from a range of Pentateuchal locations. By Eve's own admission, a clearly marked and intelligible *topos* schema is precisely what Luke lacks in his travel section, which is more like a half-sorted topical menagerie. The analogy therefore does not serve.[203] That Eve is intuitively aware of the difficulty is evident in his attempt to assimilate Philo's procedures to Luke's by describing Philo in subjective terms as composing (as Eve will conceive FH Luke doing in the travel section) by following "his own train of thought."[204] But, in fact, Philo is composing in accord with a precise schematic.

Eve on Luke's Rearrangement of Matthew in the Travel Section

Eve acknowledges that "there may be no clear overall structure to [Luke's] travel section," and elsewhere that "the rationale behind the resultant Lukan order appears less than immediately apparent."[205] Or, damning it with faint praise: "Luke's ordering of material in his travel section is not totally without rhyme or reason."[206] But as he further notes, "if there is anywhere an FH Luke would have to be conceived as working from memory it is surely in this sec-

202. Philo, *De Specialibus Legis*, trans. F. A. Colson, LCL (Cambridge, MA: Harvard University Press, 1968).

203. The present author could not forgive himself if he failed to point out that the Philo analogies accord closely with 2DH Matthew's procedure: pulling materials from his double-tradition source, which has its own internal organization, into a *topoi* sequence of his own devising.

204. Eve, *Relating the Gospels*, 52.

205. Eve, *Writing the Gospels*, 138; *Relating the Gospels*, 145.

206. Eve, "Synoptic Problem without Q?," 563.

tion."[207] The rub is that the absence of a compositional schematic in the travel section means that Luke lacks a thought-out topical system to serve as his mnemonic for retrieving and organizing Matthean materials in the building out of his own composition.

Eve exerts all his powers of ingenuity to find a way for the FH out of this quandary. Thematic eclecticism, he holds, is of the travel section's essence. Many of the materials it comprises can be construed as bearing in one way or another upon the diffuse topic of discipleship. In the nature of things they intersect thematically. It follows that "they cannot always be separated neatly out into distinct blocks and are often intertwined" (170–71). In other words, the materials of the travel section are simply not amenable to clean schematic ordering. This explains why Luke demurs at working up a schematic to engineer the incorporation of Matthean materials systematically into his own compositional design. It is at this point that Eve's associative memory-prompt expedient for Luke's Matthew utilization comes into its own. Luke, he says, nevertheless has a "train of thought" that can be followed—though admittedly it can be "elusive"—in the very ad hoc sequencing of the travel section's topical array (185, 190).

The course followed by this "train of thought" and its contingency, Eve will argue, emerges from the confluence of Luke's thematic agenda, on the one hand, and the extrinsic media and memory influences operating upon him from moment to moment in his Matthew utilization on the other. Even more importantly, recognizing the interplay of these factors will make it possible to finally meet the charge that Luke's Matthew utilization in the travel section is, to put it charitably, unsystematic (Eve himself once called it "a mental jumbling").[208] Eve will try to show that to the contrary, Luke's Matthew utilization in the travel section has a consistent forward directionality, from Matthew 8:18–22 (discipleship call chreias) to Matthew 25:14–30 (Parable of the Talents). This will confirm that in composing the travel sequence Luke sustains his consistent forward scrolling movement through Matthew.

To this end he parses out Luke's Matthean materials in the section into three sequences: (1) Luke's *direct forward use* of Matthew, (2) Luke's *forward borrowing* from Matthew, and (3) Luke's *indirect forward use* of Matthew. The "direct use" forward sequence (to begin with the first) comprises nine items from Luke 9:57–62 to Luke 19:11–27, which plot "predominantly" in Matthean order from Matthew 8:18–22 to Matthew 25:14–30 (171–72).[209] One observes

207. Eve, *Writing the Gospels*, 138.

208. Eve, "Synoptic Problem without Q?," 569.

209. There is some shuffling of order within the sequence; e.g., Luke 15:3–7 (Matt 18:12–14) and Luke 17:1–4 (Matt 18:6–7, 15–22, 21–22) invert the Matthew 18 order.

that a good chunk of the sequence—items one through five of twelve—falls into the Mission of the Seventy and its revelation postscript (9:57–62; 10:2–16, 10:21–22). More worrying for Eve though is that this "direct use" forward sequence that he isolates comprises just 13 percent of the total verses from Matthew 8:18 to Matthew 25:30. To mitigate this adverse statistic he (a) brackets the Markan parallels between Matthew 8 and Matthew 25 that are either taken over elsewhere by Luke or omitted, and (b) suspends the principled FH rejection of the DT/M distinction and brackets the M materials in Matthew 8–25 that Luke does not use, thereby reconstituting the remainder as double tradition only. This gives Eve a better statistic: of this truncated remainder Luke's direct forward-use sequence constitutes 47 percent. However, this more favorable outcome is bought at the price of introducing a Q-defined body of material ("196 double tradition Matthean verses from Mt. 8:19–25:30") (172).

Punctuating this direct forward-usage sequence is a "forward borrowing" sequence: eight items that from his advancing absolute position in his Matthew scroll Luke pulls forward from later sections of Matthew. These eight forward borrowings, which begin with Luke 10:23–24 = Matt 13:16–17 and end with Luke 14:15–24 = Matt 22:1–14, do not fall into Matthean order (Matt 13, 23, 16, 25, 24, 16, 23, 22), and five of the eight occur in Luke 12–13. Nevertheless, they correspond to Luke's "consistent" forward directionality through his Matthew source (172–73).

Eve makes his crucial move, however, with his claim that alongside Luke's *direct* forward-use sequence there exists a shadow sequence of Luke's *indirect* forward use of Matthew. In extensive segments in his travel section (also elsewhere in his gospel), Luke's direct use of Matthew in his forward progression through the scroll is not in evidence. Instead, it gives way to what to all appearances is a highly unsystematic use of M/DT passages from other locations in Matthew (e.g., the Sermon on the Mount). Extensive "gaps," that is to say, appear in Luke's direct forward utilization of Matthew, and are particularly noticeable from Matthew 12 onward. Eve observes that these gaps correspond to stretches of his Matthew source that feature either parallels to Markan passages (that Luke uses elsewhere or omits) or M sequences that Luke declines to use. But, he says, nevertheless, as Luke continues to work forward gradually through his Matthew scroll, assorted textual motifs that he encounters in these gap passages consecutively trigger his recollection and utilization of M/DT passages from other locations in Matthew. That is, the consecutive Matthean order continues to exert control over Luke's Matthew utilization *indirectly* (172–74, 182–83).

By this ingenious means Eve tries to subsume Luke's seemingly unsystematic movements around Matthew to his systematic forward progression through his Matthew source. And with the same stroke he can put to rest another solution-resistant difficulty for the FH—namely, that Luke seems to have no awareness of large amounts of very fine M materials. He is indeed aware of these materials, for they subtly control his selection of the M materials that he *does* use. One example must suffice. Eve holds that the copious materials Luke passes over in Matthew 13 (Luke's absolute position in his forward progress through his Matthew scroll at the time) cue his memory retrieval of the M materials from elsewhere in Matthew that he uses to constitute his long sequence Luke 12:1–13:29 (Mark 8:15 + Matt 10:26–33 + 10:19–20 + 6:24–25 + 6:19–21 + 10:34–36 + 5:25–26 + 7:13–14, 22–23 + 8:11–12). In Luke 12:1 ("beware the leaven of the Pharisees") the Markan parallel (8:15) is associatively prompted by the Matthean Parable of the Leaven at Matthew 13:33. Matthew 13 contains no parallel to Luke 12:2 ("nothing hidden that shall not be revealed"), but the saying may have been cued by the Matthean parallel to the Markan Parable of the Sower (Matt 13:1–8//Mark 4:1–9), which in turn cued Mark 4:22: "nothing is hidden, except to be revealed." Luke's Parable of the Rich Fool (Luke 12:16–20) is prompted by (or alternatively, composed out of) the motifs of the abundant harvest at Matthew 13:8, gathering the harvest into barns at Matthew 13:30, and the danger of riches (choking the seed) at Matthew 13:22, "perhaps coupled with the blindness of those who fail to perceive God's word at Mt. 13:34–35." Luke's retrieval of the Do Not Be Anxious instruction (Luke 12:22–32) from Matthew 6:25–34 is triggered by the motif of "burning grass of the field" in the Parable of the Tares (Matt 13:30, compare Luke 12:28). Luke's sequence on preparing for eschatological judgment is cued by the eschatological judgment scene in the Parable of the Tares (Matt 13:36–42); moreover the "weeping and gnashing of teeth" phrase (Matt 13:42b) also appears in Luke 13:28, and so may have been the prompt that triggered Luke's recollection and retrieval of Matthew 8:11–12, Luke's actual parallel. Similarly, Matthew's Parable of the Dragnet (Matt 13:47–50), "which envisages the general eschatological division of the righteous and the wicked," helps cue the Matthew 8:11 parallel (182).

In short, though Luke in composing 12:1–13:29 has been everywhere *but* Matthew 13 (excepting the Mustard Seed Parable), the materials of the chapter are the unseen hand directing Luke's utilization movements around Matthew. This is taken right from Goulder's playbook (confirmed by the density of Eve's citations to Goulder), including Goulder's extension of it to the L materials, which Eve likewise suggests are sometimes precipitated by Luke's encounter with motifs in Matthean textual matrices, perhaps in some cases even composed out of those matrices (167). Eve recycles Goulder's account, bolsters it with some associative memory theory, and reduces Luke's furious scroll spinning by elevating the level of Luke's memory control of Matthew.

One might think that the need to rely on "indirect usage" to conjure up literary agreement is injurious to the Farrer hypothesis. For his part Eve is satisfied that his case for Luke's "indirect usage" of Matthew hits the plausibility threshold, indeed, more daringly, that indirect usage is "not just plausible but probable" (194). One thing that he remains worried about, however, is the spontaneous, undeliberated nature of Luke's Matthew utilization. Source critics of Luke-depends-on-Matthew persuasions have long labored to overcome the charge that Luke's Matthew utilization is deficient in coherence, but the Goulder/Eve solution seems to concede the point, indeed, to incorporate it, to rationalize it as the workings of spontaneous memory associations. Eve tries to mitigate matters. True, Luke's abrupt reach forward from his location in Matthew 12 to Matthew 23 for the Woes is "prompted" by the invective against the Pharisees at Matthew 12:33–37, a passage Luke "has otherwise just passed over." But this is a theme that "Luke is minded to pursue in any case" (179). Or put in more general terms, "[Luke's] associations are cued *both* by what he comes across in Matthew *and* by the topical sequence he is in the course of constructing" (194, emphasis added). In other words, Luke manages to corral his associative impulses into a didactic plan of a sort.

Eve works on improving the viability of Goulder's account by reducing Luke's pell-mell scrolling around Matthew. But he pushes further and attempts to resolve Luke's use of Matthew into a consistently forward progression through his Matthew scroll. This would align FH Luke with the constraints of working with the scroll medium and the practice of other ancient writers. Hence Eve's three "Tables" that respectively itemize Luke's direct forward use of Matthew, his forward borrowing, and his indirect forward use. Conspicuous by its absence is an itemization of Luke's backward movements in Matthew. One has to create this table, which when lined up in parallel with the other three scrambles the picture of Luke's consistent forward progression through Matthew to no small extent. Eve, of course, can accommodate Luke's retrieval movements by adducing Luke's memory command of Matthew, to which he adds the claim that the seemingly random operations in question are themselves the function of Luke's indirect forward use of Matthew.

Nevertheless, Luke's movements around Matthew are rather more complex than Eve's somewhat sanitized depiction. One example will need to do. Luke encounters Matthew's parallel to the Markan controversy Plucking Grain on the Sabbath at Matthew 12:1–7 "in the course of scrolling forward from Matt 11:24" (Woes against the Galilean Cities—Matt 11:20–24//Luke 10:13–15).

Because he had earlier taken Plucking Grain on the Sabbath directly from Mark (Luke 6:1–5//Mark 2:23–26), he does not take over Matthew's addition to the Markan pericope, "Have you not read in the law . . . 'I desire mercy and not sacrifice.'" But this addition with its citation catches his eye, and it "prompt[s]" the Good Samaritan Parable, likewise concerned with the law and showing mercy (177). However, to encounter Matthew 12:1–7 (Plucking Grain on the Sabbath) Luke must be scrolling not forward from Matthew 11:24 but backward from Matthew 13:16–17 (Blessed Are the Eyes = Luke 10:23–24), and from Matthew 12:1–7 his next move is again backward, to Matthew 6:9–13 for the Lord's Prayer (Luke 11:1–5) and forward to Matthew 7:7–11 for the remainder of the Prayer instruction (Luke 11:9–13). He then moves forward past the Matthean Plucking Grain on the Sabbath to the Beelzebul controversy which commences at Matthew 12:22. Even allowing that forward borrowings and backward retrievals can be by memory, this is a rather more erratic set of utilization maneuvers than one might guess from Eve's presentation of things.[210]

In this connection one worries that, in adducing spontaneous memory association to solve one chronic problem in Luke's Matthean source utilization, Eve has created another problem. Ancient authors such as Philo relied upon cleanly defined topical schemata as the indispensable mnemonic tool to comb their sources for desired materials and to recombine them. By Eve's own admission Luke lacks clear navigational coordinates for searching out and reindexing corresponding Matthean materials; he is improvising his topical sequence off indirect associational stimuli from his present visual locations in his Matthew scroll. What then is his basis for omission of congenial materials during his passage through the Sermon on the Mount if he has in mind no definite compositional schema for the central section that he is reserving them for?

Eve: Luke's Rhetorical Emulation of Matthew

The sheer scale of Luke's reconception and rearrangement of Matthew and the prolific number of corresponding editorial motives FH defenders must impute to Luke in dissecting his individual actions means that the FH typically has needed a high estimate of Luke's independent authorial agency, one that well exceeds the creative scope normally allowed for in redaction criticism. Un-

---

210. Eve gets around this problem by having Luke "read or recall" Matthew in "blocks," which comprise several pericopes—"then [he] sometimes rearranges the Matthean material within that block." So truth be told, Luke's forward movement through Matthew is actually "block by block, rather than pericope by pericope" (*Relating the Gospels*, 171).

easy with the constant recursions to Luke's subjective intentionality, its leading figures have sought to put the appeal to Luke's authorial creativity on a firmer basis. Goulder experimented with a Luke who revises Matthew's lectionary sequence. Goodacre grounded his representation of Luke, the consummate narrative artist, in contemporary narrative criticism. Eve's forthright appraisal of the looseness and ad hoc contingency of Luke's travel section means that his Luke cannot be Goodacre's master of literary design. He finds his model for Luke's treatment of Matthew instead in the ancient rhetorical practice of *emulation*—i.e., competitive literary imitation, identifying as diagnostic instances Virgil's emulation of the *Iliad* in the *Aeneid* and *Jubilees*'s creative rewriting (versus redaction) of the Torah. The payoff for Eve—and the FH—is that literary emulation is an accommodative rubric that can encompass everything from "paraphrase" of the literary model to "more adventurous transformations." Best of all, "there were no set rules on how to imitate" (195). The utility of the analogy is that it can serve as an omnibus category that allows the FH to rationalize as "literary emulation" virtually any operation whatsoever of Luke upon his literary model, Matthew, as may be required by the hypothesis. It endows *every* utilization action of FH Luke with the property of "plausibility," so prized in FH scholarship, that assures the victory of the hypothesis (205).

Though touting literary emulation as the comprehensive model for Luke's use of Matthew, in practice Eve adduces it ad hoc, for those troublesome cases in which agreement patterns of the sort normally taken to indicate a literary relationship are weak to nonexistent. For to posit literary imitation, all that is required is "sufficient similarities between the two texts" (103). Unsurprisingly Eve uses it to legitimize his account of Luke's "indirect usage" of Matthew in the travel section, which is grounded in little more than some similar motifs. Luke's audience, he says, familiarized to Matthew and culturally attuned to literary emulation, would recognize in these "retain[ed] traces" Luke's creative emulation of the base Matthean text (197–98). Luke's Nativity likewise is a literary emulation of Matthew's Nativity, a creative transformation of Matthean motifs: Luke transforms Matthew's "in the time of Herod" to "a decree went out from Caesar Augustus," Matthew's star-guided Magi to Luke's shepherds guided by an angel, Herod's killing the infants around Bethlehem to Joseph and Mary's sacrifice of two pigeons to redeem their firstborn, Rachel weeping for her children to a sword piercing Mary's soul, and so on in this vein (98–99). With *emulatio* Eve again tacks back toward Goulder, with Luke authoring new tradition out of the textual matrices of his sources.

Anyone who spends time in the FH literature will be impressed and perhaps at first perplexed by the lengths to which its defenders go, as Eve does here, to argue Luke's dependence on Matthew in the Nativity. But Luke's Nativity has long been the litmus test for FH ingenuity. Securing Luke's dependence on Matthew here (and in his Resurrection accounts) is essential to the viability of the FH. Luke's and Matthew's patterns of agreement of the sort normally taken to be indicative of a literary relationship begin and end with Mark. But for the FH, *everything* in Luke must be derived from Matthew or Mark (with possible exceptions for L^S passages). Allow an exception, and the FH is finished. Once the slightest concession is made that Luke is not dependent upon Matthew in his Nativity and Resurrection accounts, the further inference that he did not know Matthew in these two sections is difficult to keep at bay.[211]

Eve's contribution to these FH efforts is to associate the sorts of transformations that must be imputed to Luke with ancient practices of literary emulation. *Emulatio* performs the service of converting Lukan divergences from Matthew, be they ever so great, into agreements and literary dependence. One pauses to admire, in all sincerity, the resourcefulness of FH scholarship. On the one hand, close verbal agreements are probative evidence for Luke's dependence on Matthew ("too good to be Q"); on the other hand, levels of verbal agreement that approach absolute zero are probative evidence of Luke's dependence on Matthew ("emulation"). With defenses like this, the FH is untouchable.

If Luke is taking Matthew as his model for literary emulation, the question of why he opts for Mark over Matthew for the narrative tradition, with all the source-utilization complications of that choice, becomes even more pressing. In Eve's scenario Luke's emulation of Matthew extends even to indirect usage of Matthew, and of Matthean triple-tradition parallels in particular. He holds that Luke's combined direct and indirect usage of Matthew "suggests a desire to reflect as much of Matthew as possible" (197). It is hard to see where a preference for Mark can fit into this picture. If Luke is emulating Matthew even in the latter's triple tradition, why does he not just select Matthew as his basis for emulation? One would think that a Luke capable of spinning his Nativity out of a few stray Matthean and Old Testament threads would be able to use Matthew's triple tradition, making what use he wanted of it, saving himself the trouble of reference to a Markan scroll and the source-discrimination operations that he would need to perform in Matthew. Eve's analysis of Luke's Matthew emulation would tend toward rendering Mark superfluous. Other than one or two passing comments—e.g., Luke "choosing the best of each" to

211. Thus Eve will suggest "that at Mt. 28.9 the women who meet Jesus near the tomb hold his feet, while at Lk. 24.39 the risen Jesus shows his hands and feet to his disciples and invites them to handle him" (*Relating the Gospels*, 118).

emulate (195)—Eve never engages this question, the premise of the whole FH enterprise. Put differently, literary emulation as the model for Luke's utilization of Matthew cannot be squared with the FH itself.

Eve's Memory Solution to the "Unpicking" Problem

Knowledge of ancient media realities leads Eve to abandon the visual-utilization model and embrace a memory-based model. This shift in approach itself is highly creditable, but it is not clear that Eve adequately explores its implications for the "unpicking" problem. In standard FH responses to the "unpicking" objection it is argued that Luke's so-called unpicking involves some kind of manageable visual-discrimination operation on his part. Eve recognizes that "ancient manuscripts were not particularly well suited for ready reference." But where the source has been internalized, memory can assist in identifying the passage visually and picking it out. In fact, "someone who knew the text well enough to search it in that way would hardly need to look up a passage in the first place."[212] Luke would have had this kind of memory competence in Matthew as well as Mark, in line with ancient practices of internalizing formative cultural texts. This does not exclude that he has his source scrolls at hand and could, as the occasion required, consult them.[213]

What are the implications of Luke's separating materials out, nonvisually, from their Markan contextualizations? Eve points out that "memorable" sayings are always easily separable from closely environing contexts. Luke's clean separation of "Blind Guides" from the heart of Matthew's Hand-Washing Controversy (Matt 15:1–20) would present no difficulty; similarly Luke 6:40, Disciple and Teacher, from Matthew 10:24–25. Matters get more complicated when it comes to operations such as Luke's forward borrowing of selected eschatological materials from Matthew 24 to compose a distinct discourse in 17:20–37. Here we are no longer dealing with impromptu memory associations but systematic culling and source-strand disarticulation by memory. To take the Luke 17//Matt 24 instance: the Markan elements and the M/DT elements combined in Matthew 24 are closely akin thematically. Eve's suggestion that a thematic distinction between Coming Son of Man materials and Fall of Jerusalem materials is helping to guide Luke's selection and separation of materials from Matthew 24 does not hold (192). The motifs interpenetrate, even in Luke 17, and Luke shows no interest in Matt 24:29–31//Mark 13:24–27, which

212. Eve, *Writing the Gospels*, 3–5.
213. Eve, *Writing the Gospels*, xiii, 41–42.

prominently feature "the sign of the Son of Man" appearing in the sky. As Eve notes, what Luke is in fact up to is abstracting out the M/DT elements from the baseline Mark 13 apocalyptic discourse, which he wants to bring in its unexpanded version when he arrives at its forward Mark 13 location in his Markan source. This means that not only must he borrow forward from Matthew 24 by memory; he must simultaneously cross-reference Mark 13 in memory as he makes his distinctions and selections, at the same time dealing with the complication that the Matthew 24 combination of these elements is likewise memory familiarized. Pulling off this separation of M/DT elements from Markan elements by source memory would be no small cognitive feat.[214]

The obstacles to visual discrimination of source strands in a manuscript were daunting enough. The difficulties compound if the operation is to be carried out by memory. Eve cites Virgil's procedure in the *Aeneid* 2.469–558, where the poet plucks images and phrases from two different locations in the *Iliad*, from the poet Nicander, and from his own *Georgics* to compose the sequence (66). But this is not "unpicking" but conflation: Virgil is not separating out *Iliad* strands, Nicander strands, and *Georgics* strands from the *Aeneid* 2.469–558. Luke's elimination of most Markan elements from his Beelzebul controversy is particularly diagnostic of the problems that memory utilization raises for FH Luke's unpicking actions. His surgical extraction of Matthew 12:31b and 12:32a (Blasphemy of Holy Spirit/Word against the Son of Man), the apodosis and protasis, respectively, of two Mark/M composite sayings, would be an even more astonishing feat if he managed the operation by memory.

In other problem contexts Eve imagines Luke's memory not as the precision instrument that homes in unerringly on target passages and unpicks source elements but as a highly volatile faculty of uneven reliability impinging on Luke's source utilization. The continuity errors in some of Matthew's and Luke's triple-tradition parallels that Goodacre put down to "editorial fatigue" should instead be understood, Eve says, "as a form of memory error" that is bound to occur when a writer is working from memory instead of visually from a source text (21). In the preamble (Luke 5:17) to the Healing of the Paralytic Luke "may simply have forgotten to add the Markan detail about being inside a house,"

214. Examples of similar cases include Matt 17:20b//Luke 17:6; Matt 18:7//Luke 17:1; Matt 19:28//Luke 22:28–30. In fetching Matt 25:15–29 (Parable of the Talents) Luke unerringly picks out and avoids Matthew's Markan peg Matt 25:14//Mark 13:34 (ὥσπερ γὰρ ἄνθρωπος ἀποδημῶν κ.τ.λ.), thinly squeezed between two M/DT passages, which amounts to four words in Mark, seven words in Matthew, leaving ἄνθρωπος the sole remaining three-way term.

his "cognitive resources [being] tied up in composing a new introduction."[215] In support of his thesis of Luke's "forward borrowing" in Matthew by memory Eve points out the low-agreement profile of a number of the parallels in question. The assumption is that memory is prone to error if unsupported by visual consultation with the source (172–79). Eve endorses the standard FH view that minor agreements are the consequence of unpredictable memory interference from Matthew, which leads to Luke "unconsciously conflating his text with that of Matthew's" (25).[216] As a particularly vivid example of Luke's inadvertent mental conflation of Mark and Matthew he calls attention to the jumble of cross-agreements in the Lukan Salt saying: Καλὸν οὖν το ἅλας· ἐὰν δὲ καὶ τὸ ἅλας μωρανθῇ, ἐν τίνι ἀρτυθήσεται; οὔτε εἰς γῆν οὔτε εἰς κοπρίαν εὔθετόν ἐστιν, ἔξω βάλλουσιν αὐτό (Luke 14:34–35//Matt 5:13//Mark 9:49) (85).[217] One wonders how a faculty this volatile can be up to the job of separating out source elements from each other in Matthew.

The model adduced for the operation of memory in a given instance depends on the FH problem-complex being addressed. When it happens to be a matter of the minor agreements, Luke's source memory is a volatile and cross-contaminating faculty, in need of frequent refreshing from the source scroll. When it is a matter of unpicking, it is an unerring precision instrument. On the one hand we have a Luke who cannot keep Matthew and Mark straight in his head, and on the other a Luke who can easily distinguish and separate Markan and M elements from each other and zero in on unused M/DT passages from earlier segments of his Matthew source. The chronic FH inability to attribute consistent procedures to Luke rears up again.

In line with memory being an active performative competence Eve holds that there is pronounced oral-traditional dynamic in Luke's source utilization. Luke, he says, is not so much redacting as he is reperforming, "reworking," his source texts. Indeed, he continues, Luke's actual source text, the operational referent of his composing activity, is constituted as much if not more by his sedimented memory of previous oral enactments as it is by the visible artifact before him.[218] Again, it is very difficult to see how this compelling image of Luke engaged in an active reactualization of his written, source-based tradition, in an operation grounded in memory and infused by oral modes, involv-

215. Eve, *Writing the Gospels*, 101.

216. Also *Writing the Gospels*, 142.

217. Three-way agreements = **bold**; Matt/Luke agreements = underline; Mark/Luke agreements = *italics*.

218. Eve, "Devil in the Detail," 18–19.

ing mainly ancillary contact with the written artifact, is to be squared with a Luke engrossed by meticulously distinguishing Markan and M/DT source strands from each other in his Matthean scroll. On the one hand we have Luke the tradent, on the other Luke the source critic. Oral dynamics in tradition appropriation inject a potent element of indeterminacy into source utilization that is difficult to square with the procedures the FH attributes to Luke.

Eve and Phantom Q

Can Eve's recourse to memory-based utilization and Luke's rhetorical emulation of Matthew prevent a phantom Q taking shape in the background of his utilization account? His robust model for Luke's memory-based utilization of Matthew allows him to make do with just occasional appeal to the wax tablet or notebook expedient (150–60). He cannot be charged with creating an intermediary double-tradition source. Eve however never quite relinquishes the intermediate-drafts expedient, which spreads out Luke's large-scale rearrangements of Matthew over intermediate compositional steps, which include "some degree of note-taking" (14).[219] We also saw that in mitigation of Luke's "direct forward movement" through Matthew in the travel section comprising only 13 percent of the available Matthean verses, Eve reconstitutes from the latter a double-tradition subset of material, of which the "direct forward movement" sequence comprises 44 percent (172). This is a palpable phantom Q.

Eve follows Goodacre in countenancing Luke's access to parallel sources for double-tradition passages in which source relations remain ambiguous. He recognizes that the evangelists wrote within a penumbra of living oral tradition.[220] Nevertheless he imposes strict controls on the ingress of disruptive external traditions into the FH schema. Cognizant of the risks to the FH of "too many appeals . . . to Luke's use of parallel oral traditions," he is much more intentional than Goodacre about trying to derive difficult cases redactionally from the Matthean parallel, claiming that any such account need only be "plausible" to succeed.[221]

When it comes to Matthew, this issue is further complicated by the question of the sources for Matthew's M/DT materials. Eve gestures at the possibility of Matthew drawing his additions to Mark directly from oral tradition or nondescript written sources, but in practice he construes them as Matthean compositions from Markan textual cues or worked up from motifs made pres-

219. Also *Writing the Gospels*, 144–45; "Synoptic Problem without Q?," 568.
220. Eve, "Devil in the Detail," 19.
221. Eve, "Synoptic Problem without Q?," 562.

ent to Matthew's mind by an external tradition. He is wary of opening the door too widely to pre-Matthean tradition and so derives as much M/DT as possible from Matthew's authorial activity. The same concern feeds his efforts to derive Luke's variants as much as possible from his redactions of the Matthean parallels. He is alert to how essential it is to the FH to confine Synoptic difference as much as possible to writing operations along the closed textual circuits of Matthew, Mark, and Luke. His account of the origins of the M/DT materials is effectively Goulder's with a gesture to Goodacre. Numerous of the additions to Mark are of Matthew's composition, his interpretative extensions, or "reworkings," of Markan passages, though Matthew does not cavil at taking inspiration from materials and motifs circulating in the tradition, or even more vaguely from "community memory."[222] Earlier tradition is a source of Matthew's M/DT materials, but these traditions have been filtered and heavily reprocessed through Matthean composition and invention.

Thereby Eve seeks to protect the FH zone of Synoptic literary activity from the dangerous intrusion of non-Markan tradition. Matthew's Beelzebul controversy is a case in point: there is "very little . . . that is not either derived directly from Mark or that could not plausibly be the product of Matthaean reworking, perhaps in light of other traditions circulating in his community."[223] Eve is even willing to grant that among the conglomerate of pre-Matthean, pre-Lukan tradition that is the ultimate source of "a good deal" of the M/DT and L^S material there were written sources. But he denies peremptorily that this opens the door to a Q-like source of the sort posited in the 2DH. His curious certitude about this must have its grounds in FH logics. The foundational premise of the 2DH and its hypothesized source Q is the implausibility of Luke's knowledge of Matthew. The FH account (as Eve goes to pains to show by his analyses) manages to hit the plausibility threshold. Accordingly the 2DH is otiose, vaporized by this ineluctable logic (205–9).

Phantom Q obtrudes into his analysis elsewhere. In his attempt to shoehorn the Gospel of Mark into an account that is all about Luke's rhetorical emulation of the Gospel of Matthew, Eve says that Luke selects what comprises the best of each: "roughly speaking Mark's narrative and Matthew's teaching material." That is to say, he acknowledges the sayings profile of the double tradition (195). But his theory that the ultimate source of the M/DT materials is a diffuse pre-Matthean aggregate of tradition in nondescript sources would not predict this. To get around this problem Eve would have to hold—like Goodacre did

---

222. Eve, "Devil in the Detail," 25.
223. Eve, "Devil in the Detail," 42.

in response to the same problem—that Matthew intentionally selects sayings out of the tradition, which would amount to an ersatz sayings source.

Eve's reliance upon ad hoc memory cuing and expedients such as "indirect forward use" to explain Luke's recollection and retrieval of materials scattered about his Matthew source effectively means that Luke is not really reliant upon Matthew as a *work* to access these materials. He accesses materials without regard to their Matthean contextualization and sequencing. It follows that there is no compelling reason to hold that Matthew is his source for these materials: he could just as easily be combing them direct from "communal memory," the oral tradition, or some source or conglomerate of sources. That his source is Matthew becomes just a gratuitous postulate of Eve's governing hypothesis.

Eve and the FH's Enclosed Textual Circuit

Though more alert to ancient media realities than his Farrer contemporaries Eve has difficulty breaking out of the closed-circuit textualist model. He accords recognition to memory in source utilization, but he does not operationalize memory either as a performative competence or as an instrument for systematic utilization of a source. In his view low-agreement parallels attest to memory's proneness to error when unsupported by visual contact with the source. Since he mentions this as evidence of Luke's "forward borrowing" of certain passages, he finds himself in a bind in the case of forward-borrowed passages that are high agreement (e.g., Luke 12:39–46//Matt 24:42–51; Luke 13:34–5//Matt 23:37–39). This forces him to claim that Luke has a more expert memory grasp of some Matthean passages than of others (172). Eve's recourse to memory utilization is not so much different from Goulder's. It is an ad hoc expedient to get around certain utilization difficulties raised by the postulate of Luke's literary dependence upon Matthew.

The FH is congenitally joined to the closed-circuit textualist model. This is because the viability of the hypothesis depends upon deriving the non-Markan elements in Luke textually from Matthew (exceptions made, sometimes grudgingly, for L^S materials). This explains why Eve ends up routing the non-Markan materials into the closed FH system of Synoptic sources through the filter of Matthean composition. More damningly, it also explains why one so rarely as almost never observes FH scholars leveraging their source history for a wider inquiry into the questions of the origins and history of the tradition and into Christian origins, problems that so preoccupied nineteenth- and early twentieth-century source critics. One might speculate that this is due to form criticism's severing of source criticism from these questions. But this cannot be correct. Contemporary 2DH scholarship and also contemporary revivals of the oral hypothesis are deeply invested in these questions. The reality is that the horizons of the Farrer hypothesis simply do not open out to these larger questions. Its preoccupation is to derive Luke from Matthew (and Mark) and, in this connection, to maintain at all costs the closure of this tight intra-Synoptic textual circuit. Any breach in this *cordon sanitaire* would constitute a grave danger to the hypothesis. Watson is our only exception. His L/M hypothesis opened out to rich reflections on the origins of the tradition and on the subsequent history of gospel writing, but this is because his sayings collections postulate threw open the closed FH textual circuit. The muteness of the Farrer hypothesis before these great questions is not a point in its favor.[224]

FH Luke: Source Critic or Tradent?

We return to the issue touched on above: the tension in all FH scholarship between Luke the *source critic* and Luke the *tradent*. In Eve this is a tension between a Luke immersed in his written tradition, reperforming it in oral-traditional modes, and a Luke fastidiously separating out Markan and M/DT textual strands in his Matthew source. It is a tension between Luke's memory precision in locating, discriminating, and separating source elements in his Matthew scroll on the one hand, and the cognitive volatility and associational unpredictability of his memory of his source on the other.

Ample attestation of the latter comes from study of so-called harmonization patterns in scribal transmission of the gospel manuscript tradition. When copying, scribes carried shorter or longer sequences of a source text temporarily in working memory. This created the conditions for memory interference with the text from the scribe's wider memory field. A more memory-habituated gospel formed what Pardee terms the scribe's "cognitive exemplar" that might interfere in his reproduction of the gospel at hand, leading to alignments ("substitutions, additions, omissions, transpositions") of the text of the physical exemplar to the text of the cognitive exemplar.[225] The scribe of P[45], for example, "was regularly influenced by parallel material."[226] Similarly in the Ptolemaic papyri of Homer: passages of different Homeric poems that are quite similar in wording and phrasing exert a strong attraction upon each other.[227] The effect of this reflexive cognitive process was a blurring of bound-

---

224. "A new revolutionary theory functions exactly like a new and powerful sense organ" (Karl Popper, "Evolutionary Epistemology," in Miller, *Popper Selections*, 78–86 [80]).

225. Pardee, *Scribal Harmonization*, 430.

226. Pardee, *Scribal Harmonization*, 189.

227. Jonathan Ready, *Orality, Textuality, and the Homeric Epics: An Interdisciplinary Study of Oral Texts, Dictated Texts, and Wild Texts* (Oxford: Oxford University Press, 2019), 220.

aries of sources and of versional variants—and this in an early Christian scribal enterprise in which the concern for accurate reproduction of the *Vorlage* was to the fore and the impetus to scribal performance much attenuated.

In the second- and third-century gospel manuscript tradition cognitive alignment occurred toward all three Synoptic Gospels, though the Gospel of Matthew can be observed to be the cognitive exemplar that is acting upon scribal copying of Luke or Mark with the greatest frequency.[228] Pardee notes that the interference effect of Matthew is "even stronger" in cases in which scribes are copying Mark, "given that the two texts are already so close in most passages."[229] Similarly, in P[45] the scribe's rendering of Luke's Beelzebul Accusation has been aligned to Matthean and Markan readings at a number of points.[230] This raises serious questions about the FH account of overlap passages, such as the Beelzebul controversy, where Luke follows Matthew 12 with remarkably little interference from the Mark 3 parallel or even from the Markan elements in the Matthean version. Different from the scribes of the gospel manuscript tradition, Luke is not particularly concerned for the close reproduction of his Matthean text. He is more the active tradent than the copyist, more attuned to the dynamic potentials of the tradition than to distinguishing its source variants.[231]

Even for copying scribes the "source" existed as a cognitive, oral, and aural entity as well as a visual manuscript artifact. Let there be no mistake: the written manuscript tradition was the normative center that held cognitive, oral, and aural source dynamics in its gravity. Committal of a formative tradition to writing constituted an important cultural inflection point, and the emergent written artifacts carried a heightened normativity. That said, the plural media dimensions in which the source was activated complicates the picture of a Luke who needs to cleanly disaggregate the Markan and M/DT elements in his Matthew source. This rests upon a visual paradigm of source perception and conceives the source material as a static, scholarly objectified entity.

A further confounding factor is that scribes in reproducing a work also tapped, intentionally or otherwise, into a wider performance tradition. Pardee comments that the early Christian scribe "was occasionally more influenced by the magnetism of what he remembered hearing or receiving regarding the

---

228. Pardee, *Scribal Harmonization*, 109.

229. Pardee, *Scribal Harmonization*, 173.

230. Pardee, *Scribal Harmonization*, 165.

231. See Raymond F. Person Jr., "Harmonization in the Pentateuch and Synoptic Gospels: Repetition and Category-Triggering within Scribal Memory," in *Repetition, Communication, and Meaning in the Ancient World*, ed. Deborah Beck, OLAW 13 (Leiden: Brill, 2021), 318–57 (352–53).

teachings of Jesus than by his exemplar."[232] The typical scribe of the "wild papyri" of the Homeric tradition in the Ptolemaic period worked from what Jonathan Ready describes as "multiple sources of inspiration . . . from what he had memorized; from what he internalized as he copied; and from what he absorbed as he listened to rhapsodes perform."[233] Of the Qumran scribes Molly Zahn says that "a scribe making a new copy of a text would know that text as a living tradition, and thus the new copy would reflect elements of the tradition as performed and discussed, recalled from the scribe's memory."[234] Similarly Shem Miller: "A written text, a traditional text, and a performed text all interfaced with one another in the mind of the scribe during the copying process."[235] Scribes were themselves active performers of the tradition, its cocreators in its transmission. The border between reproduction of the written tradition and its reperformance was a dynamic and shifting one. The border was especially indistinct where the written tradition still coexisted with a living oral tradition.[236]

This model exactly captures the nature of Luke's engagement with his tradition (and Matthew with his). Moreover, it illuminates the observable features of the Synoptic tradition—the curious patterns of variation and agreement that have posed for the Synoptic problem its principal explanatory challenge. The source text in front of the scribe is an instantiation, a normative baseline, of a more widely conceived tradition. The scribe can adhere to the source text or diverge from it as befits his fresh actualization of the written tradition. Source utilization is a constant negotiation between the text of the source and the writer's reactualization of the written tradition.

This reactualization is shaped by what Jonathan Ready, in reference to the Homeric papyri, aptly terms the scribe's "notional intertext." The notional intertext comprises the written artifact, the history of the tradition's oral enactment, the wider cultural memory field, local situational factors, and audience realities. Where the source text overlaps with this notional intertext the scribe will adhere to it more or less closely, and vary from it, again more or less, where

232. Pardee, *Scribal Harmonization*, 142–43.

233. Ready, *Orality, Textuality, and the Homeric Epics*, 222; Person, "Harmonization," 2–3, 28–29. Shem Miller, *Dead Sea Media: Orality, Textuality, and Memory in the Scrolls from the Judean Desert*, STDJ 129 (Leiden: Brill, 2019), writes that the scribes of the Dead Sea Scrolls "were both (1) copyists who reproduced the (written) text of compositions and (2) performers who incorporated the oral register of language into their written copies" (118).

234. Molly M. Zahn, *Genres of Rewriting in Second Temple Judaism: Scribal Composition and Transmission* (Cambridge: Cambridge University Press, 2020), 32–33.

235. Miller, *Dead Sea Media*, 265.

236. Ready, *Orality, Textuality, and the Homeric Epics*, 228. See also Geoffrey Kahn and Hindy Najman, "Performance in Ancient and Medieval Judaism," *DSD* 29 (2022): 259–91.

a gap between the source text and the notional intertext opens up to various degrees.[237] The scribe's fidelity is to the *tradition*, which includes but exceeds what is inked upon the papyrus or parchment surface of the source. This dynamic can play out "within the span of one copying event."[238] Accordingly, "although . . . it is easiest to see the performer at work when he deviates from the model, verbatim repetition does not disqualify one as a performer."[239] This clarifies the Synoptic patterns, which explore every point on a range from high agreement to low agreement, and often within a single pericope. It explains the patterns of Matthew's and Luke's major agreements with Mark: there will be numerous occasions that they coincide at points of overlap of their common Markan text with their respective "notional intertexts."

Understanding these dynamics also overcomes the false alternative of *either* visual utilization *or* memory utilization—the latter usually misunderstood, furthermore, as a more or less defective "memorization" of the static text of the exemplar. The reality is, as Jonathan Vroom puts it, a memory-manuscript interaction "that was probably in flux at any given time with any given scribe."[240] Both mediums are involved in source-utilization operations. Scroll and memory—understood as a dynamic faculty—play off one another productively.

The sum of all the foregoing is that the evangelists in their function as tradents were not sensitized to clean distinctions between the various written instantiations of their tradition, or to put the matter more simply, to clean distinctions among their parallel written sources. Presented with Matthew and Mark, it is unlikely that FH Luke would have understood them as anything other than variant instantiations of a single normative tradition, not as sources with clean textual boundaries to be discriminated and disaggregated source critically.[241]

An analogy is the various recensions of the Qumran Community Rule. Shem Miller points out that these resist organization into a recensional history (similarly the manuscript attestations to the Self-Glorification Hymn). Instead they appear to be variant witnesses to an underlying set of core traditions.[242] David

237. Ready, *Orality, Textuality, and the Homeric Epics*, 278–79.

238. Ready, *Orality, Textuality, and the Homeric Epics*, 228; also David Andrew Teeter, *Scribal Laws: Exegetical Variation in the Textual Transmission of Biblical Law in the Late Second Temple Period*, FAT 92 (Tübingen: Mohr Siebeck, 2014), 269: "[Scribal] tradents took their orientation in the *meaning* of the gapped, laconic, and polyvalent text before them" (emphasis original).

239. Ready, *Orality, Textuality, and the Homeric Epics*, 213.

240. Jonathan Vroom, "The Role of Memory in *Vorlage*-Based Transmission: Evidence from Erasures and Corrections," *Textus* 27 (2018): 258–73 (273).

241. This principle is nicely articulated by Person, "Harmonization," 352–53.

242. Miller, *Dead Sea Media*, 245 (the Hodayot), 259–60 (Community Rule).

Teeter says that, when it comes to the phenomenon of textual plurality more generally at Qumran, it is likely that the scribes "neither thought about this plurality in text-critical terms, nor . . . necessarily recognized multiple 'text-types' or 'recensions' as such."[243] In regard to the gospel manuscript tradition Pardee notes that the procedure of scribes "check[ing] their exemplar of one Gospel against a manuscript or several manuscripts of another Gospel" cannot be attested prior to the fifth century. "This type of procedure," he continues, "was restricted to the creation of Gospel Harmonies."[244] The performing scribes of the "wild" Homeric papyri would not have viewed their own and parallel papyri as anything other than instantiations of the still half-oralized Homeric tradition, in Graeme Bird's words, as "reflect[ing] a text not yet normalized, and closer to the fluctuating state of the rhapsodic epic."[245] This immersive relationship to the written tradition is entirely alien to its scholarly objectification that one encounters in the scholars of the Alexandrian Library, whose cultural project was to establish the authorized text of the Homeric epics. Here we find qualitative ranking of versions, sorting of sources, collation of variant manuscripts.[246] Textual normalization enterprises like this lie considerably downstream from the period when a culturally formative tradition is cultivated in more immanent modes.

But to come to the point: the Farrer hypothesis combines in FH Luke two incommensurable models, two incommensurable approaches. It is hard to see that this is a conflict that can be resolved (though if we have learned anything in the course of this long chapter, it is to not underestimate the resourcefulness of Farrer scholarship). Our long and detailed treatment of the Farrer hypothesis has been essential to the project of this book, which is to recoup for the Synoptic problem its central role in inquiry into the origins and history of the tradition and, thereby, into Christian origins. The FH is a sterile hypothesis; it does not open out to these larger questions. Measured against ancient media realities, it also turns out not to be a viable hypothesis.

243. Teeter, *Scribal Laws*, 19–20.
244. Pardee, *Scribal Harmonization*, 431.
245. Graeme D. Bird, *Multitextuality in the Homeric Iliad: The Witness of the Ptolemaic Papyri*, Hellenic Studies 43 (Cambridge, MA: Harvard University Press, 2010), 58.
246. Ready, *Orality, Textuality, and the Homeric Epics*, 245; Bird, *Multitextuality*, 30–31.

CHAPTER 6

The Primitive Community Reborn:
The "Galilean Q People"

TWO-DOCUMENT SCHOLARSHIP has been affected by the same defective media models that we have assessed in preceding chapters. Their application, however, has not posed any existential threat to the 2DH itself. When measured against ancient media realities the 2DH comes out quite well.[1] There will always be 2DH debates that an informed media framework can help settle, a case in point being the dispute not long ago over whether Q was oral, written, or some admixture of both, which itself just recycles a debate that goes back to the Oxford Seminar and indeed back to Herder. But the Q postulate itself is not dependent on the resolution of that debate, any more than Markan priority rides on whether the gospel is a sophisticated narrative production or—as recently argued—a provisional draft, a *hypomnema*, polished up by Matthew and Luke.[2]

For our purposes there is therefore little to be gained by an inquiry into the media frameworks that have been operative within twentieth-century 2DH scholarship. Instead, we will look at the reappearance of a fixture of nineteenth-century source criticism: the "primitive Palestinian congregation," the *Urgemeinde*, reborn as the Galilean Q community. Our critique will lead us back—not to Galilee—but to the formation of the sayings tradition and

---

1. For inquiry into 2DH source utilization in the framework of ancient media practices, see Alan Kirk, *Q in Matthew: Tradition, Memory, and Early Scribal Transmission of the Jesus Tradition*, LNTS 564 (London: Bloomsbury/T&T Clark, 2016); Derrenbacker, *Ancient Compositional Practices*, 212–58.

2. On Mark as a provisional *hypomnema*, see Matthew D. C. Larsen, *Gospels before the Book* (New York: Oxford University Press, 2018); as a sophisticated narrative, Sandra Hübenthal, *Das Markusevangelium als kollektives Gedächtnis*, FRLANT 253 (Göttingen: Vandenhoeck & Ruprecht, 2014); English translation *Reading Mark's Gospel as a Text from Collective Memory* (Grand Rapids: Eerdmans, 2020).

narrative tradition in Jesus commemoration within the primitive Jerusalem community. We will see that, respectively, the narrative tradition and sayings tradition are artifacts of the commemoration of Jesus along the narrative and normative (i.e., ethical) vectors that eventually converge in Matthew's and Luke's source consolidation projects. As the nineteenth-century source critics grasped, it is by means of Synoptic-problem inquiry that we are able to anatomize the memory-tradition nexus and find our way back to the very beginnings of the gospel enterprise.

THE PRIMITIVE COMMUNITY OF THE SOURCE CRITICS: A REVIEW

The "Galilean Q community" is the contemporary incarnation of the romanticized primitive community (*Urgemeinde*) of nineteenth-century source criticism. For Herder the primitive Palestinian community (*älteste Christusgemeinde*) was the point of origination for his oral Urgospel. Inquiry into these traditions of the primitive community, Herder said, reveals to us the pure, universalizing religion of Jesus: simple childlike trust in the loving fatherhood and provident care of God, over against Pharisaic legalism and empty cultic ritualism. This is the religiosity of the humble village folk of Galilee, "far from Judea and haughty Jerusalem."[3] The counterposing of Galilean simplicity and folk universalism to particularistic Judean legalism and ritualism appears here, right at the outset of critical enquiry into the Synoptic problem.

With occasional gestures to romanticized Galilean origins many nineteenth-century critics focused on the Jerusalem community, like Herder taking it as the place of privileged memory access to the authentic Jesus and where the simple religion of Jesus took expression in oral tradition and in primitive sources. Gieseler's oral Urgospel, formulated in the primitive community, was constituted of living utterances of the apostolic eyewitnesses: humble, unschooled Galilean fishermen, simple "Orientals" for whom the "dead letters" of the scribes and their productions were alien.[4] Schleiermacher's multiple-collection Synoptic sources of 1817, by 1832 reduced to a proto-Markan collection and the Logia source, were "collections of individual apostolic memories."[5] For D. F. Strauss the principal generative force in the formation of the Synoptic oral saga was myth, myth being the default cognitive mode of Jesus's Galilean following, of the "simple and energetic minds of Galilee, less

3. See Herder, "Vom Erlöser," 641–42.
4. Gieseler, *Versuch*, 66.
5. Schleiermacher, "Zeugnisse," 254.

fettered by priestcraft and Pharisaism."⁶ The luminous exception is the sayings tradition, which unlike the narrative tradition has not been spun out by myth. The sayings are the most stable, authentic, and most primitive elements of the tradition, the germs of its subsequent narrative developments.

In C. H. Weisse's view the Logia source is not "tradition" but the unmediated outflow of apostolic memory. It captures Jesus's very utterances. The narrative tradition on the other hand is prone to deformation by myth. It is the words of Jesus in the Logia that capture the essence of his ministry unsullied and serve as the criterion for evaluating the Markan narrative materials.⁷ F. C. Baur's earliest source was an Urmatthew: an instructional text consisting mainly of sayings that originated in the primitive Jewish-Christian community. Its materials, issuing from the mouth of Jesus, are the pristinely authentic elements of the Synoptic tradition. The source projected a spiritualized Judaism, purified of legalism and religious dogmatism. It incubated a universalizing potentiality that transcended narrow Jewish particularism, and thereby an innate developmental tendency toward Gentile Christianity.⁸ The *Tendenz*-critic Köstlin likewise identified this primitive Matthean Urgospel as in fact a logia collection, written by an apostolic eyewitness, and thus of pristine authenticity. Jewish-Christian in complexion with universalizing accents, it was a work of the ur-primitive *Galilean* community (*die älteste galilaischen Christengemeinde*). It contained a Galilean stream of primitive tradition grounded in the living memory of Jesus's activity in the region. In its anti-Pharisaic elements it reflected regional Galilean aversion to the elite scribal Judaism of Jerusalem.⁹

For Weizsäcker likewise the proto-Matthean didactic source is an artifact of apostolic memory that circulated within the Palestinian community.¹⁰ Similarly for Holtzmann's Logia source, which is much superior in its authenticity to Urmarkus (Source A). Origins in the Palestinian geographical sphere, the privileged zone of memory, elevates the Logia over Urmarkus.¹¹ For its part the narrative tradition gathered into Urmarkus, generated by the dogmatic conviction that the Messiah died "for us," emerged belatedly. The Logia source therefore is "the true treasure of the primitive community"; it forms "the deepest grounds

6. Strauss, *Life of Jesus*, 270.
7. Weisse, *Geschichte*, 1:46–47, 69–70; 2:3; *Evangelienfrage*, 132–34.
8. Baur, *Kritische Untersuchungen*, 578–87, 602–20.
9. Köstlin, *Ursprung*, 32–34, 46–57, 112–13, 394–400.
10. Weizsäcker, *Untersuchungen*, 118–27.
11. Holtzmann, *Evangelien*, 379, 418, 443–51, 503–4.

of its religious consciousness."[12] Holtzmann asserts the priority of the sayings tradition over the narrative tradition, logia Christology over narrative Christology. The Logia source expresses the authentic teaching of Jesus: that the relation to God is purely an ethical one, not mediated through temple and cult.

For Wernle Q—more precisely, its earliest layer (*Grundstock*)—is the authentic memory source beyond compare, directly mediating Jesus and his preaching with just a light tincturing by the simple messianic Christology of the primitive community. It preserves "the essence of the gospel in its unadulterated clarity and its freedom."[13] The Gospel of Mark on the other hand is infested with dogma. The burden of mediating Jesus's simple Galilean piety and the outlook of the primitive Palestinian community falls on the earliest layer of Q, in which one can hear Jesus speaking of simple trust in God, of yearning after purity of heart, mercy, and humility.[14] For Johannes Weiss likewise the most primitive layer of the sayings tradition conserves the simple theological orientation of the *Urgemeinde*. Lacking any independent cultic life, this community is oriented wholly toward eschatological moral transformation in anticipation of the impending kingdom of God, to this end cultivating Jesus's sayings. It attests to a Jesus opposed to rigid Jewish legalism and purity codes, teaching a joyful piety founded in simple trust in God as heavenly father, on God's providential goodness manifest everywhere in the natural world.[15] In Jülicher's view the most high-yield vein for authentic materials will be the sayings tradition.[16] Indeed, starting from its "primitive core" (*älteste Kern*) of sayings Q gradually grows and evolves toward the form of a narrative gospel, such that it amounts to a *Halbevangelium*, a gospel *manqué*.[17] The sayings tradition enjoys an evolutionary, tradition-history priority over the narrative gospel form.

Harnack, we recollect, intensified the standard privileging of the sayings tradition over the narrative tradition into a sharp christological antithesis between the narrative gospel Mark, with its materials aligned forward to the Passion and Resurrection narrative, and the sayings source Q, a memory-authentic presentation of Jesus's teachings, wholly untouched by febrile apocalypticism and Passion theology. The antithesis has a geographical correlate: between Q, with its horizons circumscribed by Galilee, and Mark, whose Passion narrative

12. Holtzmann, *Hand-Commentar*, 22.
13. Wernle, *Quellen*, 73.
14. Wernle, *Synoptische Frage*, 202–3, 231–33; *Quellen*, 52, 86–87.
15. Weiss, "Die drei älteren Evangelien," 51, 64–65, 256–57.
16. Jülicher, *Neue Linien*, 6, 73.
17. Jülicher, *Einleitung* (1906), 322.

unfolds in Judea and Jerusalem.[18] Like his nineteenth-century predecessors Harnack romanticizes a Galilean natural piety, expressed in Jesus's teaching in Q, over against Judean cult ritualism and Pharisaic legalism. Narrative interest in Jesus's crucifixion, which develops into the narrative gospel form, is a degenerate dogmatic development. The projects of Matthew and Luke are attempts to subsume the authentic Jesus of Q and the simple messianic Christology of the primitive Palestinian community to the dogmatic agenda of the Passion narrative gospel.[19]

In Bultmann's form criticism this pattern finds its most influential expression. In the sayings source the consciousness of the primitive Palestinian community is manifest. It contains the simple moral teaching of Jesus, subsumed to the primitive community's enthusiastic Easter faith: God demands radical obedience rather than mere conformity to codified law; cult and ritual are excluded from the demands of God. Jesus "sets free the purely religious relation to God in which man stands only as one who asks and receives, hopes and trusts."[20] Bultmann therefore forms the bridge from nineteenth-century source criticism to the "Q community" of contemporary 2DH scholarship.

BIRTH OF THE "GALILEAN Q PEOPLE"

H. E. Tödt's Second Sphere of Christological Reflection

Many Q scholars celebrate H. E. Tödt's 1956 volume (ET *The Son of Man in the Synoptic Tradition*) as the new point of departure that has led to the rediscovery of the autonomous Galilean Q community, soteriologically centered on the sayings tradition, and to a revolution in Christian origins scholarship that decenters the Passion and Resurrection narratives.[21] This sounds suspiciously like the nineteenth-century liberal Protestant trope of privileging the sayings over the narrative tradition and its reification in a social formation,

---

18. Harnack, *Sprüche*, 118–19.
19. Harnack, *Sprüche*, 171–74.
20. Bultmann, *Theology*, 13.
21. H. E. Tödt, *The Son of Man in the Synoptic Tradition*, trans. D. M. Barton (Philadelphia: Westminster, 1965); e.g., John S. Kloppenborg, "'Easter Faith' and the Sayings Gospel Q," in *Synoptic Problems: Collected Essays*, WUNT 329 (Tübingen: Mohr Siebeck, 2014), 179–203 (178); Jens Schröter, *Erinnerung an Jesu Worte. Studien zur Rezeption der Logienüberlieferung in Markus, Q und Thomas*, WMANT 76 (Neukirchen-Vluyn: Neukirchener Verlag, 1997), 91–93; William Arnal, "The Trouble with Q," *Forum* 3rd Series 2 (2013): 7–77 (8).

the primitive Palestinian community (*Urgemeinde*). One therefore has reason to be skeptical that Tödt marks any such new point of departure at all. That he refuted Dibelius's notion that the sayings source was just a nondescript paraenetic appendage to the Passion and Resurrection kerygma can be readily granted. But Tödt is best understood as mediating the Q of Bultmann's form criticism and Bultmann's primitive Palestinian congregation to contemporary Q scholarship.

Tödt's analysis rests upon form-critical assumptions about the history of the tradition. The second sphere of soteriological reflection that he identifies, a sphere oriented "almost exclusively" to Jesus's "word," is in its essentials indistinguishable from Bultmann's narrative-deficient Palestinian community centered upon a traditional Son of Man eschatology.[22] Tödt takes over the form-critical conception of Q as a stratum of tradition: not a *Schrift* (written work) but a *Schicht* (layer of tradition).[23] He rejects Harnack's view that this body of tradition has literary origins in the initiative of an author or redactor. Instead, and channeling Bultmann, he identifies it as the immanent manifestation of a social formation, the primitive "post-Easter" Palestinian congregation.[24] The Q "stratum of tradition" has a "sociological concomitant" (as Arnal aptly puts it).[25] It follows that because this Q stratum of tradition contains no Passion and Resurrection narrative ("it is nowhere referred to"), the Passion and Resurrection kerygma had no purchase, indeed no presence in the Palestinian community.[26] Correspondingly, the force that coalesces this mass of tradition is christological: the community's post-mortem identification of Jesus, the earthly Son of Man, with the coming Son of Man. This is to be inferred from Q's stock of earthly and coming Son of Man sayings and its lack of suffering Son of Man sayings. Accordingly, it must be the definitive Christology of the "post-Easter" community. The soteriological significance of Jesus therefore lay in his sayings, his *word*, which the primitive community now takes up and proclaims anew as the word of the exalted and imminently appearing Son of Man.[27]

Tödt's account is no better than the questionable form-critical assumptions upon which it is based. This can be pushed further. Tödt's analysis is basically

22. Tödt, *Son of Man*, 249–50.
23. Martin Dibelius: "The present state of research on Q justifies our speaking of Q as more of a stratum of tradition (*Schicht*) than a written work (*Schrift*)" (*Formgeschichte*, 236). Tödt cites Dibelius (*Son of Man*, 237).
24. Tödt, *Son of Man*, 237, also 249–50.
25. Arnal, "Trouble with Q," 8 n. 8.
26. Tödt, *Son of Man*, 243.
27. Tödt, *Son of Man*, 218–19, 234–35, 249.

a further christological glossing of Bultmann's views of Q and the primitive community. It is therefore unsurprising that Tödt will claim that "a gulf" thus opens up in between the sayings-oriented, exalted Son of Man soteriology of the primitive community of Q ("no passage . . . mentions the passion"), and the Christology and soteriology that find expression in the Markan Passion kerygma.[28] This reprises Bultmann's distinction between Palestinian Christianity, with its primitive Son of Man Christology, and Hellenistic Christianity, formed around the Christ cult of death and resurrection.

Tödt however has abandoned the *religionsgeschichtliche* schema that for Bultmann supplied his history of the tradition and its evolutionary trajectory with its warrants. That is, he has abandoned the grounds for the distinction between the primitive Palestinian community and the kerygmatic communities in the first place. This explains why his schema is no longer dynamic and developmental, like Bultmann's, but static: Q now represents a second sphere of christological cognition. Like Bultmann's primitive community this second sphere remains identified with the "post-Easter" Palestinian congregation. But without the enabling *religionsgeschichtliche* schema, the distinction, the "two spheres," is gratuitous. Tödt's two spheres are debris of this collapsed framework. The most that can be said of it is that it resets to the practice of nineteenth-century source criticism of privileging the sayings tradition over the narrative tradition.

It is difficult to argue that Tödt has supplied alternative grounds for his second sphere in an analysis of Q's Christology, namely, from its lack of suffering Son of Man sayings. This makes the text an epiphenomenon of a Christology instead of the artifact of a cultural-formation enterprise. Taking Q as a christological-history entity owes something to interpreters like Tödt being trained as theologians. But more directly, Tödt's argument is predicated on form-critical assumptions about the generative relationship of sociological setting to the tradition and on a superannuated *religionsgeschichtliche* schema that designates the Passion and Resurrection kerygma a later development of Hellenistic syncretism. The "stratum of tradition" conception allows Tödt to understand Q as the theological and christological shadow cast by the primitive community. As soon as it is recognized as a work (*Schrift*) and not a stratum of tradition (*Schicht*), genre analysis is triggered, and it can no longer be taken as the textual simulacrum of a sociological formation. The issue of text-pragmatic function and of the nonnarrative profile of an instructional genre moves to the fore. Perhaps it is really not so remarkable that suffering

---

28. Tödt, *Son of Man*, 232–33.

Son of Man sayings, which portend a narrative resolution, are not present in a work executed within the genre parameters of an instructional work.[29]

Sensing the problem, Tödt declares that though Q materials may indeed have been useful for exhortation, they were only "secondarily" so. What he has in mind when he says "exhortation," however, is Dibelius's dubious catechetical supplement to the kerygma. Seemingly non-instructional elements such as John the Baptist's preaching, the Beelzebul Accusation, and the Woes indicate that the "primary motive to . . . collect this material" was "not . . . a need for exhortation."[30] Rather, it was the reauthorization of the word of the earthly Jesus as the word of the eschatological Son of Man that explains the coalescing of this "stratum" of tradition. But Tödt has no working conception of the genre factor. His inferences to a second sphere of christological and soteriological reflection are unsound.

Tödt engineered the shift from conceiving Q and the narrative kerygma as the remote extremities of a *religionsgeschichtliche* trajectory to their being separate spheres of christological cognition. The consequence is that maintaining Q's insularity from kerygmatic theologizing suddenly becomes an acute problem. Tödt solves it by retaining a residue of Bultmann's kerygmatic trajectory: the primitive "post-Easter" community, whose outlook is registered by Q, knew of Jesus's passion, and they also believed he had been raised—his exaltation to Son of Man. But this was not yet kerygma, which was a subsequent theological development. Jesus's exaltation as Son of Man is a sufficient christological catalyst for their renewed proclamation of his word of the imminent kingdom. Jesus's "word" is the soteriological center, not the kerygma of suffering, death, and resurrection.[31]

From Tödt to the "Galilean Q People"

Subsequent Q scholarship will recognize that the synchronic implications of Tödt's second-sphere schema require a reckoning. This will entail sharpening

---

29. A case can be made that the suffering Son of Man is the implicit premise of the martyrdom paraenesis in Q 12:2–12. To all intents and purposes the setting projected in the sequence Q 12:8–9, 10, 11–12 is indistinguishable from that of Jesus before the High Priest's tribunal in Mark 14:62, which Tödt sums up as follows: "That Jesus possesses full authority in spite of the external powerlessness in which he stands before his earthly judges will become clearly visible when the Son of Man, ruling at God's side, comes with the clouds of heaven" (40). In Mark 14:62 this situation finds narrative representation, in Q 12:2–12 paraenetic application.

30. Tödt, *Son of Man*, 247.

31. Tödt, *Son of Man*, 250–52.

the Q group's differences vis-à-vis kerygmatic Christianity—that is, making the distinctions more categorical. Daniel Smith will neatly pose the only two possible alternatives: "Did Q know, but diverge from, kerygmatic approaches to Jesus's death? Or did Q's silence result from ignorance of, or even isolation from, such approaches?"[32] He opts for the former. Because the kerygma of Christ's soteriological suffering "for us" originates early, the group whose views are laid down in the Q source stands consciously in difference from kerygmatic communities. Smith construes this community not as pre-kerygma, as Tödt does, but as non-kerygma. For him as it was for Tödt it is probative that Q contains no references either to Jesus's suffering as soteriological or to his resurrection. To be sure, he acknowledges, "eschatological resurrection forms part of the belief structure evidenced by Q" (7:22; 11:31–32). But because Q lacks a resurrection narrative, the tradent group simply could not have conceived Jesus's post-mortem vindication in terms of resurrection.[33] Therefore another model must be sought. Smith finds this in the Jewish tradition of assumption, a motif which he argues can be found in 13:34–35: "you will no longer see me."[34] Weighing the merits of Smith's analysis of Jesus's post-mortem vindication in Q cannot occupy us here.[35] For our purposes it suffices to note that though he gestures at Q not being exhaustive of the tradent group's beliefs, in the long tradition of making the Q tradition coterminous with the primitive community, now the Q community, Smith excludes anything not attested or implied in Q from the tradent group's belief structure.

By far the more common strategy in the face of this "second sphere" problem, however, has been to isolate the Q community geographically in Galilee.[36] For Arnal it is clear, given the extent of its christological and soteriological differences, that "Q is not in conversation with other groups of Jesus people."[37] He is in agreement with Arland Jacobson: it must have been an isolated com-

---

32. Daniel A. Smith, *The Post-Mortem Vindication of Jesus in the Sayings Gospel Q*, LNTS 338 (London: T&T Clark, 2006), 18–19.

33. Smith, *Vindication*, 21–24, 51–52.

34. Smith, *Vindication*, 51–52.

35. Smith must plead the special case for Q that the assumption model is an *alternative* to the resurrection schema (169–70). Tödt did not have this problem, because he had no difficulty with resurrection belief as the backdrop to Q's exalted Son of Man Christology.

36. See Simon Joseph's trenchant observations on this: "The Quest for the 'Community' of Q: Mapping Q within the Social, Scribal, and Textual Landscape(s) of Second Temple Judaism," *HTR* 111 (2018): 90–114 (99).

37. William Arnal, "The Q Document," in *Jewish Christianity Reconsidered: Rethinking Ancient Groups and Texts*, ed. Matt Jackson-McCabe (Minneapolis: Fortress, 2007), 119–54 (135).

munity.[38] The template for this is Walter Bauer's correlation of theological divergence to distinct geographical regions and cultural spheres.[39] Bultmann's Jerusalem location for the primitive Palestinian church will not do because of the manifest inter-connectedness of the Jerusalem community and the kerygmatic community of Antioch.[40] In Q scholarship therefore the primitive community gets dissociated from Jerusalem and the Jerusalem community and moved north to Galilee—and loaded up with all the positive qualities that liberal Protestant sensibility imputed to "Galilean religiosity."

The newly born "Galilean Q community" thereby becomes the new focal point for the old liberal Protestant ideological project. John Kloppenborg describes the message of Q (more precisely, of his Q^1) thus: "Q^1 is full of confidence in divine providence, in God's loving surveillance, and the possibility of transformed human relationships; but there is no indication whatsoever that this is mediated by Torah or Temple or the priestly hierarchy."[41] This echoes Bultmann's description of Jesus's message: Jesus protested against a relationship with God mediated by "codified law"; he "excluded from the commands of God . . . all cultic and ritual regulations, so that along with ethics Jesus sets free the purely religious relation to God in which man stands only as one who asks and receives, hopes and trusts."[42] In its essentials this is nineteenth-century natural religion, the universalistic ethical religion of liberal Protestantism, that resurfaces in contemporary Q scholarship as the message of the Galilean Q community. Moreover, in its renewed proclamation of Jesus's "word" in all its pristine originality over against the legalistic cult religion of Judea on the one hand and the Passion soteriology of the eucharistic communities on the other, Q becomes, as Francis Watson puts it, "the definitive expression of liberal Protestant ambivalence toward catholic Christianity."[43]

---

38. Arland D. Jacobson, *The First Gospel: An Introduction to Q* (Sonoma, CA: Polebridge, 1992), 260.

39. Helmut Koester, "The Synoptic Sayings Gospel Q in the Early Communities of Jesus' Followers," in *From Jesus to the Gospels: Interpreting the New Testament in Its Context* (Minneapolis: Fortress, 2007), 72–83 (73); "Conclusion: The Intention and Scope of Trajectories," in *Trajectories through Early Christianity* (Philadelphia: Fortress, 1971), 269–79 (273, 276).

40. Koester, "Synoptic Sayings Gospel," 74.

41. Kloppenborg, *Excavating Q*, 199.

42. Bultmann, *Theology*, 13.

43. Watson, *Gospel Writing*, 117; similarly Marco Frenschkowski, "Welche biographischen Kenntnisse von Jesus setzt die Logienquelle voraus? Beobachtungen zur Gattung von Q im Kontext antiker Spruchsammlungen," in *From Quest to Q: Festschrift James M. Robinson*, ed. Jón Ma. Ásgeirsson, Kristin de Troyer, and Marvin W. Meyer, BETL 146 (Leuven: Leuven University Press/Peeters, 2000), 3–42 (21–22).

Galilee's regional boundedness fulfills the crucial function of distancing the Q community from Judean cult and ritual practice (temple centered) and Judean scribal legalism. In contemporary Q scholarship Galilee as a region reprises the role Galilee played in nineteenth-century source criticism—namely, to dissociate Jesus the Galilean from his Judaistic context.[44] Kloppenborg maintains that the "sheer distance between Galilee and the Temple" would render the loyalties of Galileans to the temple cult tenuous.[45] For Burton Mack likewise it is a matter of great significance that Galilee "was not contiguous to Judea." Indeed, he exclaims, "it was even further removed from Jerusalem than Samaria." Since Samaria is manifestly hostile to the Judean cult, *a fortiori* so is Galilean religiosity.[46] Kloppenborg alleges that in ignoring the sacrificial system and the Decalogue Q registers the resistance of an "indigenous Galilean piety" to the "incursion" of Judaean and priestly influence."[47] Q, he holds, attributes no efficacy to the redemptive media of Torah and Temple cult. Its proclamation is grounded in rational appeals to universal experience of the Creator's providential presence observed in the natural world and in everyday human interactions.[48] "In Q^1," says Arnal, "the *particularities* of Judean religion" are "entirely absent."[49] The Q community's geographical isolation in Galilee does double duty, safely segregating it not only from orthodox Judaism in Judea but also from kerygmatic Jesus groups like the Antioch community and from the Jewish-Christian community in Jerusalem.[50] In Q scholarship Galilean geographical isolation, in concert with Q group's absolute valorization of Jesus's rational "word," takes over the function Bultmann's *Religionsgeschichte* played in his tradition history: to set up a polarity between the Q group's simple eth-

44. Roland Deines, "Galilee and the Historical Jesus in Recent Research," in *Life, Culture, and Society*, vol. 1 of *Galilee in the Late Second Temple and Mishnaic Periods*, ed. David A. Fiensy and James Riley Strange (Minneapolis: Fortress, 2014) 11–48 (13, 37–38); "Jesus the Galilean: Questioning the Function of Galilee in Recent Jesus Research," in *Acts of God in History: Studies Towards Recovering a Theological Historiography*, ed. Christoph Ochs and Peter Watts, WUNT 317 (Tübingen: Mohr Siebeck, 2013), 53–93 (55–56, 70).

45. Kloppenborg, *Excavating Q*, 227.

46. Burton Mack, *The Lost Gospel: The Book of Q and Christian Origins* (San Francisco: HarperSanFrancisco, 1993), 52.

47. Kloppenborg, *Excavating Q*, 206.

48. John S. Kloppenborg, "Literary Convention, Self-Evidence, and the Social History of the Q People," in *Synoptic Problems*, 237–65 (245); "Nomos and Ethos in Q," in *Synoptic Problems*, 204–21 (213–18); *Excavating Q*, 199, 388.

49. Arnal, "Q Document," 145, emphasis original.

50. Joseph, "Quest," 99.

ical religion and the sacramental piety of kerygmatic Christianity, and to give the former priority over the latter.

The other essential function of Galilee, scene of Jesus's activity, is to bring the Galilean Q community into privileged proximity to the historical Jesus. Galilee serves to position Q as the authentic source over against the narrative gospels, which with their Passion and Resurrection kerygma all but obliterate the historical Jesus. Galilee is the authentic memory zone, and Q, textual simulacrum of the Galilean Q community, registers that memory with least distortion. Once again it is Kloppenborg who expresses this view with directness. He uses "the Q people" and "the earliest Jesus movement" interchangeably.[51] The Q group is "geographically, culturally, and chronologically proximate to the historical Jesus."[52] It is "not likely to have been discontinuous with the social catchment of Jesus and his followers."[53] To be sure, he says, as a work it is the product of community perspectives and rhetoric. Thus it permits no naïve inferences to the historical Jesus without redactional expansions of its formative materials being recognized and bracketed.[54] But with that caveat, so sterling are Q's authenticity credentials that it can serve as the criterion for the authenticity of elements of the narrative gospels. Any matter that Q does not explicitly refer to is presumptively historically questionable. Its complete silence on Jesus carrying out a programmatic critique of Sabbath practice, for example, renders this Markan motif historically dubious.[55] As it was for the nineteenth-century source critics, the sayings tradition is here the translucent medium for the historical Jesus, a tradition unsullied by narrative, ritual, and dogmatic elaboration. Q's Galilean regionalism, its embodiment in "the Galilean Q community," secures this claim. Simon Joseph in his critique puts the point trenchantly: "Q and Galilee . . . function as literary-geographical *symbols* for Jesus."[56]

As noted, the Galilean Q community is the symbolic antipode to the cultic and ritualistic practices of Judean Judaism on the one hand and kerygmatic,

51. Kloppenborg, *Excavating Q*, 414.

52. Kloppenborg, *Excavating Q*, 442–44; also "The Sayings Gospel Q and the Quest of the Historical Jesus," *HTR* 89 (1996): 307–44 (343).

53. John S. Kloppenborg, "Discursive Practices in the Sayings Gospel Q and the Quest of the Historical Jesus," in *The Sayings Source Q and the Historical Jesus*, ed. A. Lindemann, BETL 158 (Leuven: Leuven University Press/Peeters, 2001), 149–51 (171 n. 70).

54. Kloppenborg, "Sayings Gospel Q," 322–26, 344; *Excavating Q*, 351.

55. Kloppenborg, "Sayings Gospel Q," 333–34.

56. Simon Joseph, *Jesus, Q, and the Dead Sea Scrolls: A Judaic Approach to Q*, WUNT 333 (Tübingen: Mohr Siebeck, 2012), 77.

narrative-gospel Jesus groups on the other. In it rematerializes the romanticized primitive community of nineteenth-century source criticism, liberal Protestantism's ancient precursor. It is Herder's "älteste Christusgemeinde" reborn, witness to the universalizing religion of Jesus and the religiosity of humble village folk of Galilee, to a religion of simple childlike trust in the provident care of God and abjuring Pharisaic legalism and the empty cultic ritualism of faraway Judea.[57] The Q of the Galilean Q group is Gieseler's oral Urgospel, the faithful testimony of unschooled Galilean fishermen, simple "Orientals," to whom the "dead letters" of the scribes and their productions are alien. It is Köstlin's proto-Matthean logia collection of the oldest Galilean Jesus community, grounded in the living memory of Jesus in Galilee and bristling with all the regional aversion to the alien scribal Judaism of Jerusalem. It is the re-embodiment of Wernle's lay Galilean piety of simple intuitive moral response to God's will, untrammeled by the legalism, purity codes and cultic ritualism of elite Judean religion. The Galilean Q community is Johannes Weiss's *Urgemeinde*, oriented not to cult but to eschatological moral transformation, bearing witness to a Jesus opposed to rigid Jewish legalism and purity codes and teaching a joyful piety of simple trust in God's providential goodness manifest everywhere in the natural world. It is the bearer of Harnack's sayings tradition—bounded by Galilean horizons and untouched by dogmatic Passion theology, the ever-luminous contradiction to Mark, whose Passion narrative unfolds in Judea and Jerusalem.[58] The Galilean Q community of contemporary Q scholarship is a retro-manifestation of this liberal Protestant myth-making activity centered on the *Urgemeinde*. It is a vestige of the theological and cultural program of nineteenth-century source criticism, a testament to the ability of a scholarly paradigm to persist even after its warrants are gone.

But an additional element is required in the mix for the specifically *Galilean* Q community to materialize—as we noted, Walter Bauer's sorting of alleged theological differences in second-century Christianity into distinct geographical regions—Asia Minor, eastern Syria, western Syria, Egypt, and Rome.[59] "Walter Bauer was right," Koester says in his concluding essay in *Trajectories through Early Christianity*, "when he singled out particular regions for his description of orthodoxy and heresy. Further probing into the question of geographical distinctions within cultural and religious developments is certain

57. Herder, "Vom Erlöser," 641–42.
58. Harnack, *Sprüche*, 118–19.
59. Walter Bauer, *Orthodoxy and Heresy in Earliest Christianity*, trans. Philadelphia Seminar on Christian Origins (Miffletown, PA: Sigler, 1996).

to yield significant results."[60] The "Galilean Q community" is the vehicle for the attempt to import Bauer's paradigm of widely divergent theological vectors right back into the earliest period in Christian origins. The most determined application of this agenda is Burton Mack's correlation of the different *forms* of the Synoptic tradition to different *social identities*. Mack inflates the erstwhile *Sitze* of the form critics to the prodigious proportions of "diverse Jesus movements" and distributes them out among different geographical regions.[61] This agenda explains the curious resistance of Q scholars to letting go of the "Galilean" designation even in the face of its mounting difficulties. Dissociating the "Q group" from Galilee means abandoning the larger Christian origins revisionist project. It means surrendering the alleged "differentness" of the Q tradition.

The existence of a regional Galilean piety inimical to Judean temple cult, ritual purity practices, and law is fanciful. Archaeological, historical, and literary evidence gives us a predominantly Jewish Galilee oriented socially, religiously, and culturally toward Judea and Jerusalem—resettled from Judea in the Hasmonean period, halakhically observant.[62] The notion of a Galilean

60. Koester, "Conclusion," 273.

61. Burton L. Mack, *A Myth of Innocence: Mark and Christian Origins* (Philadelphia: Fortress, 1988). Pronouncement stories are the tradition of a "synagogue reform" Jesus movement; a "congregation of Israel" Jesus movement cultivates the miracle stories; eucharistic meal traditions are associated with the Hellenistic Christ cult located in western Asia Minor and Greece; the aphoristic tradition is associated with Q group in Galilee. By means of a Passion narrative the Markan evangelist combines the eponymous traditions of these diverse Jesus groups with the eucharistic traditions of the Asia Minor and Greece Christ-cult communities to give us Christianity—though somehow the aphoristic tradition (Q) eludes Mark's net. This is transparently a retrieval and update of Bultmann's narrative of Mark combining the "Palestinian tradition" with the syncretistic *kyrios*-cult kerygma of the Hellenistic churches.

62. Deines, "Jesus the Galilean," 92–93. See Mark A. Chancey, *Greco-Roman Culture and the Galilee of Jesus*, SNTS Monograph Series 134 (Cambridge: Cambridge University Press, 2005), 38; Jürgen K. Zangenberg, "From the Galilean Jesus to the Galilean Silence: Earliest Christianity in the Galilee until the Fourth Century CE," in *The Rise and Expansion of Christianity in the First Three Centuries of the Common Era*, ed. Clare K. Rothschild and Jens Schröter, WUNT 301 (Tübingen: Mohr Siebeck, 2013), 75–108 (75); Mordechai Aviam, "Distribution Maps of Archaeological Data from the Galilee: An Attempt to Establish Zones Indicative of Ethnicity and Religious Affiliation," in *Religion, Ethnicity, and Identity in Ancient Galilee: A Region in Transition*, ed. Jürgen Zangenberg, Harold W. Attridge, and Dale B. Martin, WUNT 201 (Tübingen: Mohr Siebeck, 2007), 115–32 (132); Sean Freyne, "Galilean Studies: Old Issues and New Questions," in *Religion, Ethnicity, and Identity in Ancient Galilee*, 13–29 (26–27); John S. Kloppenborg, "Q, Bethsaida, Khorazin, and Capernaum," in *Q in Context II: Social Setting and Archeological Background of the Sayings Source*, ed. Markus

Q group embodying a simple Galilean religiosity alien to Judean Judaism is the legacy of an Orientalizing discourse that puts the natural religion of an enlightened universalism in sharp contrast with Jewish legalistic, cultic, and ethnic particularism.[63]

Thus Mack, for example, paints a picture of a cosmopolitan, Hellenized, Greek-capable Galilee, conscious of its ancient Israelite heritage but experiencing Jerusalem-based Judaism as a recent and alien imposition, and he finds his leading analogy to Jesus and the Galilean "people of Q" in a philosophical movement with its origins on the Greek mainland, the Cynics. Mack's principal argument for a Hellenized Galilee is the nearby presence of the urban foundations in the Decapolis.[64] Warwick Ball points out, however, that "it would be a mistake to view the Decapolis as somehow Hellenistic ... [Nabatean] Arabs probably formed the bulk of the population [of these cities]. . . . The old Semitic names of the cities were either retained or lay just below the surface throughout, resurfacing the moment Roman rule ended ... [and] the temples and cults were to local Semitic deities."[65] Similarly David F. Graf: "Nothing suggests the cities were large Greek enclaves, insulated from the surrounding culture," and he notes as well that the cultural formation of the Gadara-born poet Meleager occurred in Tyre.[66] "The royal [i.e., Seleucid] foundations," Graf says, "were more political gestures than real transformations of the indigenous villages."[67] Urban development in the Decapolis along Hellenistic lines, he continues, is a post-Augustan development, but "this urbanisation trend did not become

Tiwald, BBB 173 (Bonn: Vandenhoeck & Ruprecht; Bonn University Press, 2015), 61–90 (85); Giovanni B. Bazzana, *The Kingdom of Bureaucracy: The Political Theology of Village Scribes in the Sayings Gospel Q*, BETL 274 (Leuven: Peeters, 2015), 14. Also see Andrea M. Berlin and Paul J. Kosmin, eds., *The Middle Maccabees: Archaeology, History, and the Rise of the Hasmonean Kingdom* (Atlanta: SBL Press, 2021), especially Uzi Leibner, "Galilee in the Second Century BCE: Material Culture and Ethnic Identity," 123–45; Andrea M. Berlin, "The Upper Galilee and the Northern," 145–76; and Danny Syon, "The Hasmonean Settlement in Galilee: A Numismatic Perspective," 177–92.

63. Deines, "Jesus the Galilean," 57–58, 70.

64. Mack, *Lost Gospel*, 57–59.

65. Warwick Ball, *Rome in the East: The Transformation of an Empire* (London: Routledge, 2000), 181.

66. David F. Graf, "Hellenisation and the Decapolis," *ARAM* 4 (1992): 1–48 (5–7, quotation 7). Social and religious relations between Gadara and Galilee were antagonistic; see Thomas M. Weber, "Gadara and the Galilee," in Zangenberg, et al., *Religion, Ethnicity, and Identity in Ancient Galilee*, 449–77 (454–60, 476).

67. Graf, "Hellenisation," 11–12.

really prevalent until the reigns of Trajan and Hadrian." In any case, "during the Roman era the cities possessed the municipal forms of the Greek city without the basic political substance or spirit of the Greek civic legacy."[68]

Similarly, in John Kloppenborg's reconstruction the Q group moves in a compressed social history (Q^1, Q^2, Q^3) from a universal sapiential outlook, with a religiosity grounded in God's providence manifested universally in nature, to a Jewish particularism of Torah and Temple.[69] Arnal explicitly characterizes Q's social history as a re-Judaization trajectory: "In Q^1, the *particularities* of Judean religion" are "entirely absent." Q becomes "*more* ideologically Jewish over time . . . it appears to have developed more and more 'typical features' of Jewish religious belief at each stage of its development."[70] The Galilean Q group plays the same role vis-à-vis Judaism that Sufism does in past and present Orientalizing discourses on Islam. Sufism—so it is claimed—is enlightened, nonlegalistic, unritualistic, interior, and tolerant, "an Oriental version of a Kantian universal faith," in contrast to Islamic orthodoxy, which is Semitic, legalistic, obsessed with Sharia, dogmatic, ritualistic, intolerant, coercive, and politicized.[71]

Developments in understanding the material culture of Galilee have killed off the notion of a distinctive, non-Judean Galilean religiosity. However, so ideologically fixed has become the putative Q-Galilee connection and so cognitively habituated the second-sphere model for interpreting the Q source that scholars look for alternative grounds to posit the distinctive Galilean Q group. Jonathan Reed, after acknowledging the religious, social, and material connections between Galilean Jews and Judea nevertheless asserts, on the basis of Q's positive appraisal of the northern Israelite prophet Jonah, that the Q community "shared with the northern prophets a common geographical and spiritual distance from the center of Jerusalem."[72] Michael Labahn finds no trace of any anti-Jerusalem disposition in Q, but he nevertheless asserts its Galilean provenance on the grounds of the agrarian texture of its traditions and the sense of

---

68. Graf, "Hellenisation," 27, 34–35.

69. Kloppenborg, *Excavating Q*, 199.

70. Arnal, "Q Document," 138–39, 145, emphasis original.

71. G. A. Lipton, "Secular Sufism: Neoliberalism, Ethnoracism, and the Reformation of the Muslim Other," *The Muslim World* 101 (2011): 427–40 (427). I am indebted to my colleague Dr. Cyril Uy for an illuminating discussion of this and for directing me to Lipton's article. To be clear, this is simply a matter of our inherited paradigms as scholars standing in the European intellectual tradition.

72. Jonathan L. Reed, *Archaeology and the Galilean Jesus: A Re-examination of the Evidence* (Harrisburg, PA: Trinity Press International, 2000), 60.

immediacy in the Woes on the Galilean Cities (10:13–15), allegedly absent in the Announcement and Oracle of Judgment over Jerusalem (11:49–51; 13:34–35).[73] Arguments that find Q's Galilean provenance in the local Galilean color of its traditions play a large role in contemporary Q scholarship.

The "Galilean Q People": From Radical Itinerants to Village Scribes

Scholarship of "the Galilean Q community" persuasion owes a great deal to Gerd Theissen's identification of a hypothesized Q tradent group with radical itinerants in Galilee. Theissen stands in the long tradition of reifying the Q tradition into a particular Jesus group—that is, a particular social formation, an *Urgemeinde*. This tradent group's constitutive ethos is defined not by the Passion narrative, which Q lacks, but by the sayings tradition, and by the Q 10 Mission Instruction in particular. The Mission Instruction plays an outsized role in Theissen's identification of the tradent group with radical itinerants based in Galilee. Theissen holds that while Galilee is likely the group's local base, by virtue of its itineracy it is not territorially confined to Galilee but has a more widely radiating sphere of activity, likely extending into southern Syria.[74] That Q is a *written* source, however, gives him pause: this is hard to square with a band of subliterate itinerants. Perhaps a literate member of the itinerant band wrote down the group's formative tradition to serve as a handbook for itinerants. Or alternatively, a member of one of the settled communities wrote it for community use. This would explain its escape from the itinerant *Sitz* and its eventual incorporation, "against its intention," into Matthew and Luke.[75] Theissen seems to imagine Q here as a kind of *Aufzeichnung*, a rough and ready collection of loosely cohering oral traditions.

73. Michael Labahn, *Der Gekommene als Wiederkommender: Die Logienquelle als erzählte Geschichte*, ABG 32 (Leipzig: Evangelische Verlagsanstalt, 2010), 95–97, 378.

74. Gerd Theissen, *The Gospels in Context: Social and Political History in the Synoptic Tradition*, trans. Linda M. Maloney (London: T&T Clark, 1992), 233–34; "The Sayings Source Q and Itinerant Radicalism," in Tiwald, ed., *Q in Context II*, 93–110 (100, 110). Similarly Koester, "Synoptic Sayings Gospel," 77. Koester notes that Son of Man motifs overlapping with the Markan Apocalypse connects Q with wider circles of tradition. He fixes the Q group's location in "southern Syria/Palestine." He keeps Q and its message of "salvation through Jesus of Nazareth's saving words" segregated from Mark and the kerygmatic communities by identifying the Mark 13 Apocalypse, with its coming Son of Man sayings, as a non-Markan source.

75. Theissen, "Sayings Source Q," 103–5, 110. Richard Horsley likewise conceives Q as a stratum of frequently performed oral tradition with a veneer of scribality, and on the grounds of its Galilean place-names he locates its tradent group in Galilean and southern

Theissen's itinerant-radicals account is vulnerable at two points in particular. First, it cannot encompass the reality that the source is more comprehensive in its topical content than a mission instruction. Second, it will be undermined by any elucidation of the literary features of the work. Our interest at present is in the latter. No one has done more to shift the conception of Q from "stratum of tradition," or *Kleinliteratur*, to that of a literary work shaped by specific genre conceptions, instructional genres in particular, than John Kloppenborg.[76] His 1987 volume sent a shock wave through scholarship of the Galilean Q community persuasion, for the provenance of a work can be different from the provenance of its constituent materials.[77] With this shift, therefore, came the urgent need to reimagine the sociology of the tradent group, while at all costs keeping it localized in Galilee. Kloppenborg managed this by correlating what he held to be the modest level of Q's literary formation with the modest literary capabilities of *Galilean village scribes*.[78] The village scribe *Sitz* also had the advantage of being able to accommodate the Galilean and agrarian topicality of the Q materials.[79]

Galilean village scribes now become *the* tradent group, *the* Galilean community. This curious development is to some degree a matter of the cognitive habit of assimilating the tradition to social setting: the tradition has a "social concomitant," now conceived of as a network of village scribes. The literary profile of the work is reified into a literary tradent group. The more particular reason is that Q as a Greek work employing the "relatively learned" scribal instructional genre would not find any reception among the Aramaic-speaking agrarians of Galilee.[80] The Galilean Q community therefore reduces to this

---

Syrian villages; see *Whoever Hears You Hears Me: Prophets, Performance, and Tradition in Q*, with Jonathan Draper (Harrisburg, PA: Trinity Press International, 1998), 46, 146, 167, 248; "The Language(s) of the Kingdom: From Aramaic to Greek, Galilee to Syria, Oral to Oral-Written," in *A Wandering Galilean: Essays in Honour of Seán Freyne*, ed. Zuleika Rogers et al. (Leiden: Brill, 2009), 401–25 (416).

76. Kloppenborg, *Formation of Q*, passim.

77. Noted pointedly by Marco Frenschkowski, "Galiläa oder Jerusalem? Die topographischen und politischen Hintergründe der Logienquelle," in Lindemann, ed., *Sayings Source Q and the Historical Jesus*, 535–59 (536).

78. Kloppenborg, "Literary Convention," 245–47; "Variation and Reproduction of the Double Tradition and an Oral Q?," in *Synoptic Problems*, 91–119 (115–18).

79. John S. Kloppenborg, "The Sayings Gospel Q: Recent Opinion on the People behind the Document," *CurBR* 1 (1993) 9–34 (25); *Excavating Q*, 200. On this exigent need to re-engineer the sociology of Galilean tradent group, see Joseph, "Quest," 113.

80. Kloppenborg, "Literary Convention," 245–46. On the unintelligibility of a Greek work in agrarian Galilee, see Christopher Tuckett, "The Community of Q," in *Shadowy Characters and Fragmentary Evidence: The Search for Early Christian Groups and Movements*,

specialized and low-density occupational group. Remnants of the old "itinerant radical" model can be seen in Arnal's depiction of these "scribal figures . . . attempting to disseminate that agenda . . . among their fellow administrators in neighboring villages."[81] Arnal is trying to reconcile a scribal tradent group with the Q 10 Mission Instruction: it is a mission to fellow village scribes. The consequence of identifying scribes *per se* as the Galilean Q group is, ironically, to disengage Q and the Q materials from the concrete exigencies of rural life in Galilee. Q now records the solipsistic "musings of displaced bureaucrats."[82]

But it also leads to urban creep overtaking the original village scribes tradent group. Due to Q's "relatively learned" instructional profile Kloppenborg ends up associating it with "the lower administrative sectors" not only of the villages but also of Tiberius and Sepphoris.[83] "Galilean village scribes" turns out to be an unstable category, and in consequence Q's localization in Galilee becomes increasingly arbitrary.[84] Willi Braun upgrades the village scribes to "grammarian/scribes . . . Galilean small town scribal intelligentsia," with the social liminality of grammarians serving to explain the social alienation of the Q tradent group.[85] Bazzana uses "village scribes/administrators" and "village/rural sub-elites" interchangeably, and these at times morph into "intellectual and social elites."[86] Braun and Bazzana are surely on target in finding the originators of Q as a work in the sub-elite scribal cohort. But since the grounds for Kloppenborg's attribution of Q to Galilean village scribes in the first place—its

ed. Joseph Verheyden, Tobias Nicklas, and Elisabeth Hernitscheck, WUNT 388 (Tübingen: Mohr Siebeck, 2015), 5–26 (21).

81. William E. Arnal, *Jesus and the Village Scribes: Galilean Conflicts and the Setting of Q* (Minneapolis: Fortress, 2001), 94. Markus Tiwald's solution to this difficulty is to embrace Theissen's suggestion that someone with scribal abilities in a supportive community wrote down the oral traditions of the radical itinerants; see "The Brazen Freedom of God's Children: 'Insolent Ravens' (Q 12:24) and 'Carefree Lilies' (Q 12:27) as Response to Mass Poverty and Social Disruption?," in Tiwald, *Q in Context II*, 111–31 (121–22).

82. Arnal, "Trouble with Q," 69.

83. Kloppenborg, "Literary Convention," 246–50. Reed argues that the "impersonal passive" in Q 6:44 ("*they* do not gather figs from thorns") reveals the nonrural positionality of the tradents of the Q materials—i.e., "a scribal perspective . . . at home in the larger villages or cities of Galilee" (*Archaeology*, 191–92).

84. See Alan Kirk, "Who Are the Q Scribes? Questioning the Village Scribes Hypothesis," in *Bridges in New Testament Interpretation: Interdisciplinary Advances*, ed. Neil Elliott and Werner H. Kelber (Lanham, MD: Lexington/Fortress Academic, 2018), 67–96.

85. Willi Braun, "Socio-mythic Invention, Graeco-Roman Schools, and the Sayings Gospel," *MTSR* 11 (1999): 210–35 (223).

86. Bazzana, *Kingdom of Bureaucracy*, 24–25, 263, 281–83, 313–18.

literary modesty—have been abandoned, their continued localization of this cohort to Galilee is gratuitous.

From Village Scribes to Authors: Rollens and Walsh

Sarah Rollens and Robyn Walsh follow out the logic of this course of development set in motion by the identification of "the Q people" with the circles of sub-elite scribal composers. Rollens tries to come to grips with the conundrum thereby created—a work of a nonpeasant tradent group that is replete with peasant concerns.[87] To this end she analogizes the Q scribes to the cross-cultural social type of the "peasant intellectual": socially alienated but educated persons who give articulation to social critiques from below. This allows her to bring the scribal tradent group of Q into proximity to the Galilean agrarian population while at the same time cleanly separating it off as a distinct social formation with its own interests. In Q this "middling" group of alienated village administrators is pursuing its own ideological agenda, appropriating the markers and tropes of a hard-pressed peasantry to invest itself with a rhetoric of social marginality.[88] Again we are left with a "Galilean Q people" with only a notional connection to the socioeconomic realities and experiences of the actual Galilean population. In invoking the "peasant intellectual" model Rollens comes close to an explanation of the scribal origins of Q as a work: the scribal "broker" who mediates a living tradition into the written medium, framing it in scribal genres.[89] But she is limited by a media model that is unable to take account of the interface between orality and writing, and thus of scribes as boundary figures between the oral medium and the written medium.[90] In consequence we have a scribal "Q people," composing materials reflective of its own ideological interests out of peasant tropes and separated from the Galilean peasantry by a line as sharp as that separating writing from orality in the binary media model.

Subsequently—and inexorably—this pulls Rollens toward an explicitly authorial model for Q origins and the severing of its materials from connections of any significance with any feeder Jesus tradition and with the historical Jesus. By the same token, it leads to her retreating from taking Q as the corporate

---

87. Sarah Rollens, *Framing Social Criticism in the Jesus Movement: The Ideological Project in the Sayings Gospel Q*, WUNT 374 (Tübingen: Mohr Siebeck, 2014).

88. Rollens, *Framing Social Criticism*, 53, 139, 174, 195–96.

89. Rollens, *Framing Social Criticism*, 64.

90. Rollens *Framing Social Criticism*, 197.

expression of a community at all.[91] Q and its materials are generated by a literary, rhetorical strategy in service to a social agenda. She identifies Stanley Stowers' critique of the typical functionalist modeling of the relation of Paul's letters to the so-called Pauline communities as crucial to this evolution in her thinking. Stowers argues that Paul's letters are not so much reflections of the social realities of the communities addressed as they are Paul's rhetorical interventions to promote the formation of Paul's imagined community.[92] Rollens applies Stowers' critique to call into question the reflexive tendency to connect Q to a corresponding Q community of which it is supposedly the immanent expression. Instead, like the Pauline authorships and letters, it is a rhetorical intervention into a contingent social situation to engineer a social reality imagined by its author or authors. It does not so much reflect a social identity as it seeks to construct an imagined social identity.[93] "The rhetoric of Q," she says, "is evidence for the *effort* it took to fashion a new identity around Jesus."[94]

This is a consequential and long overdue break with the old form-critical model. In key respects it lines up with the approach that we develop later in this chapter. But there is something suspect about the unqualified adoption of the Pauline authorial model for Q origins, the severing of Q's connection with a tradition, the reimagining Q's "text" as "a discursive space dealing with identity and authority . . . perhaps entirely disconnected from any coherent community."[95] An approach that leads Rollens to claim that the "so-called" Mission Instruction and its "harsh rhetoric" against the Galilean towns is best interpreted in terms of competition among competing scribal groups, as a kind of "exaggerated rhetorical metonymy," gives one pause.[96] The problem is traceable to Stowers' assimilation of the project of tradition formation and gospel writing to the Pauline authorial model, to the epistolary enterprise of the apostle.[97] These are two very different sorts of cultural projects, governed by different practices. Tradition, in all its semiotic potency, is the principal

91. Sarah E. Rollens, "The Kingdom of God Is among You: Prospects for a Q Community," in *Christian Origins and the Establishment of the Early Jesus Movement*, ed. Stanley E. Porter and Andrew W. Pitts, ECHE 4 (Leiden: Brill, 2018), 224–41 (225, 240).

92. Stanley Stowers, "The Concept of 'Community' and the History of Early Christianity," *MTSR* 23 (2011): 238–56 (242–50).

93. Rollens, "Kingdom of God," 231–33.

94. Rollens, "Kingdom of God," 237.

95. Sarah E. Rollens, "The Anachronism of 'Early Christian Communities,'" in *Theorizing Religion in Antiquity*, ed. Nickolas Roubekas (London: Equinox, 2019), 307–21 (307).

96. Rollens, "Kingdom of God," 237.

97. Stowers, "Concept of 'Community,'" 248.

force in the formation of a cultural identity. Tradition is densely concentrated cultural information, and it operates to transmit and reproduce the forms of a cultural life. Stowers does not work with any robust model for tradition, a deficiency in his analysis that gets taken over in Rollens's application of it over to the Q source. In consequence she subsumes the Q tradition to specialist authorial rhetoric; it is diminished to a "common discourse about Jesus," a resource for rhetorical enterprises.[98] On the other hand, that Q is a protreptic rhetorical project aimed at bringing into existence a certain kind of imagined social identity and social formation is an indispensable observation.[99] Attention to the genre of the work—and with genre its text-pragmatic directionality—is the way forward in reconciling its rhetorical intentionality with the cultural potency of the Jesus tradition that it incorporates.

It falls to Robyn Walsh (likewise influenced by Stowers) to follow out the authorial model for Q's origins to its endpoint.[100] Taking the practices of leisured Greco-Roman authors in their elite literary salons as normative for ancient writing, she defines Q as an individual authorial composition, though granting that its author or authors are not literati of the first rank like Pliny.[101] The "community" dimension of its existence fades away. Q is not the collective voice of a particular community, and especially not of any hypothesized scribal group in Galilee. Hellenistic literary practice, she says, does not bear narrow localization to Galilee, and in any case, village clerks were not capable of the evident literary achievement that Q represents. Making Q the textual residue of the tradition of some anonymous community and its social history is a vestige of form criticism and the creative community of the Romantic imagination.[102] The Q "community" is now to be reconfigured, in Walsh's words, as the Q author's "critical writing 'circle' of fellow elite cultural producers that is the most immediate and formative social context for the production of literature."[103] Just like the literary works issuing from elite Greco-Roman

98. Rollens, "Anachronism," 322–23.

99. Rollens, "Kingdom of God," 235.

100. Robyn Faith Walsh, *The Origins of Early Christian Literature: Contextualizing the New Testament within Greco-Roman Literary Culture* (Cambridge: Cambridge University Press, 2021).

101. Robyn Faith Walsh, "Q and the 'Big Bang' Theory of Christian Origins," in *Redescribing the Gospel of Mark*, ed. Barry S. Crawford and Merrill P. Miller (Atlanta: SBL Press, 2017), 483–33 (487); *Origins*, 13. Walsh applies the identical model to Q ("'Big Bang' Theory") and the Gospel of Mark (*Origins*) without any differentiation.

102. Walsh, "'Big Bang' Theory," 489–90, 520–22.

103. Walsh, "'Big Bang' Theory," 498; also *Origins*, 55.

authorships Q is a creative work that originates principally in the thoughts and reflections of an autonomous author eclectically nourished by various cultural sources and models, mainly literary, and an interest in Jesus. Perhaps he has some connection to a group of Jesus people, but this is incidental to his literary undertaking—his principal reference group is his literary coterie and network. The social reality that Q projects is an ideological experiment, an imagined community.[104]

The most striking consequence of Walsh's application of the autonomous Greco-Roman authorial model is its all but complete erasure of any entity that might be called a tradition, in all of its culture-formative potency. Inherently it is a literary account from beginning to end. Like her Markan author, Walsh's Q author is a social isolate, composing autonomously in no relationship to any larger project of cultural and social formation. His principal orientation can only be to his present. Memories of John and Jesus as subversives vis-à-vis official Judaism, for instance, are simply convenient symbols for commenting on the post-70 crisis in Judaism.[105] This media model is incapable of detecting the tradition-boundedness of the work, let alone accounting for it. It takes the media binary to the unusual extreme of facing off tradition and authorial literary production against each other as mutually exclusive alternatives.[106] One needs to go back to Wilke and Bruno Bauer to find a similar model for gospel writing.

It is therefore not surprising to find Walsh all but rejecting any constraint from tradition upon the creative literary autonomy of the author. Indeed, on the grounds of missing literary (i.e., Pauline) evidence for a pre-70 tradition oriented to an interest in the figure of Jesus as a biographically noteworthy teacher, she suggests that the profile of Jesus in Q and Mark is in the main the product of post-70 literary invention.[107] The narrow authorial model causes her to lose touch with the cultural phenomenon of tradition altogether, with cultural identity formation among emergent groups, of which tradition cultivation is the base dynamic. One is left wondering how these writings of autonomous authors found any traction, how social movements were even precipitated by them. Similarly conspicuous by its absence is any engagement of Walsh's Greco-Roman literary *Sitz* for the production of gospel literature with Synoptic variation and agreement—that is, how this Greco-Roman authorial model

104. Walsh, "'Big Bang' Theory," 509, 514–15; *Origins*, 131.
105. Walsh, "'Big Bang' Theory," 524.
106. Walsh, *Origins*, 135.
107. Walsh, "'Big Bang' Theory," 488, 517–18, 525.

for Q and Markan origins might explain the observable Synoptic utilization patterns. Like so many ambitious theories of gospel origins it does not engage with the Synoptic profile. In a seminal essay John Kloppenborg showed that the Synoptic patterns of variation and agreement are strikingly out of synch with the literary canons of Greco-Roman authorship.[108] This calls in question the adequacy of this *Sitz* for Q's genesis as a work. Walsh has a clear eye for the defects of the form critics' anonymous creative community as the source for the tradition. But lacking an alternative she substitutes the creative author.

Our differences with Rollens and Walsh are chiefly over their media assumptions and the inability of their approaches to cope with tradition as a tangible cultural phenomenon. That Q is the artifact of a skilled literary and rhetorical enterprise is even more securely nailed down by their analyses. The effect is to further loosen Q, understood as a literary production, from any necessary connection to a so-called Galilean Q community, a development fatefully set in motion by the tremor of John Kloppenborg's 1987 elucidation of Q's literary profile. Walsh's grasp of the defects of the form-critical model upon which the "Q community" association is based doubtless helps explain why she is more primed than Rollens to abandon this connection—though it has to do mainly with her transfer of Q completely into the Greco-Roman sphere of elite literary production. But by virtue of placing the work's origins in the specialized cultural sphere of literary production she injects genres and literary models into the discussion. In turn this brings the question of Q's text-pragmatic function—the ends to which it is calibrated as an instructional genre—to the forefront. The ground now shifts considerably: Q understood as a genre-bound work with a particular function *within* a community rather than a proxy *for* a community. Rollens, on the other hand, with her "peasant intellectuals" analogy has a model in hand much superior to Walsh's in its capacity to size up Q as the literary mediation of a tradition that is culturally and morally formative for networks of Jesus followers. It also maintains Jewish Palestine as its likely place of origins. In this connection she also points to the activity of scribes in its literary instantiation. Rollens sizes Q up for what it in fact is: *a work of Second Temple Judaism*, accordingly to be explained with reference to the literary conventions and tradition-cultivation practices richly attested for Jewish Palestine.

Naturally, Q's connection with "the Galilean Q people" is not about to be abandoned so easily by those who hold to it. A Galilean Q group is indis-

108. Kloppenborg, "Variation," 101, 112, 116–18.

pensable to maintaining Q's "difference" and the revisionist Christian origins reconstructions that are predicated upon it. The final line of defense for contemporary Q scholars of this persuasion (including Rollens) is to invoke Jonathan Reed's arguments for a Galilean Q group and claim that Reed has settled the matter of provenance.

Jonathan Reed's Argument for Galilean Provenance

Reed bases his case on the place names in Q. One observes that references to Jerusalem in the south and to Capernaum, Bethsaida, and Chorazin in the north enjoy equal representation in Q. Likewise, both Jerusalem in the south and the Galilean towns in the north are denounced. Therefore, to the innocent eye Q appears to have an ecumenical perspective on Jewish Palestine. How does Reed nevertheless manage a Galilean Q group centered in Capernaum, Bethsaida, and Chorazin? Q, he claims, views Jerusalem "with suspicion," as "remote," as "a pretentious city . . . spiritually barren" (one hears echoes here of Herder's "haughty Jerusalem"). Q rejects the temple's claim to "house the divine presence." Indeed, Q shows "little awareness of the inner workings of the Temple cult," and it ignores the law.[109] Reed's claim that Jerusalem is a "remote," a "distant" presence on the Q group's social map seems a rather obvious begging of the question. For its part the corollary claim that Jerusalem, temple cult, and the law are "alien" entities is based on the old and tendentious notion of an indigenous Galilean religiosity—in Reed's own words, "a Galilean perspective"—characterized by resistance or indifference to Judean cult ritualism and Judea-based Pharisaic legalism.[110] This, of course, is not to say that these are not problematized by the tradition.

Reed also argues that because the place names Capernaum, Bethsaida, and Chorazin (10:13–15) are (a) redactional, and (b) not products of an imagined narrative world that one would find in a narrative genre, it follows that they represent "the unreflective spatial imagination of the Q community."[111] This

109. Reed, *Archaeology*, 187; "The Sign of Jonah (Q 11:29–32) and Other Epic Traditions in Q," in *Reimagining Christian Origins: A Colloquium Honoring Burton L. Mack*, ed. Elizabeth A. Castelli and Hal Taussig (Valley Forge, PA: Trinity Press International, 1996), 130–43 (137). Galilean Q group advocates rely very heavily on arguments from silence—taking it as a matter of great significance that Q does not refer to "x," "y," or "z."

110. Reed, *Archaeology*, 178, 196. As Christopher Tuckett points out, the Q 13:34–35 oracle seems to envision a glorious return of the speaker to Jerusalem ("Community of Q," 19).

111. Reed, *Archaeology*, 182, also 187.

argument relies on Kloppenborg's theory that Q 10:13–15 is an element of a redactional layer overlaying and obtruding into a formative collection of sayings, and thus unlike the elements of the formative collection not potentially an utterance of Jesus. It will carry little weight for anyone not subscribing to that redaction history. But taken on its own terms the claim that place markers in a sayings collection mark out the geographical horizons of the tradent group is dubious. Besides taking tradition to be the immanent—i.e., "unreflective"—efflux of a social formation, it depends on the genre-purity assumption that narrative framework markers in a sayings collection are intrusive. This assumption likewise informs Reed's belief that Q as a sayings collection would lack reference to an ambient narrative world.[112]

Reed's principal strategy, however, is to sort the place names in Q into a "symbolic map" of three concentric circles. The effect of the superimposition of this map is to relativize Q's non-Galilean place names. He places Capernaum, Bethsaida, and Chorazin in the center circle. These towns have no particular symbolic significance in Jewish epic or prophecy. For Reed it follows that they define the Q group's concrete social world. Into the second circle Reed brings Tyre, Sidon, and Jerusalem, classifying them, that is, as elements of the Q group's *symbolic* world. Different from the Galilean towns, each of these geographically "mid-range" cities carries a symbolic charge in Jewish Scripture and history. By this ingenious means Reed removes Jerusalem from the Q group's concrete world. Into the third circle go Sodom and Nineveh, cities of mythic stature drawn from the Jewish epic tradition. Surveying this map, Reed finds its convergence on Capernaum confirmation of the Q group's locale on the north rim of the lake.[113]

Again, it is difficult to see anyone not predisposed to do so taking this cleverly engineered "symbolic map" as a compelling argument for a Galilean Q group. Kloppenborg rejects it as an artificial imposition, pointing out that Q 10:12–15 "juxtaposes the 'real' cities of Tyre and Sidon (Reed's second circle) with Sodom (the third circle) without making any distinction between them."[114] With the failure of Reed's arguments there are really no grounds remaining for postulating a "Galilean Q people," preaching "salvation through Jesus of Nazareth's words" (Koester).[115] One is, of course, not so naïve as to

---

112. Reed, *Archaeology*, 181.
113. Reed, *Archaeology*, 181–87.
114. Kloppenborg, *Excavating Q*, 174.
115. Koester, "Synoptic Sayings Gospel," 77.

CHAPTER 6

think that the Galilean Q group will disappear—scholarship has too much invested in its existence.[116] But we are now in a position to reopen the question of the place of Q within primitive Christianity—the perennial question of the sayings tradition and the *Urgemeinde*.

EARLY CHRISTIAN JESUS COMMEMORATION AND THE TWO DOCUMENT HYPOTHESIS

Knowledge of ancient media realities and research on cultural practices of commemoration allow us to map the 2DH onto a compelling account of Christian origins and the formation of early Christian cultural identity.

Ambient Field of Tradition

The first step is to be rid of the dichotomy "sayings gospel" and "narrative gospel" and with it the literary-critical and print-culture notion of closed textual boundaries. Q and Mark emerge from a wider matrix, a wider register, of tradition, and they remain permeable to that matrix.[117] At innumerable points the Q materials intersect with and summon up this ambient world of tradition and memory. The partial inventory assembled by Luz suffices to make the point: Jesus calls disciples; he performs healings and exorcisms; his lifestyle contrasts with John's; he is criticized for eating with sinners; he is homeless and itinerant;

---

116. An argument advanced by Milton Moreland illustrates the point: "This observation [no second or third century evidence for a Galilean Jesus movement] has no significant effect on the question of the original provenience of Q. In fact, it is reasonable to argue that the *only* type of Jesus group that makes sense in a Galilean context is something like what we see represented in the Q sayings. If a Jesus or Christos group formed in Galilee, with a similar Christos ideology to those found in the canonical Gospels or Paul's letters, it is probable that we would know of that group from one of our second or third century Christian authors" ("Provenience Studies and the Question of Q in Galilee," in Tiwald, *Q in Context II*, 43–60 [55]). In a word: that we have no evidence of the existence of a Galilean Q group is consistent with its existence. Actually, such evidence as we have of Christianity in Galilee is of Christ-believers and correlates to details in the Gospel of Mark; see Anders Runesson, "Architecture, Conflict, and Identity Formation: Jews and Christians in Capernaum from the First to the Sixth Century," in Zangenberg et al., *Religion, Ethnicity, and Identity in Ancient Galilee*, 231–57 (240–46); also Cilliers Breytenbach, *The Gospel according to Mark as Episodic Narrative*, NovTSup 182 (Leiden: Brill, 2020), especially chap. 5: "Mark and Galilee: Text World and Historical World."

117. Werner H. Kelber, "The Case of the Gospels: Memory's Desire and the Limits of Historical Criticism," *OT* 17 (2002): 55–86 (75).

he is rejected and killed in Jerusalem.[118] To be sure, as Labahn establishes, as an articulated work Q fashions a text-internal world of meaning superbly interpretable in terms of its textual reference points.[119] But, he continues, not only do "Jesus' instructional speeches constitute excerpts from his total ministry and from a wider external world," knowledge of that wider narrative world is indispensable to the recipients' cognition of the sayings-oriented work.[120]

This is only to be expected. Labahn points out that narrative is a universal anthropological category. Narrative is the fundamental means for the cognitive organization of human existence into meaningful patterns, for orienting human existence in time.[121] Along these same lines Samuel Byrskog observes that the notion in New Testament scholarship has been that early Christian memory is a matter of "memorization of isolated items, especially Jesus-sayings." This produced "a strange dichotomy between sayings material and narrative material." In fact, he says, memory is an inherently narrativizing faculty.[122] Community identity is grounded in memory, which means that it is grounded in narrative. A nonnarrative community identity—that is, grounded in sayings—is an oxymoron. A "Q community" without a narrative identity would be an anomaly, existing without a narrative orientation to reality.

In this connection it is noteworthy that the single occurrence of the verb εὐαγγελίζεσθαι in Q is at 7:22—that is, at the point of intersection with narrative elements of the Synoptic tradition, Jesus's healings in particular. As Kloppenborg puts it, Q 7:22 "characterizes Jesus' *discourse* and the *events* attending his ministry as salvific in a manner analogous to what the use of the term εὐαγγέλιον accomplishes in Mark."[123] He aligns this to his view that Q is a "sayings gospel" in the way that Mark is a "narrative gospel." However, it cuts the other direction as well, and in fact better: Q is understood by those who put it together as intersecting crosswise with narrative elements of the "good news." There is an *instructional dimension* to the "good news," a corollary *ethos*.

---

118. Ulrich Luz, "Looking at Q through the Eyes of Matthew," in Foster et al., *New Studies in the Synoptic Problem*, 571–89 (587–88).

119. Labahn, *Gekommene*, 460–61.

120. Labahn, *Gekommene*, 564 (quotation), 567.

121. Labahn, *Gekommene*, 16–17, 135, 160.

122. Samuel Byrskog, "From Memory to Memoirs: Tracing the Background of a Literary Genre," in *The Making of Christianity: Conflicts, Contacts, and Constructions: Essays in Honor of Bengt Holmberg*, ed. M. Zetterholm and S. Byrskog, ConBNT 47 (Winona Lake, IN: Eisenbrauns, 2012), 1–21 (19).

123. Kloppenborg, *Excavating Q*, 405.

Didactic and Narrative Vectors in Synoptic Source Formation

The pronounced instructional profile of the double tradition points us to the genre factor in appraising the circumstances of Q's origins within primitive Christianity. Genre has either been neglected or applied patchily in Q scholarship. It is hard to imagine a more critical neglect. Genre supplies "the generative rules for the production of texts."[124] A work originates within a constellation of genre conventions. Tödt, the godfather of contemporary Q studies, did not conceive Q as having a genre. It was a tradition-mass, a "stratum of tradition," a notion he took over from Bultmann and Dibelius (who themselves had trouble squaring their *Kleinliteratur* model for Q with its genre indicators). For him its ontogenesis was theological; it was the hypostatization of a particular group's Christology, of a second sphere of christological cognition. Subsequent Q scholarship has proceeded by trying to splice genre secondarily into Tödt's tradition-history entity, remaining wholly within the form-critical framework. In their 1971 work, *Trajectories through Early Christianity,* Koester and Robinson perpetuated the form-critical error of connecting a "form," now understood as *Gattung*, generatively with a corresponding *Sitz im Leben*. The different *Sitze* were reconceived as diverse Jesus movements, or "trajectories," each with a different Christology and ethos defined by a corresponding *Gattung*.[125] Mack took this to its extreme, but it is present already as a controlling conception in Dieter Lührmann's 1969 *Redaktion der Logienquelle*.[126] From this conceptual framework comes the notion of a Q community, with Q as its gospel.

The reality is that a community will make use of a range of genres—though to be sure, a particular genre may be emblematic of a subcultural group's ethos. Genres exist as a cultural repertoire that individuals and groups draw upon and combine to accomplish certain social tasks and achieve certain ends that a particular set of genre conventions is calibrated for.[127] There is no exclu-

124. Klaus W. Hempfer, "Generische Allgemeinheitsgrade," in *Handbuch Gattungstheorie,* ed. Rüdiger Zymner (Stuttgart & Weimar: Metzler, 2010), 15–19 (17).

125. James M. Robinson, "*LOGOI SOPHON*: On the Gattung of Q," in *Trajectories,* 71–113. For critique see Schröter, *Erinnerung,* 25–26, 59; also Buss, *Form Criticism,* 26, pointing out that Bultmann's and Dibelius's construal of *Sitz im Leben* as a concrete historical-social setting is a misapplication of Gunkel, for whom the *Sitz im Leben* concept addressed the question, "To what kind of problem is this [form] an answer? . . . What kind of situation would occasion such an expression?"

126. "The question arises whether or not along with the different tendencies of the individual traditions, which are made evident in form-critical analysis of the respective 'Sitz im Leben,' also widely diverse Christologies have shaped the Synoptic tradition" (*Redaktion,* 95).

127. John Frow, *Genre,* 2nd ed. (London: Routledge, 2015), 135.

sive correspondence of a genre with a particular community social setting, that is, *Sitz*, and conversely, diverse genres can be deployed in a single social setting.[128] A genre is a recurrent strategy for bringing about particular social and cultural outcomes. Genre "shapes strategies for occasions; it gets a certain kind of work done . . . it is a 'typified' action."[129] The recurrent form of the genre summons up the recurrent social task, and the corresponding typical social situation, to which it is the strategic response. Viewed in this light the question then becomes: what social and cultural task or tasks do the cluster of genre conventions that are shaping Q fit it for? What social and cultural end is it strategically calibrated to achieve? What tangible social reality is it aimed at bringing into existence?

The answer is that as an instructional genre its pragmatic directionality is toward *ethos inculcation*. A further implication then is that a set of genre conventions will place constraints on a work like Q, making it one kind of a work, and not another, binding it to certain types of content, and not others. Its pragmatic orientation to the ends of norm inculcation should therefore make one wary of inferring more from its genre than warranted. As an instance, it is difficult to see how Q's instructional framework genre, which necessarily centers Jesus as direct speaker, might incorporate a narrative of Jesus's suffering and death. Q cross-references Jesus's death, as Labahn shows.[130] Its elliptical manner of doing so, however, is a consequence of the constraints of the genre.[131] To associate it to a narrative of suffering one would need to incorporate it into a narrative framework genre of the *bios* type. Matthew and Luke oblige us by doing just that, each coming up with his own solution to the formidable technical difficulties thereby posed. Genre constraints likewise explain why Q is thin in pronouncement stories, disputes, and healings and exorcisms, and why its two instances of the latter (7:2–13; 11:14–23) have had their narrative elements curtailed and been converted into discourses.[132] Simon Joseph and Olegs Andrejevs point out that Q in its wisdom profile and pragmatic orientation to formation of a community ethos is closely cognate with other Second Temple instructional works, with *4QInstruction* in

128. Schröter, *Erinnerung*, 25.

129. Frow, *Genre*, 14–15.

130. Labahn, *Gekommene*, 127, 173, 233–34, 572.

131. A point that has been made repeatedly; e.g., Birger A. Pearson, "A Q Community in Galilee?," *NTS* 50 (2004): 476–94 (487); Frenschkowski, "Galiläa oder Jerusalem?," 558.

132. Lucian's *Life of Demonax* can describe the death of the sage only by adopting a *bios* framework genre and rendering the instructional materials in chreiic (i.e., narrative) format, thereby maintaining third-person reference to the hero.

particular.[133] Q belongs among an attested subset of Second Temple Jewish didactic writings.

Here our genre-based line of analysis begins to connect up promisingly with the Synoptic problem, and with the 2DH in particular. Sandra Hübenthal remarks on the oft-noticed oddity that the Gospel of Mark makes frequent reference to Jesus as διδάσκαλος, to his teaching activity, and to reactions stirred up by his διδαχή, but recounts very few of the "many things" (6:34) that he taught (διδάσκειν αὐτοὺς πολλά). Mark presents Jesus's teaching activities (*Lehrtätigkeit*), she observes, strictly in an episodic, narrative (*erzählerisch*) mode.[134] The didactic elements that Mark does contain are shaped to the narrative line, and they are frequently chreiic in form. Mark throws the opening line of his Mission Instruction into indirect speech (Mark 6:8–9), thereby grafting it into the narrative ductus. He selects elements from the sayings and chreiic tradition, such as the Beelzebul Accusation (3:22–30) and the ritual purity controversy (7:1–13), that lend themselves to integration into his narrative arc of escalating conflict.[135]

The contrast with Q—as sparse in narrative elements, pronouncement stories, and healing stories as Mark is replete with them; as dense in didactic elements as Mark is scarce in them—is too symmetrical to be coincidence. We are in touch here with a *narrative vector* and a *didactic vector* in Synoptic source formation, vectors that we can extrapolate back to the origins of the tradition in the commemorative practices of primitive Christianity. We are in touch with a dynamic of cultural memory formation that the 2DH uniquely is able to elucidate, for this dynamic ramifies out into Synoptic source utilization.

Jesus Commemoration, Synoptic Source Formation, and the 2DH

Q and the Gospel of Mark are, respectively, the downstream artifacts of the dual didactic and narrative impulses in primitive Christianity's commemoration of Jesus. Mark's extended narrative project circa AD 70 builds around a core Passion narrative, the formation of which occurred in narrative practices connected with early, eucharistic-type ritual settings commemorating Jesus's shocking, violent death by crucifixion.[136] It takes shape as the master

133. Joseph, "Quest," 124; Olegs Andrejevs, *Apocalypticism in the Synoptic Sayings Source*, WUNT 499 (Tübingen: Mohr Siebeck, 2019), 55–56.
134. Hübenthal, *Markusevangelium*, 181, 261.
135. Dibelius, *Formgeschichte*, 226–27, 260–62.
136. Adela Yarbro Collins, "The Composition of the Passion Narrative in Mark," *STRev*

commemorative narrative—the essential *Grunderzählung*—that is formative of primitive Christian cultural (or better, subcultural) identity.[137] In this commemoration historical reality, cognitive processes of memory and narrative formation converge in an urgent hermeneutical project of working out the *significance* of Jesus's crucifixion, to this end drawing upon the rich semantic resources available within ancient Judaism's cultural register.[138]

But commemoration is also a *normative* enterprise. The commemorated past has an indelible moral complexion. In particular, the deaths of significant persons give rise to commemorative activities concentrated upon the moral vision these individuals embodied in life and to which they bore witness in their death. Martyrs, by definition heroic individuals who have displayed steadfast commitment—to the death—to a set of emblematic virtues, engender intense cults of commemoration. The martyr's death itself is instrumental in establishing the urgent normative claims of the moral vision he or she embodied and died exemplifying, and in mobilizing a movement cohering around those norms.[139] Ritual contexts of narrative commemoration therefore will also be sites of norm inculcation.[140] Though precipitated out in different genres, narrative and normative vectors are indivisibly elements—the x and y axes—of a unitary commemorative enterprise. Q as a downstream written

---

36 (1992): 57–77 (76–77); Joel B. Green, *The Death of Jesus: Tradition and Interpretation in the Passion Narrative*, WUNT 33 (Tübingen: Mohr Siebeck, 1988), 215.

137. Hübenthal, *Markusevangelium*, 454. The term "master commemorative narrative" is Yael Zerubavel's; see *Recovered Roots: Collective Memory and the Making of Israeli National Tradition* (Chicago: University of Chicago Press, 1995), 4–9.

138. For a detailed study of this dynamic see Alan Kirk, *Memory and the Jesus Tradition*, RJFTC 2 (New York: Bloomsbury, 2018), especially chap. 5, "The Formation of the Synoptic Tradition: Cognitive and Cultural Approaches to an Old Problem"; chap. 9, "The Memory of Violence and the Death of Jesus in Q"; and chap. 11, "Cognition, Commemoration, and Tradition: Memory and the Historiography of Jesus Research."

139. Assmann, *Gedächtnis*, 16–17, 76, 141–42; *Religion und kulturelles Gedächtnis: Zehn Studien* (Munich: Beck, 2000), 127–28; Zerubavel, *Recovered Roots*, 148; Maurice Halbwachs, *On Collective Memory*, ed. and trans. Lewis A. Coser (Chicago: University of Chicago Press, 1992), 59.

140. One example in a large literature: Chang-tai Hung, "The Cult of the Red Martyr: The Politics of Commemoration in China," *Journal of Contemporary History* 43 (2008): 279–304. The cult of the red martyr "was created . . . to legitimize armed conflict as means of fighting enemies; to comfort the bereaved and help them cope with personal loss; to help heal collective psychic wounds; and . . . *to educate future generations*" (282, emphasis added). It was a manifestation of the "cult of the fallen soldier," which "turned dead soldiers into martyrs, making them objects of national worship and transforming sacrifice in battle into *a great didactic exercise* to forge national cohesion" (302, emphasis added).

artifact therefore has its origins in the normative impulses that coexisted with narrative impulses in primitive Christian commemoration of Jesus's death.

The channeling of the commemorative impulse into narrative and normative vectors and the corresponding genres is a recurrent cross-cultural phenomenon. A case in point is the various collections of "Sayings of Imam Hussein," grandson of Muhammad and the Shi'ite martyr of Karbala, whose murder at the hands of the Umayyad tyrant Yazid is commemorated in the annual Shi'ite festival the Mourning of Muharram. In his book on commemoration of the Twelve Imams in Shi'ism, Matthew Pierce describes the symbiotic relationship between "collections of sayings and teachings of the imams" and their early sacred biographies, the latter genre incorporating elements of the former, "rearranging them into a birth-to-death chronology that removed from them legal questions and placed them in the realm of history."[141] The "little red book" containing the quotations of Mao Zedong, propagated by Mao and the Communist Party during the Cultural Revolution to displace Confucianism as the normative basis for Chinese society, was a crucial element of the cult of Mao alongside Mao narrative hagiography, for example the heroic Long March.[142] The genres transmitting the tradition of the Ba'al Shem Tov (the "Besht"), the eighteenth-century founder of Hasidism, include a hagiographical collection of 250 anecdotes and "sayings quoted in the name of the Besht in the books [of his disciple] Jacob Joseph."[143] It is uniquely the virtue of the 2DH that it aligns with these cultural dynamics. Synoptic scholarship's disciplinary isolation in biblical and theological studies has been a hindrance to its benefiting from these comparative resources.

The normative enterprise of cultivating instructional traditions proceeds in tandem with early narrative practices behind the formation of the Passion narrative. The Gospel of Mark, taken as a work, is a distinct cultural project: a strategic reaction at the generational turning point to the passing of the cohort of the living carriers of memory, which precipitates an acute memory crisis: the dissolution of constitutive memories and with it the dissolution of the social movement for which those memories supply the cohesion. The crisis issues in a programmatic shift to the written medium and the consolidation of

141. Matthew Pierce, *Twelve Infallible Men: The Imams and the Making of Shi'ism* (Cambridge, MA: Harvard University Press, 2016), 18.
142. See Barbara Mittler, *A Continuous Revolution: Making Sense of Cultural Revolution Culture*, Harvard East Asia Monographs 343 (Cambridge, MA: Harvard University Press, 2012), 173, 187–97, 249–54.
143. Moshe Rosman, *Founder of Hasidism: A Quest for the Historical Ba'al Shem Tov*, 2nd ed. (Oxford: Littmann Library of Jewish Civilization, 2013), xxv.

the dispersed episodic tradition into a narrative sequence, issuing in the written gospel artifact, which provides the basis for reconstituting memory and for the cross-generational reproduction of cultural identity.[144] Prior to this, Hübenthal says, "the individual episodes formed an unconnected narrative net as regards temporality and structure."[145] The episodic, i.e., apophthegma, tradition formed separately from the Passion narrative, in the distillation of remembered historical realities out into their christological and moral essentials, that is, to the elements salient to the identity of commemorating community, to constituting its moral and symbolic world.[146]

As C. H. Weisse observed long ago, the Passion story—as the primordial gospel narrative pattern—provides the orientation point for Mark's comprehensive narrative, for his arrangement of the episodic tradition into a more or less connected narrative arc.[147] As Hübenthal puts it, the Passion narrative acts "retroactively" back upon Mark's alignments of the episodic materials.[148] It could not be otherwise. Eucharistic commemoration constituted the ritual actualization of the social and cultural identity of the new community, an identity that—just as with Jewish identity and the Passover narrative—is symbolically refracted through the corresponding narrative. As the quintessential primitive narrative pattern, the Passion is the magnetic pole pulling the apophthegma tradition into its narrative alignment.

This explains why a connected-up narrative of the activities, of the ministry, of Jesus, would not have appeared prior to its being formulated by the first evangelist. The general course and turning points of Jesus's ministry would have been known, and its geographical theaters. But all that would have been of consequence for the moral and christological formation of the believers would have been the individual episodes: healings, pronouncement stories, and the like. It matters little for the inculcation of community identity that Jesus entered a synagogue and taught on the second Sabbath after the first, or whether he called the first disciples after the Nazareth rejection or before. Only with the composition of a gospel does the exigency present itself of sorting these materials into a more or less cohering narrative order. As a matter of inevitability, therefore, the evangelist's narrative project would be oriented to the master commemorative narrative, the Passion.

144. Assmann, *Gedächtnis*, 11, 50, 218–21; *Religion und kulturelles Gedächtnis*, 29, 53–54; Hübenthal, *Reading Mark's Gospel*, 172–78, 510–12.

145. Hübenthal, *Reading Mark's Gospel*, 185, 511.

146. For discussion see Kirk, *Memory and the Jesus Tradition*, especially chaps. 5 and 11.

147. See Weisse, *Geschichte*, 1:16–22.

148. Hübenthal, *Reading Mark's Gospel*, 221.

In this connection we recollect from chapter five that Mark's hard-won narrative solution to this crisis of cultural identity is a case of what art histo- rian George Kubler calls an "entrance" of an innovative cultural form, which in turn initiates a sequence of further developments out of the potentialities of the form. "A work of art," he says, "is not only the residue of an event but it is its own signal, directly moving other makers to repeat or improve its solu- tion."[149] This dynamic exhausts its momentum in the Gospel of John, where the elements of the Passion narrative—and the sacramental elements them- selves—are now diffused throughout the entire account of Jesus's ministry in chapters 2–11, effectively turning the entire gospel into an extended Passion narrative. In the Gospel of John the project inaugurated by the Markan cultural *novum* rapidly reaches the endpoint of its immanent potentiality for develop- ment. This accounts for why second-century gospels seem either derivative or reactive. As Hübenthal points out, the programmatic proportions of Mark's cultural memory project, and its nature as a written consolidation of an oral gospel proclamation, make it "almost perforce a new *Gattung*."[150] Doubtless Mark does not write without influence from genre patterns circulating in the surrounding culture—for example, the Greco-Roman *bios*—but to take the evangelist as a Greco-Roman author setting out to write a *bios* of his subject in the manner of a Plutarch is to fail to grasp the urgent cultural exigencies that are converging to originate and drive his project.[151]

Matthew's and Luke's subsequent consolidation of the instructional tradi- tion with the narrative gospel form is the natural further development of this cultural-identity enterprise. As Hübenthal establishes, the exigency at the crisis generational turning point is to provide a durable narrative basis for Christian identity, thus a Mark-like project that binds the Passion narrative with the loose episodic tradition in the written medium. But the Gospel of Mark every- where signals its cognizance of the διδαχή dimension of the commemoration of Jesus, of his identity as διδάσκαλος, which cuts across the narrative at points

149. Kubler, *Shape of Time*, 5–7, 19 (quotation), 30–34, 57, 79–80.

150. Hübenthal, *Markusevangelium*, 455–56.

151. On the present retreat of the once-dominant *bios* genre model for Mark see various of the essays in Robert Matthew Calhoun, David P. Moessner, and Tobias Nicklas, eds., *Mod- ern and Ancient Literary Criticism of the Gospels: Continuing the Debate on Gospel Genre(s)*, WUNT 451 (Tübingen: Mohr Siebeck, 2020), for example, Elizabeth E. Shively, "Critique of Richard Burridge's Genre Theory: From a One-Dimensional to a Multi-Dimensional Approach to Gospel Genre," 97–112; Werner H. Kelber, "On Mastering Genre," 57–76. See also Elizabeth Shively, "The Eclipse of the Markan Narrative: On the (Re)cognition of a Coherent Story and Implications for Genre," *EC* 12 (2021): 369–87.

as numerous as the crosswise references in the Q materials to a wider narrative tradition. These gaps (*Leerstellen*) in Mark prime the gospel for a subsequent consolidation of the parallel commemorative traditions, the narrative and the instructional.[152] Put differently, Synoptic source utilization, Matthew's and Luke's independent integration of the Q materials into the Markan narrative baseline, is a dynamic project of *cultural memory consolidation* of normative tradition.[153] The 2DH is a virtuous hypothesis. The 2DH scenario is wholly intelligible when viewed in the light of the early Christian commemorative enterprise, its corresponding practices, and its conceivable lines of development. It allows us to find our way back to the forge of early Christian memory.

Q AND THE PRIMITIVE COMMUNITY

Q Origins in the Early Jerusalem Community

We are back perforce to the question of the sayings tradition and the "primitive community" (*Urgemeinde*). Simon Joseph shows that in the profile and disposition of its materials, in its leading motifs, and in its ritual incorporative function Q's closest relatives are Second Temple sectarian works such as CD and *4QInstruction*. The social matrix of Q's origins is Judean sectarianism. Like these other works its text-pragmatic function is the formation of a particular subcultural, i.e., particularistic, identity. Its problematization of the temple and the temple establishment is likewise intelligible within the framework of Judean movements and in fact "remarkably similar to the position taken at Qumran, where the community regarded itself as having already replaced the Temple."[154] Q's cultural and social resonance with Judean particularism is congruent with origins in the early Jerusalem community. The evidence we have in fact confirms the existence of a close connection between the Je-

---

152. Hübenthal, *Markusevangelium*, 181 n. 64.

153. Mark's narrative orientation to conflict and to Jesus's suffering naturally limits the extent and sorts of paraenetic materials he thinks he can incorporate. Matthew solves this problem by making Jesus a rabbi and creating extensive teaching sequences. Luke solves it with a travel narrative device, which as a teaching and discipleship vehicle is oriented to the culminating event of Jesus's martyrdom on the cross. The circumstances of the written consolidation of instructional tradition in Q as a work are unclear. Some light may be cast on this in our later discussion of the pragmatic effects of the work—i.e., how it operates.

154. Joseph, *Jesus*, 31, 84 (quotation), 89, 150; also Andrejevs, *Apocalypticism*, 73. For analysis of how the *topoi* sequence in Q 3–6 conforms to the conventions of Jewish wisdom texts see Alan Kirk, "Some Compositional Conventions of Hellenistic Wisdom Texts and the Juxtaposition of 4:1–13; 6:20b–49; and 7:1–10 in Q," *JBL* 116 (1997): 235–57.

rusalem church and the Galilean Jesus tradition. Galatians 1–2 corroborates the information of Acts 1–2 that the bearers of the Galilean tradition—Jesus's Galilean disciples and his Nazareth kin—are its charter members and leaders.[155] In addition, Christopher Tuckett points out that Q's Jewish-Christian complexion, in particular its interest in upholding the practice of the law, "fits . . . with the picture one has from Paul's letters (and Acts) of the Jerusalem Christian church as self-consciously Torah-observant."[156] These considerations support Q's provenance in the Jerusalem church.

Q's scribal profile also accords with Judean provenance. We saw that the Galilean-village-scribes theory was an adjustment to the recognition that Q's relatively learned literary form and its decent Greek made it an awkward fit with a tradent group of "itinerant radicals" missionizing in Aramaic-speaking Galilee. The consequence, however, was to reduce Q to a solipsistic work of Galilean village administrators nursing their bureaucratic resentments. The recognition that even with this adjustment Q composition exceeded the capabilities of village clerks induced advocates of village scribes provenance to expand the category to include urban administrators, intellectuals, grammarians, scholars, and the like, effectively attributing Q to Greek-capable scribal sub-elites, a trans-local cohort found throughout the eastern Mediterranean. In Jewish Palestine the existence of a scribal cohort of this sort is securely attested for Judea and Jerusalem and for subgroups like Qumran that questioned the legitimacy of the current Temple hierarchy and viewed contemporary events through apocalyptic lenses.[157] In Jewish Palestine the cultivation of literature in Greek was, in Michael Wise's words, "inherently and intentionally elitist."[158] Q's literary framers, that is, are to be found among Richard Horsley's dissident scribes, loyal to nationalistic traditions, and with affinities to apocalyptically charged programs.[159]

In short, if a Jewish Palestinian provenance is to be sought for Q, the indicators converge on Jerusalem.[160] It is in Jerusalem that one finds bilingual

---

155. Ernst Lohmeyer, *Galiläa und Jerusalem* (Göttingen: Vandenhoeck & Ruprecht, 1936), 82–83, 90; Bultmann, *Theology*, 52–53 ("representatives of the Galilean tradition").

156. Tuckett, "Community of Q," 24; see also Marcus Tiwald, *Commentary on Q* (Stuttgart: Kohlhammer, 2020), noting that "in Q there is no contrast between Jesus and Torah" (25).

157. Full analysis in Kirk, "Who Were the Q Scribes?"

158. Michael Owen Wise, *Language and Literacy in Roman Judaea: A Study of the Bar Kokhba Documents*, AYBRL (New Haven, CT: Yale University Press, 2015), 336.

159. See Richard A. Horsley, *Revolt of the Scribes: Resistance and Apocalyptic Origins* (Minneapolis: Fortress, 2010), 3–4, 15, 197–98; also Andrejevs, *Apocalypticism*, 215.

160. Similarly Joseph, *Jesus*, 82–86; "Quest," 111; also Tuckett, "Community of Q," 23; Pearson, "Q Community," 492.

population sectors and capably bilingual scribes that like their counterparts in the Egyptian *metropoleis* were fiercely loyal to national traditions. In Jerusalem one also finds a city deeply networked into the Diaspora communities, a city where, in Fergus Millar's words, "visitors or long-term immigrants, including proselytes . . . encountered a Jewish society . . . which was less unlike a Diaspora community than we might have supposed."[161] Q's existence in Greek and its emergence in Diaspora-networked Jerusalem point to its being the artifact of a movement that has begun to open out onto the cosmopolitan Greco-Roman world. In Q we see these unknown scribes carrying out a momentous cultural and media conversion: mediating the normative moral tradition of a Galilean, Aramaic-speaking movement into the wider Greco-Roman cosmopolitan world. Q constitutes a scribally brokered, complex media conversion of that tradition into a not unsophisticated literary artifact.

This again connects directly to the 2DH. It explains with simplicity how Q comes to be diffused along early Christian social networks throughout the eastern Mediterranean such that it comes to be received independently by the Matthean and Lukan evangelists, within Jewish-Christian and Pauline Gentile churches, respectively. Explaining Q's reception by Matthew and Luke has always presented a puzzle for scholars of the "Galilean Q community" persuasion, for whom it is axiomatic that Q is the charter expression of a socially autonomous, theologically alien, and isolated Jesus movement. The stubborn empirical reality of Matthew's and Luke's full incorporation of the work and its evident normativity for both of them is a standing challenge to this view. It forces those who hold it—and who choose not to gloss over the difficulty—back upon aetiological tales of "suppression" or "domestication" of simple Q Christianity by hegemonic kerygmatic Christianity.[162] In antiquity a work was propagated, however, along social networks constituted of close personal relationships (*se fait en "circuit fermé"*).[163] This reality accords with

161. Fergus Millar, "Jerusalem and the Near Eastern Diaspora in the Early Imperial Period," *SCI* 33 (2014): 139–54 (153).

162. E.g., James M. Robinson, "The Matthean Trajectory from Q to Mark," in *Ancient and Modern Perspectives on the Bible and Culture: Essays in Honor of Hans Dieter Betz*, ed. Adela Yarbro Collins (Atlanta: Scholars Press, 1998), 122–55 (124–25, 129, 132, 145). Bultmann also struggled to explain why the syncretistic "Hellenistic" churches took over the "Palestinian" didactic tradition as an addendum to their *kyrios* cult. He finally just issues one of his dicta: Jesus "*obviously* would have to be made . . . a διδάσκαλος to Gentile Christians, in spite of his primary cultic significance" (*History*, 369, emphasis added).

163. Catherine Salles, *Lire à Rome* (Paris: Les Belles Lettres, 1992), 156; also Raymond J. Starr, "The Circulation of Literary Texts in the Roman World," *ClQ* 37 (1987): 213–23; Loveday Alexander, "Ancient Book Production and the Circulation of the Gospels," in *The*

Q provenance in the Jerusalem community, with its open Diaspora networks, with its connections to the Antioch church, the Antioch church in turn with the churches of the Pauline mission.[164] It accounts economically for its reception by Matthew and Luke, representative of Jewish Christianity and Pauline Christianity, respectively. It invites us to take a rather different view of Christian origins than the one projected by the "Galilean Q people" scenario.

Q's Identity-Formation Project in the Jerusalem Community

Q is gripped by conviction of eschatological crisis, of an inbreaking eschatological reality that radically reconditions existence, that therefore takes tangible social form in a new ethos. This inbreaking eschatological reality breaks down normal temporal boundaries between present and future; thus it redefines present existence totally. It means that the social existence of Jesus followers has a fundamentally different quality from those who are simply existing in the present world, for whom the future is not present other than as a vague uncertainty. Q is the artifact of a concerted effort toward tangible social actualization of this new eschatological reality, this new mode of existence, in its ethical dimension.

Q's instructional genre, and especially its active element the deliberative speech, is calibrated toward achieving this effect, toward bringing this new social and moral reality into embodied existence in those toward whom it is directed. It shares in the sectarian apocalyptic outlook that conceives the cosmos "as a domain of anomie and lawlessness, thus lending itself to constructive identity formation."[165] Q's paraenetic genre configurations are strategies for the transformation of identity through norm-inculcation.[166] The origins of this project lie in commemoration of Jesus's proclamation of the kingdom in its ethical dimension. Q is the artifact of the memory of Jesus as the proclaimer of a new social and moral reality, with its dominant symbol the kingdom of God. It aims at instantiating that memory through a program of transformation of the ethos of its addressees.

Gospels for All Christians: Rethinking the Gospel Audiences, ed. Richard Bauckham (Grand Rapids: Eerdmans, 1998), 71–111 (104).

164. Joseph, Jesus, 83–84.

165. Andrejevs, Apocalypticism, 53.

166. See Benjamin G. Wright III, "Joining the Club: A Suggestion about Genre in Early Jewish Texts," DSD 17 (2010): 289–314 (298–99); Kloppenborg, Excavating Q, 197; Labahn, Gekommene, 88–89.

This program commences right away, in the sharply disorienting effects of John's threshold address to the "brood of vipers." By obliterating their status as children of Abraham, John detaches them from their previously secure social position, defined by covenant, election, and birth. The point of such verbal beating down, such radical questioning of supposedly secure status positions, is to render the work's projected recipients *prima materia* out of which may be fashioned persons reintegrated into the new social and moral order that the Q materials project.[167] Form critically, John's address is paraenetic and protreptic: a "scolding word" (*Scheltwort*), followed by a double admonition, creating a deliberative discourse intended to move its addressees to decisive moral action. It is an instance of an instructional convention, widely attested in wisdom literature of the ancient Mediterranean world, of an instructor who assumes a threatening demeanor to arrest the attention of complacent, wayward students, disabuse them of their delusions, and motivate them to attach themselves to a wise instructor able to impart to them the wisdom requisite for a successful life. It is the dismantling operation that is propaedeutic to the reconstruction project.[168] Notably, at Q 6:40 stands the conventional invitation of the sage to the unlearned to discipleship, holding out the promise of the corresponding transformation of status. Appropriately it stands at the center of Q's threshold discourse like a gateway to the alternative moral and symbolic universe that opens out in Q.[169] We see that its opening section enacts a conventional protreptic sequence. Its intent is to secure participation in this new moral, social, and soteriological reality.

The opening sequence stirs up the sharp debate about covenant, Torah observance, and the boundary markers of the true Israel, confirming that the

167. For detailed discussion see Alan Kirk, "Crossing the Boundary: Liminality and Transformative Wisdom in Q," *NTS* 45 (1999): 1–18, with particular reference to Victor Turner, *The Ritual Process: Structure and Anti-Structure* (Chicago: Aldine, 1969), 95; "Variations on a Theme of Liminality," in *Secular Ritual*, ed. Sally F. Moor and Barbara G. Myerhoff (Amsterdam: van Gorcum, 1977), 36–52; Leo G. Perdue, "Liminality as a Social Setting for Wisdom Instructions," *ZAW* 93 (1981): 114–26; "The Social Character of Paraenesis and Paraenetic Literature," in *Paraenesis: Act and Form*, ed. Leo G. Perdue and John J. Gammie, Semeia 50 (Atlanta: Scholars Press, 1990), 5–39.

168. Elisabeth Sevenich-Bax, *Israels Konfrontation mit dem letzten Boten der Weisheit*, MThA 21 (Altenberge: Oros, 1993), 291–92, 298–99. For analysis see Alan Kirk, "Upbraiding Wisdom: John's Speech and the Beginning of Q," *NovT* 40 (1998): 1–16; "Crossing the Boundary."

169. See Leo G. Perdue, "The Wisdom Sayings of Jesus," *Forum* 2.3 (1986): 3–35 (20); Hans Dieter Betz, *The Sermon on the Mount*, Hermeneia (Minneapolis: Fortress, 1995), 622–25.

social and cultural setting for the work is Second Temple Jewish sectarianism. Q's affinities are to Second Temple movements that combine a particularistic definition of covenant boundary requirements with a prescriptive way of life grounded in a distinct interpretation of Torah. It was characteristic of Second Temple parties to reject the adequacy of birth as a criterion for drawing covenant boundaries and to shift focus to obedience in accordance with a set of ethical precepts and purity rules drawn from particularistic Torah interpretation. Incorporation into the true covenant community constitutes movement and transformation within corporate Israel as people respond to sectarian protreptic and paraenesis.[170]

Against a backdrop of coming wrath John's address draws a map of covenant boundaries based upon rejection of the adequacy of Abrahamic descent, instead emphasizing repentance, obedience, and a particular eschatological agent. Shortly thereafter follows Jesus's Inaugural Sermon (6:20b–49), a sapiential epitome of the law.[171] Joseph puts matters succinctly: "Q provides us with a classic example of nascent sectarian identity formation. It defines who belongs to 'Israel' (Q 3:8; 13:29, 28; 13:30; 14:11; 14:16–23); polarizes its self-definition (Q 11:23); criticizes other Jews (Q 11:42, 30b, 43–44, 46b, 52, 47–48) . . . pronounces judgment on Israel (Q 13:34–35); intensifies its practice of Mosaic law (Q 16:18) . . . [requires] renouncing family ties in order to join the new family of Jesus people (Q 12:53) . . . and . . . exalt[s] Jesus to the status of the son of God (Q 10:22)."[172] Q's genre configuration primes it to carry out this ritual incorporative operation, to make the social vision that it projects a social reality.

We are back full circle to Bultmann's association of the sayings source with the Jerusalem community and his positioning of the eschatological congregation within Jewish sectarianism.[173] Where Bultmann erred was in denying to the

170. Ellen Juhl Christiansen, *The Covenant in Judaism and Paul: A Study of Ritual Boundaries as Identity Markers*, AGJU 27 (Leiden: Brill, 1995), 108, 143–44; also Andrejevs, *Apocalypticism*, 215.

171. Kirk, "Compositional Conventions," 235–57.

172. Joseph, *Jesus*, 89. For a compelling statement on Q's sectarian ethos grounded in intensified Torah interpretation, see Andrejevs, *Apocalypticism*, 208–9.

173. Bultmann, *Theology*, 37. The possibility of a Q provenance in the Antioch church can be entertained, if it is a matter of the origins of Q as a *work*, as opposed to the instructional enterprise from which it issues, the origins of which lie in the very earliest Jesus commemoration. In addition to being Greek-speaking the Antioch community was closely networked with Jerusalem-based Jewish Christianity on the one side and Gentile Christianity on the other, which accounts efficiently for Q's diffusion and independent reception by the Matthean and Lukan evangelists. That Q's formative cultural environment is Jewish sectarianism is simply a commentary on the socio-cultural origins of early Christianity,

primitive community intense narrative identity-formation activity, throwing the latter to the remote terminus of his *religionsgeschichtliche* trajectory. Primitive Jesus commemoration has a narrative dimension as surely as it has a normative dimension. Notwithstanding its later Markan redactional workup, the Passion narrative in fact contains a number of indicators, catalogued by Gerd Theissen, of early origins in the narrative practices in the Jerusalem community.[174] This confirms what cultural-memory theory would predict: the emergence of a master commemorative narrative is as basic to the formation of a community identity as the normative project of inculcating the corresponding ethos.

These dual elements, the narrative and the normative, are both of them inherent in the commemoration of Jesus in his violent death by crucifixion. The Passion narrative emerges as the baseline cultural narrative through which the community's identity is focalized; the normative enterprise inculcates the corresponding ethos. That Jesus died a violent death as a martyr opens up the soteriological dimension of early Jesus commemoration. The reception of the pre-Pauline kerygmatic formula in 1 Corinthians 15:3 that Christ died "for our sins" attests to the soteriological thrust of primitive Jesus commemoration. What we might reasonably identify as the Jerusalem-Antioch kerygma cannot be simply identified with the Pauline kerygma, but neither is the distinction between them to be exaggerated.

For our purposes the point is this: the Q traditions, and then further on Q as a work, flow from the normative dimension of early Christian commemoration of Jesus occurring along the Jerusalem-Antioch axis that is attested in Galatians 1–2. This project exists in symbiosis with the narrative impulse that has generated the Passion narrative and its cognate kerygmas. Though the christological focalization and sociocultural contextualization of Q and Mark, respectively, are anything but identical, the normative and narrative elements of primitive Christian commemoration are not capable of being prised apart. The "Q community" turns out to be the Jerusalem *Urgemeinde* and those in its radiating range of influence, just as the nineteenth-century source critics surmised.[175]

The two document hypothesis was birthed from the concerted nineteenth-century effort to recover the origins of the Synoptic tradition in the memory of

---

a rapidly propagating movement of Second Temple Judaism. To decide between Jerusalem or Antioch is not important. One can think of it emerging along the Jerusalem-Antioch axis.

174. Theissen, *Gospels in Context*, 179–83, 189; see also Green, *Death of Jesus*, 162–63.

175. For similar reflections see Joseph, "Quest," 101–2.

Jesus. The Gospel of Mark and Q are the downstream artifacts of the narrative and normative impulses of earliest Jesus commemoration. Uniquely the 2DH is able to lead us back to the primitive beginnings of the formation of Christian cultural memory in the early community, to the complex cultural and cognitive conversion of memories of Jesus into the observable instructional and narrative elements of the tradition. Progress in understanding cultural processes of commemoration in the convergence of cognitive, cultural, and social dimensions of memory puts in our reach the solution to the vexed memory-tradition nexus problem. With lines of inquiry reoriented away from "the Galilean Q community," the 2DH opens out to the wider questions of Christian origins, recovering its position as the essential support for generating elegant accounts of the early history of the Jesus movement and its development. The Synoptic problem finds its natural place as the principal avenue of approach to questions of Christian origins and the historical Jesus.

Bibliography

Alexander, Loveday. "Ancient Book Production and the Circulation of the Gospels." Pages 71–111 in *The Gospels for All Christians: Rethinking the Gospel Audiences*. Edited by Richard Bauckham. Grand Rapids: Eerdmans, 1998.

Andrejevs, Olegs. *Apocalypticism in the Synoptic Sayings Source*. WUNT 499. Tübingen: Mohr Siebeck, 2019.

Arnal, William. *Jesus and the Village Scribes: Galilean Conflicts and the Setting of Q*. Minneapolis: Fortress, 2001.

———. "The Q Document." Pages 119–54 in *Jewish Christianity Reconsidered: Rethinking Ancient Groups and Texts*. Edited by Matt Jackson-McCabe. Minneapolis: Fortress, 2007.

———. "The Trouble with Q." *Forum* 2.1 (third series) (2013): 7–77.

Assmann, Jan. *Das kulturelle Gedächtnis: Schrift, Erinnerung und politische Identität in frühen Hochkulturen*. Munich: Beck, 1992.

———. *Religion und kulturelles Gedächtnis: Zehn Studien*. Munich: Beck, 2000.

Ball, Warwick. *Rome in the East: The Transformation of an Empire*. London: Routledge, 2000.

Barker, James W. "Ancient Compositional Practices and the Gospels: A Reassessment." *JBL* 135 (2016): 109–21.

Bauer, Bruno. *Kritik der evangelischen Geschichte der Synoptiker*. 3 vols. Leipzig: Otto Wiegand, 1841.

Bauer, Walter. *Orthodoxy and Heresy in Earliest Christianity*. Translated by the Philadelphia Seminar on Christian Origins. Miffletown, PA: Sigler, 1996.

Baur, F. C. *Das Markusevangelium nach seinem Ursprung und Charakter, nebst einem Anhang über das Evangelium Marcions*. Tübingen: Fues, 1851.

———. *Kritische Untersuchungen über die kanonischen Evangelien: Ihr Verhältnis zu einander, ihren Charakter und Ursprung*. Tübingen: Fues, 1847.

Bazzana, Giovanni B. *The Kingdom of Bureaucracy: The Political Theology of Village Scribes in the Sayings Gospel Q*. BETL 274. Leuven: Peeters, 2015.

Berlin, Andrea M., and Paul J. Kosmin, eds. *The Middle Maccabees: Archaeology, History, and the Rise of the Hasmonean Kingdom*. Atlanta: SBL Press, 2021.

Betz, Hans Dieter. *The Sermon on the Mount*. Hermeneia. Minneapolis: Fortress, 1995.

Bird, Graeme D. *Multitextuality in the Homeric Iliad: The Witness of the Ptolemaic Papyri*. Hellenic Studies 43. Cambridge, MA: Harvard University Press, 2010.

Bousset, Wilhelm. *Kyrios Christos*. Translated by John E. Steely. Nashville: Abingdon, 1970.

Braun, Willi. "Socio-mythic Invention, Graeco-Roman Schools, and the Sayings Gospel." *MTSR* 11 (1999): 210–35.

Breytenbach, Cilliers. *The Gospel according to Mark as Episodic Narrative*. NovTSup 182. Leiden: Brill, 2020.

Bultmann, Rudolf. *Die Geschichte der synoptischen Tradition*. 4th ed. Göttingen: Vandenhoeck & Ruprecht, 1958.

———. *The History of the Synoptic Tradition*. Translated by John Marsh. Rev. ed. New York: Harper & Row, 1968.

———. *Jesus and the Word*. Translated by Louise Pettibone Smith and Erminie Huntress Lantero. New York: Charles Scribner's Sons, 1958.

———. "The New Approach to the Synoptic Problem." *JR* 6 (1926): 337–62.

———. *Primitive Christianity in Its Contemporary Setting*. Translated by Reginald H. Fuller. Philadelphia: Fortress, 1980.

———. *Theology of the New Testament*. Translated by Kendrick Grobel. New York: Charles Scribner's Sons, 1951.

———. "What the Sayings Source Reveals about the Early Church." Pages 23–34 in *The Shape of Q: Signal Essays on the Sayings Gospel*. Translated and edited by John S. Kloppenborg. Minneapolis: Fortress, 1994. Originally published as "Was lässt die Spruchquelle über die Urgemeinde erkennen." *Oldenburgische Kirchenblatt* 19 (1913): 35–37, 41–44.

Bultmann, Rudolf, and Karl Kundsin. *Form Criticism*. Translated by F. C. Grant. New York: Harper, 1962.

Buss, Martin J. *The Changing Shape of Form Criticism: A Relational Approach*. Sheffield: Sheffield Academic, 2010.

Byrskog, Samuel. "From Memory to Memoirs: Tracing the Background of a Literary Genre." Pages 1–21 in *The Making of Christianity: Conflicts, Contacts, and Constructions: Essays in Honor of Bengt Holmberg*. Edited by M. Zetterholm and S. Byrskog. ConBNT 47. Winona Lake, IN: Eisenbrauns, 2012.

Calhoun, Robert Matthew, David P. Moessner, and Tobias Nicklas, eds. *Modern and Ancient Literary Criticism of the Gospels: Continuing the Debate on Gospel Genre(s)*. WUNT 451. Tübingen: Mohr Siebeck, 2020.

Carlston, Charles E., and Dennis Norlin. "Statistics and Q—Some Further Observations." *NovT* 41 (1999): 108–23.

Chancy, Mark A. *Greco-Roman Culture and the Galilee of Jesus.* SNTS Monograph Series 134. Cambridge: Cambridge University Press, 2005.

Chapman, John. *Matthew, Mark, and Luke: A Study in the Order and Interrelation of the Synoptic Gospels.* London: Longmans and Green, 1937.

Christiansen, Ellen Juhl. *The Covenant in Judaism and Paul: A Study of Ritual Boundaries as Identity Markers.* AGJU 27. Leiden: Brill, 1995.

Collins, Adela Yarbro. "The Composition of the Passion Narrative in Mark." *STRev* 36 (1992): 57–77.

Crawford, Matthew R. "The Diatessaron, Canonical or Non-Canonical? Rereading the Dura Fragment." *NTS* 62 (2016): 253–77.

———. "Rejection at Nazareth in the Gospels of *Mark, Matthew, Luke*—and Tatian." Pages 97–124 in *Connecting Gospels: Beyond the Canonical/Non-Canonical Divide.* Edited by Francis Watson and Sarah Parkhouse. Oxford: Oxford University Press, 2018.

Credner, Karl August. *Einleitung in das Neue Testament.* Halle: Buchhandlung des Waisenhauses, 1836.

Deines, Roland. "Galilee and the Historical Jesus in Recent Research." Pages 11–48 in *Life, Culture, and Society*, vol. 1 of *Galilee in the Late Second Temple and Mishnaic Periods.* Edited by David A. Fiensy and James Riley Strange. Minneapolis: Fortress, 2014.

———. "Jesus the Galilean: Questioning the Function of Galilee in Recent Jesus Research." Pages 53–93 in *Acts of God in History: Studies Towards Recovering a Theological Historiography.* Edited by Christoph Ochs and Peter Watts. WUNT 317. Tübingen: Mohr Siebeck, 2013.

Derrenbacker, Robert A., Jr. *Ancient Compositional Practices and the Synoptic Problem.* BETL 186. Leuven: Leuven University Press; Peeters, 2005.

———. "Greco-Roman Writing Practices and Luke's Gospel: Revisiting 'The Order of a Crank.'" Pages 61–83 in *The Gospels according to Michael Goulder: A North American Response.* Edited by Christopher A. Rollston. Harrisburg, PA: Trinity Press International, 2002.

De Wette, Wilhelm Martin Leberecht. *An Historico-critical Introduction to the Canonical Books of the New Testament.* Translated by Frederick Frothingham. Boston: Crosby & Nichols, 1858.

———. *Lehrbuch der historisch kritischen Einleitung in die Bibel Alten und Neuen Testaments.* Berlin: Reimer, 1826.

———. *Lehrbuch der historisch kritischen Einleitung in die Bibel Alten und Neuen Testaments.* 2nd ed. Berlin: Reimer, 1830.

———. *Lehrbuch der historisch kritischen Einleitung in die Bibel Alten und Neuen Testaments*. 4th ed. Berlin: Reimer, 1842.

Dibelius, Martin. *Die Formgeschichte des Evangeliums*. 6th ed. Tübingen: Mohr Siebeck, 1971.

Downing, F. Gerald. "Disagreements of Each Evangelist with the Minor Close Agreements of the Other Two." *ETL* 80 (2004): 445–69.

———. "A Paradigm Perplex: Luke, Matthew, and Mark." *NTS* 38 (1992): 15–36.

———. "Plausibility, Probability, and Synoptic Hypotheses." *ETL* 93 (2017): 313–37.

———. "Waxing Careless: Poirier, Derrenbacker, and Downing." *JSNT* 35 (2013): 388–93.

Eichhorn, Johann Gottfried, *Einleitung in das Neue Testament*. 2nd ed. 2 vols. Leipzig: Weidmann, 1820.

———. "Ueber die drey ersten Evangelien: einige Beyträge zu ihrer künftigen kritischen Behandlung." Pages 760–996 in *Allgemeine Bibliothek der biblischen Literatur*, vol. 5. Leipzig: Weidmann, 1794.

Eve, Eric. "The Devil in the Detail: Exorcising Q from the Beelzebul Controversy." Pages 16–43 in *Marcan Priority without Q: Explorations in the Farrer Hypothesis*. Edited by John C. Poirier and Jeffrey Peterson. LNTS 455. London: Bloomsbury/T&T Clark, 2015.

———. *Relating the Gospels: Memory, Imitation, and the Farrer Hypothesis*. LNTS 592. London: T&T Clark, 2021.

———. "The Synoptic Problem without Q?" Pages 551–70 in *New Studies in the Synoptic Problem*. Edited by P. Foster, A. Gregory, J. S. Kloppenborg, and J. Verheyden. BETL 239. Leuven: Peeters, 2011.

———. *Writing the Gospels: Composition and Memory*. London: SPCK, 2016.

Ewald, Heinrich. "Ursprung und Wesen der Evangelien." *Jahrbücher der biblischen Wissenschaft* 1 (1848): 113–54; 2 (1849): 180–224.

Farrer, A. M. "On Dispensing with Q." Pages 55–88 in *Studies in the Gospels: Essays in Honour of R. H. Lightfoot*. Edited by D. E. Nineham. Oxford: Blackwell, 1957.

Fascher, Erich. *Die formgeschichtliche Methode: Eine Darstellung und Kritik, zugleich ein Beitrag zur Geschichte des synoptischen Problems*. Gießen: Töpelmann, 1924.

Fiske, Susan T., and Shelley E. Taylor. *Social Cognition*. New York: McGraw Hill, 1984.

Foster, Paul. "Is It Possible to Dispense with Q?" *NovT* 45 (2003): 313–37.

———. "The Rise and Development of the Farrer Hypothesis." Pages 85–128 in *The Q-Hypothesis Unveiled: Theological, Church-Political, Socio-Political, and*

Hermeneutical Issues behind the Sayings Source. Edited by Markus Tiwald. BWANT 225. Stuttgart: Kohlhammer, 2020.

Frenschkowski, Marco. "Galiläa oder Jerusalem? Die topographischen und politischen Hintergründe der Logienquelle." Pages 535–59 in *The Sayings Source Q and the Historical Jesus*. Edited by A. Lindemann. BETL 158. Leuven: Leuven University Press/Peeters, 2001.

———. "Welche biographischen Kenntnisse von Jesus setzt die Logienquelle voraus? Beobachtungen zur Gattung von Q im Kontext antiker Spruchsammlungen." Pages 3–42 in *From Quest to Q: Festschrift James M. Robinson*. Edited by Jón Ma. Ásgeirsson, Kristin de Troyer, and Marvin W. Meyer. BETL 146. Leuven: Leuven University Press/Peeters, 2000.

Frow, John. *Genre*. 2nd ed. London: Routledge, 2015.

Gieseler, Johann Carl Ludwig. *Historisch-kritischer Versuch über die Entstehung und die frühesten Schicksale der schriftlichen Evangelien*. Leipzig: Engelmann, 1818.

———. "Ueber die Entstehung und frühesten Schicksale der schriftlichen Evangelien." Pages 31–87 in *Analekten für das Studien der exegetischen und schematischen Theologie*. Edited by Carl August Gottlieb Keil and Heinrich Gottlieb Tzschirner. 3.1. Leipzig: Johann Ambrosius Barth, 1816.

Goodacre, Mark S. *The Case against Q: Studies in Markan Priority and the Synoptic Problem*. Harrisburg, PA: Trinity Press International, 2002.

———. "Farrer Hypothesis Response." Pages 127–38 in *The Synoptic Problem: Four Views*. Edited by Stanley E. Porter and Bryan R. Dyer. Grand Rapids: Baker, 2016.

———. "Fatigue in the Synoptics." *NTS* 44 (1998): 45–58.

———. *Goulder and the Gospels: An Examination of a New Paradigm*. JSNTSup 133. Sheffield: Sheffield Academic, 1996.

———. "On Choosing and Using Appropriate Analogies: A Response to F. Gerald Downing." *JSNT* 26 (2003): 237–40.

———. "Q, Memory, and Matthew: A Response to Alan Kirk." *JSHJ* 15 (2017): 224–33.

———. "Re-walking the 'Way of the Lord': Luke's Use of Mark and his Reaction to Matthew." Pages 26–43 in *Luke's Literary Creativity*. Edited by Jesper Tang Nielsen and Mogens Müller. LNTS 550. London: Bloomsbury/T&T Clark, 2016.

———. "The Synoptic Jesus and the Celluloid Christ: Solving the Synoptic Problem through Film." *JSNT* 80 (2000): 31–43.

———. *The Synoptic Problem: A Way through the Maze*. London: T&T Clark, 2001.

———. "The Synoptic Problem: John the Baptist and Jesus." Pages 177–92 in *Method and Meaning: Essays on New Testament Introduction in Honor of Harold W. Attridge.* Edited by Andrew B. McGowan. Atlanta: SBL Press, 2011.

———. "Taking Our Leave of Mark-Q Overlaps: Major Agreements and the Farrer Theory." Pages 201–22 in *Gospel Interpretation and the Q-Hypothesis.* Edited by Mogens Müller and Heike Omerzu. LNTS 573. London: T&T Clark, 2018.

———. "Too Good to Be Q: High Verbatim Agreement in the Double Tradition." Pages 82–100 in *Marcan Priority without Q: Explorations in the Farrer Hypothesis.* Edited by John C. Poirier and Jeffrey Peterson. LNTS 455. London: Bloomsbury/T&T Clark, 2015.

———. "What Does *Thomas* Have to Do with Q? The Afterlife of a Sayings Gospel." Pages 81–89 in *Writing the Gospels: A Dialogue with Francis Watson.* Edited by Catherine Sider Hamilton. LNTS 606. London: T&T Clark, 2019.

———. "A World without Q." Pages 174–79 in *Questioning Q: A Multidimensional Critique.* Edited by Mark Goodacre and Nicholas Perrin. Downers Grove, IL: InterVarsity Press, 2004.

Goulder, Michael. "Is Q a Juggernaut?" *JBL* 115 (1996): 667–81.

———. *Luke: A New Paradigm.* 2 vols. JSNTSup 20. Sheffield: JSOT Press, 1989.

———. "Luke's Compositional Options." *NTS* 38 (1993): 150–52.

———. "Luke's Knowledge of Matthew." Pages 143–61 in *Minor Agreements: Symposium Göttingen 1991.* Edited by George Strecker. Göttingen: Vandenhoeck & Ruprecht, 1993.

———. "Michael Goulder Responds." Pages 137–52 in *The Gospels according to Michael Goulder: A North American Response.* Edited by Christopher A. Rollston. Harrisburg, PA: Trinity Press International, 2002.

———. *Midrash and Lection in Matthew.* London: SPCK, 1974.

———. "On Putting Q to the Test." *NTS* 24 (1978): 218–34.

———. "The Order of a Crank." Pages 111–30 in *Synoptic Studies: The Ampleforth Conferences of 1982 and 1983.* Edited by C. M. Tuckett. JSNTSup 7. Sheffield: JSOT Press, 1984.

Graf, David F. "Hellenisation and the Decapolis." *ARAM* 4 (1992): 1–48.

Gratz, Alois, *Neuer Versuch, die Entstehung der drey ersten Evangelien zu erklären.* Tübingen: Fues, 1812.

Green, Joel B. *The Death of Jesus: Tradition and Interpretation in the Passion Narrative.* WUNT 33. Tübingen: Mohr Siebeck, 1988.

Gunkel, Hermann. *Genesis.* Translated by Mark E. Biddle. Macon, GA: Mercer University Press, 1997.

———. "The Literature of Ancient Israel." Pages 26–83 in *Relating to the Text: Interdisciplinary and Form-Critical Insights on the Bible.* Translated by Armin

Siedlecki. Edited by Timothy J. Sandoval, Carleen Mandolfo, and Martin Buss. JSOTSup 384. London: T&T Clark, 2003.

Hägerland, Tobias. "Editorial Fatigue and the Existence of Q." *NTS* 65 (2019): 190–206.

Halbwachs, Maurice. *On Collective Memory*. Translated and edited by Lewis A. Coser. Chicago: University of Chicago Press, 1992.

Harnack, Adolf von. *Sprüche und Reden Jesu*. Beiträge zur Einleitung in das Neue Testament 2. Leipzig: Hinrichs, 1907.

Haupt, Walther. *Worte Jesu und Gemeindeüberlieferung: Eine Untersuchung zur Quellengeschichte der Synopse*. UNT 3. Leipzig: Hinrichs, 1913.

Hempfer, Klaus W. "Generische Allgemeinheitsgrade." Pages 15–19 in *Handbuch Gattungstheorie*. Edited by Rüdiger Zymner. Stuttgart & Weimar: Metzler, 2010.

Herder, Johann Gottfried. "Regel der Zusammenstimmung unsrer Evangelien, aus ihrer Entstehung und Ordnung." Pages 1–68 in *Sämmtliche Werke: Religion und Theologie*, vol. 1. Edited Johann Georg Müller. 1797. Repr., Carlsruhe: Büreau der deutschen Classiker, 1829.

———. "Vom Erlöser der Menschen: nach unsern drei ersten Evangelien." Pages 609–724 in *Johann Gottfried Herder Theologische Schriften; Johann Gottfried Werke*, vol. 9.1. Edited by Christoph Bultmann and Thomas Zippert. 1796–1797. Repr., Frankfurt am Main: Deutsche Klassiker Verlag, 1994.

———. "Von Gottes Sohn, der Welt Heiland: nach Johannes Evangelium." Pages 1–273 in *Christliche Schriften von J. G. Herder. Dritte Sammlung*. Riga: Hartnoch, 1797.

Hilgenfeld, Adolf. *Das Markus-Evangelium nach seiner Composition, seiner Stellung in der Evangelien-Literatur, seinem Ursprung und Charakter*. Leipzig: Breitkopf & Härtel, 1850.

———. *Die Evangelien nach ihrer Entstehung und geschichtlichen Bedeutung*. Leipzig: Hirzel, 1854.

Holtzmann, H. J. *Das messianische Bewusstsein Jesu: Ein Beitrag zur Leben-Jesu-Forschung*. Tübingen: Mohr Siebeck, 1907.

———. *Die synoptischen Evangelien: Ihr Ursprung und geschichtlicher Charakter*. Leipzig: Engelmann, 1863.

———. "Die synoptischen Evangelien nach den Forschungen von Bernhard Weiss." *Protestantische Kirchenzeitung* 24 (1877): 820–27.

———. *Hand-Commentar zum Neuen Testament. Die Synoptiker*. 3rd ed. Tübingen: J. C. B. Mohr (Paul Siebeck), 1901.

———. *Lehrbuch der historisch-kritischen Einleitung in das Neue Testament*. 3rd ed. Freiburg im Breisgau: J. C. B. Mohr (Paul Siebeck), 1892.

———. *Lehrbuch der neutestamentlichen Theologie*. Edited by Adolf Jülicher and Walter Bauer. 2nd ed. Freiburg im Breisgau: J. C. B. Mohr (Paul Siebeck), 1911.

———. "Zur synoptischen Frage." *Jahrbücher für protestantische Theologie* 4 (1878): 328–82, 533–68.

Horsley, Richard A. "The Language(s) of the Kingdom: From Aramaic to Greek, Galilee to Syria, Oral to Oral-Written." Pages 401–25 in *A Wandering Galilean: Essays in Honour of Seán Freyne*. Edited by Zuleika Rogers, Margaret Daly-Denton, and Anne Fitzpatrick-McKinley. Leiden: Brill, 2009.

———. *Revolt of the Scribes: Resistance and Apocalyptic Origins*. Minneapolis: Fortress, 2010.

———. *Whoever Hears You Hears Me: Prophets, Performance, and Tradition in Q*. With Jonathan Draper. Harrisburg, PA: Trinity Press International, 1998.

Hübenthal, Sandra. *Das Markusevangelium als kollektives Gedächtnis*. FRLANT 253. Göttingen: Vandenhoeck & Ruprecht, 2014.

———. *Reading Mark's Gospel as a Text from Collective Memory*. Grand Rapids: Eerdmans, 2020. Translation of *Das Markusevangelium als kollektives Gedächtnis*.

Huggins, Ron. "Q Doesn't Go Away, It Only Changes Shape." Paper presented at the Annual Meeting of the Society of Biblical Literature, San Diego, November 2014.

Hultgren, Stephen. *Narrative Elements in the Double Tradition: A Study of Their Place within the Framework of the Gospel Narrative*. BZNW 113. Berlin: de Gruyter, 2002.

Hung, Chang-tai. "The Cult of the Red Martyr: The Politics of Commemoration in China." *Journal of Contemporary History* 43 (2008): 279–304.

Jacobson, Arland D. *The First Gospel: An Introduction to Q*. Sonoma, CA: Polebridge, 1992.

Jameson, H. G. *Origins of the Synoptic Gospels: A Revision of the Synoptic Problem*. Oxford: Blackwell, 1922.

Joseph, Simon. *Jesus, Q, and the Dead Sea Scrolls: A Judaic Approach to Q*. WUNT 333. Tübingen: Mohr Siebeck, 2012.

———. "The Quest for the 'Community' of Q: Mapping Q within the Social, Scribal, and Textual Landscape(s) of Second Temple Judaism." *HTR* 111 (2018): 90–114.

Jülicher, Adolf. *Einleitung in das Neue Testament*. 5th ed. Tübingen: J. C. B. Mohr (Paul Siebeck), 1906.

———. *An Introduction to the New Testament*. Translated by Janet Penrose Ward. London: Smith and Elder, 1904.

———. *Neue Linien in der Kritik der evangelischen Überlieferung*. Giessen: Topelmann, 1906.

Jülicher, Adolf, and Erich Fascher. *Einleitung in das Neue Testament*. 7th ed. Tübingen: J. C. B. Mohr (Paul Siebeck), 1931.

Kelber, Werner H. "The Case of the Gospels: Memory's Desire and the Limits of Historical Criticism." *OT* 17 (2002): 55–86.

———. *The Oral and the Written Gospel: The Hermeneutics of Speaking and Writing in the Synoptic Tradition, Mark, Paul, and Q*. 1983. Repr., with a new introduction by Werner H. Kelber. Bloomington: Indiana University Press, 1997.

Kirk, Alan. "Crossing the Boundary: Liminality and Transformative Wisdom in Q." *NTS* 45 (1999): 1–18.

———. *Memory and the Jesus Tradition*. RJFTC 2. London: Bloomsbury, 2018.

———. "Memory, Tradition, and Synoptic Sources: The Quest of Holtzmann and Wernle for a Pre-Dogma Jesus." Pages 53–70 in *Theological and Theoretical Issues in the Synoptic Problem*. Edited by John S. Kloppenborg and Joseph Verheyden. LNTS 618. London: Bloomsbury/T&T Clark, 2020.

———. *Q in Matthew: Tradition, Memory, and Early Scribal Transmission of the Jesus Tradition*. LNTS 564. London: Bloomsbury/T&T Clark, 2016.

———. "Some Compositional Conventions of Hellenistic Wisdom Texts and the Juxtaposition of 4:1–13; 6:20b–49; and 7:1–10 in Q." *JBL* 116 (1997): 235–57.

———. "Upbraiding Wisdom: John's Speech and the Beginning of Q." *NovT* 40 (1998): 1–16.

———. "Who Are the Q Scribes? Questioning the Village Scribes Hypothesis." Pages 67–96 in *Bridges in New Testament Interpretation: Interdisciplinary Advances*. Edited by Neil Elliott and Werner H. Kelber. Lanham, MD: Lexington/Fortress Academic, 2018.

Kloppenborg, John S. "Assimilation, Harmonization, Conflation: Comments on James Barker's 'Ancient Compositional Practices and the Gospels.'" Paper presented at the Annual Meeting of the Society of Biblical Literature, San Diego, November 2014.

———. "Discursive Practices in the Sayings Gospel Q and the Quest of the Historical Jesus." Pages 149–90 in *The Sayings Source Q and the Historical Jesus*. Edited by A. Lindemann. BETL 158. Leuven: Leuven University Press/Peeters, 2001.

———. "'Easter Faith' and the Sayings Gospel Q." Pages 179–203 in *Synoptic Problems: Collected Essays*. WUNT 329. Tübingen: Mohr Siebeck, 2014.

———. *Excavating Q: The History and Setting of the Sayings Gospel*. Minneapolis: Fortress, 2000.

———. "The Farrer/Mark without Q Hypothesis: A Response." Pages 226–44 in *Marcan Priority Without Q: Explorations in the Farrer Hypothesis*. Edited by John C. Poirier and Jeffrey Peterson. LNTS 455. London: Bloomsbury/T&T Clark, 2015.

————. *The Formation of Q: Trajectories in Ancient Wisdom Collections.* Philadelphia: Fortress, 1987.

————. "Literary Convention, Self-Evidence, and the Social History of the Q People." Pages 237–65 in *Synoptic Problems: Collected Essays.* WUNT 329. Tübingen: Mohr Siebeck, 2014.

————. "Nomos and Ethos in Q." Pages 204–21 in *Synoptic Problems: Collected Essays.* WUNT 329. Tübingen: Mohr Siebeck, 2014.

————. "On Dispensing with Q? Goodacre on the Relation of Luke to Matthew." *NTS* 49 (2003): 210–36.

————. "Q, Bethsaida, Khorazin, and Capernaum." Pages 61–90 in *Q in Context II: Social Setting and Archeological Background of the Sayings Source.* Edited by Markus Tiwald. BBB 173. Bonn: Vandenhoeck & Ruprecht; Bonn University Press, 2015.

————. "The Sayings Gospel Q and the Quest of the Historical Jesus." *HTR* 89 (1996): 307–44.

————. "Variation and Reproduction of the Double Tradition and an Oral Q?" Pages 91–119 in *Synoptic Problems: Collected Essays.* WUNT 329. Tübingen: Mohr Siebeck, 2014.

Koester, Helmut. "Conclusion: The Intention and Scope of Trajectories." Pages 269–79 in *Trajectories through Early Christianity.* Philadelphia: Fortress, 1971.

————. "The Synoptic Sayings Gospel Q in the Early Communities of Jesus' Followers." Pages 72–83 in *From Jesus to the Gospels: Interpreting the New Testament in Its Context.* Minneapolis: Fortress, 2007.

Köstlin, Karl Reinhold. *Der Ursprung und die Komposition der synoptischen Evangelien.* Stuttgart: Carl Mäcken, 1853.

Kubler, George. *The Shape of Time: Remarks on the History of Things.* 1962. Repr., New Haven, CT: Yale University Press, 2008.

Labahn, Michael. *Der Gekommene als Wiederkommender: Die Logienquelle als erzählte Geschichte.* ABG 32. Leipzig: Evangelische Verlagsanstalt, 2010.

Lachmann, Karl. "De ordine narrationum in evangeliis Synopticis." Translated by N. H. Palmer in "Lachmann's Argument." *NTS* 13 (1967): 368–78. Originally published in *TSK* 8 (1835): 570–90.

Larsen, Matthew D. C. *Gospels before the Book.* New York: Oxford University Press, 2018.

Lessing, Gotthold Ephraim. "New Hypothesis concerning the Evangelists Regarded as Merely Human Historians." Pages 65–81 in *Lessing's Theological Writings.* Translated by Henry Chadwick. 1784. Repr., Stanford: Stanford University Press, 1957.

Lipton, G. A. "Secular Sufism: Neoliberalism, Ethnoracism, and the Reformation of the Muslim Other." *The Muslim World* 101 (2011): 427–40.

Lohmeyer, Ernst. *Galiläa und Jerusalem*. Göttingen: Vandenhoeck & Ruprecht, 1936.

Lüdemann, Gerd, and Alf Özen. "Religionsgeschichtliche Schule." *TRE* 28 (1997): 618–24.

Lührmann, Dieter. *Die Redaktion der Logienquelle*. WMANT 33. Neukirchen: Neukirchener Verlag, 1969.

Lummis, Edward W. "A Case against 'Q.'" *HibJ* 24 (1925–1926): 755–65.

———. *How Luke Was Written*. Cambridge: Cambridge University Press, 1915.

Luz, Ulrich. "Looking at Q through the Eyes of Matthew." Pages 571–89 in *New Studies in the Synoptic Problem*. Edited by P. Foster, A. Gregory, J. S. Kloppenborg, and J. Verheyden. BETL 239. Leuven: Peeters, 2011.

Mack, Burton L. *The Lost Gospel: The Book of Q and Christian Origins*. San Francisco: HarperSanFrancisco, 1993.

———. *A Myth of Innocence: Mark and Christian Origins*. Philadelphia: Fortress, 1988.

Marsh, Herbert. *A Dissertation on the Origin and Composition of Our Three First Canonical Gospels*. Cambridge: Burges, 1801.

Mattila, Sharon Lea. "A Question Too Often Neglected." *NTS* 41 (1995): 199–217.

Meyer, Heinrich A. W. *Kritisch exegetisches Handbuch über das Evangelium des Matthäus*. 3rd ed. Göttingen: Vandenhoeck & Ruprecht, 1853.

Midgley, Mary. *The Myths We Live By*. London: Routledge, 2011.

Millar, Fergus. "Jerusalem and the Near Eastern Diaspora in the Early Imperial Period." *SCI* 33 (2014): 139–54.

Miller, Shem. *Dead Sea Media: Orality, Textuality, and Memory in the Scrolls from the Judean Desert*. STDJ 129. Leiden: Brill, 2019.

Mittler, Barbara. *A Continuous Revolution: Making Sense of Cultural Revolution Culture*. Harvard East Asia Monographs 343. Cambridge, MA: Harvard University Press, 2012.

Moreland, Milton. "Provenience Studies and the Question of Q in Galilee." Pages 43–60 in *Q in Context II: Social Setting and Archeological Background of the Sayings Source*. Edited by Markus Tiwald. BBB 173. Bonn: Vandenhoeck & Ruprecht; Bonn University Press, 2015.

Nineham, D. E. "Eyewitness Testimony and the Gospel Tradition." *JTS* 9 (1958): 13–25.

Olson, Ken. "The Lord's Prayer (Abridged Edition)." Pages 101–18 in *Marcan Priority without Q: Explorations in the Farrer Hypothesis*. Edited by John C. Poirier and Jeffrey Peterson. LNTS 455. London: Bloomsbury/T&T Clark, 2015.

——. "Unpicking on the Farrer Theory." Pages 127–50 in *Questioning Q: A Multidimensional Critique*. Edited by Mark Goodacre and Nicholas Perrin. Downers Grove, IL: InterVarsity Press, 2004.

Palmer, N. H. "Lachmann's Argument." *NTS* 13 (1967): 368–78.

Pardee, Cambry G. *Scribal Harmonization in the Synoptic Gospels*. NTTSD 60. Leiden: Brill, 2019.

Parker, D. C., D. G. K. Taylor, and M. S. Goodacre. "The Dura-Europos Gospel Harmony." Pages 192–228 in *Studies in the Early Text of the Gospels and Acts*. Edited by D. G. K. Taylor. Atlanta: SBL Press, 1999.

Paulsen, Henning. "Traditionsgeschichtliche Methode und religionsgeschichtliche Schule." *ZTK* 75 (1978): 20–55.

Pearson, Birger A. "A Q Community in Galilee?" *NTS* 50 (2004): 476–94.

Perdue, Leo G. "The Wisdom Sayings of Jesus." *Forum* 3 (2nd series) (1986): 3–35.

Person, Raymond F., Jr. "Harmonization in the Pentateuch and Synoptic Gospels: Repetition and Category-Triggering within Scribal Memory." Pages 318–58 in *Repetition, Communication, and Meaning in the Ancient World*. Edited by Deborah Beck. OLAW 13. Leiden: Brill, 2021.

Pierce, Matthew. *Twelve Infallible Men: The Imams and the Making of Shiʿism*. Cambridge, MA: Harvard University Press, 2016.

Poirier, John C. "The Composition of Luke in Source-Critical Perspective." Pages 209–26 in *New Studies in the Synoptic Problem: Essays in Honour of Christopher M. Tuckett*. Edited by P. Foster, A. Gregory, J. S. Kloppenborg, and J. Verheyden. BETL 239. Leuven: Peeters, 2011.

——. "Delbert Burkett's Defense of Q." Pages 191–225 in *Marcan Priority without Q: Explorations in the Farrer Hypothesis*. Edited by John C. Poirier and Jeffrey Peterson. LNTS 455. London: Bloomsbury/T&T Clark, 2015.

——. "Introduction: Why the Farrer Hypothesis? Why Now?" Pages 1–15 in *Marcan Priority Without Q: Explorations in the Farrer Hypothesis*. Edited by John C. Poirier and Jeffrey Peterson. LNTS 455. London: Bloomsbury/T&T Clark, 2015.

——. "The Roll, the Codex, the Wax Tablet, and the Synoptic Problem." *JSNT* 35 (2012): 3–30.

Popper, Karl. "Evolutionary Epistemology." Pages 78–86 in *Popper Selections*. Edited by David Miller. Princeton: Princeton University Press, 1985.

——. "The Problem of Demarcation." Pages 118–30 in *Popper Selections*. Edited by David Miller. Princeton: Princeton University Press, 1985.

Ready, Jonathan. *Orality, Textuality, and the Homeric Epics: An Interdisciplinary Study of Oral Texts, Dictated Texts, and Wild Texts*. Oxford: Oxford University Press, 2019.

Reed, Jonathan L. *Archaeology and the Galilean Jesus: A Re-examination of the Evidence*. Harrisburg: Trinity Press International, 2000.

———. "The Sign of Jonah (Q 11:29–32) and Other Epic Traditions in Q." Pages 130–43 in *Reimagining Christian Origins: A Colloquium Honoring Burton L. Mack*. Edited by Elizabeth A. Castelli and Hal Taussig. Valley Forge, PA: Trinity Press International, 1996.

Reitzenstein, Richard. *Die hellenistischen Mysterienreligionen: ihre Grundgedanken und Wirkungen*. 2nd ed. Leipzig: Teubner, 1919.

Reuss, Eduard. *Die Geschichte der heiligen Schrift: Neuen Testaments*. 2nd ed. Braunschweig: Schwetschke, 1853.

Ritschl, A. "Über den gegenwärtigen Stand der Kritik der synoptischen Evangelien." *Theologische Jahrbücher* 10 (1851): 480–538.

Robinson, James M. "*LOGOI SOPHON*: On the Gattung of Q." Pages 71–113 in *Trajectories through Early Christianity*. Philadelphia: Fortress, 1971.

———. "The Matthean Trajectory from Q to Mark." Pages 122–55 in *Ancient and Modern Perspectives on the Bible and Culture: Essays in Honor of Hans Dieter Betz*. Edited by Adela Yarbro Collins. Atlanta: Scholars Press, 1998.

Rollens, Sarah. "The Anachronism of 'Early Christian Communities.'" Pages 307–21 in *Theorizing Religion in Antiquity*. Edited by Nickolas Roubekas. London: Equinox, 2019.

———. *Framing Social Criticism in the Jesus Movement: The Ideological Project in the Sayings Gospel Q*. WUNT 2.374. Tübingen: Mohr Siebeck, 2014.

———. "The Kingdom of God Is among You: Prospects for a Q Community." Pages 224–41 in *Christian Origins and the Establishment of the Early Jesus Movement*. Edited by Stanley E. Porter and Andrew W. Pitts. ECHE 4. Leiden: Brill, 2018.

Rosman, Moshe. *Founder of Hasidism: A Quest for the Historical Baʿal Shem Tov*. 2nd ed. Oxford & Portland: Littmann Library of Jewish Civilization, 2013.

Rouse, Richard H., and Mary A. Rouse. "Wax Tablets." *Language and Communication* 9 (1989): 175–91.

Rubin, David C. *Memory in Oral Traditions: The Cognitive Psychology of Epic, Ballads, and Counting-Out Rhymes*. New York: Oxford University Press, 1995.

Runesson, Anders. "Architecture, Conflict, and Identity Formation: Jews and Christians in Capernaum from the First to the Sixth Century." Pages 231–57 in *Religion, Ethnicity, and Identity in Ancient Galilee: A Region in Transition*. Edited by Jürgen Zangenberg, Harold W. Attridge, and Dale B. Martin. WUNT 210. Tübingen: Mohr Siebeck, 2007.

Salles, Catherine. *Lire à Rome*. Paris: Les Belles Lettres, 1992.

Sanders, E. P. *Jesus and Judaism*. Philadelphia: Fortress, 1985.

Sartorius, Ernst. "Ueber die Entstehung der drey ersten Evangelien." Pages 9–126 in *Drey Abhandlungen über wichtige Gegenstände der exegetischen und systematischen Theologie.* Göttingen: Dieterische Buchhandlung, 1820.

Saunier, Heinrich. *Ueber die Quellen des Evangelium des Markus: Ein Beitrag zu den Untersuchungen über die Entstehung unsrer kanonischen Evangelien.* Berlin: Dümmler, 1825.

Schleiermacher, Friedrich D. E. "Über die Zeugnisse des Papias von unsern beiden ersten Evangelien." Pages 229–54 in *Friedrich Daniel Ernst Schleiermacher: Exegetische Schriften.* Edited by Hermann Patsch and Dirk Schmid. 1832. Repr., Berlin & New York: de Gruyter, 2000.

———. "Ueber die Schriften des Lukas: Ein kritischer Versuch." Pages 1–179 in *Friedrich Daniel Ernst Schleiermacher: Exegetische Schriften.* Edited by Hermann Patsch and Dirk Schmid. 1817. Repr., Berlin: de Gruyter, 2001.

Schmid, Ulrich B. "The Diatessaron of Tatian." Pages 115–42 in *The Text of the New Testament in Contemporary Research: Essays on the Status Quaestionis.* Edited by B. D. Ehrman and M. W. Holmes. 2nd ed. Leiden: Brill, 2013.

Schmidt, Karl Ludwig. *Der Rahmen der Geschichte Jesu: Literarkritische Untersuchungen zur ältesten Jesusüberlieferung.* Berlin: Trowitzsch & Sohn, 1919.

———. *The Place of the Gospels in the General History of Literature.* Translated by Byron R. McCane. Columbia: University of South Carolina Press, 2002.

Schröter, Jens. *Erinnerung an Jesu Worte. Studien zur Rezeption der Logienüberlieferung in Markus, Q und Thomas.* WMANT 76. Neukirchen-Vluyn: Neukirchener Verlag, 1997.

Schwegler, A. "Die Hypothese vom schöpferischen Urevangelisten in ihrem Verhältniss zur Traditionshypothese." *Theologische Jahrbücher* 2 (1843): 203–78.

Sevenich-Bax, Elisabeth. *Israels Konfrontation mit dem letzten Boten der Weisheit: Form, Funktion und Interdependenz der Weisheitselemente in der Logienquelle.* MThA 21. Altenberge: Oros, 1993.

Shively, Elizabeth E. "The Eclipse of the Markan Narrative: On the (Re)cognition of a Coherent Story and Implications for Genre." *EC* 12 (2021): 369–87.

Sieffert, Friedrich Ludwig. *Ueber den Ursprung des ersten kanonischen Evangeliums: Eine kritische Abhandlung.* Königsberg: Bon, 1832.

Simons, Eduard. *Hat der dritte Evangelist den kanonischen Matthäus benutzt?* Bonn: Universitäts-Buchdruckerei von Carl Georgi, 1880.

Smith, Daniel A. *The Post-Mortem Vindication of Jesus in the Sayings Gospel Q.* LNTS 338. London: T&T Clark, 2006.

Starr, Raymond J. "The Circulation of Literary Texts in the Roman World." *ClQ* 37 (1987): 213–23.

Storr, Gottlob Christian. *Ueber den Zweck der evangelischen Geschichte und der Briefe Johannis.* Tübingen: Herbrandt, 1786.

Stowers, Stanley. "The Concept of 'Community' and the History of Early Christianity." *MTSR* 23 (2011): 238–56.

Strauss, David Friedrich. *The Life of Jesus Critically Examined.* Translated by George Eliot. 1846. Repr., Philadelphia: Fortress, 1972. Originally published as: *Das Leben Jesu: Kritisch bearbeitet.* 2 vols. Tübingen: C. F. Osiander, 1835–1836.

Streeter, Burnett Hillman. *Four Gospels: A Study of Origins.* London: Macmillan, 1924.

Teeter, David Andrew. *Scribal Laws: Exegetical Variation in the Textual Transmission of Biblical Law in the Late Second Temple Period.* FAT 92. Tübingen: Mohr Siebeck, 2014.

Theissen, Gerd. *The Gospels in Context: Social and Political History in the Synoptic Tradition.* Translated by Linda M. Maloney. London: T&T Clark, 1992.

———. "The Sayings Source Q and Itinerant Radicalism." Pages 93–110 in *Q in Context II: Social Setting and Archeological Background of the Sayings Source.* Edited by Markus Tiwald. BBB 173. Bonn: Vandenhoeck & Ruprecht; Bonn University Press, 2015.

Tiwald, Markus. "The Brazen Freedom of God's Children: 'Insolent Ravens' (Q 12:24) and 'Carefree Lilies' (Q 12:27) as Response to Mass Poverty and Social Disruption?" Pages 111–31 in *Q in Context II: Social Setting and Archaeological Background of the Sayings Source.* Edited by Markus Tiwald. BBB 173. Bonn: Vandenhoeck & Ruprecht; Bonn University Press, 2015.

———. *Commentary on Q.* Stuttgart: Kohlhammer, 2020.

Tödt, H. E. *The Son of Man in the Synoptic Tradition.* Translated by D. M. Barton. Philadelphia: Westminster, 1965.

Tuckett, Christopher M. "The Community of Q." Pages 5–26 in *Shadowy Characters and Fragmentary Evidence: The Search for Early Christian Groups and Movements.* Edited by Joseph Verheyden, Tobias Nicklas, and Elisabeth Hernitscheck. WUNT 388. Tübingen: Mohr Siebeck, 2015.

———. "The Existence of Q." Pages 1–41 in *Q and the History of Early Christianity.* Edinburgh: T&T Clark, 1996.

———. "The Reception of Q Studies in the UK: No Room at the Inn?" Pages 62–85 in *The Q Hypothesis Unveiled: Theological, Sociological, and Hermeneutical Issues behind the Sayings Source.* Edited by Marcus Tiwald. BWANT 225. Stuttgart: Kohlhammer, 2020.

Turner, James. *Philology: The Forgotten Origins of the Modern Humanities.* Princeton, NJ: Princeton University Press, 2014.

Veit, Karl. *Die synoptischen Parallelen und ein älterer Versuch ihrer Enträtselung.* Gütersloh: Bertelsmann, 1897.

Vroom, Jonathan. "The Role of Memory in *Vorlage*-based Transmission: Evidence from Erasures and Corrections." *Textus* 27 (2018): 258–73.

Walsh, Robyn Faith. *The Origins of Early Christian Literature: Contextualizing the New Testament within Greco-Roman Literary Culture*. Cambridge: Cambridge University Press, 2021.

———. "Q and the 'Big Bang' Theory of Christian Origins." Pages 483–533 in *Redescribing the Gospel of Mark*. Edited by Barry S. Crawford and Merrill P. Miller. Atlanta: SBL Press, 2017.

Watson, Francis. "The Archaeology of the Q Hypothesis: The Case of H. J. Holtzmann." Pages 37–52 in *Theological and Theoretical Issues in the Synoptic Problem*. Edited by John S. Kloppenborg and Joseph Verheyden. LNTS 618. London: T&T Clark, 2020.

———. "Braucht Lukas Q? Ein Plädoyer für die L/M Hypothese." *ZNT* 22 (2019): 61–77.

———. *Gospel Writing: A Canonical Perspective*. Grand Rapids: Eerdmans, 2013.

———. "Luke Rewriting and Rewritten." Pages 79–95 in *Luke's Literary Creativity*. Edited by Jesper Tang Nielsen and Mogens Müller. LNTS 550. London: Bloomsbury/T&T Clark, 2016.

———. "Q and the *Logia*: on the Discovery and Marginalizing of P. Oxy. 1." Pages 97–113 in *Gospel Interpretation and the Q-Hypothesis*. Edited by Mogens Müller and Heike Omerzu. LNTS 573. London: T&T Clark, 2018.

———. "Q as Hypothesis: A Study in Methodology." *NTS* 55 (2009): 397–415.

———. "A Reply to My Critics." Pages 227–48 in *Writing the Gospels: A Dialogue with Francis Watson*. Edited by Catherine Sider Hamilton with Joel Willitts. LNTS 606. London: T&T Clark, 2019.

———. "Seven Theses on the Synoptic Problem, in Disagreement with Christopher Tuckett." Pages 139–47 in *Gospel Interpretation and the Q-Hypothesis*. Edited by Mogens Müller and Heike Omerzu. LNTS 573. London: T&T Clark, 2018.

Weaks, Joseph. "Mark without Mark: Problematizing the Reliability of a Reconstructed Text of Q." PhD diss., Brite Divinity School, 2010.

Weber, Thomas M. "Gadara and the Galilee." Pages 449–77 in *Religion, Ethnicity, and Identity in Ancient Galilee: A Region in Transition*. Edited by Jürgen Zangenberg, Harold W. Attridge, and Dale B. Martin. WUNT 201. Tübingen: Mohr Siebeck, 2007.

Weiss, Bernhard. *Die Quellen der synoptischen Überlieferung*. Leipzig: Hinrichs, 1908.

———. *Die Quellen des Lukasevangeliums*. Stuttgart: J. G. Cotta, 1907.

———. "Zur Entstehungsgeschichte der drei synoptischen Evangelien." *TSK* 34 (1861): 29–100, 646–713.

Weiss, Johannes. *Das älteste Evangelium: Ein Beitrag zum Verständnis des Markus-evangeliums und der ältesten evangelischen Überlieferung.* Göttingen: Vandenhoeck & Ruprecht, 1903.

———. "Die drei älteren Evangelien." Pages 31–525 in *Die Schriften des Neuen Testaments.* Edited by Johannes Weiss. 2nd ed. Göttingen: Vandenhoeck & Ruprecht, 1907.

Weisse, Christian Hermann. *Die Evangelienfrage in ihrem gegenwärtigen Stadium.* Leipzig: Breitkopf and Härtel, 1856.

———. *Die evangelische Geschichte kritisch und philosophisch bearbeitet.* 2 vols. Leipzig: Breitkopf and Härtel, 1838.

Weizsäcker, Carl. *Untersuchungen über die evangelische Geschichte: Ihre Quellen und den Gang ihrer Entwicklung.* 1864. Repr., Tübingen: J. C. B. Mohr (Paul Siebeck), 1901.

Wellhausen, Julius. *Einleitung in die drei ersten Evangelien.* 2nd ed. Berlin: Reimer, 1911.

Wernle, Paul. *Die Quellen des Lebens Jesu.* 3rd ed. Tübingen: J. C. B. Mohr (Paul Siebeck), 1906.

———. *Die synoptische Frage.* Tübingen: J. C. B. Mohr (Paul Siebeck), 1899.

Wilke, Christian Gottlob. *Der Urevangelist, oder exegetisch kritische Untersuchung über das Verwandtschaftsverhältniß der drei ersten Evangelien.* Dresden: Fleischer, 1838.

———. "Ueber die Parabel von den Arbeitern im Weinberge Matth. 20, 1–16." *ZWT* 1 (1829): 71–109.

Wise, Michael Owen. *Language and Literacy in Roman Judaea: A Study of the Bar Kokhba Documents.* AYBRL. New Haven, CT: Yale University Press, 2015.

Wrede, William. *The Messianic Secret.* Translated by J. C. G. Greig. London: James Clarke & Co., 1971.

Wright, Benjamin G., III. "Joining the Club: A Suggestion about Genre in Early Jewish Texts." *DSD* 17 (2010): 289–314.

Zahn, Molly M. *Genres of Rewriting in Second Temple Judaism: Scribal Composition and Transmission.* Cambridge: Cambridge University Press, 2020.

Zangenberg, Jürgen K. "From the Galilean Jesus to the Galilean Silence: Earliest Christianity in the Galilee until the Fourth Century CE." Pages 75–108 in *The Rise and Expansion of Christianity in the First Three Centuries of the Common Era.* Edited by Clare K. Rothschild and Jens Schröter. WUNT 301. Tübingen: Mohr Siebeck, 2013.

Zerubavel, Yael. *Recovered Roots: Collective Memory and the Making of Israeli National Tradition.* Chicago: University of Chicago Press, 1995.

Index of Authors

Index of Subjects

Index of Scripture References